Hiking Georgia

A Guide to the State's Greatest Hiking Adventures

Fourth Edition

Donald W. Pfitzer and Jimmy Jacobs
Photography by Polly Dean

FALCON GUIDES

GUILFORD, CONNECTICUT
HELENA, MONTANA

AN IMPRINT OF GLOBE PEQUOT PRESS

To Billie S. Pfitzer and Martha E. Pfitzer

FALCONGUIDES®

FalconGuides is an imprint of Globe Pequot Press.
Falcon, FalconGuides, and Outfit Your Mind are registered trademarks of Morris Book Publishing, LLC.
All interior photographs by Polly Dean unless otherwise credited.

Maps by Design Maps Inc. © Morris Book Publishing, LLC
Project editor: Julie Marsh
Layout: Mary Ballachino

Library of Congress Cataloging-in-Publication Data
Pfitzer, Donald W.
Hiking Georgia / Donald W. Pfitzer —3rd ed.
p. cm. — (A Falconguide)
ISSN-13: 978-0-7627-3642-3
ISBN-10: 0-7627-3642-9
1. Hiking—Georgia—Guidebooks. 2. Family recreation—Georgia—Guidebooks. 3. Backpacking—Georgia—Guidebooks. 4. Georgia—Guidebooks. I. Title. II. Series.
GV199.42.G46P46 2006
796.5109758—dc22 2006015901

ISBN 978-0-7627-8243-7

Printed in the United States of America

10 9 8 7 6 5 4 3 2 1

Contents

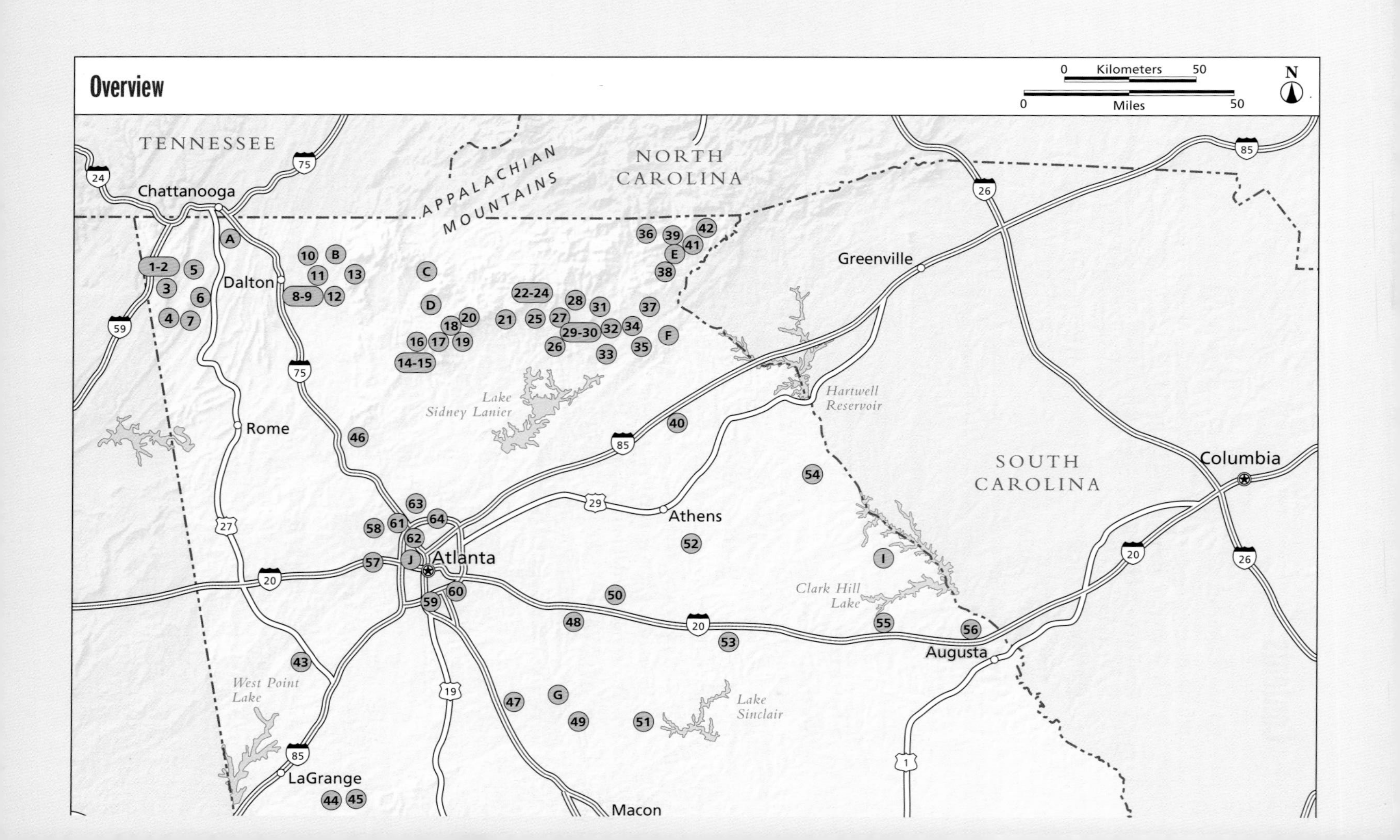

Overview
0 Kilometers 50
0 Miles 50
N
TENNESSEE
NORTH CAROLINA
APPALACHIAN MOUNTAINS
SOUTH CAROLINA
Chattanooga
Dalton
Rome
Atlanta
Athens
Greenville
Columbia
Augusta
LaGrange
Macon
Lake Sidney Lanier
Hartwell Reservoir
Clark Hill Lake
Lake Sinclair
West Point Lake

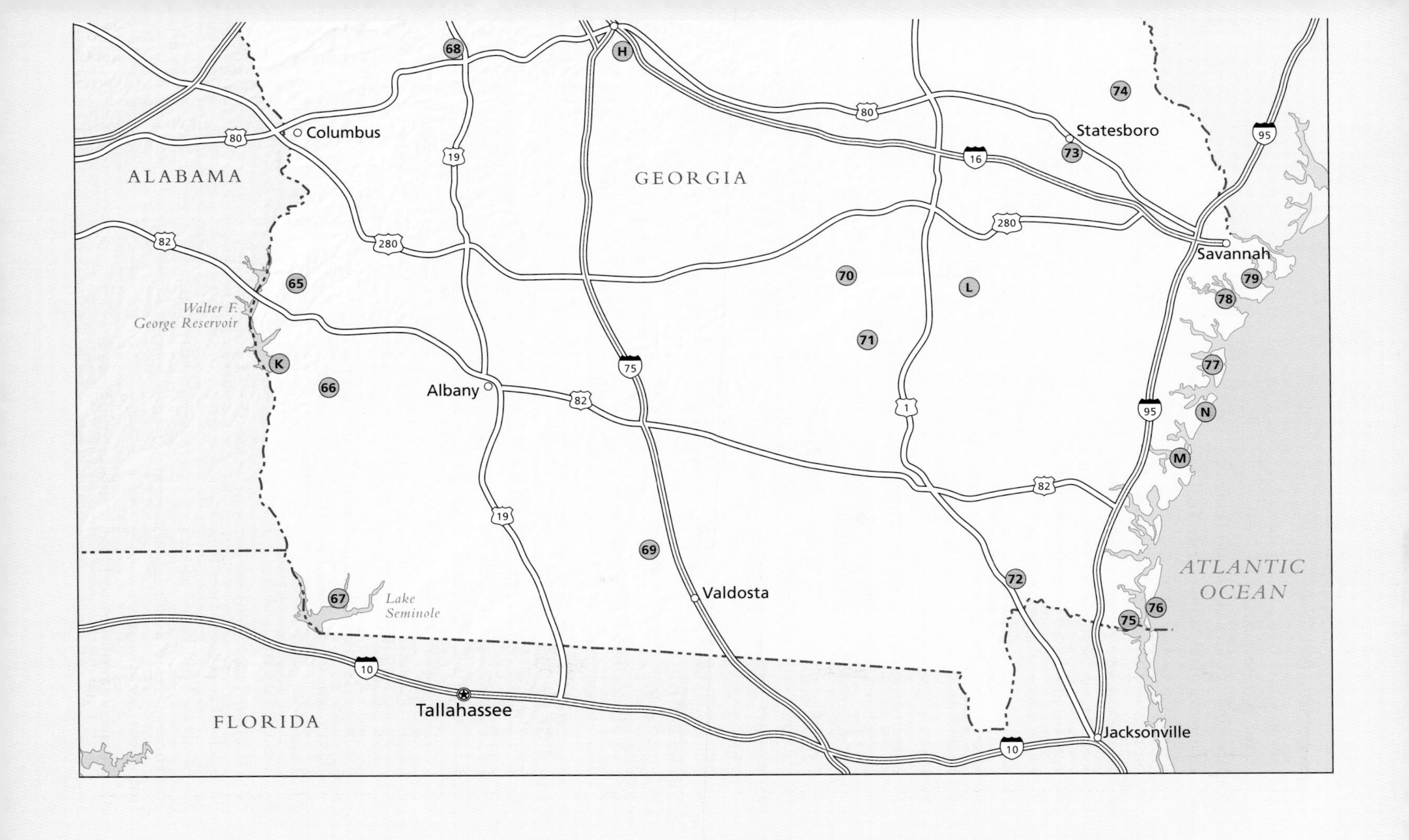
ALABAMA
GEORGIA
FLORIDA
ATLANTIC OCEAN
Columbus
Statesboro
Savannah
Albany
Valdosta
Tallahassee
Jacksonville
Walter F. George Reservoir
Lake Seminole
80
19
16
280
82
75
1
95
10
65
66
67
68
69
70
71
72
73
74
75
76
77
78
79
H
K
L
M
N

ACKNOWLEDGMENTS

Producing a guidebook such as this always is a group project, dependent on the efforts and input of many individuals and agencies. The groundwork laid by Don Pfitzer with the encouragement and editing of Billie Pfitzer was the foundation upon which this newest edition rests.

The aid of the staff of the Georgia Department of Natural Resources and especially the help of Kim Hatcher of the State Parks & Historic Sites Division proved invaluable. The US Department of Agriculture Forest Service, National Park Service, and US Fish and Wildlife Service also provided important input in producing this book.

I am most grateful to Polly Dean for adding her photography to the effort, hiking the trails for long hours, and in general keeping the entire project headed in the right direction.

INTRODUCTION

Georgia has everything to delight the hiker. The largest state east of the Mississippi has more than 1,000 miles of hiking trails. Those paths run along wild mountain streams, through rolling foothills, among the towering pines of the coastal plain, and on pristine beaches of the Atlantic Coast barrier islands. Hundreds of species of animals and thousands of species of plants can be discovered and enjoyed along the trails of Georgia.

Hikes vary in length and difficulty from easy walks along quiet nature trails in state parks to an 80-mile trek on the Appalachian Trail, from strolls along sandy beaches on undeveloped islands to treks amid sheer sandstone cliffs in the mountains.

All of the more than 800 miles of trails discussed in this guide are on public land. Although most are in the mountains and hills of North Georgia, there also are interesting and challenging hikes in Central and South Georgia.

Whatever your interests, there is probably a trail on Georgia public lands that will help you experience them.

Physiographic Regions and Natural History

Five major physiographic provinces span Georgia from south to north: Coastal Plain, Piedmont, Blue Ridge, Ridge and Valley, and Cumberland Plateau. The Coastal Plain is the most extensive. It extends from numerous subtropical barrier islands of the Atlantic Coast north to the very irregular "fall line," which crosses the state from Augusta through Milledgeville and Macon to Columbus.

White-tailed deer are encountered on many of Georgia's hiking trails.

Lying north of the ancient seashore of the fall line is the Piedmont Plateau. The region's rolling foothills rise gradually from 500 to about 1,700 feet of elevation, before abutting the mountains about 50 miles north of Atlanta.

Three smaller regions lie north of the Piedmont: the Cumberland Plateau, the Ridge and Valley, and the Blue Ridge. The Blue Ridge region in Georgia's northeast is part of the Appalachian Mountain system, considered to be among the oldest mountains in the world. The mountains here rise to the greatest height in Georgia—4,783 feet at Brasstown Bald.

The Cumberland Plateau is in the extreme northwest corner of the state. Part of the Allegheny Mountain system, it is represented by Lookout and Sand Mountains, which reach to 2,364 feet.

Between those two regions lies the Ridge and Valley, which extends from the Georgia-Tennessee line southwest 75 miles toward Cedartown.

Georgia has outstanding plant and animal diversity. More than 150 species of trees and 400 species of shrubs and vines grow in the state. Add an almost countless number of flowering herbaceous plants, ferns, mosses, liverworts, lichens, and mushrooms to the list and the sum equals a plant community as diverse as anywhere in the country. Also known to occur in Georgia are more than 65 species of mammals, 75 species of snakes and lizards, and 120 species of salamanders, toads, frogs, and turtles.

Zero Impact Hiking

Reward the thousands of volunteers who create and help maintain the trails and allow those who follow your footsteps to enjoy their own wilderness experience by leaving an area as pristine as you found it—or better. The following guidelines can help ensure enjoyable hiking experiences for years to come:

- Pack it in; pack it out. Few things are more irritating than finding aluminum cans, candy wrappers, and other litter along the trail. Pack out what you pack in—and carry an extra garbage bag on hikes for carting out litter left behind by others.
- Stay on the trail. Designated paths limit the impact on natural areas. Taking shortcuts or straying off the blazed trail can cause damage to sensitive areas that can take years to heal.

Leaving no trace should be the goal of every hiker passing along the trails.

- Respect other trail users. If you are on a multiuse trail that allows horses, remember that they have the right-of-way. Step aside quietly, off the trail if necessary, and let horse and rider pass. Although hikers generally have right-of-way on trails shared with mountain bikers, it's probably best to yield for safety's sake—especially on narrow or steep trail sections.

To learn more about leaving no trace, visit www.LNT.org.

Be Prepared

Should I Drink from That Stream?

In Georgia the answer is no—unless the water has been treated by boiling, filtered with a reliable filter/purifier, or treated with an effective chemical purifier.

From the mountains to the sea, there is no real shortage of water in Georgia. However, water quality can be a problem. Day hikers should bring sufficient water for drinking unless potable water is known to be available. All Georgia state parks and most USDA Forest Service campgrounds and recreation areas have potable running water. Only occasionally will you find yourself several miles from surface water from a spring, stream, or lake. On long trails like the Appalachian Trail, water sources are marked both by signs and on trail maps. Again, this water must be treated before it is considered safe to drink.

Do not drink water directly from streams, no matter how remote they are or how clean and pure they seem to be.

No matter how pretty and inviting a stream may look, you should never drink the water without first boiling, filtering, or chemically treating it.

First Aid

A first-aid kit should be part of every hiker's backpack, whether you're on a day hike or a longer trek. There are many good lightweight, compact kits on the market. Be especially prepared to take care of hike-spoiling blisters by carrying moleskin, gauze, and tape or adhesive bandages.

Dangers

Wear sunscreen (SPF 15 or higher), protective clothing, a wide-brimmed hat, and sunglasses when you are hiking. If you get sunburn, treat the area with aloe vera gel, and protect the area from further sun exposure. Don't let overcast skies fool you into thinking you're safe—you can burn even when you cannot see the sun.

Bear encounters are extremely rare, except at campsites where garbage has been allowed to accumulate. At some shelters along the Appalachian Trail, where hundreds of campers a year spend the night, bears may become night visitors looking for food. You will seldom, if ever, see black bears while walking trails. They will usually run before you get close enough to see them.

The fields and woodlands of Georgia are home to a staggering array of insect life.

Stinging insects represent the greatest and most frequently encountered danger on Georgia's trails. Wasps build nests on bridge handrails or under benches. Running the hand against a wasp nest or brushing against a nest hanging on low vegetation can cause stings that are fortunately only temporarily painful for most people. However, for those few who are allergic to bee and wasp stings, the problem can be life threatening. Know your sensitivity—or the sensitivity of anyone in your hiking party—and prepare for it. Know what to do in the event of a sting, and carry the appropriate antihistamines or other medication in your first-aid kit to use immediately if stung.

Chiggers (red bugs), mosquitoes, biting flies, and gnats are common throughout the state. They are most annoying during the warmer months and during twilight and nighttime hours. In parts of southern Georgia and in the coastal counties, mosquitoes can be very annoying during the day. Be sure to use an effective all-around repellent. The most effective repellents contain at least 30 percent DEET. Other repellents are available for those who are sensitive to DEET, including young children.

Ticks are another problem in Georgia. These bugs can transmit two diseases: Lyme disease and Rocky Mountain spotted fever. Lyme disease occurs throughout Georgia but is most prevalent in the southern two-thirds of the state. It is transmitted by the tiny deer tick. The larger wood tick can transmit spotted fever. A few spotted fever cases are reported each year, while Lyme disease has become much more prevalent.

The best way to avoid ticks on the trail is to use an effective repellent before you head out. DEET is effective against ticks. Another highly effective repellent, which also kills ticks, is Permanone. It should not be applied directly to the skin but is very effective when applied to clothes and footwear before going into tick-infested areas. Wear a long-sleeved shirt and long pants tucked into your footwear. Examine yourself carefully immediately after a day hike and once a day or more on longer hikes. The tiny deer tick nymphs, the most active carrier of the Lyme disease spirochete, may be picked up even during mild winter months in Central and South Georgia.

Removing an attached tick in the first 8 to 10 hours is important. To remove the tick, use forceps or tweezers to grasp the tick as close to the skin as possible; gently but firmly pull the tick away, trying not to leave its mouthparts in the skin. Squeezing the tick's body can act like a syringe, forcing the tick's body fluids into your body and increasing the potential for Lyme disease. In about half the cases of Lyme disease, redness occurs around the bite and may take on a bull's-eye appearance. This should be reported to a doctor as soon as possible. Treated early, Lyme disease is quickly cured.

Venomous snakes in Georgia run from the small, secretive coral snake to the eastern diamondback rattlesnake, our largest North American snake. The coral snake

Most Georgia snakes are harmless and quite beneficial to the ecosystem.

The copperhead is the state's most common venomous snake.

occurs in both dry and moist sandy-loam areas of the southern third of Georgia. The timber rattlesnake occurs throughout the state from the mountains through the Coastal Plain. It may be called the canebrake rattlesnake in the southern part of the state. Coral snakes and rattlesnakes are rarely seen.

Both the northern and southern copperheads occur in Georgia. The larger southern copperhead is found throughout the Piedmont, along the fall line, and in the Coastal Plain. The northern copperhead is generally found in the Piedmont and all the mountain regions.

The cottonmouth, or water moccasin, is found from the fall line south throughout the Coastal Plain along streams, river swamps, and marshes.

Many new hikers in Georgia seem to fear snakes more than other hazards along the trail, carrying snakebite kits with little knowledge of how to use them. Most of these kits have blades to cut the fang puncture, a tourniquet, disinfectant, and other things—none of which are practical first aid for a venomous snakebite. The best first aid for venomous snakebite is get to medical help as soon as possible.

To reduce your risk of snakebite, don't put your foot or hand anywhere without looking first. Be cautious stepping over logs. Keep your hands and feet out of cavities around boulders. Since many snakes are nocturnal, carry and use a flashlight if you need to walk on trails at night during warm weather. Even nonvenomous snakebites can be painful and prone to infection.

Poison ivy is present on many trails in Georgia. It is most obvious in late spring and throughout the summer months. Learn to recognize it and avoid it: "Leaves of three, let it be." Washing exposed skin with soap and water as soon as possible after contact is the best way to prevent irritation.

Hypothermia has been called the number-one killer of all outdoor injuries. The lowering of internal body temperature from exposure to cold, wind, rain, or immersion in cold water, hypothermia can occur even when outdoor temperatures are not very cold. Learn to recognize the symptoms and know that injuries increase the risk of hypothermia. First signs include shivering, followed by no shivering, disorientation, and confusion. Later the person may appear apathetic and moody. As hypothermia becomes more advanced, the victim may lapse into a coma.

The first step in treatment of hypothermia, after making all possible arrangements to get the person to expert medical attention, is to reduce heat loss. Get the victim out of the wind and into dry clothes and/or a windproof shell like a poncho or space blanket (a good addition to your first-aid kit). Pay special attention to covering the head and back of the neck with a cap, hat, or anything windproof and warm. Next try to produce heat in the body core. If the victim can drink, give him/her warm, sweet fluids—not alcohol.

After applying dry clothing and a windproof outer covering, get the victim walking, with support if necessary. Exercise is the best way to improve internal organ heat. If you are alone and recognize hypothermia, drink hot fluids like sweet hot chocolate, get into dry clothes, protect yourself from the wind, and keep moving. Movement is crucial. Obviously, it's important to be able to recognize the condition before you become disoriented or confused.

Planning Your Trip

For safety's sake, always leave your hike itinerary with someone before you head out. It should include where you will be hiking, where you will park, your estimated time of completing the trip, and whom to contact if necessary. "Trail Contacts" for each trail description list phone numbers and websites that can be used to contact park personnel should emergencies arise.

There are registers on the Appalachian Trail (AT) at the Springer Mountain trailhead (hike 16) and at many of the shelters. It is a good idea to leave pertinent information at these points. For the AT and some other trails, you must register with the appropriate land-managing agencies.

The Coosa Backcountry Trail, which originates at Vogel State Park (hike 20); Tallulah Gorge State Park, Stoneplace Trail (hike 37); and the Pine Mountain Trail at F. D. Roosevelt State Park (hike 44) are other trails requiring registration to obtain a free permit to hike or camp along these paths. Advanced reservations for ferry passage and camping are needed at Cumberland Island National Seashore (hike 76).

Comfortable clothing and footwear will do more to make a hike pleasant than almost anything else. The great variety of hiking and walking situations makes it impossible to cover all personal needs, but two important ones are to dress in layers and dress for safety in hunting season. The first allows you to remove or add layers to suit the weather. The second involves wearing blaze orange to make you visible to hunters in the area.

Everyone seems to have a different idea about what type of footwear to wear for hiking. Footwear boils down to personal preference, but it should be sturdy and supportive. Many people still wear good leather boots for serious hiking; others prefer

Wearing a blaze orange cap is a wise decision when hiking during hunting seasons.

Packing a rain jacket is wise because Georgia's changeable weather can bring clouds rolling in.

lighter-weight boots with breathable, water-resistant fabrics. The best advice for the beginner is to visit a good outdoor outfitter and try on several styles before finally deciding.

There are many types and styles of backpacks. For day hiking, the smaller daypack type is all you need. It should fit and have padded shoulder and hip pads. Make sure they are wide enough to be comfortable. The pack should have external pockets for easy access to items like camera, water, and maps. External straps are handy to lash things like a jacket or poncho. The main bag should be large enough for lunch or other bulky things. Don't burden yourself with a daypack that is too large. You may find that a fanny pack or a photo vest will carry all you want or need.

Hiking in Georgia is a year-round activity, with many good hiking days in winter. Wintertime snow and cold or freezing rain in the mountains and spring and summer showers and thunderstorms throughout the state are about the only weather conditions that hamper your comfort on the trail. Fall weather is best, and September through November is the most popular time to hike.

Be aware of changing weather conditions. If thunderstorms are in the forecast, recognize that lightning in forest cover can be dangerous. Do not hike along ridgetops and on mountain crests with large exposed rock formations during electrical storms, especially with metal-frame backpacks.

Wintertime hikes can be especially beautiful in the limited snow that falls in the Georgia mountains. Plans for snow hiking should include adequate footwear and clothing to tolerate the cold, wet conditions in case an emergency occurs. Being wet and cold invites hypothermia, a potentially life-threatening condition.

Navigation

Maps

US Geological Survey (USGS) 7.5-minute series topographic quadrangles, scale 1:24,000, referred to in the text for each hike, are the best and most dependable maps for long hikes and wilderness backpack trip planning. Learn how to read them, and then learn to rely on them for keeping oriented on the trail. This is especially important for any cross-country hikes requiring good orienteering techniques. These USGS quadrangles are available at most outdoor shops that cater to hikers' needs. They can be purchased from the US Geological Survey National Mapping Division at USGS.gov/pubprod/.

Page-size maps of the trails in most of the state parks can be obtained free of charge from the respective parks or downloaded from www.gastateparks.org. These maps may not be to scale, but they will keep you oriented. They also can help you take advantage of all the special natural and historical points of interest along the way.

The Georgia Appalachian Trail Club offers a small-scale map with helpful hints for hiking the AT. The *Appalachian Trail Guide to North Carolina–Georgia* contains maps, trail mileages, water and shelter locations, and side trails; it can be purchased at hiking and backpacking outfitters and stores or from the Appalachian Trail Conservancy, www.atctrailstore.org.

The comprehensive website of the Benton MacKaye Trail Association (www.bmta.org) contains excellent information on this newest of the long trails in Georgia and other trails throughout the mountains of northeast Georgia.

Compass

The compass is probably the most valuable tool you can have to stay properly oriented in unfamiliar terrain. Some characteristics to look for in a compass are a rectangular base with detailed scales, a liquid-filled protective housing, a sighting line on the mirror, and luminous arrows. Learn to use the compass so well that you don't even think about disbelieving it.

Global Positioning System (GPS)

This is possibly the most useful navigation gadget to come along for the serious hiker. As with all such tools, you must learn how to use a GPS accurately. Most brands are sold with good instructions that anyone with computer experience should be able to master. Practice with your GPS until you are comfortable with it before you go into the backcountry on an extended hike. If you use a mapping program, you can come home from a hike and download the GPS data into your computer for a permanent record of your hike.

All GPS products use the same satellite support base. The real difference among products is in the quality of satellite reception. All are limited when in mountainous terrain with deep valleys and under dense deciduous tree cover. (Deciduous tree leaves are notorious for diffusing radio signals.) Of course as time passes, technology is catching up with those problems

The trail tracks used to create the maps in this volume were made with Garmin GPSMAP 62stc or touch-screen Garmin RINO 665t units. In more than 500 miles of trekking, the units lost satellite contact only once. That occurred in the bottom of a deep, solid rock grotto in Cloudland Canyon State Park.

Modern GPS units add a new dimension to navigating through the woodlands.

Hiking with Children

Children learn by example. Hiking trips are excellent opportunities to teach young ones to tread lightly and minimize their imprint upon the environment. Many state parks have nature trails ideal for beginning hikers and offer interpretive programs for children and adults conducted by park naturalists and program specialists.

Kids can enjoy the backcountry as much as their parents, but they see the world from a different perspective. It's the little things adults barely notice that are so special to children. Bugs scampering across the trail, spider webs dripping with morning dew, lizards doing push-ups on a trailside boulder, skipping rocks on a lake, watching sticks run the rapids of a mountain stream, exploring animal tracks in the sand—these are but a few of the natural wonders kids will enjoy while hiking backcountry trails.

To make the trip fun for the kids, let the young ones set the pace. Until they get older and are able to keep up with you, forget about that 30-mile trek to your favorite backcountry campsite. Instead, plan a destination that is only a mile or two from the trailhead. Kids tire quickly and become easily sidetracked, so don't be surprised if you don't make it to your destination.

Hikers with Special Needs

State and federal land management agencies in Georgia are putting a great deal of effort into making their facilities accessible to visitors with special needs. A number of parks and other areas covered in the following chapters have wheelchair-accessible paths or trails. These are highlighted where relevant.

Volunteering

Georgia is home to several hiking clubs and conservation organizations that are involved in hiking. Some devote a large amount of their time to trail maintenance. The Georgia Appalachian Trail Club, Benton MacKaye Trail Club, and the Pine Mountain Trail Association plan regular outings to work on these trails. The Georgia Department of Natural Resources, USDA Forest Service, National Park Service, and US Fish and Wildlife Service also welcome volunteers who are willing to help maintain and mark trails. The forest service's "Adopt-A-Trail" program is especially suited to volunteer efforts. See Appendix B for agency contact information.

Using This Guide

Hiking Georgia is divided into six sections: Northwest Georgia, Northeast Georgia, Central Georgia, Metro Atlanta, Southwest Georgia, and Southeast Georgia. All the trails are on public land, including national forest and national park lands, Georgia Department of Natural Resources' (DNR) State Park & Historic Sites and Wildlife Resources Division lands, and other political groupings. As much as possible they are listed in these areas from west to east.

Degrees of difficulty are based on the grade or incline of the trail. A flat trail with very little elevation change is designated easy whether it is 0.5 mile or 5.0 miles long. A moderate hike will have a moderately steep grade for extended distances. A strenuous trail may have steep grades for 0.5 mile or more. Degree of difficulty may be expressed with two or three ratings, as easy to moderate or moderate with strenuous stretches. Where a trail is uneven and footing is more difficult because of boulders or other obstacles, this will be discussed in the description of the hike.

All but a very few trails described in this guide are marked in some fashion. A paint mark (blaze) on a tree is the most frequent trail marker. One trail will be marked or blazed throughout with one color paint. In a state park with several different trails, a different color may be used for each trail. A few trails are marked with a white 3- to 4-inch diamond-shaped piece of metal nailed to trees and posts along the trail instead of paint blazes. The Chattooga River

Blazes can be metal or plastic strips nailed to trees, or they may simply be painted on the trunk.

National Wild and Scenic River Trail (hike 38) is marked this way. Carsonite stakes, flat fiberglass posts about 4 inches wide and 4 to 5 feet tall, are being used to mark some trailheads and occasionally along some trails. These are less vulnerable to vandalism and are marked with decals designating trail use and activities not permitted on the trail.

It has become standard to mark sudden changes in direction of a trail with two blaze marks, one above the other on the same tree. Most trails are marked so that you should not travel more than 0.25 mile without seeing a blaze. Because of dense vegetation, state park and many USDA Forest Service trails are marked with paint blazes much more frequently. Where two trails occasionally join for a distance, two colors or types of blazes are used until the trails separate again.

Trail Finder

	Backpacker	Waterfall	Geology	Great View	Lake Lover	History Lover	Wildlife Viewing	Wildflowers
Northwest Georgia								
1. Cloudland Canyon State Park, West Rim Trail			•	•				
2. Cloudland Canyon State Park, Waterfalls/Sitton Gulch Trails		•	•					
3. Crockford–Pigeon Mountain Wildlife Management Area Trails	•		•	•				
4. James H. (Sloppy) Floyd State Park Trails		•	•	•	•	•		
5. Chickamauga Creek Trail				•			•	•
6. Johns Mountain Wildlife Management Area Trails			•	•				•
7. Arrowhead Wildlife Interpretive Trail							•	•
8. Fort Mountain State Park, Old Fort Loop				•		•	•	•
9. Fort Mountain State Park, Gahuti Trail	•			•			•	•
10. Lake Conasauga Recreation Area Trails				•			•	•
11. Emery Creek Trail		•		•				
12. Pinhoti Trail	•			•			•	•
13. Benton MacKaye Trail	•			•			•	•
Northeast Georgia								
14. Amicalola State Park, Appalachian Approach Trail	•	•		•			•	•
15. Amicalola State Park, Len Foote Hike Inn Trail		•		•				•

	Backpackers	Waterfalls	Geology	Great Views	Lake Lovers	History Lovers	Wildlife Viewing	Wildflowers
16. Appalachian Trail in Georgia	●			●			●	●
17. Cooper Creek Wildlife Management Area Trails	●			●				●
18. Lake Winfield Scott Recreation Area Trails	●			●	●		●	●
19. DeSoto Falls Scenic Area Trails		●						●
20. Vogel State Park Trails	●			●	●		●	●
21. Raven Cliffs Trail		●	●					
22. Brasstown Bald, Arkaquah Trail				●				●
23. Brasstown Bald, Jacks Knob Trail	●			●				●
24. Brasstown Bald, Wagon Train Trail			●	●				
25. Dukes Creek Falls Trail		●	●					
26. Smithgall Woods State Park Trails			●			●	●	●
27. Andrews Cove Recreation Area Trail						●	●	
28. High Shoals Scenic Area Trail	●	●						●
29. Anna Ruby Falls Recreation Area Trails		●	●			●	●	●
30. Unicoi State Park Trails				●	●		●	●
31. Moccasin Creek Trails		●					●	●
32. Lake Rabun Beach Recreation Area Trail		●						

	Backpackers	Waterfalls	Geology	Great Views	Lake Lovers	History Lovers	Wildlife Viewing	Wildflowers
33. Lake Russell State Recreation Area Trails		●			●		●	●
34. Panther Creek Trail	●	●						
35. Lake Russell Wildlife Management Area Trail							●	●
36. Black Rock Mountain State Park Trails	●	●		●	●			●
37. Tallulah Gorge State Park Trails	●	●	●	●		●		●
38. Chattooga National Wild and Scenic River Trail	●	●		●				●
39. Bartram National Recreation Trail	●			●				●
40. Victoria Bryant State Park Trails							●	●
41. Three Forks Trail	●	●						
42. Ellicott Rock Wilderness Trail	●	●		●		●		●
Central Georgia								
43. Chattahoochee Bend State Park Trails				●			●	●
44. F. D. Roosevelt State Park, Pine Mountain Trail	●			●			●	●
45. F. D. Roosevelt State Park, Dowdell Knob Loop	●			●		●		●
46. Red Top Mountain State Park Trails				●	●	●	●	●
47. High Falls State Park Trails		●			●	●		●
48. Charlie Elliott Wildlife Center Trails			●		●		●	●

	Backpackers	Waterfalls	Geology	Great Views	Lake Lovers	History Lovers	Wildlife Viewing	Wildflowers
49. Piedmont National Wildlife Refuge Trails					•		•	•
50. Hard Labor Creek State Park Trails							•	•
51. Twin Bridges Trail					•		•	•
52. Watson Mill Bridge State Park Trails					•	•		•
53. Hamburg State Outdoor Recreation Area Trails					•	•	•	•
54. Richard B. Russell State Park Trails				•	•	•		•
55. Mistletoe State Park Trails	•		•		•			•
56. Augusta Canal National Heritage Area Trail			•	•		•	•	•
Metro Atlanta								
57. Sweetwater Creek State Park Trails		•	•		•	•	•	•
58. Kennesaw Mountain National Battlefield Park Trails			•	•		•	•	•
59. Panola Mountain State Park Trails			•	•			•	•
60. Davidson–Arabia Mountain Nature Preserve Trails			•	•	•	•		•
61. West Palisades Trail			•	•		•	•	•
62. East Palisades Trail			•	•			•	•
63. Johnson Ferry North Trail							•	•
64. Island Ford Trail						•	•	•

	Backpackers	Waterfalls	Geology	Great Views	Lake Lovers	History Lovers	Wildlife Viewing	Wildflowers
Southwest Georgia								
65. Providence Canyon State Outdoor Recreation Area Trails	•		•	•		•		•
66. Kolomoki Mounds State Historic Park Trails					•	•	•	•
67. Seminole State Park Trails					•		•	•
68. Sprewell Bluff Wildlife Management Area Trails			•	•			•	•
69. Reed Bingham State Park Trails					•	•	•	•
Southeast Georgia								
70. Little Ocmulgee State Park Trails			•		•		•	•
71. General Coffee State Park Trails					•	•	•	•
72. Okefenokee National Wildlife Refuge Trails						•	•	•
73. George L. Smith State Park Trails					•	•	•	•
74. Magnolia Springs State Park Trails					•	•	•	•
75. Crooked River State Park Trails				•			•	•
76. Cumberland Island National Seashore Trails	•			•		•	•	
77. Harris Neck National Wildlife Refuge Trails					•	•	•	
78. Fort McAllister State Historic Park Trails				•		•	•	
79. Skidaway Island State Park Trails				•		•	•	

Map Legend

Transportation

- 85 Interstate Highway
- 76 US Highway
- 28 State Highway
- 2658 Forest/Local Road
- Unpaved Road
- Paved Trail/Bike Path

Trails

- Featured Trail
- Trail
- Appalachian Trail

Water Features

- Body of Water
- River/Creek
- Spring
- Waterfall

Land Management

- State Line
- National Forest
- State Park

Symbols

- Boat Ramp
- Bridge
- Campground
- Campsite (backcountry)
- Dam
- Gate
- Ford
- Mountain Peak/Summit
- P Parking
- Pass/Gap
- Picnic Area
- Point of Interest/Structure
- Ranger Station
- Town
- 1 Trailhead
- 5 Trail Direction
- Restroom
- Viewpoint/Overlook
- ? Visitor/Information Center

Northwest Georgia

Sitton Gulch Creek in Cloudland Canyon State Park is a good example of Northwest Georgia streams (hike 2).

1 Cloudland Canyon State Park, West Rim Trail

Because so little of the Cumberland Plateau touches the state, Cloudland Canyon State Park's 3,488 acres have a unique geological feature in Georgia. The flatter tops of the plateau provide sharp contrast to the sheer canyon walls, all softened by an almost complete cover of trees and shrubs that adds color to the ancient sandstone cliffs. The myriad shades of green as the different species of trees begin to leaf out in spring is just as striking as the multicolor display when the same trees take on their autumn hues. In winter, the leafless trees expose the cliffs for a fresh and different look.

The park contains five trails offering almost 17 miles of hikes. The featured West Rim Trail provides a hike along the top of the Cloudland plateau offering great views of Sitton Gulf.

Start: On the paved walkway leading from the parking lot at the East Rim Overlook day-use area
Distance: 4.9-mile lollipop
Hiking time: About 2.5 hours
Difficulty: West Rim Trail, moderate with a few short, steep, rocky places
Trail surface: Mostly earthen, with some exposed stone; metal and stone stairway to waterfalls
Best season: Year-round
Other trail users: Hikers only
Canine compatibility: Leashed dogs permitted
Land status: Georgia DNR, State Parks & Historic Sites Division
Nearest town: Trenton
Fees and permits: Daily parking fee
Schedule: Park hours 7 a.m.–10 p.m., year-round; trails close at sunset
Maps: USGS Durham; page-size map available in the park office or from the website
Trail contacts: Cloudland Canyon State Park, 122 Cloudland Canyon Park Rd., Rising Fawn 30738; (706) 657-4050; www.gastateparks.org
Special considerations: You are cautioned to stay on the trail and not climb on rocks or around the waterfalls. The rocks can be very slippery and dangerous.

Caution is also advised for people with heart problems and those in poor physical condition using the waterfalls stairway. From the bottom of the canyon back to the rim, there are 587 metal or stone steps. That's not counting the ones on the 2 side trails to the waterfalls.

Finding the trailhead: From Trenton on I-59, take exit 11 and go east 6.3 miles on SR 136 to the park entrance. Continue 1.2 miles to East Rim Overlook day-use area. The trailhead is at the overlook parking lot. Trailhead GPS: N34 50.038' / W85 28'

The Hike

The West Rim Trail runs west from the trailhead at the parking lot at the East Rim Overlook; it has yellow blazes. It goes behind several cabins and begins the descent to Daniel Creek, which forms the waterfalls. The trail passes the junction with Waterfalls Trail, which descends on metal steps to the right. The West Rim Trail continues, reaching a picturesque footbridge over fast-flowing and cascading Daniel Creek.

Sitton Gulf in early spring from the overlook on the West Rim Trail

Catawba rhododendron and mountain laurel thickets interspersed with sourwood, dogwood, and larger oaks, hickories, hemlocks, and maples shade the trail.

After crossing the bridge, which is only about 30 or 40 yards above the highest falls, you begin climbing up to the plateau top. Mosses, ferns, and many wildflowers line the trail in spring and summer.

Traveling through switchbacks in an area of large sandstone boulders, the path passes a pair of rock overhangs that form natural shelters. The first is the largest, and the second is smaller and cave-like. Once on the plateau top, you reach the first of the six designated overlooks on the rim of the gulf, or canyon.

Soon the trail leaves the canyon rim and comes to a fork in the trail beside the bridge over Whiteoak Spring. The return loop crosses this span to rejoin the trail. Continuing to the left, in a clockwise direction, the hike goes upstream along Whiteoak Spring through the oak-hickory forest of the Cumberland Plateau. There is a steady rise in elevation for the next mile. Blueberries, dogwood, and sourwood grow under the larger trees. Dwarf iris, pipsissewa, spring beauty, phlox, and bird's-foot violets grow in the well-drained sandy soil and along the small stream drainages.

Shortly, the white-blazed trail to the Walk-in Camp intersects from the left. You next cross the paved park road and reach the junction with a trail from the West Rim Access parking area entering from the left. The parking lot is 0.1 mile down that path.

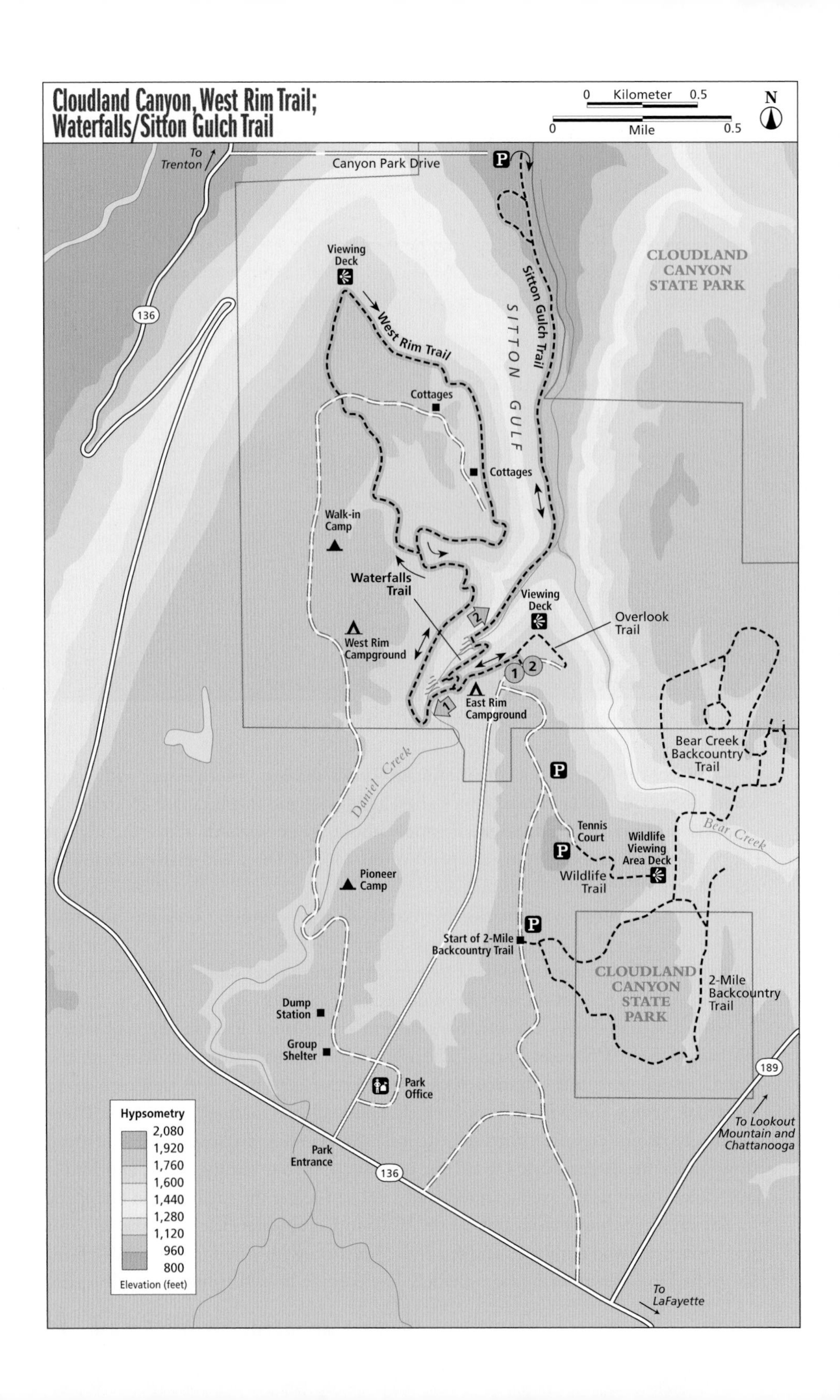
Cloudland Canyon, West Rim Trail; Waterfalls/Sitton Gulch Trail
0 Kilometer 0.5
0 Mile 0.5
N
To Trenton
Canyon Park Drive
P
CLOUDLAND CANYON STATE PARK
Viewing Deck
136
West Rim Trail
SITTON GULF
Sitton Gulch Trail
Cottages
Cottages
Walk-in Camp
Waterfalls Trail
Viewing Deck
Overlook Trail
West Rim Campground
East Rim Campground
1
2
Bear Creek Backcountry Trail
Daniel Creek
Bear Creek
Tennis Court
Wildlife Viewing Area Deck
Wildlife Trail
Pioneer Camp
Start of 2-Mile Backcountry Trail
CLOUDLAND CANYON STATE PARK
2-Mile Backcountry Trail
Dump Station
Group Shelter
Park Office
189
To Lookout Mountain and Chattanooga
Hypsometry
2,080
1,920
1,760
1,600
1,440
1,280
1,120
960
800
Elevation (feet)
Park Entrance
136
To LaFayette

From here the path provides a view of the eastern side of the Lookout Mountain escarpment. The town of Trenton in Lookout Valley is visible more than 1,200 feet below. The trail continues north along this rim to stone steps and a spectacular rocky point overlook. On a clear day you can see to the Tennessee River, where it forms Moccasin Bend at Chattanooga, Tennessee.

Climb back up the rocky steps and continue to the left along the western rim of Sitton Gulf. The path leads to several beautiful overlooks along the way.

Almost anytime during the day you will see hawks or vultures soaring on the wind currents along the steep escarpments. You will pass several spur paths on the right that lead to cabins.

Leaving the canyon bluff, you come to Whiteoak Spring; cross the bridge and turn left to return to the trailhead.

Miles and Directions

0.0 Start from the trailhead at the parking area.

0.2 Pass the junction with the Waterfalls Trail; follow the yellow blazes to the left.

0.4 Cross a footbridge over Daniel Creek.

0.5 Pass a rock shelter on the hillside.

0.6 Reach a second smaller, cave-like rock shelter.

1.0 Enjoy the first of six overlooks of the canyon from the west rim.

1.2 At the fork in the trail, take the left path along the creek bank.

1.5 The trail to the Walk-in Camp enters from the left.

2.1 Cross the paved park road.

2.2 The trail from West Overlook parking lot enters from the left.

2.4 Arrive at a grand overlook to the north toward Chattanooga, Tennessee.

3.7 Cross the bridge over Whiteoak Springs to close the loop and turn left.

4.9 Arrive back at the parking area.

2 Cloudland Canyon State Park, Waterfalls / Sitton Gulch Trail

While the West Rim Trail meanders along the brink of Sitton Gulf, the Waterfalls / Sitton Gulch Trail provides an adventure down in the chasm. The descent and hike through the gulf offers a close look at the structure of this Cumberland Plateau geophysical region. Hiking this trail presents a steadily changing variety of flora and fauna.

This featured hike is a combination of the Waterfalls Trail and the longer Sitton Gulch Trail. The Waterfalls Trail climbs down the rocky cliffs of the gulf, then the Sitton Gulch Trail follows the course of Daniels and Sitton Gulch Creeks to the lower end of the gulf.

See map on page 22.
Start: On the paved walkway leading from the parking lot at the East Rim Overlook day-use area
Distance: Waterfalls Trail, 0.8 mile one way to the second falls; Sitton Gulch Trail, 2.8-mile one-way trail to the lower trailhead or 5.0 miles out and back using the side loop
Hiking time: About 1.25 hours one way or 2.25 hours out and back
Difficulty: Easy to moderate, but strenuous on the climb out on the stairs section
Trail surface: Mostly earthen, with some exposed stone; metal and stone stairway to waterfalls
Best season: Year-round
Other trail users: Hikers only
Canine compatibility: Leashed dogs permitted
Land status: Georgia DNR, State Parks & Historic Sites Division
Nearest town: Trenton
Fees and permits: Daily parking fee
Schedule: Park hours 7 a.m.–10 p.m., year-round; trails close at sunset
Maps: USGS Durham; page-size map available in the park office or from the website
Trail contacts: Cloudland Canyon State Park, 122 Cloudland Canyon Park Rd., Rising Fawn 30738; (706) 657-4050; www.gastateparks.org
Special considerations: You are cautioned to stay on the trail and not climb on rocks or around the waterfalls. The rocks can be very slippery and dangerous.

Caution is also advised for people with heart problems and those in poor physical condition using the waterfalls stairway. From the bottom of the canyon back to the rim, there are 587 metal or stone steps. That's not counting the ones on the 2 side trails to the waterfalls.

Finding the trailhead: On I-59 from Trenton, take exit 11 and go east 6.3 miles on SR 136 to the park entrance. Continue 1.2 miles to East Rim Overlook day-use area. The trailhead is at the overlook parking lot. Trailhead GPS: N34 50.038' / W85 28'

For the lower trailhead of the Sitton Gulch Trail, go 4.5 miles west of the park entrance on SR 136. Turn right on Canyon Park Road and travel 0.3 mile to Canyon Park Drive. Turn right and go 0.1 mile to the entrance drive for the lot. Trailhead GPS: N34 51.598' / W85 29.068'

Hemlock Falls is the larger of the two cascades on Daniel Creek.

The Hike

The Waterfalls / Sitton Gulch Trail can be separated into two parts, but we recommend you tackle the entire route. This hike begins by sharing the path with the West Rim Trail. At the point it forks off to the right, the trail descends on a series of metal and stone steps.

The flowers growing on the steep canyon face are outstanding. Jack-in-the-pulpit, windflower, hydrangea, foamflower, Solomon's seal, long-spurred violet, dwarf crested iris, bellwort, and great patches of trilliums bloom in the spring. Several species of ferns, including maidenhair and marginal, grow among the other lush vegetation. Magnificent yellow poplars, hemlocks, and buckeyes thrive on the lower levels of the gulch.

Side trails to the upper Cherokee Falls and lower Hemlock Falls on Daniel Creek are encountered to the left along the descent. The quantity of water over the falls varies greatly from season to season. The water falls into large splash pools and then continues to cascade down over the boulder-strewn streambed during wet weather. In periods of normal rainfall, the falls and creek can have just a trickle of water.

A strenuous climb back up the stairs from the lower falls provides a 1.6-mile total hike on the Waterfall Trail.

At the intersection with the lower falls side trail, the blue-blazed Sitton Gulch Trail continues over a bridge across Daniel Creek. Just downstream from the bridge, Whiteoak Spring tumbles down the canyon wall after heavy rains, forming a set of falls that are more than 500 feet high. In drier periods, these falls can be completely dry.

The path then meanders through a veritable rock garden of sandstone boulders beneath the forest canopy. Mountain laurel is prevalent along the stream course, with Christmas ferns at trailside.

Shortly, Bear Creek joins Daniel Creek from the east to form Sitton Gulch Creek. The stream then continues beside the path, either tumbling over the boulders after rains, or meandering around them in drier times. Through this stretch the trail is moderate as it descends and drops over bluffs along the creek.

As the trail reaches more level ground, Lunch Table Rock appears on the right. This flat outcrop of sandstone juts over the creek and is a favorite rest and picnic spot for hikers.

At normal water levels, just before reaching Lunch Table, the creek forms a couple of deep pools called "blue holes." The creek then goes completely dry. The only time the rest of the streambed has a flow is after heavy downpours.

The remaining portion of the trail is relatively flat and easy as it runs along an old roadbed through a mixed oak, hickory, poplar, sweet gum, and maple forest. Along here a side trail splits off to the left. Following it creates a clockwise loop that rejoins the main trail. Using this loop and then heading back upstream creates a strenuous hike that totals 5.0 miles.

Halfway around the loop you encounter a sign announcing a Georgia Department of Natural Resources Special Permit Area. Looking up the rock cliff to the left, the entrance to a cave with a metal grating over it is visible. That cave, along with others in the area, is home to several species of bats.

If you chose to make the hike a one-way venture, when the loop rejoins the main trail, turn left and continue to the lower trailhead and parking lot.

Miles and Directions

0.0 Start from trailhead at the parking area.

0.2 Turn right on the Waterfalls Trail into the canyon.

0.3 Pass through the large rock shelter and reach the side trail to Cherokee Falls.

0.7 Take the side trail to Hemlock Falls to the left, or follow the blue blazes across the Daniel Creek bridge for the Sitton Gulch Trail.

0.9 Cross Whiteoak Spring bed at the foot of the seasonal waterfalls.

1.1 Reach the junction of Daniel and Bear Creeks at the head of Sitton Gulch Creek.

2.0 Pass Lunch Table Rock.

2.2 The loop trail splits off to the left.

2.3 The loop trail rejoins the main path.

2.8 Reach the lower trailhead.

The Daniel Creek bridge on the Sitton Gulch Trail

Options

The **2-Mile Backcountry Trail** is a loop beginning at a parking area for the group lodge and tennis courts. This red-blazed trail is designed for backpacking and camping. Eleven primitive campsites are situated along the trail.

The trailhead for the 2-Mile Backcountry Trail is 0.3 mile past the tennis courts at the end of the road.

The **Bear Creek Backcountry Trail** is the newest in the park. It is a permit-only, 9.0-mile lollipop trail that crosses the Bear Creek valley to the ridge to the north. In the process it traverses some private land between sections of the park. This path is moderate to strenuous. To reach the trail, walk 0.5 mile in a clockwise direction on the 2-Mile Backcountry Trail. Then take the orange-blazed trail to the left.

The **Overlook Trail** runs east 0.3 mile from the East Overlook parking area. This path to the overlook is paved and wheelchair accessible.

Local Information

Accommodations

Cloudland Canyon State Park has 72 regular campsites, 11 backcountry campsites, and 16 rental cottages. For information and reservations go to www.gastateparks.org.

3 Crockford–Pigeon Mountain Wildlife Management Area Trails

Most of Pigeon Mountain is in the 19,951-acre Crockford–Pigeon Mountain Wildlife Management Area (WMA) under the supervision of the Department of Natural Resources' (DNR) Wildlife Resources Division. The name comes from the now-extinct passenger pigeon, which once roosted here in great numbers, and the late Jack Crockford, former director of the Wildlife Resources Division.

The mountain is noted for its many extensive caves that honeycomb the limestone formations under the plateau. The best known of those is Ellison Cave, with exceptionally deep pits. Be aware, however, that spelunking is by permit only.

This area has a dozen marked trails stretching well over 40 miles. Many are rated for hiking, biking, and equestrian use. The longest is the West Brow Trail at more than 11 miles, and the shortest is the Shirley Miller Wildflower Trail, composed of an 800-foot, wheelchair-accessible boardwalk.

The Pocket Loop Trail is featured because it provides a microcosm of what Pigeon Mountain has to offer hikers.

Start: At the parking area at the end of Pocket Road
Distance: 9.6-mile loop
Hiking time: About 5.5–6 hours
Difficulty: Moderate to strenuous
Trail surface: Gravel, sandy loam, and exposed rocky areas
Best season: Mar–Dec
Other trail users: Equestrians and hunters in season
Canine compatibility: Leashed dogs permitted
Land status: Georgia DNR, Wildlife Resources Division
Nearest town: Lafayette
Fees and permits: All users must have a wildlife management area hunting license or a Georgia Outdoor Recreation Pass.
Schedules: All trails are closed to equestrians and bicycles during firearms deer season and before 10 a.m. during archery, deer, and turkey seasons (for current hunting seasons: www.gohuntgeorgia.com).
Maps: USGS Cedar Grove and Lafayette; page-size map of the management area available at the check station or from the Department of Natural Resources
Trail contacts: Office of Regional Supervisor, Department of Natural Resources, Wildlife Resources Division, 2592 Floyd Springs Rd., Armuchee 30105; (706) 295-6041; www.gohuntgeorgia.com

Finding the trailhead: For the Pocket Loop Trail go west for 8.9 miles from Lafayette on SR 193 from its junction with SR 136. Turn south on Hog Jowl Road, drive 2.7 miles to Pocket Road and turn left. This turn is difficult to see; it is at the top of a rise just past the Mount Herman Baptist Church.

After 0.4 mile on pavement, Pocket Road changes to gravel for 0.8 mile. The parking area is on the left where the road reaches a dead end, just after fording Pocket Branch. The trailheads are at the gate on the gravel road. Trailhead GPS: N34 42.741' / W85 22.791'

View from the rock overlook at High Point on the top of Pigeon Mountain

The Hike

The Pocket Loop Trail begins at 890 feet elevation and climbs to 2,293 feet. It traverses an excellent wildlife and birding area with fine scenery, especially in winter.

The trail begins with a walk up a service road paralleling Pocket Branch to a grassy wildlife clearing. Along the way the left side is lined with layered sedimentary rock that hints of its origins on the floor of a prehistoric sea. The trail also passes on the right what would be an impressive 50-foot waterfall, except that it is dry for most of the year. Usually, Pocket Branch bubbles up out of the rocks at its foot.

In the clearing the trail forks into a loop. Turn to the right to walk the trail counterclockwise.

The blue-blazed trail crosses Pocket Branch to pass through a hardwood forest of oaks, hickories, red cedars, yellow poplars, buckeyes, and mulberries. The undergrowth is dogwoods, redbuds, sourwoods, mountain laurel, sweet shrub, wild hydrangea, spicebush, blueberry, and azalea.

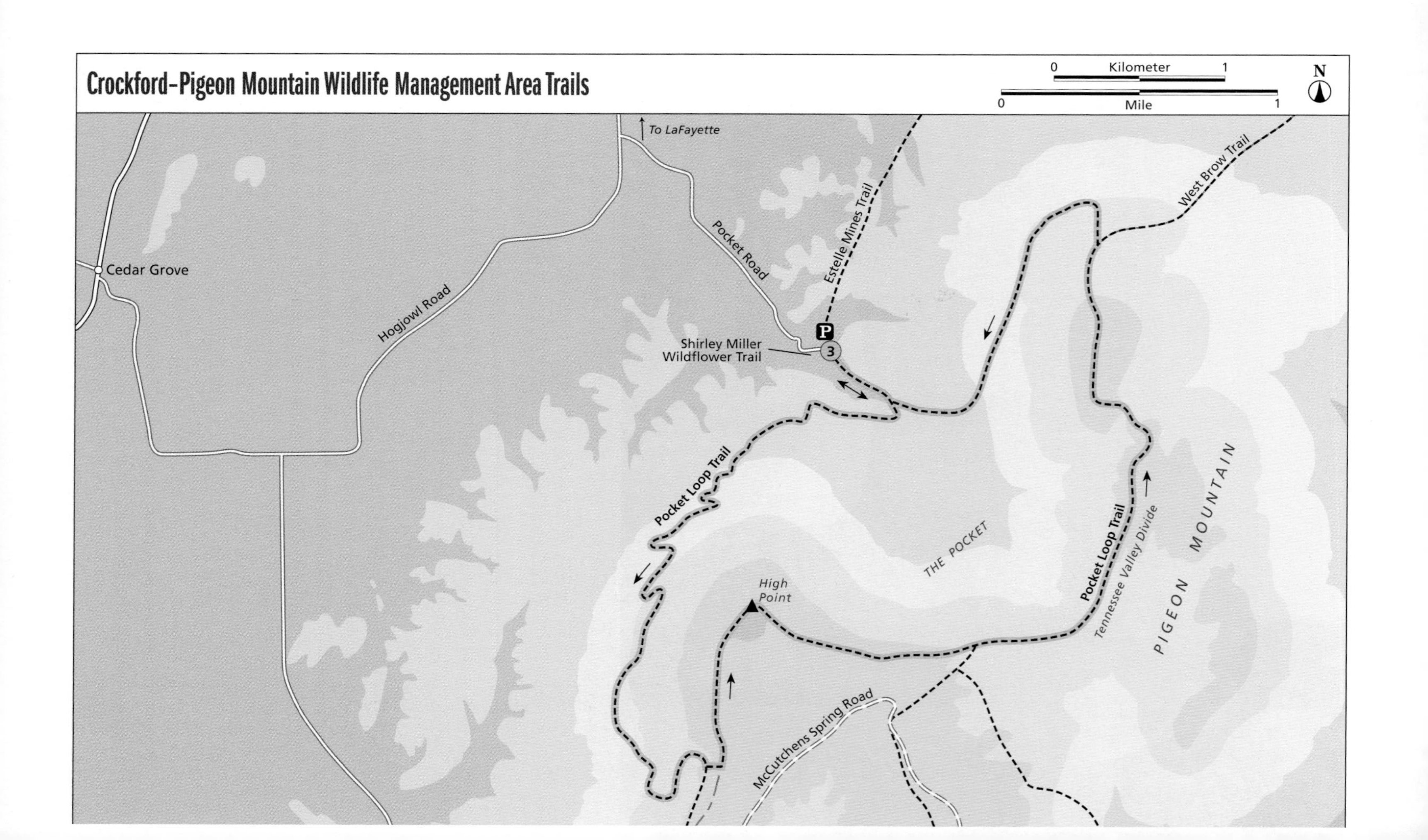
Crockford–Pigeon Mountain Wildlife Management Area Trails
0
Kilometer
1
0
Mile
1
N
To LaFayette
West Brow Trail
Estelle Mines Trail
Pocket Road
Cedar Grove
Hogjowl Road
P
3
Shirley Miller
Wildflower Trail
Pocket Loop Trail
THE POCKET
High
Point
Pocket Loop Trail
Tennessee Valley Divide
PIGEON MOUNTAIN
McCutchens Spring Road

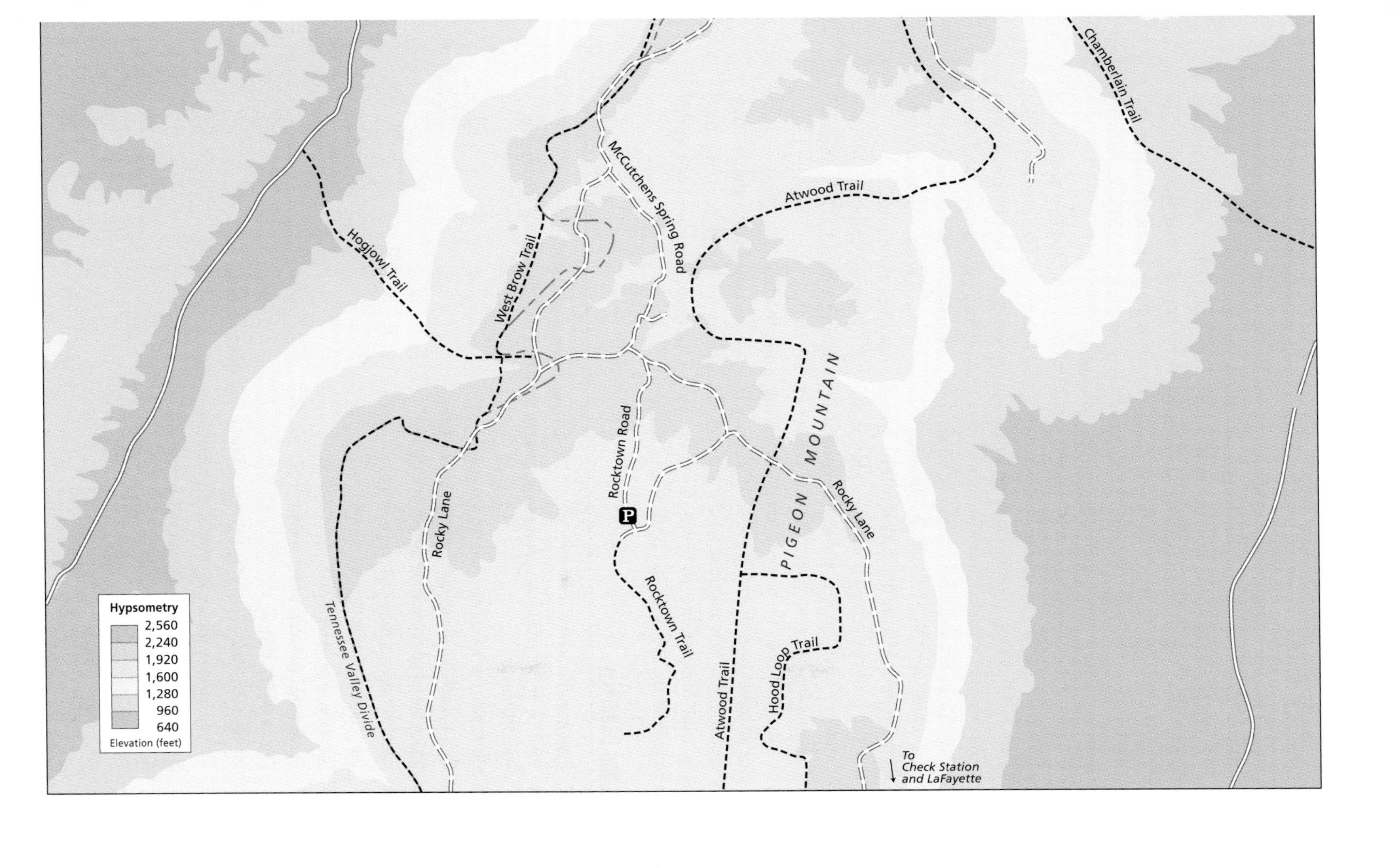
Chamberlain Trail
Atwood Trail
McCutchens Spring Road
Hogjowl Trail
West Brow Trail
PIGEON MOUNTAIN
Rocktown Road
P
Rocky Lane
Rocky Lane
Rocktown Trail
Atwood Trail
Hood Loop Trail
Tennessee Valley Divide
To Check Station and LaFayette
Hypsometry
2,560
2,240
1,920
1,600
1,280
960
640
Elevation (feet)

The path climbs for the next 3.2 miles to High Point, which is the crest of Pigeon Mountain. There are no long, steep grades, and switchbacks keep the climb moderate, although you gain more than 1,400 feet of elevation.

At the top of the first short climb the trail passes beneath a black walnut tree on the left, with a very deep erosion gully on the right. A bit later the path goes through the first of several dry spring beds. This one is framed by huge boulders above and below the trail. You also pass a small sinkhole opening on the left of the trail, confirming the porous nature of the substratum on the mountain.

At the top of the ridge, the path intersects the West Brow Trail, marked with white blazes. Turn left to continue up the combined trails to High Point. This portion of the walk passes stunted Virginia pines and abundant blueberry bushes. Just before getting to that crest there is a rocky overlook facing west that offers a great year-round view.

Passing through a wildlife clearing at High Point, the trail then skirts the edge of the massif on the west side of Pigeon Mountain for the next 2.7 miles. Along the way it passes the junction with the Atwood Trail, which joins from the right.

Once the trail turns down off the ridge, it follows a long rock wall on the left. Many boulders have broken loose from this face, forming unique and interesting shapes. The rock face ends where the trail crosses Pocket Branch high in its dry headwater region. The path then turns steeply downhill along the branch.

Once it levels out, the trail crosses the branch again and passes through a large grassy clearing. Just beyond that field a small pond appears on the right of the trail. Entering a second clearing, the path closes the loop. Continue straight ahead at this point to follow the service road back to the trailhead.

Miles and Directions

0.0 Start from the parking area. Step around the bar gate in the service road.

0.4 Pass the dry waterfall and start the loop, going to the right out of the clearing and crossing Pocket Branch.

0.6 Climb past the walnut tree and erosion gully.

1.1 Pass through the dry streambed with huge boulders.

1.5 Reach the small sinkhole on the left of the path.

3.1 Intersect the West Brow Trail and turn left.

3.7 The year-round overlook is on the left.

3.8 Cross the peak of High Point.

4.9 The Atwood Trail enters from the right.

5.9 Enter a wildlife clearing.

6.0 The West Brow Trail splits off to the right at the far end. Continue to the left.

6.5 The trail begins to descend down off the mountain.

7.3 The rock face appears on the left side of the trail.

8.2 Reach the end of the rock face.

8.3 Cross Pocket Branch.

8.8 Recross Pocket Branch and enter a wildlife clearing.

8.9 Pass the pond on the right and enter the second clearing.

9.1 Close the loop and continue down the service road.

9.6 Arrive back at the trailhead.

Options

The **Rock Town Trail** is a 2.2-mile out-and-back hike over a flat, easy course. The main attraction of the path is the collection of huge brownish-red rock formations known as Rock Town that sits at its end. The trailhead is on top of Pigeon Mountain at the end of Rock Town Road.

The **Shirley Miller Wildflower Trail** is an 800-foot boardwalk through a small mixed hardwood cove. Eleven plants found almost nowhere else in the state are present along the route.

The **Estelle Mines Trail** covers 4.8 miles, extending from the trailhead on SR 193 at the north end of the WMA to the parking area for the Pocket Loop Trail. Old tunnels from iron mining in the early twentieth century are located along this orange-blazed trail.

The **West Brow Trail** has white blazes and runs for 11.8 miles from the Estelle Mines trailhead to Rape Gap in the southern portion of the WMA. The first 3.3 miles of the path is also called the **Cane Trail** as it climbs Pigeon Mountain. Once on the top, the trail continues along the western edge of the massif.

The **Chamberlain Trail** starts at a trailhead on Chamberlain Road, climbing the eastern side of the mountain. Blazed red, the pathway runs for 2.7 miles.

At 10.7 miles in length, the **Atwood Trail** is the second longest on the tract. Its southern trailhead is in Rape Gap. The path runs up the central portion of the mountain crest, connecting to the Chamberlain and West Brow Trails. This trail is marked with orange blazes.

The **Hogjowl Trail** climbs 2.5 miles up the western side of Pigeon Mountain from its trailhead on Hogjowl Road. The path has red blazes. It intersects the West Brow Trail and ends at the Sawmill Lake camping area.

The **Hood Loop Trail** spans 6.2 miles beginning at the Hood Overlook. This overlook is a popular launch point for hang gliders and parasailers. The trail runs concurrent with a portion of the Atwood Trail and then curls to the east to form a loop in the upper Allen Creek watershed.

4 James H. (Sloppy) Floyd State Park Trails

This state park is in the Ridge and Valley district of northwest Georgia, just to the south of the city of Summerville. The facility was named for local politician Sloppy Floyd, who served in the Georgia General Assembly from 1953 to 1974.

The park lies in a region of steep ridges separated by wide valleys that frequently contain springs. The flora is dominated by hardwood forests, with pines more prevalent in areas that have be cleared and reforested. Old mines also dot the terrain in and around the park.

Recent additions have brought the trail system to a total of more than 5.5 miles in the state park. The park trails also connect with a section of the 330-mile Pinhoti Trail that runs through northern Alabama and Georgia. The featured hike is the Marble Mine Loop, combining the Jenkins Gap and Marble Mine Trails with portions of the Upper Lake Loop and Pinhoti Trail.

Start: At the Jenkins Gap Trailhead in the parking area for the Pinhoti Trail approach at the southwest end of Upper Lake
Distance: 3.8-mile loop
Hiking time: About 3.5–4 hours
Difficulty: Moderate to strenuous
Trail surface: Hard-packed soil, with gravel in old roadbeds and some exposed rock on the ridge
Best season: Mar–June; Oct–Dec
Other trail users: Anglers on the portion of the Upper Lake Loop
Canine compatibility: Leashed dogs permitted
Land status: Georgia DNR, State Parks & Historic Sites Division
Nearest town: Summerville
Fees and permits: Daily parking fee
Schedule: Park hours 7 a.m.–10 p.m., year-round
Maps: USGS Summerville; color map of trails available at the park office
Trail contacts: James H. (Sloppy) Floyd State Park, 2800 Sloppy Floyd Lake Rd., Summerville 30747; (706) 857-0826; www.gastateparks.org

Finding the trailhead: Take US 27 east from Summerville for 2.6 miles. Turn right (south) on Sloppy Floyd Lake Road and continue 3.1 miles to the park entrance on the left. After passing the park office on the right, continue to the end of Upper Lake on the left. The Pinhoti Trail parking lot is on the left. Trailhead GPS: N34 25.997' / W85 20.474'

The Hike

The Marble Mine Loop Trail features an old marble mine, a 700-foot change of elevation in climbing up and back down from Taylor Ridge, and a walk along the flat lakeshore.

The hike begins on the 1.1-mile Jenkins Gap Trail, which is also used as an approach to the Pinhoti Trail. From the gravel parking area, begin following the blue-blazed trail to the southeast. In the first few yards the trail is lined with Christmas ferns and foamflowers that have stalks of white blossoms in the early spring. The forest cover is composed of white and chestnut oaks, mixed with hickory, maple, sweet gum, elm, yellow poplar, dogwood, buckeye, and pines.

Pool and boardwalk at the entrance to Marble Mine

Shortly the trail enters an old roadbed and begins climbing toward Taylor Ridge. After 0.2 mile the trail leaves the road, and near this point a white-blazed connector trail runs off to the left to the Marble Mine Trail.

Continuing to follow the blue blazes, the path climbs more steeply and passes another white-blazed connector on the left. This trail leads to the old Marble Mine, creating a shorter loop.

As the Jenkins Gap Trail heads on up toward Taylor Ridge, the incline increases dramatically, becoming very steep and rocky in the final 0.2 mile. Through here the trail features the purple blossoms of spiderwort and white flowers of black cohosh in June. Also along the path are heartleaf, Virginia creeper, blackberry, and greenbrier.

Once on the ridge at the end of the Jenkins Gap Trail, turn left and follow the Pinhoti Trail on an old dirt road. There are no blazes along this trail, but boundary signs for the state park property are posted along the left side of the road.

This ridgetop walk provides some good wintertime views of the surrounding landscape. The path is bordered by buckeyes and Virginia pines, with abundant blueberries and wild petunias that bloom purple in the summer.

At the intersection with the Marble Mine Trail, turn left and begin steeply descending Taylor Ridge on another old roadbed. The trail through here is lined by

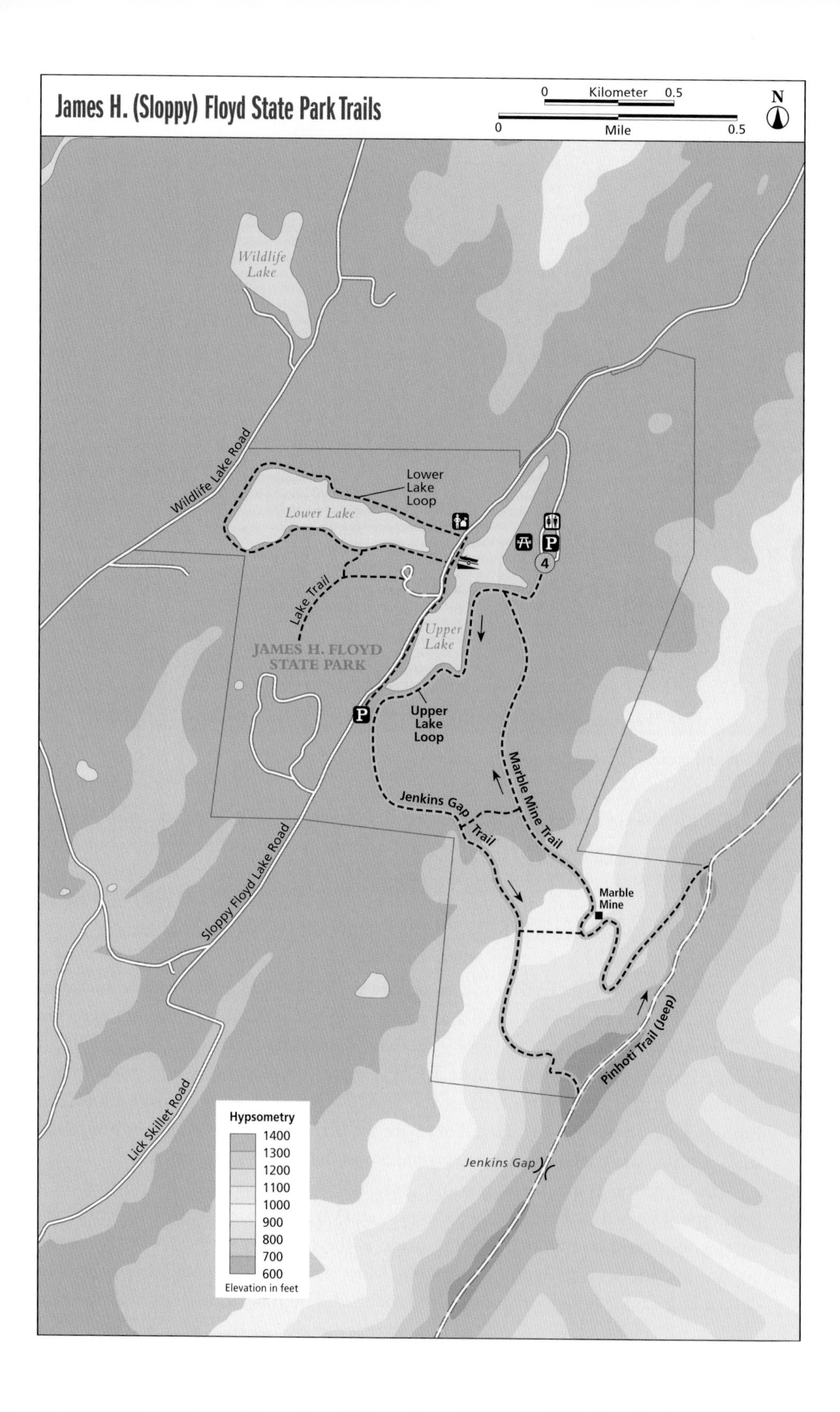
James H. (Sloppy) Floyd State Park Trails
0 Kilometer 0.5
0 Mile 0.5
N
Wildlife Lake
Wildlife Lake Road
Lower Lake Loop
Lower Lake
Lake Trail
Upper Lake
JAMES H. FLOYD STATE PARK
Upper Lake Loop
4
Marble Mine Trail
Jenkins Gap Trail
Marble Mine
Sloppy Floyd Lake Road
Pinhoti Trail (Jeep)
Lick Skillet Road
Jenkins Gap
Hypsometry
1400
1300
1200
1100
1000
900
800
700
600
Elevation in feet

small red maple trees. As you walk watch for the purple flowers of wild bergamot in the summer, as well as the brown-stemmed spleenwort.

This 1.5-mile trail passes the old Marble Mine, which has a reflecting pool and a boardwalk built across the openings of the twin shafts back into the mountain. Even on the hottest day a cool breeze comes from these caverns. A small stream dropping over the lip from the top of the cave creates a tiny waterfall dripping into the pool below.

From here the trail follows a gravel service road, which is still in use, as it passes through more open woodlands that contain a few red cedars. On the right you pass a tiny concrete building that has no windows and is the only remaining structure from the mining operation.

Reaching the junction with the Upper Lake Loop, turn left and follow this 0.5-mile pink-blazed pathway along the lakeshore. The trail crosses two footbridges and then emerges in an open grassy area at the end of the lake. Just before the Upper Lake Loop crosses a footbridge, a blue-blazed trail runs into the forest on the left. This leads back to the parking area and trailhead for the Jenkins Gap Trail.

Miles and Directions

0.0 Start at the Pinhoti Access Trailhead on the Jenkins Gap Trail.

0.1 Enter an old roadbed.

0.3 Exit the roadbed and pass the connector to the Marble Mine Trail on the left.

0.5 Pass the connector trail on the left running to the Marble Mine and begin the steep ascent up Taylor Ridge.

1.1 Reach the end of the Jenkins Gap Trail and turn left on the Pinhoti Trail.

1.7 Turn left onto the Marble Mine Trail.

2.4 Pass the east end of the white-blazed connector path from the Jenkins Gap Trail.

2.5 Reach the Marble Mine on the right of the trail.

2.8 Pass the second white-blazed connector on the left for the Jenkins Gap Trail.

3.0 The small concrete building is on the right of the trail.

3.2 At the junction with the Upper Lake Loop, turn to the left on that trail, or turn right and cross the bridge for the trailhead of the Marble Mine Trail.

3.7 Turn left onto the blue-blazed trail leading back to the trailhead.

3.8 Arrive back at the trailhead parking lot.

Options

The **Lower Lake Loop** runs around the shore of Lower Lake. This 1.0-mile path provides a flat, easy walk.

The **Upper Lake Loop** is a 1.0-mile trail circling the western half of the Upper Lake. It crosses a footbridge over the lake near the park office.

The **Lake Trail** is a short path connecting the campground to the fishing area on the south side of Lower Lake.

5 Chickamauga Creek Trail

The trail lies in the Chattahoochee National Forest, straddling the ridgeline that separates the Tennessee and Alabama River watersheds. Ponder Branch flows south to the Alabama River system. East Chickamauga Creek flows north before emptying into the Tennessee and Mississippi River system. The protected watersheds for these small permanent streams lie completely within the national forest.

The length and diversity of this trail makes for a nice half-day excursion as you hike up and down two ridges with moderately steep grades. There are no grand views, but there is plenty of wildlife, wildflowers, and forest types. The streams, hardwood forests mixed with pine and laurel thickets, ridgetops, and valleys make this trail an exceptionally good birding area. There's also a good population of deer, turkey, and other small game.

Start: At the Ponder Creek Road trailhead
Distance: 6.3-mile loop
Hiking time: About 3–4 hours
Difficulty: Moderate
Trail Surface: Mostly earth, with some rocks
Best season: Year-round
Other trail users: Hunters in season
Canine compatibility: Dogs permitted
Land status: Chattahoochee National Forest
Nearest town: Lafayette
Fees and permits: None
Schedules: Open year-round
Maps: USGS Catlett; *Trail Guide to the Chattahoochee-Oconee National Forests*
Trail contacts: USDA Forest Service, Conasauga Ranger District, 3941 US 76, Chatsworth 30705; (706) 695-6736; www.fs.usda.gov/conf
Special considerations: Wearing a blaze-orange cap or vest is advised during fall deer and spring turkey hunting seasons.

Finding the trailhead: Go west from I-75 at Resaca on SR 136 for 21 miles. Turn right (north) on Ponder Creek Road and travel 0.6 mile on the paved road, and then angle off to the right onto unpaved FS 219. Go 1.7 miles to the end of the road, fording small Ponder Branch on the way. At the end of FS 219 is a turnaround and primitive camping area. From the parking area there is no indication which way the trail runs. Facing toward the end of the road, the trail runs to the right (east), following Ponder Branch upstream. Trailhead GPS: N34 42.748' / W85 09.736'

The Hike

The Chickamauga Creek loop trail can be hiked in either direction. This hike starts at the Ponder Branch trailhead and travels clockwise on the loop. A short path leads from the parking area across Ponder Branch to the loop trail. At the loop junction the trail passes across a power line right-of-way.

On the opposite side of the right-of-way, a lime-green metal blaze can be seen marking where the trail reenters the woods. As you hike up Ponder Branch through Baker Hollow, the path crosses the stream several times.

The trail passes through a hardwood forest containing many big American beech trees. During the spring, beneath the canopy the white blossoms of milkweed, orange

Sandstone rock formations are fairly common along the crest of Dick Ridge.

butterfly weed, and purple spiderwort are common. Other prevalent plants are sassafras, greenbrier, and Virginia creeper, with mountain laurel along the streambed.

Soon the path leaves Ponder Branch and begins gently climbing toward the ridge to the right. Upon cresting the ridge at the Tennessee Valley Divide, the trail reaches the crossing at the junction of FS 250 and FS 250A. The path crosses the intersection diagonally, and it may require a bit of searching to find where it enters the woods again. That point has a trail marker, but it is not easy to see.

The path next descends down to East Chickamauga Creek, where it follows an old roadbed downstream. This small stream flows through limestone rocks. The water is clear, and many snails—called periwinkles—can be seen attached to the stones. Wildflowers are abundant along the creek, as are Christmas and New York ferns.

The trail next turns sharply uphill to the right to ascend a number of switchbacks up onto Dick Ridge. Along the climb the path passes through patches of wild bergamot that bloom pale lavender in the spring.

Just before reaching the crest of the ridge, the trail enters an abandoned logging road. Once on top the old road and trail turn sharply south along Dick Ridge.

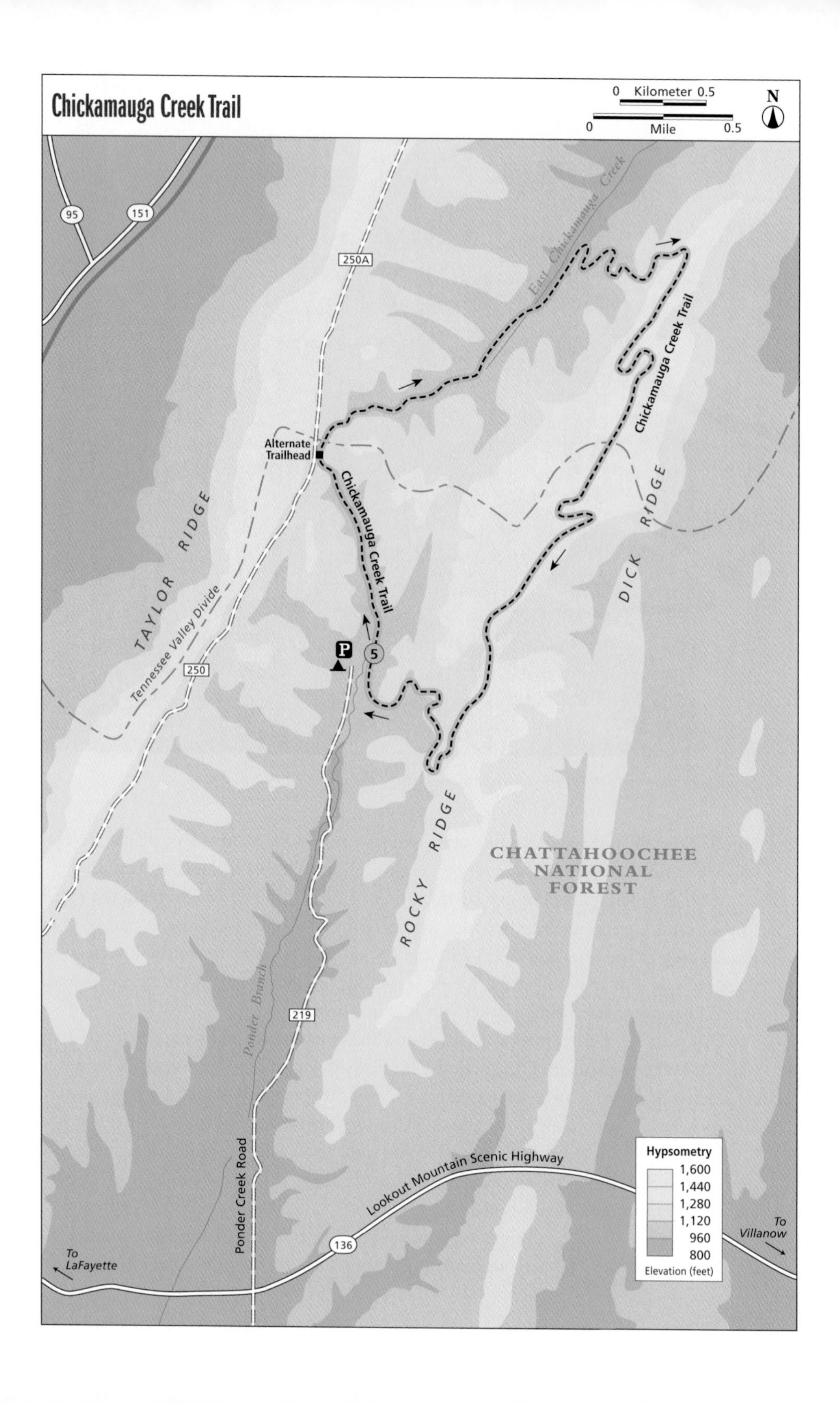

Chickamauga Creek Trail
0 Kilometer 0.5
0 Mile 0.5
N
95
151
250A
East Chickamauga Creek
Chickamauga Creek Trail
Alternate Trailhead
Chickamauga Creek Trail
TAYLOR RIDGE
Tennessee Valley Divide
250
5
P
DICK RIDGE
ROCKY RIDGE
CHATTAHOOCHEE NATIONAL FOREST
Ponder Branch
219
Ponder Creek Road
Lookout Mountain Scenic Highway
136
To LaFayette
To Villanow
Hypsometry
1,600
1,440
1,280
1,120
960
800
Elevation (feet)

A formation of sandstone rocks lines the crest of the ridge to the right of the path. Stunted Virginia pines grow from crevices amid these boulders.

As you walk along the crest, keep an eye out for the yellow-and-brown-patterned shells of box turtles. The reptiles are fairly abundant along the ridge.

The trail next passes through a couple of switchbacks to reach the highest point on Dick Ridge at 1,562 feet. From there the path continues on the logging road, passing through a more open forest.

The bright orange displays of butterfly weed brighten the path in the spring.

After turning off the road to the right, the trail snakes its way off Dick Ridge, passing across the power line right-of-way again. All trees have been cleared from beneath the transmission lines, and this open area attracts deer.

Next the trail climbs up to the crest of Rocky Ridge and then continues gently down its side through coves of mountain laurel. When the path again reaches the power line, turn to the left and walk about 30 yards. Another left turn closes the loop and heads back to the parking area.

Miles and Directions

- **0.0** Start to the east from the parking area and cross Ponder Branch to begin the loop at 100 yards.
- **0.6** The trail leaves the headwaters of Ponder Branch.
- **0.9** Reach FS 250 and FS 250A.
- **1.1** East Chickamauga Creek appears to the left of the trail.
- **2.1** The trail leaves the creek and ascends sharply up switchbacks to Dick Ridge.
- **2.7** Enter the bed of the old logging road, continuing to the left.
- **2.9** Reach the crest of Dick Ridge and turn south. The sandstone rock formation is now on the right.
- **3.2** Pass the end of the rock formation.
- **3.8** Reach the rounded crest on the west side of Dick Ridge and begin to descend.
- **4.3** Exit the logging road.
- **4.8** Cross the power line right-of-way.
- **6.3** Close the loop and turn left to the parking area.

6 Johns Mountain Wildlife Management Area Trails

The Johns Mountain Wildlife Management Area (WMA) is a 24,589-acre tract of land within the Chattahoochee National Forest.

The WMA is located in the unique Ridge and Valley physiographic province, which terminates just to the west in Alabama. To the northeast this type of terrain and habitat extends through Tennessee, Virginia, Maryland, Pennsylvania, and New York. It is characterized by porous limestone and sandstone sedimentary rock formations, with many smaller streams that go completely dry during warmer months.

The Johns Mountain WMA has three main hiking trails. The Johns Mountain Trail circles the crest of its namesake. The Keown Falls Trail climbs up to the falls from which it takes its name and back down the side of the mountain to form a loop. Farther south, the Pocket Recreation Area Trail provides an easy lowland alternative hike.

A portion of the Pinhoti Trail also crosses the WMA and joins the path of both the Johns Mountain and Keown Falls Trails for short distances.

The Johns Mountain Trail is the featured hike.

Start: At the parking area at the end of FS 208
Distance: 3.1-mile loop
Hiking time: About 2.5 hours
Difficulty: Easy to moderate
Trail surface: Dirt, with some rocky portions
Best season: Oct–June
Other trail users: Hunters in season
Canine compatibility: Dogs permitted
Land status: Chattahoochee National Forest
Nearest town: Lafayette
Fees and permits: None
Schedule: Trails open year-round
Maps: USGS Sugar Valley, Calhoun; Chattahoochee National Forest Map
Trail contacts: USDA Forest Service, Conasauga Ranger District, 3941 US 76, Chatsworth 30705; (706) 695-6736; www.fs.usda.gov/conf
Special considerations: There is some type of hunting season open on the tract during most of the year. When hiking during hunting seasons, stay on the trails and wear blaze-orange apparel, such as a cap or jacket. Check www.gohuntgeorgia.com for the exact dates for hunting on the WMA.

Finding the trailhead: To get to the Johns Mountain Trailhead from I-75 at Resaca, go west on SR 136 for 14.0 miles and turn left on Pocket Road. Go 3.9 miles south to FS 208 and turn right. Continue 2.1 miles to the parking area for the Johns Mountain Overlook. The trailhead is at the parking lot. Trailhead GPS: N34 37.383' / W85 05.895'

The Hike

The Johns Mountain Trail begins at a well-designed observation deck on one of the highest points on this ridge. In fact, the deck is the signature site on this hike. Great sunsets are common from this vantage point. The view extends to Taylor Ridge, Pigeon, and Lookout Mountains to the west across the Armuchee Valley.

The Johns Mountain Overlook is located at the trailhead parking area.

The Johns Mountain Overlook deck is wheelchair accessible from the parking area.

Although the direction sign for the trail indicates walking counterclockwise, the trek is much easier when walked clockwise. To do so, start at the trailhead directly across the parking area from the observation deck.

The trail immediately begins descending to the east side of the ridge. On the section from the parking area to the Keown Falls Overlook, the path is blazed green, but it also has the white, turkey-track blazes of the Pinhoti Trail. The Pinhoti follows a portion of the approach road, before joining the Johns Mountain trail at the parking lot.

The right side of the first part of the trail is lined by a thick hardwood forest. On the left the woods are much thinner out to the steep drop to the east. The forest through here shows the scars of storm damage in the last few years. Watch for a stone outcropping on the crest of the ridge in this open area. It offers a great view to the east toward Furnace Valley and Horn Mountain.

As the descent levels out, the Keown Falls observation deck appears on the left. The deck provides a good view of the top of the falls. Keown Falls, a 60-foot straight

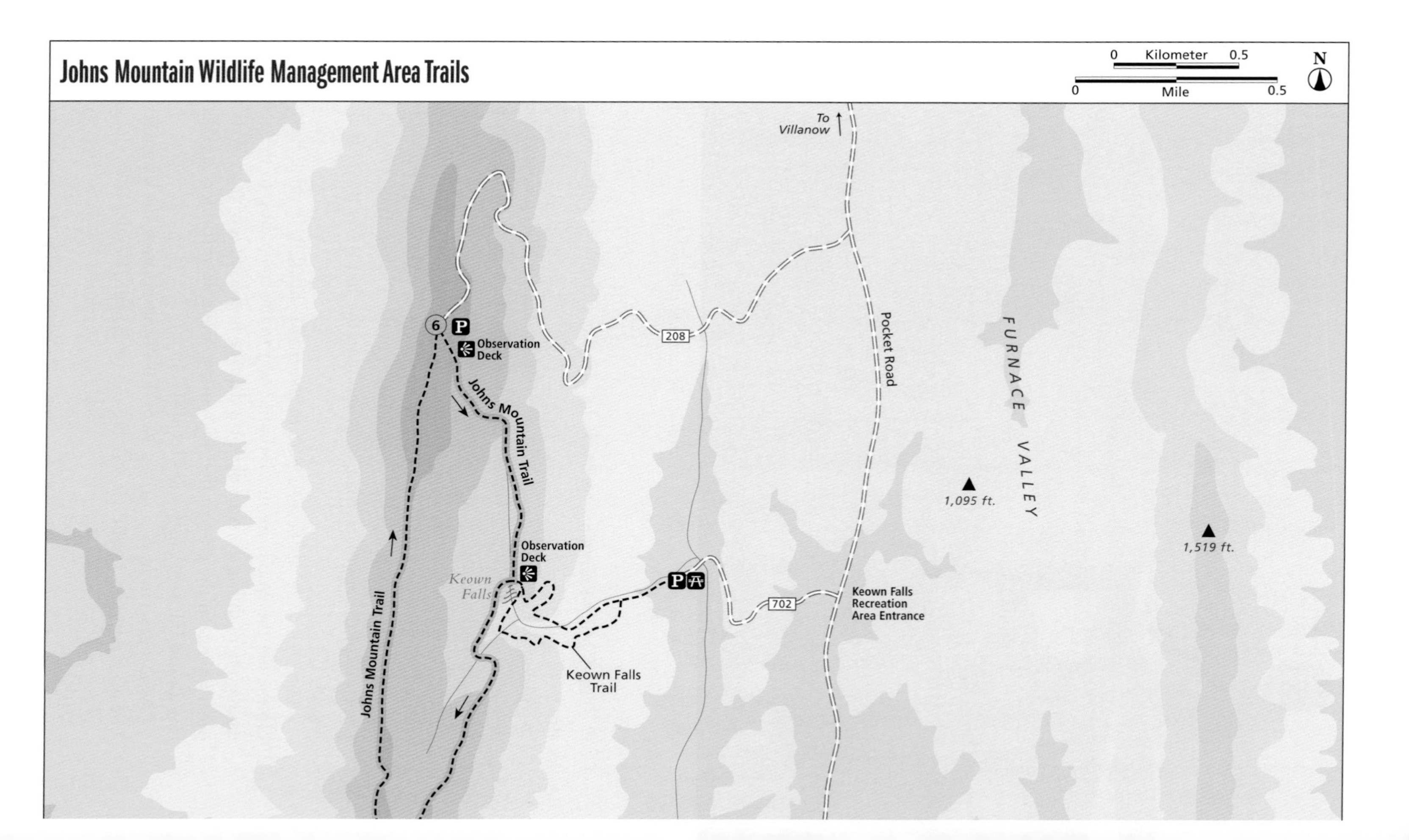
Johns Mountain Wildlife Management Area Trails
0 Kilometer 0.5
0 Mile 0.5
N
To Villanow
Pocket Road
FURNACE VALLEY
1,095 ft.
1,519 ft.
208
702
Observation Deck
Johns Mountain Trail
Observation Deck
Keown Falls
Keown Falls Trail
Keown Falls Recreation Area Entrance
Johns Mountain Trail
6

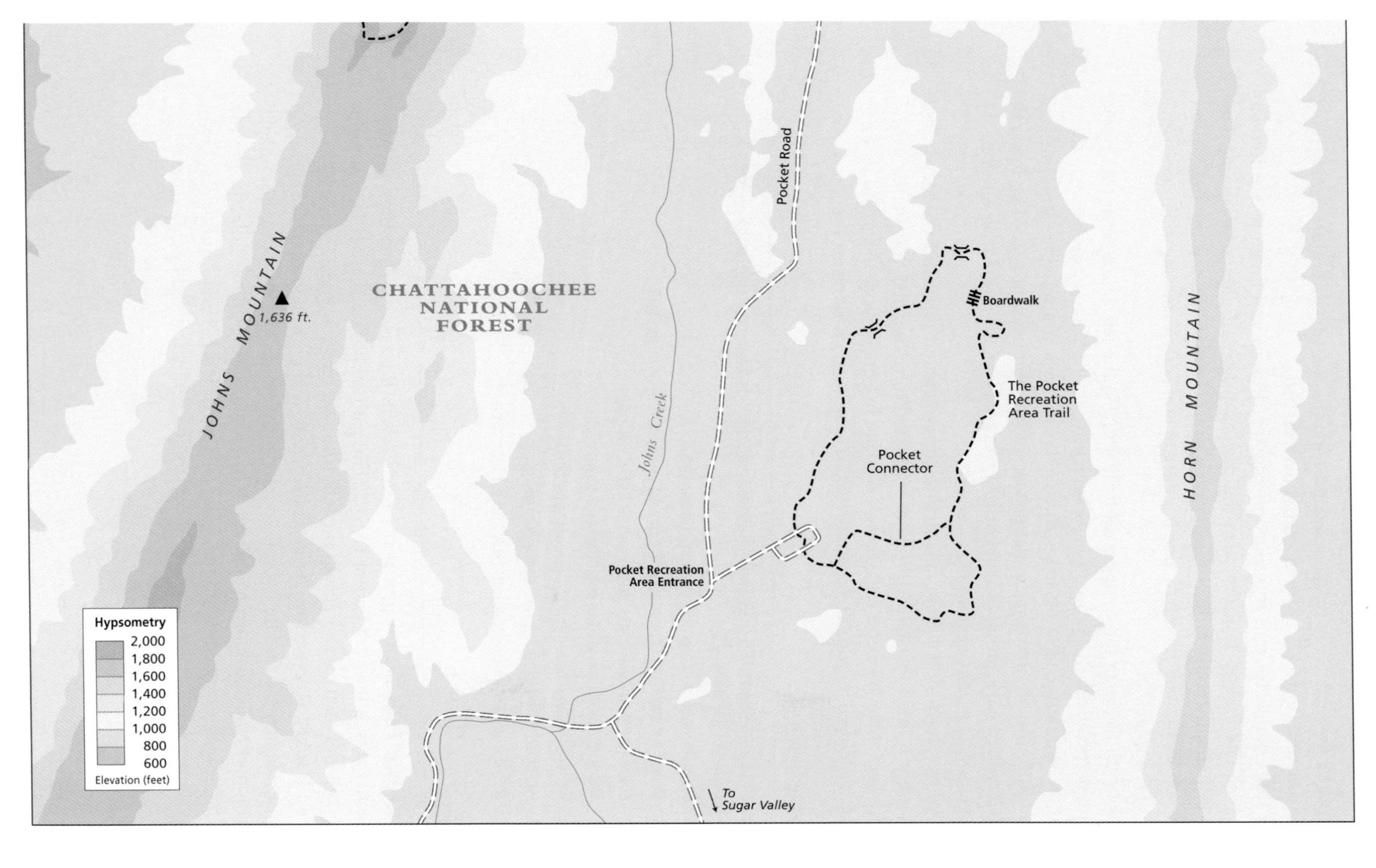

JOHNS MOUNTAIN
1,636 ft.
CHATTAHOOCHEE NATIONAL FOREST
Johns Creek
Pocket Road
Boardwalk
The Pocket Recreation Area Trail
Pocket Connector
Pocket Recreation Area Entrance
HORN MOUNTAIN
To Sugar Valley
Hypsometry
2,000
1,800
1,600
1,400
1,200
1,000
800
600
Elevation (feet)

drop over a rock ledge, can be spectacular during the wet season. Unfortunately, most of the time only a trickle of water comes over the falls.

A short connector trail also splits off past the deck to lead down to the Keown Falls Trail. The Pinhoti Trail also takes this path as it descends the mountainside. The Johns Mountain Trail continues south over a short boardwalk across the tiny stream at the top of the falls. The trail also begins to climb, often running right along the edge of the ridge.

The path passes an interesting rock formation on the left. Three large, thin boulders jut perpendicularly up from the ground, leaving very narrow cuts between them.

At the southern end of the ridge, the trail curves back around to the west side and turns north. You are now on the flat plateau of the mountain in a parklike forest of smaller, twisted oaks, pines, and hickories. Occasional breaks in the trees allow peeks of the same view you get from the overlook.

The west brow of the mountain on the left is steep, and about halfway back to the trailhead, it is lined for about 100 yards with sandstone boulders. Just before reaching the end of the hike, the trail passes a clearing holding a radio tower and its small service building. The path then completes the loop at the parking area trailhead.

Miles and Directions

0.0 Start at the end of FS 208 and the observation deck, following the trail at the southeast corner of the parking lot.

0.6 Pass the rock outcrop and overlook on the left.

0.8 Reach Keown Falls Observation Deck and connector trail on the left.

1.3 Three perpendicular rocks jut up on the left of the path.

1.7 The trail rounds the end of the ridge and turns north.

2.6 Reach the large boulders on the west face of the ridge.

3.0 Go through the clearing with the radio tower.

3.1 Arrive back at the observation deck and parking area.

Options

The **Keown Falls Trail** begins at the Keown Falls Recreation Area from the day-use picnic area at the west end of FS 702. The path climbs up the east face of Johns Mountain and then passes beneath the falls in a counterclockwise 1.7-mile loop.

The **Pocket Recreation Area Trail** begins at the campground and spring in a popular camping area. The Pocket is a valley surrounded by the horseshoe-shaped formation of Mill and Horn Mountains. The natural spring gushes from the ground to form a small stream through the facility. The trail is a 2.8-mile, mostly level loop that is white blazed. It provides access to a unique geological and botanical area.

7 Arrowhead Wildlife Interpretive Trail

Located on the 400-acre Arrowhead Wildlife Management Area, this trail runs through a tract formerly used as a state fish hatchery. This easy, level hike winds in and out of a dozen or more different wildlife habitat types, including open fields, forest, forest edge, and water. This trail provides a short course in wildlife management for both game and nongame animals. Interpretive signs strategically placed along the path explain what has been done to improve the diversity of animals and plants. The trail is short enough for a quick morning or evening walk and has enough variety to keep you busy for a day of watching and photography.

Start: At the parking area with an information board
Distance: 1.8-mile loop
Hiking time: About 1.5 hours
Difficulty: Easy
Trail surface: Earthen, with sod in places
Best season: Year-round
Other trail users: Hunters in season
Canine compatibility: Leashed dogs permitted
Land status: Georgia DNR, Wildlife Resources Division
Nearest town: Rome
Fees and permits: None
Schedule: Dawn to dusk, year-round
Maps: USGS Armuchee; Wildlife Resources Division trail map available in the headquarters office
Trail contacts: Georgia Wildlife Resources Division, Game Management Section, 2592 Floyd Springs Rd., Armuchee 30105; (706) 295-6041; www.gohuntgeorgia.com
Special considerations: Managed archery deer hunts, as well as small game and waterfowl hunts, are held here in the fall and winter. For specific dates visit www.georgiawildlife.com/hunting.

Finding the trailhead: From Rome go north about 10 miles on US 27. Turn right (east) onto SR 156. Go 2.4 miles and turn left (north) onto Floyd Springs Road. Drive 1.9 miles to a special parking area just before the main entrance to the DNR Wildlife Resources Division Northwest Regional Game Management Headquarters. The trailhead is at the gravel parking area on the right of the road, along with a large sign with orientation information and a map of the trail. Trailhead GPS: N34 26.387' / W85 09.051'

The Hike

A number of marked points on the trail are interpreted in a brochure available in the Region Office. Presently, however, many of the signs along the trail are very faded or missing.

The wide, easy-to-follow path begins at the corner of the parking area. The trail begins by overlooking the old fish hatchery ponds that are now managed for waterfowl. The path goes through an open area past the first interpretive sign that provides information about waterfowl and wading birds. The trail also passes a platform overlooking a small pond on the right of the trail. A wood duck nest box is mounted on a post in the willow- and alder-lined pool.

A small deck offers view of a waterfowl pond near the start of the trail.

At the junction where the end of the loop rejoins the trail, take the right fork and pass a pole with gourds for martin nest boxes. Next you enter into a wooded area, where the trail is marked with blue blazes.

At first this stretch is a pure pine stand, where dwarf iris blooms beside the path in April. This is a good area for spotting some of the white-tailed deer population.

The trees soon transition into a hardwood forest as the path follows a dirt roadbed that was created as a firebreak. Blueberries are abundant where prescribed burns have encouraged their growth.

The trail next passes through a small field of grasses, clover, and a few small shrubs. This is a planted opening in the forest to provide food for a number of different animals. The edge of the opening is important to many birds not otherwise found in the woods, and many other animals take advantage of these grassy openings.

The path goes back into the woods, through a wet area, and passes a sign discussing the important practice of prescribed burning.

As you enter another open field, a small pond appears on the right. Nest boxes for wood ducks are located here. Bluebirds also thrive in these old open fields, which have nest boxes for those songbirds.

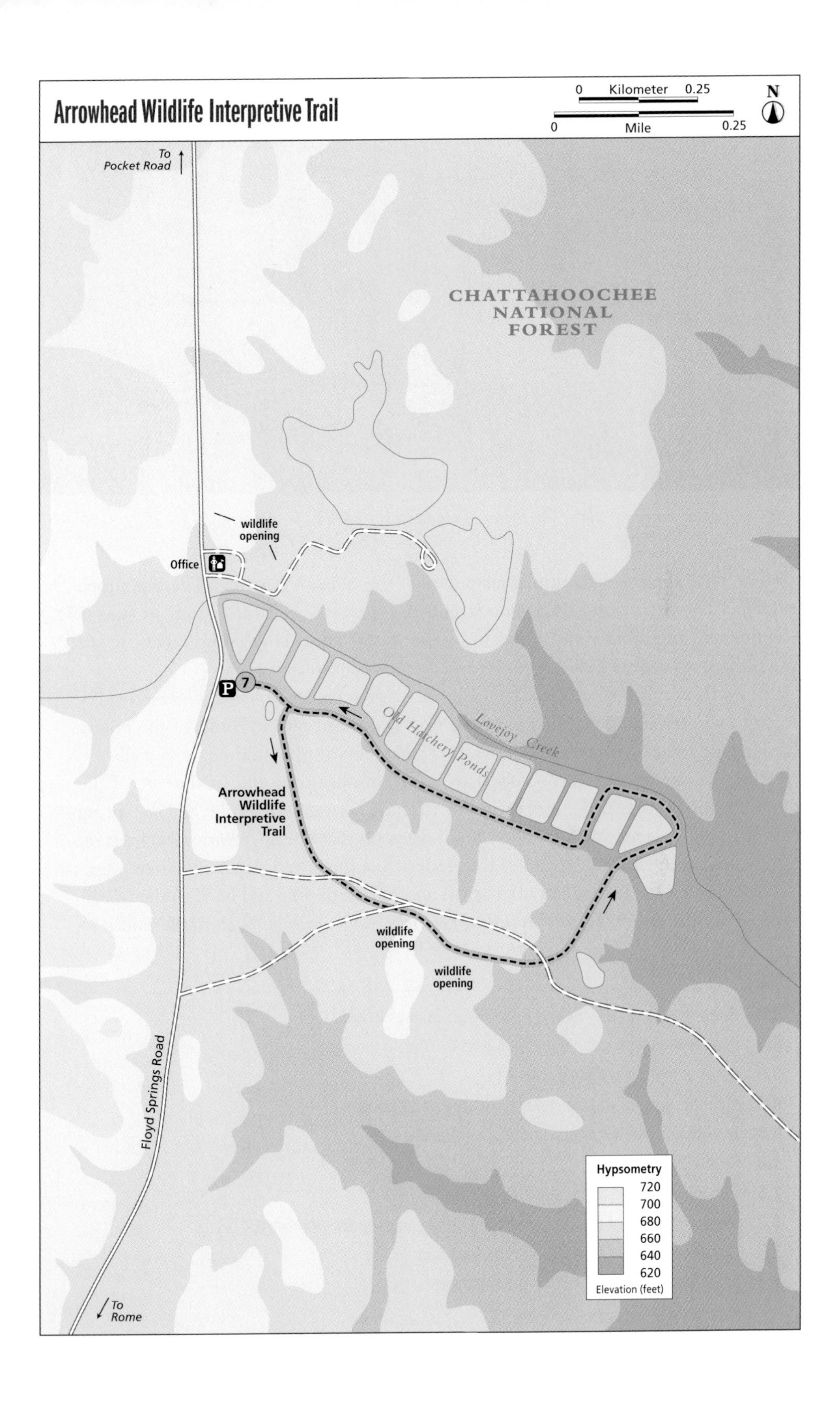

Arrowhead Wildlife Interpretive Trail
0 Kilometer 0.25
0 Mile 0.25
N
To Pocket Road
CHATTAHOOCHEE NATIONAL FOREST
wildlife opening
Office
7
P
Old Hatchery Ponds
Lovejoy Creek
Arrowhead Wildlife Interpretive Trail
wildlife opening
wildlife opening
Floyd Springs Road
To Rome
Hypsometry
720
700
680
660
640
620
Elevation (feet)

The interpretive trail runs along the shores of old hatchery ponds.

The hike continues to the larger ponds of the old fish hatchery. There is much wildlife to be seen along these ponds, and the species vary from season to season. Reptiles and amphibians are abundant by the water's edge. The careful hiker can see and photograph many kinds of plants and animals on this trail.

In April watch for nesting Canada geese at these water holes. The geese readily adapt to this environment and nest right on the ground on the banks of the ponds. Red-winged blackbirds nest in the willows and alders at the pond edges as well.

The trail crosses the earth dike dam at the southeastern end of the last of the ponds. Beyond the dam, the trail turns left, running between the ponds and the spring run of Lovejoy Creek. Beavers often build dams on that stream, creating backwaters. Many other animals, both aquatic and terrestrial, use the beaver ponds and their edges.

The trail makes a sharp left turn across another earth dike and back to the southwest side of the ponds. There the path turns right and continues back to the trailhead.

Miles and Directions

0.0 Begin the hike at the parking lot on Floyd Springs Road.

0.1 Reach the junction where the loop begins. Walk to the right.

0.5 Arrive at the first wildlife clearing.

0.8 Enter the second wildlife clearing with the small pond.

0.9 The old fish hatchery ponds appear on the left.

1.0 Reach Lovejoy Creek.

1.1 Turn left back across the dike between ponds.

1.2 Make a sharp right turn to parallel the pond shores to the northwest.

1.7 Close the loop and turn right for the trailhead.

1.8 Arrive back at the parking lot and trailhead.

8 Fort Mountain State Park, Old Fort Loop

Fort Mountain State Park trails offer an assortment of natural and human history subjects. The park lies on the southwestern edge of the southern Appalachian range and melds into the Ridge and Valley province, giving it a wide variety of habitat types and geological diversity, including old gold mines and active talc mines.

There are 14 miles of hiking trails of varying lengths and difficulty—from a short walk along the ancient stone wall from which the mountain got its name to a backpacking trail with campsites. Additionally there are miles of bike and horse trails. The seven hiking trails are well marked, interesting, and easy to follow.

One of the featured hikes in the park is the Old Fort Loop, which is a composite of portions of the West Overlook, North Stone Tower, Tower, Stone Wall, and CCC Stone Tower Trails.

Start: At the Old Fort Picnic Area parking lot
Distance: 2.1-mile loop
Hiking time: About 1–1.5 hours
Difficulty: Easy to moderate
Trail surface: Mostly dirt; some paved or unpaved roads
Best season: Mar–Dec
Other trail users: Mountain bikers on portions of Gahuti Trail
Canine compatibility: Leashed dogs permitted
Land status: Georgia DNR, State Parks & Historic Sites Division
Nearest town: Chatsworth
Fees and permits: Daily parking fee
Schedule: Park hours 7 a.m.–10 p.m., year-round
Maps: USGS Crandall; page-size map showing all trails, lengths, and blaze colors available at park office
Trail contacts: Fort Mountain State Park, 181 Fort Mountain Park Rd., Chatsworth 30705; (706) 695-2621; www.gastateparks.org

Finding the trailhead: From SR 515 in Ellijay, go west on SR 52 for 19 miles. The park entrance is on the right. The trailhead for the Old Fort Loop is at the Old Fort parking area on the north end of the park. Trailhead GPS: N34 45.701' / W84 42.542'

The Hike

All access trails connecting the main trails to campgrounds or to other trails are marked with red blazes. The Pinhoti Connector Trail links to the park's trail system, beginning across SR 52 at the park entrance.

This composite loop path takes in several of the most popular trails in the park. Along the way it leads to the West Overlook, which is one of the most impressive in the Georgia highlands, passes the stone fire tower, built by the Civilian Conservation Corps (CCC) in the 1930s, and runs along the ancient stone wall from which the park takes its name.

The CCC Stone Tower was constructed on the peak of Fort Mountain in the 1930s.

Many generations of explorers, archaeologists, geologists, historians, and sightseers have wondered about the identity of the unknown builders and the purpose of the stone wall. From the brink of the cliff on the east side of the mountain, the wall extends 855 feet to another precipice on the west side. Its highest part measures about 7 feet, but generally it rises to a height of 2 to 3 feet. There are twenty-nine pits scattered fairly regularly along the wall, with the wings of a gateway at one point.

Speculation regarding the builders and their purpose includes references to sun worship and last-ditch defense by prehistoric white peoples, bloody warfare between rival Indian tribes, defense fortification by Spanish conquistadors hunting gold, and honeymoon havens for Cherokee Indian newlyweds. Nobody knows which of the many legends and theories is true or false. The true answer still lies buried somewhere in antiquity and may never be unearthed.

At the beginning of the trail, a large metal plaque placed in 1968 by the state parks system tells of the mystery and legends of the stone wall and the mountain.

From the trailhead walk north along the yellow-blazed West Overlook Trail. The pathway skirts the precipice of the mountain, until passing through a large outcropping of rocks marking the western end of the old stone wall. Shortly you reach a fork in the path. Turn left onto the red-blazed connector trail leading toward the West Overlook.

Upon reaching the wooden observation deck, the overlook provides a sweeping 270-degree vista to the west and north. From the deck climb several flights of wood and metal steps up to the junction with the North Stone Tower and Tower Trails. Turn left and follow the yellow blazes of the North Stone Tower Trail around the north face of Fort Mountain. This portion of the walk offers a number of great views down the mountainside.

Once around the face of the mountain, you reach the junction at the other end of the Tower Trail.

Turn right and follow the red blazes uphill to the crest of Fort Mountain and the old stone fire tower. The trees on the Fort Mountain summit show the weathering of wind, rain, ice, and snow and are much older than they look.

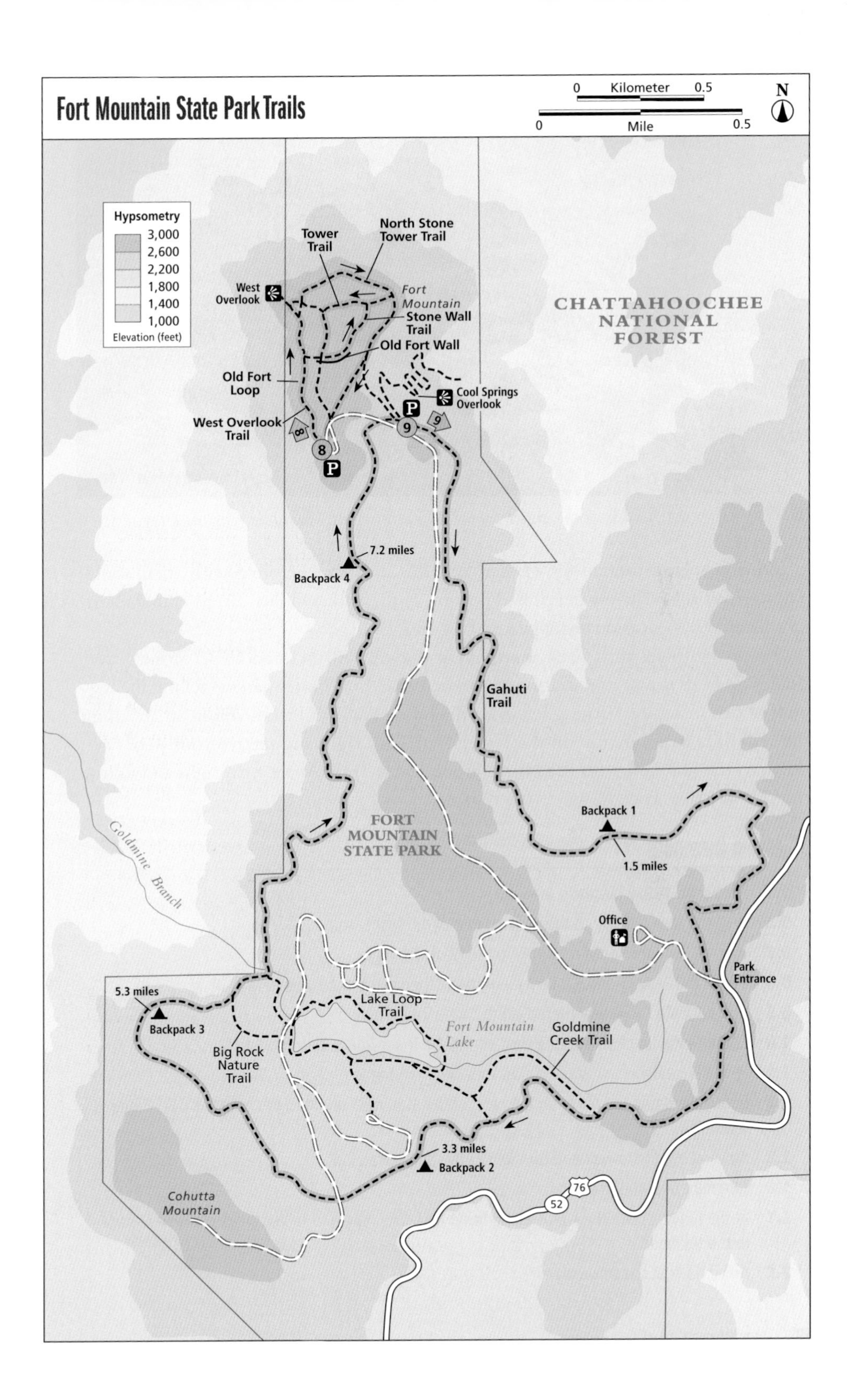

Fort Mountain State Park Trails
0 Kilometer 0.5
0 Mile 0.5
N
Hypsometry
3,000
2,600
2,200
1,800
1,400
1,000
Elevation (feet)
Tower Trail
North Stone Tower Trail
West Overlook
Fort Mountain
Stone Wall Trail
Old Fort Wall
Old Fort Loop
West Overlook Trail
Cool Springs Overlook
CHATTAHOOCHEE NATIONAL FOREST
8
9
7.2 miles
Backpack 4
Gahuti Trail
Backpack 1
1.5 miles
FORT MOUNTAIN STATE PARK
Goldmine Branch
Office
Park Entrance
5.3 miles
Backpack 3
Big Rock Nature Trail
Lake Loop Trail
Fort Mountain Lake
Goldmine Creek Trail
3.3 miles
Backpack 2
76
52
Cohutta Mountain

The identity of the builders of the ancient stone wall across Fort Mountain remains a mystery.

During spring migrations of warblers, this area can be alive with their songs. Though this is a relatively developed portion of the park, wildlife can be abundant. In fact, black bears occasionally appear in this area.

From the tower turn back south along the well-maintained CCC Stone Tower Trail. This leads down to the stone wall, where you find more markers telling the legends of this structure. Turning left onto the Stone Wall Trail takes you in an arc along the wall back to a junction on the Tower Trail. Turn right and retrace your steps back down to the junction with the North Stone Tower Trail. Again turn right and follow the yellow blazes back down to the trailhead.

Miles and Directions

0.0 Follow the yellow blazes to the left.

0.2 Pass the rock outcrop at the western end of the stone wall.

0.3 Turn left onto the red-blazed trail to the West Overlook.

0.5 Reach the West Overlook observation deck. Then climb the stairs to the left.

0.6 Turn left onto the yellow-blazed North Stone Tower Trail.

1.0 Come to the junction with the east end of the Tower Trail and turn right.

1.1 Pass the junction with the Wall Trail entering from the left.

1.2 Reach the stone fire tower on the crest of the mountain and turn left onto the CCC Stone Tower Trail.

1.3 Arrive at the stone wall and turn left on the Stone Wall Trail.

1.6 Turn right onto the Tower Trail.

1.7 At the junction with the North Stone Tower Trail, turn right and follow the yellow blazes back to the trailhead.

2.1 Arrive back at the trailhead.

9 Fort Mountain State Park, Gahuti Trail

The Gahuti Trail offers the most comprehensive look at the geology, flora, and fauna of Fort Mountain State Park. Its path completely circles the crest of the mountain, traversing a number of habitats and featuring frequent vistas of the surrounding country. Additionally, the trail provides the opportunity for a multi-day trek using the backcountry campsites provided along the way.

The Gahuti Trail backcountry loop is one of the featured hikes in the park and takes advantage of more than half of the 14 miles of walking trails in the state park. Hiking the Gahuti offers a long tour of the natural history of the park. The other six shorter trails provide a mixture of the natural and human history of the area.

See map page 53.
Start: At the Cool Springs Overlook parking area
Distance: 8.2-mile loop
Hiking time: About 4–4.5 hours
Difficulty: Mostly easy to moderate; some strenuous stretches
Trail surface: Mostly dirt; some paved or unpaved roads
Best season: Mar–Dec
Other trail users: Mountain bikers on portions
Canine compatibility: Leashed dogs permitted
Land status: Georgia DNR, State Parks & Historic Sites Division
Nearest town: Chatsworth
Fees and permits: Daily parking fee; free permit required for camping
Schedule: Park hours 7 a.m.–10 p.m., year-round
Maps: USGS Crandall; page-size map showing all trails, lengths, and blaze colors available at park office
Trail contacts: Fort Mountain State Park, 181 Fort Mountain Park Rd., Chatsworth 30705; (706) 695-2621; www.gastateparks.org

Finding the trailhead: From SR 515 in Ellijay, go west on SR 52 for 19 miles. The park entrance is on the right. The trailhead for the Gahuti Trail is at the Cool Springs Overlook parking area. Trailhead GPS: N34 46.726' / W84 42.325'

The Hike

This 8.2-mile loop is the park's backcountry camping trail. The orange-blazed path travels around the crest of Fort Mountain. Begin from the Cool Springs Overlook parking area, walking in a clockwise direction.

A grand view of the Cohutta Mountains and Wilderness Area greets you at the very beginning. During late fall, winter, and early spring, the colors and vistas are exceptional.

For the most part, the trail is easy to moderate; however, there are some short steep climbs and descents as the trail leads through ravines and around the ridge crests. These can be slippery when wet or when covered with snow. Four campsites are strategically located along the trail for backpackers. Free permits must be obtained

The West Overlook on the Fort Mountain Loop offers one of the most spectacular panoramas in the Georgia mountains.

from the park office for use of these campsites. No permit is necessary for day use of the trail.

At Campsite 1 a mountain-bike trail joins the Gahuti and shares the path along a level stretch through a tunnel of rhododendron in a creek bottom. After crossing the first of two bridges over Mill Creek, turn to the right. The trail to the left has a sign marking it as a Permit Only Area. Next the bicycle trail branches off, and the Gahuti crosses a second bridge over Mill Creek. At this point the path begins climbing out of the creek valley. Purple spiderwort and phlox bloom along this part of the trail in the summer.

After the trail crosses the park's entrance drive, it then follows an old dirt roadbed. Upon reaching the first of two junctions with the white-blazed Goldmine Creek Trail, Campsite 2 is on the left of the path.

Once past the point that the Goldmine Creek Trail leaves the path, the Gahuti next crosses a paved road, goes under a power line, and crosses a small creek before reaching Campsite 3. A bit farther the trail crosses a bridge and intersects the Big Rock Trail, sharing the path for a short stretch.

The final portion of the trail running north along the west rim of the mountain passes Campsite 4 and crosses a paved park road.

Finally the trail leads up some steps to the Cool Springs Overlook, providing a great vista to the east. From there a short paved walk runs from the observation deck to the parking lot and trailhead.

Miles and Directions

- **0.0** Start at the trailhead at the Cool Springs Overlook parking area.
- **1.5** Reach Campsite 1.
- **1.6** Stay right after crossing the bridge over Mill Creek.
- **1.8** Pass the junction where the bicycle trail splits off.
- **1.9** Cross the second bridge over Mill Creek.
- **2.6** Cross the Fort Mountain Park Road at the park entrance.
- **3.3** The Goldmine Creek Trail is on the right and Campsite 2 is on the left; look for white blazes.
- **3.7** The Goldmine Creek Trail forks off to the right; leave white blazes.
- **4.3** Cross Fort Mountain Park Road again.
- **4.6** Pass beneath a power line.
- **4.9** Cross a small brook.
- **5.3** Reach Campsite 3, with a great view to the north and west.
- **5.5** Cross a bridge and reach the junction with the yellow-blazed Big Rock Trail.
- **5.7** Leave the yellow-blazed Big Rock Trail, and cross over Goldmine Creek.
- **6.1** The trail crosses another bridge and reaches the first white-blazed campground connector trail.
- **6.2** Pass the second campground connector trail to the right.
- **7.2** Campsite 4 is on the left.
- **7.8** Cross paved Old Fort Road.
- **8.2** Arrive back at the Cool Springs Overlook, trailhead, and parking area.

Options

The **Lake Loop Trail** is a 1.2-mile loop running around the shore of the park's lake. The blue-blazed path is flat, passing by the beach swimming area and boat rental dock. Along the northeast shore many of the plants have identification labels on them.

The **Big Rock Nature Trail** runs in a loop, with both ends joining the Lake Trail. The western end of the loop shares the path with the Gahuti Trail. The yellow-blazed 0.5-mile pathway runs beside some small waterfalls on Goldmine Creek and has a couple of short steep sections.

The white-blazed **Goldmine Creek Trail** forms a loop on the north side of the Gahuti Trail and just east of the park's lake. The path runs along Goldmine Creek, through a bottom filled with Christmas, New York, and cinnamon ferns.

10 Lake Conasauga Recreation Area Trails

The Lake Conasauga Recreation Area, located in the Chattahoochee National Forest very near the Tennessee state line, provides a variety of hiking opportunities. The elevation remains above 3,000 feet, making this a relatively cool place in summer.

Campgrounds, picnic areas, a boat launching ramp, and beautiful mountain forests make this a popular getaway place. The region offers exceptional birding, wildflowers, mountain scenery, wildlife, and lake fishing.

The area has three trails, combining for 4.6 miles of paths. The featured Grassy Mountain Tower hike is a composite of the Grassy Mountain Tower and Songbird Trails.

Start: At the trailhead for the Grassy Mountain Tower and Songbird Trails at the overflow campground parking area
Distance: 4.6-mile loop
Hiking time: About 2 hours
Difficulty: Easy to moderate
Trail surface: Sandy loam with leaf litter; some grassy old roadbeds; gravel roads
Best season: Mar–Dec
Other trail users: Hikers only
Canine compatibility: Dogs permitted
Land status: Chattahoochee National Forest
Nearest town: Chatsworth
Fees and permits: Fees for camping only
Schedule: Trails open year-round; campground open mid-Apr to the end of Oct
Maps: USGS Crandall; page-size map of the Songbird and Lake Trails with the beginning of the Grassy Mountain Tower Trail, available from the campground host's trailer.
Trail contacts: USDA Forest Service, Conasauga Ranger District, 3941 US 76, Chatsworth 30705; (706) 695-6736; www.fs.usda.gov/conf

Finding the trailhead: From SR 515 at Ellijay go 11 miles west on SR 52. Turn right to go north on Conasauga Road. At 1.3 miles, at a fork where the road turns to gravel, stay to the right as it becomes FS 18. Continue another 2.3 miles, and then turn right on FS 68. Climb steeply up to the junction with FS 64 at the top of Potato Patch Mountain. Stay to the left and follow FS 68 for 12.8 miles to the intersection with FS 68D at the Lake Conasauga Recreation Area. Another 0.8 mile brings you to a fork in the road; FS 68 goes right. Take the left fork on FS 49 for 0.4 mile to the overflow campground parking area on the left and the trailhead for the Songbird and Grassy Mountain Tower Trails. Trailhead GPS: N34 51.708' / W84 40.195'

The Hike

From the trailhead on FS 49, the Songbird and Grassy Mountain Tower Trails run on the same path. Cross the road and go through the campground. Continue down the gravel bed of FS 49A that has been blocked to vehicular traffic.

This first portion of the hike is through the 120-acre Songbird Management Tract, developed cooperatively by the USDA Forest Service and the Georgia Wildlife Resources Division, Nongame–Endangered Wildlife Program.

A beaver pond, rhododendron thickets, and mature forests provide habitat diversity that attracts a wide range of bird species. Experienced birders have recorded 125 species present at some time of the year, including migrating sandhill cranes, red crossbills, nesting rose-breasted grosbeaks, scarlet tanagers, and chestnut-sided warblers.

This cove drains into the stream on which beavers have built a dam, creating a 10-acre pond. Rhododendron and mountain laurel line the pathway to the pond. Watch for deer, feral pig, or black bear tracks in the soft ground along this road. Bat boxes have been placed along the trail. After passing the junction of the return trail loop of the Songbird Trail on the left, you reach the pond on the left.

An observation deck over the water provides a good place to watch for wood ducks, which nest in cavities in dead trees or in the artificial nest boxes that have been placed on poles in the pond. Belted kingfishers use this area well.

A fire lookout tower stands on the peak at the end of the Grassy Mountain Tower Trail.

At the lower end of the beaver pond, the trail passes the junction with a connector path from the Lake Trail on the right. Continuing along the beaver pond, you cross the small stream below the dam on a footbridge and begin the climb through thick rhododendron for about 100 yards to where the Grassy Mountain Tower Trail takes off to the right. The left fork is the return leg of the Songbird Trail. Turning onto it creates a 1.8-mile loop hike.

Continue through this intersection on the Grassy Mountain Tower Trail as it climbs at a moderate grade through a tunnel of rhododendron and then opens into a beautiful mixed-hardwood forest. Upon reaching a rocky, dry creek bed, a large glade of New York, wood, and other ferns stretches up the cove to the left. Large clumps of Christmas ferns are scattered about the east- and north-facing slopes as well.

This section of the trail is an exceptional wildflower area. Lady's slippers, showy orchids, rattlesnake plantain, and other orchids are present at different times throughout spring and summer. Also present are Solomon's seal, false lily of the valley, bellwort, wood lily, several species of trillium, mayapple, wild geranium, violets, squawroot,

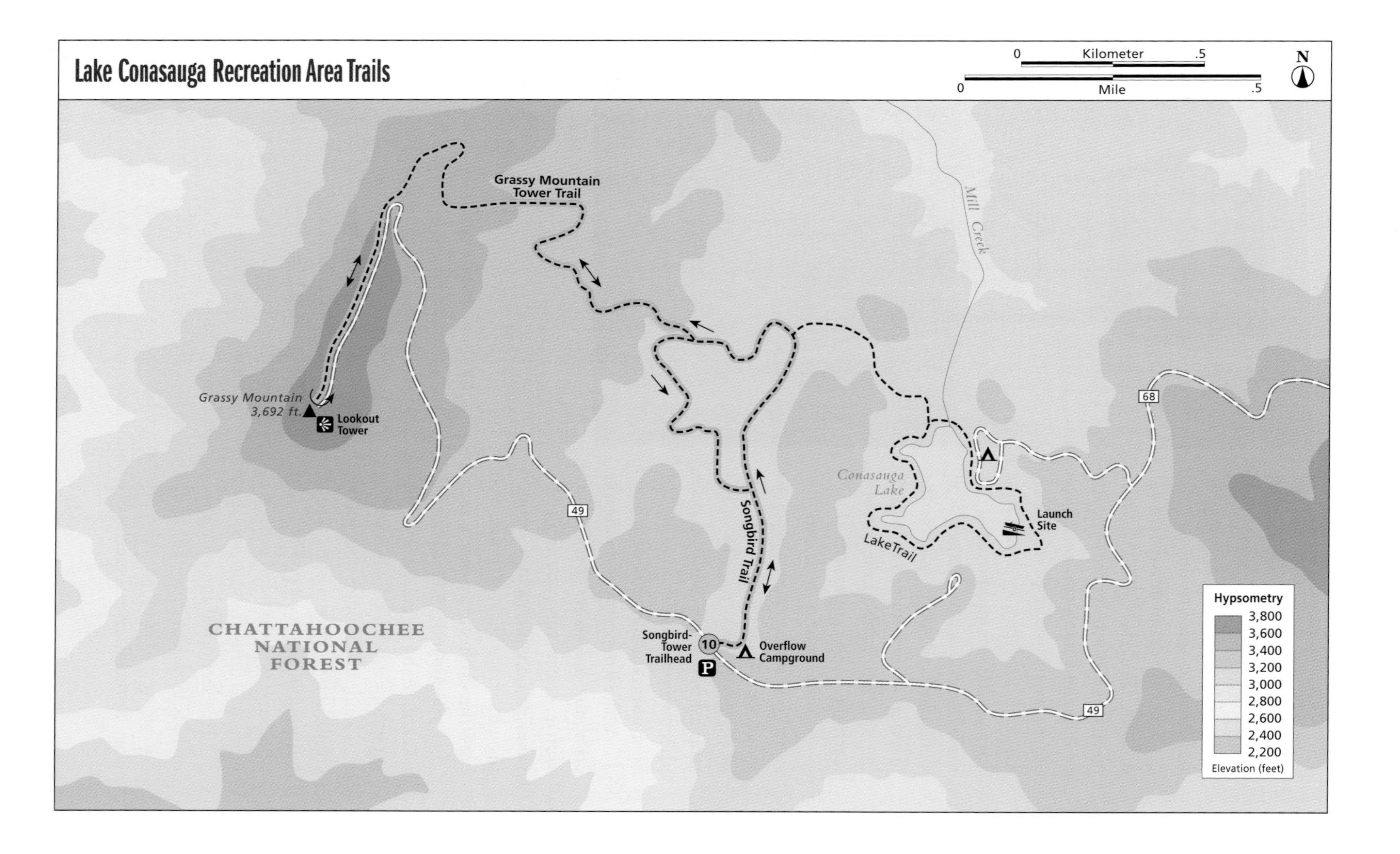
Lake Conasauga Recreation Area Trails
0
Kilometer
.5
0
Mile
.5
N
Grassy Mountain Tower Trail
Mill Creek
Grassy Mountain
3,692 ft.
Lookout Tower
49
Songbird Trail
Conasauga Lake
Launch Site
LakeTrail
68
CHATTAHOOCHEE NATIONAL FOREST
Songbird-Tower Trailhead
10
P
Overflow Campground
49
Hypsometry
3,800
3,600
3,400
3,200
3,000
2,800
2,600
2,400
2,200
Elevation (feet)

one-flowered cancer root, flame azaleas, galax, and wild ginger. At this elevation, the blooming season is two or three weeks behind lower elevations in the mountains.

The trail next reaches the crest of the ridge and then the road to the fire tower at the top of Grassy Mountain. Where the trail joins the road, continue straight ahead up the gravel road to the tower. Here the forest is made up of smaller, somewhat stunted southern red and other oak trees. Blackberries grow abundantly along the road in the open sun, along with beardtongue, Indian pinks, fire pinks, daisies, asters, Queen Anne's lace, phlox, and black-eyed Susans.

The fire lookout tower at the top is a throwback to the days before satellites and cell phone technology. From 1900 to 1970 such towers were staffed with lookouts who used an instrument called an Osborne Fire Finder to plot the azimuth and distance to smoke plumes from wildfires. Carrier pigeons and later radios were used to send that information to fire suppression teams. The tower on Grassy Mountain is no longer staffed.

At the fire tower you can climb to the first landing for a grand view of the mountains to the northeast in the Cohutta Wilderness, the Ridge and Valley province to the west, and south to Fort Mountain State Park.

This is a great place to watch for migrating hawks in the fall and sandhill cranes in spring and fall.

Afterward, return down the road and path to the junction with the Songbird Trail. Turn right on the Songbird Trail and walk along the hillside through thick rhododendron, mountain laurel, and dog-hobble beneath white pine, yellow poplar, and buckeye trees. Hemlocks are also present, but virtually all of them are dead or dying from woolly adelgid infestations.

You pass over two footbridges before the beaver pond appears on the left. Along the pond edge expect to see towhees, cardinals, catbirds, brown thrashers, indigo buntings, and other open-habitat species. Benches at strategic places along the trail afford excellent, quiet viewing places. Besides birds and mammals, the pond attracts turtles, salamanders, frogs and toads, dragonflies, damselflies, crane flies, and butterflies, all of which can be seen while you're taking advantage of the benches.

The trail crosses the upper end of the beaver pond on yet another footbridge and closes the loop of the Songbird Trail. Turn to the right and walk up FS 49A to the trailhead.

Miles and Directions

0.0 Walk across FS 49 from the parking area and through the overflow campground.

0.4 The trail on the left is the end of the Songbird Trail loop; continue straight.

0.5 Reach the boardwalk to the observation platform.

0.7 Come to the connecter path on the right, running to the Lake Trail; just beyond, cross the footbridge at the beaver dam.

0.9 At this intersection, continue on the right fork onto the Grassy Mountain Tower Trail; the left fork is the return loop of the Songbird Trail.

1.3 Pass through a rocky, dry streambed with a large glade of New York and wood ferns on the left.

1.8 Reach the crest of the ridge, where the trail turns south.

1.9 Meet the gravel road to the fire tower.

2.3 Reach the Grassy Mountain Tower (3,692 feet elevation). Climb the tower and enjoy the view before retracing your steps to the intersection with the Songbird Trail.

3.8 At the Songbird Trail junction, turn right and cross a footbridge over a small stream at 100 yards.

4.0 Reach a bridge over a dry creek bed.

4.1 Get the first view of the pond from the west shore.

4.2 Cross the pond on a footbridge and close the loop portion of the Songbird Trail; turn to the right on FS 49A.

4.6 Arrive back at the parking area and trailhead.

Options

The **Lake Trail** is best walked from the boat ramp on FS 68C. It is a level, quiet path with views of the water all the way around as it passes through the campground and picnic areas.

The 19-acre lake is usually crystal clear and is the highest-elevation pond in Georgia. The 1.2-mile trail is an ideal morning or evening exercise stroll or birding walk.

Nineteen-acre Lake Conasauga is the highest-elevation pond in Georgia.

11 Emery Creek Trail

The Emery Creek Trail is located on the southern edge of the massive, 96,503-acre Cohutta Wildlife Management Area (WMA). The Cohutta Mountains are some of the oldest on Earth and are characterized by mountain peaks of more than 4,000 feet dropping sharply to valley floors.

This trail leads up the southwest flank of Bald Mountain to Potato Patch Mountain Road, running along the ridgeline. On the opposite side of the ridge is the Cohutta Wilderness Area, a 36,977-acre roadless tract that is the second-largest federally mandated wilderness in Georgia.

The forest road follows a major travel corridor used by the Cherokee Indians and early settlers.

Start: At the day-use area at Holly Creek on Old CCC Camp Road (FS 18)
Distance: 6.2 miles one way
Hiking time: About 2.5–3.5 hours, one way
Difficulty: Strenuous
Trail surface: Dirt and firm loam
Best season: Mar–Dec
Other trail users: Hunters in season
Canine compatibility: Leashed dogs permitted
Land status: Chattahoochee National Forest
Nearest town: Chatsworth
Fees and permits: None
Schedule: Open year-round
Maps: USGS Crandall; a Cohutta WMA map is available online at www.gohuntgeorgia.com.
Trail contacts: USDA Forest Service, Conasauga Ranger District, 3941 US 76, Chatsworth 30705; (706) 695-6736; www.fs.usda.gov/conf

Georgia Wildlife Resources Division, Regional Office, 2592 Floyd Springs Rd., Armuchee 30105; (706) 295-6041
Special considerations: Wearing blaze orange during hunting seasons is recommended.

Finding the trailhead: For the lower trailhead, from the town square in Chatsworth take US 411 north for 6 miles to Eton. Turn right onto Old CCC Camp Road and go 7 miles to the day-use area on Holly Creek and the Emery Creek Trailhead parking lot. Trailhead GPS: N34 48.765' / W84 39.076'

The Hike

The Emery Creek Trail has green metal blazes nailed on trees, but not enough of them. At some junctures the path can be difficult to discern, particularly in the fall when leaves are thick on the ground. In the lower portion of the trail, some old white paint blazes are also present and helpful. You need to pay attention to make sure you don't lose the pathway.

Emery Creek features five distinct waterfalls. Three of those can easily be seen from the trail. Emery Creek Falls is at the end of a short side trail, while the uppermost two cascades are visible on the left of the main trail. Getting near the other two requires some bushwhacking.

Pools holding wild rainbow trout, like the one at the foot of Emery Creek Falls, encourage hikers to bring along a fishing rod.

The trail begins at the day-use area on Holly Creek. Near the parking area Holly Creek is a medium-size mountain stream that offers trout fishing and some deep holes used for swimming in warmer months. From the parking area for the trail, the path begins on an abandoned roadbed following the east side of Holly Creek.

At the junction where Emery Creek empties into Holly from the far side, a rather difficult ford must be negotiated to get across both of the streams. It is possible to rock hop in dry weather, but expect to get wet if the creeks have normal to high flows.

The trail next begins a gentle climb along the western side of Emery Creek up to another ford. At this point a huge boulder on the left overshadows the creek crossing. This is the first of more than half a dozen times that the trail crosses Emery. There are no bridges on this path, which follows abandoned logging roads on its entire lower half.

Just shy of a mile farther, the trail fords the creek again and pops out onto a jeep road. Turn right on this dirt and gravel track. At 0.1 mile on this road and just before it fords the creek, the trail turns sharply to the north (left) to pick up another logging road.

The trail continues to follow Emery Creek uphill through a forest of oak, hickory, hemlock, and buckeye trees. Rhododendron is abundant along the stream, but the mountain laurel that usually accompanies it is virtually absent in this valley.

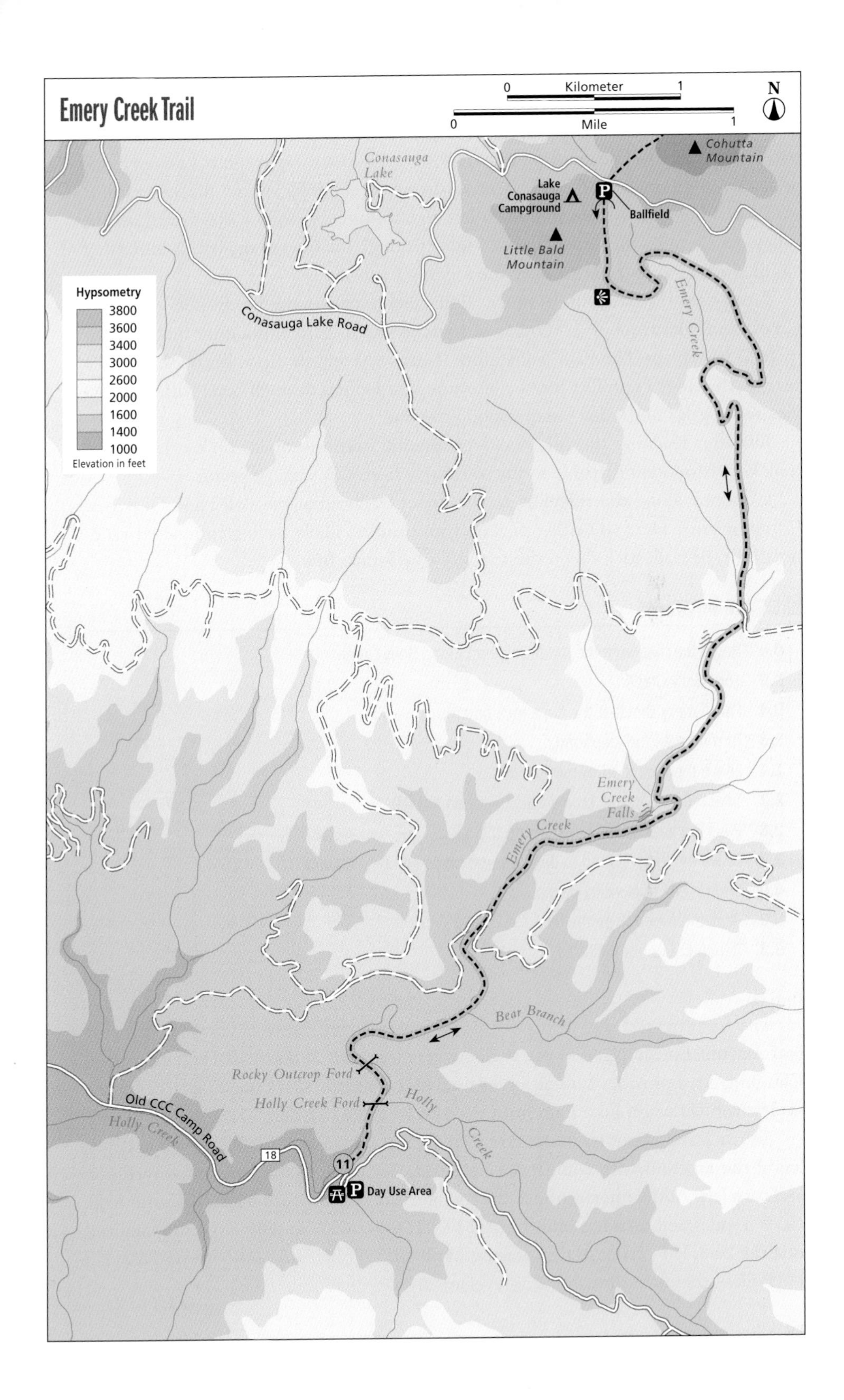
Emery Creek Trail
0
Kilometer
1
0
Mile
1
N
Cohutta Mountain
Conasauga Lake
Lake Conasauga Campground
Ballfield
Little Bald Mountain
Hypsometry
3800
3600
3400
3000
2600
2000
1600
1400
1000
Elevation in feet
Conasauga Lake Road
Emery Creek
Emery Creek Falls
Emery Creek
Bear Branch
Rocky Outcrop Ford
Holly Creek Ford
Holly Creek
Old CCC Camp Road
Holly Creek
18
11
Day Use Area

A bit more than 2.0 miles into the trek, a wooden sign for EMERY CREEK FALLS marks a side trail running off to the left. It is a 0.1-mile out-and-back detour to the base of that cascade. The creek plummets down a 40-foot rock face into a small plunge pool. A second smaller fall can be seen upstream by climbing around the lower one.

Returning to the main trail, turn left and continue to follow the stream up the valley. At 2.8 miles the upper falls are visible through the trees to the left. A bit farther along, the trail veers right to leave the logging road.

From here the path climbs much more steeply, crosses the headwaters of Emery Creek, and goes through a number of switchbacks to gain altitude up the shoulder of Bald Mountain. The path gains more than 1,500 feet of elevation by the time it reaches the ridge crest. The forest adds more white pines through here, with frequent patches of galax and some sassafras along the trail.

Just after reaching the ridgetop, a panoramic overlook opens on the left of the trail. Fort Mountain is visible to the southwest from this vantage point.

Continue along the ridgeline to the upper trailhead at the Ball Field Dispersed Camping Area. Here you either pick up your shuttle vehicle, having completed a 6.2-mile hike, or walk back down the trail for a 12.3-mile trek.

Miles and Directions

0.0 Begin the hike from the lower trailhead along Holly Creek.

0.2 Ford Holly Creek.

0.4 Ford Emery Creek at the huge rock outcrop.

1.3 Turn right on the jeep road.

1.4 Leave the jeep road by turning left.

2.2 Take the side trail to Emery Creek Falls on the left.

2.8 Pass the final upper waterfalls on the left.

3.3 Leave the logging road to the right and begin climbing steeply.

4.0 Enter a series of switchbacks.

5.9 Pass the overlook on the left.

6.2 Reach the upper trailhead.

Options

Starting the Emery Creek hike at the upper trailhead at the Ball Field Dispersed Camping Area provides a much easier downhill walk. Or it is a good place to leave a shuttle vehicle when hiking up from the lower end.

To reach the upper trailhead, take Old CCC Camp Road for 11.5 miles and stay left at the junction with Mulberry Gap Road. Continue to the junction with FS 68 and turn left. At the intersection at the top of the mountain, turn left staying on FS 68. Go 3.5 miles and turn left into the Ball Field Dispersed Camping Area; the trailhead is at the back left corner of the clearing. Trailhead GPS: N34 51.604' / W84 38.211'

Follow the directions above in reverse.

12 Pinhoti Trail

The Pinhoti Trail is a 335-mile pathway that runs from Flagg Mountain near Weogufka, Alabama, to a junction with the Benton MacKaye Trail in northwest Georgia near the town of Blue Ridge. The trail enters Georgia in the Ridge and Valley geophysical region of the state, just west of Cedartown. As it progress to the northeast, it enters the Blue Ridge Mountain region to end in the Cohutta Mountains.

The 145.2 miles of trail in Georgia make the Pinhoti the longest hiking path located entirely within the state. Though the statistics are impressive, they also are misleading. For roughly 60 miles of that distance, the path runs along major roadways, and many more miles are on county or gravel roads. On the actual woodland trails, much of the Pinhoti is on Chattahoochee National Forest lands in the Conasauga Ranger District.

The featured portion of the trail is the most northerly part, which is composed almost exclusively of woodland paths in the Cohutta Mountain region.

Start: At the parking area for the Rock Creek ATV Trail on FS 3A
Distance: 31.6 miles one way
Hiking time: A minimum of 2–3 days
Difficulty: Moderate to strenuous
Trail surface: Dirt and loam in the woodland sections; short gravel road stretches
Best season: Mar–Dec
Other trail users: Hunters in season
Canine compatibility: Dogs permitted; leashed dogs permitted on wildlife management area sections
Land status: Chattahoochee National Forest
Nearest towns: Chatsworth, Ellijay
Fees and permits: None
Schedule: Open year-round
Maps: USGS Talking Rock, Crandell, Dyer Gap, Hemp Top
Trail contact: The Pinhoti Trail Alliance, pinhoti trailalliance.org

Finding the trailhead: From Chatsworth go south on US 76/411 for 5.4 miles. Turn left on US 76 when it splits off to the left. At 100 yards turn right as US 76 joins SR 282. Immediately turn left onto Old Federal Highway. Go 2.3 miles and turn right on Peeple Road. There is no road sign, but a sign for the Rock Creek ATV Trail No. 175 is at the intersection. At 5.7 miles reach the Rock Creek ATV Trail parking area on the left. Trailhead GPS: N34 44.805' /W84 40.509'

The Hike

The original plan in 1925 for the Appalachian Trail called for a spur to run from the Georgia terminus into northern Alabama. Over the years the Pinhoti Trail was developed in the Talladega National Forest of that state, but it did not make the Georgia connection.

The completion of the Benton MacKaye Trail through northwest Georgia in the 1980s spurred renewed interest in the Pinhoti as an Appalachian Trail (AT) connector.

The Georgia Pinhoti Trail Association was founded in 1985, and work began on laying out a route connecting the Alabama pathway to the AT via the Benton MacKaye Trail.

Today that route exists, but the trail is not complete in the sense that much of it still uses paved and gravel roadways to connect the actual woodland trail portions. In essence, the Pinhoti is a work in progress.

A variety of blazes mark portions of the trail. A light blue rectangle was adopted as the standard in 2007, but some sections bear older blazes. These may be silver metal or white plastic with a turkey track on them, white painted turkey tracks, or simply white rectangles.

Miles and Directions

0.0 Begin walking northwest on FS 3A from the parking area.

1.1 Turn right onto Rock Creek Road (FS 10) and then follow the trail when it splits off the road to the right.

7.6 Turn east on paved SR 52.

8.1 Turn left off SR 52 and pass the Cohutta Overlook.

12.3 Turn right on Mulberry Gap Road.

13.4 Leave the road to turn onto the trail to the north.

17.0 Turn left on FS 90B.

17.5 Turn left on FS 90 and at 0.2 mile farther, turn left onto a wildlife clearing access road.

21.5 Intersect the Bear Creek Trail.

22.2 Pass to the right of the Gennett Poplar. At 100 feet tall and with a circumference of 20 feet, it is listed as the second-largest tree in North Georgia.

22.6 Intersect the Bear Creek Loop Trail.

24.6 Intersect the Mountain Creek Trail.

28.5 Cross FS 64.

31.3 Intersect South Fork Trail and ford the South Fork of the Jacks River.

31.6 Reach the end of the Pinhoti Trail at the intersection with the Benton MacKaye Trail. Turn right and walk 2.2 miles to the Dyer Gap parking area.

Portions of the Pinhoti Trail in Georgia are blazed with white diamonds bearing a turkey track.

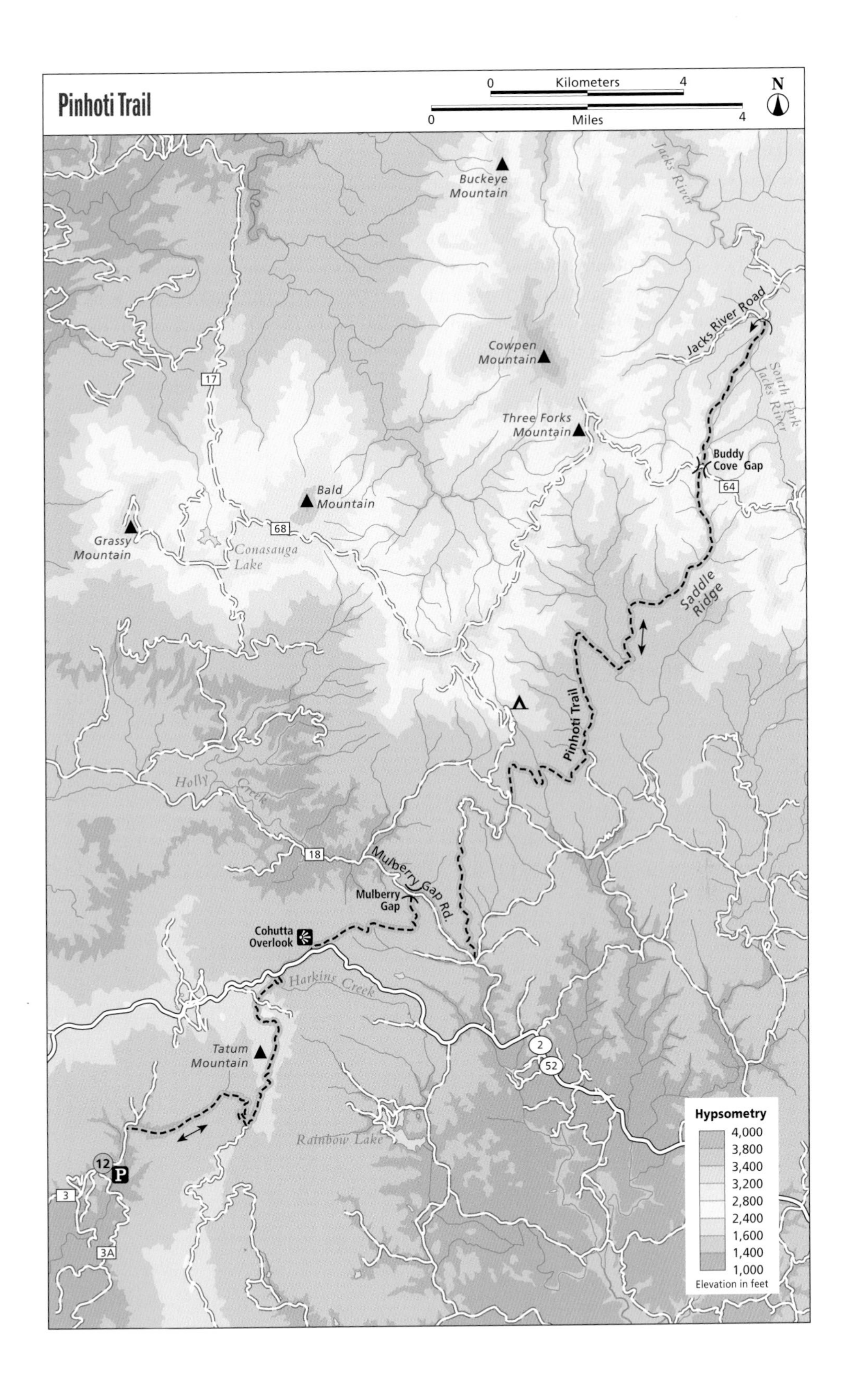
Pinhoti Trail
0 Kilometers 4
0 Miles 4
N
Buckeye Mountain
Jacks River
Jacks River Road
Cowpen Mountain
South Fork Jacks River
Three Forks Mountain
Buddy Cove Gap
64
17
Bald Mountain
68
Grassy Mountain
Conasauga Lake
Saddle Ridge
Pinhoti Trail
Holly Creek
18
Mulberry Gap Rd.
Mulberry Gap
Cohutta Overlook
Harkins Creek
2
52
Tatum Mountain
Rainbow Lake
12
P
3
3A
Hypsometry
4,000
3,800
3,400
3,200
2,800
2,400
1,600
1,400
1,000
Elevation in feet

Options

Hikers preferring to tackle the Pinhoti Trail in a north to south direction can start at the trail's junction with the Benton MacKaye Trail.

For the northern terminus of the Pinhoti, from SR 515 in Blue Ridge, go northwest on SR 5 for 3.8 miles. Turn left on SR 2 and follow the road for 9.3 miles to the end of the pavement. Continue another 1.2 miles to Watson Gap. Take the left fork of the road at the gap and drive 3.3 miles to Dyer Gap. The parking area is on the right at the Dyer Gap Cemetery. Walk 2.2 miles north from this trailhead on the Benton MacKaye Trail to the junction at the terminus of the Pinhoti Trail. Trailhead GPS: N34 52.133' / W84 30.880'

13 Benton MacKaye Trail

Named for Benton MacKaye, who provided the inspiration for establishing the Appalachian Trail (AT), this path provides a challenge for any serious hiker. The trail extends in a sweeping S shape to the north and west through Georgia from the trail-head on Springer Mountain that it shares with the AT. The trail lies mostly in the Chattahoochee National Forest.

The total length of the Benton MacKaye Trail (BMT) is 287.6 miles, of which 75.4 are in Georgia. Crossing through Tennessee and North Carolina, the pathway ends at Big Creek, where it rejoins the AT in the Great Smoky Mountains National Park. All but 10 miles of the BMT are located on public lands.

Returning to Springer Mountain on the AT provides a 521-mile lopsided figure-eight hike.

Start: At the Springer Mountain AT parking area on FS 42, then walk 0.9 mile to the trailhead
Distance: 75.4 miles
Hiking time: About 6–7 days
Difficulty: Moderate to strenuous
Trail surface: Mostly dirt or forest loam, with some rocks or gravel and paved roads
Best season: Mar–June; Oct–Dec
Other trail users: Vehicles, equestrians, and mountain bikes for short stretches on forest roads; hunters in season
Canine compatibility: Dogs permitted; leashed dogs permitted on wildlife management areas
Land status: Mostly Chattahoochee National Forest
Nearest towns: Blairsville, Blue Ridge, Dahlonega, Ellijay
Fees and permits: None
Schedule: Open year-round
Maps: USGS Nimblewill, Noontootla, Wilscot, Blue Ridge, Cashes Valley, Dyer Gap, Hem Top
Trail contacts: Benton MacKaye Trail Association, PO Box 53271, Atlanta 30355-1271; www.bmta.org

Chattahoochee National Forest, 1755 Cleveland Hwy., Gainesville 30501; (770) 297-3000; www.fs.usda.gov/conf

Finding the trailhead: From SR 515 in Ellijay, go east on SR 52 for 5.3 miles. Turn left onto Big Creek Road and continue for 12.4 miles. Along the way the name changes to Doublehead Gap Road. At Doublehead Gap turn right on FS 42 and go 6.7 miles to the Appalachian Trail parking lot on the left. Follow the AT to the southwest for 0.9 mile to the crest of Springer Mountain and the beginning of the Benton MacKaye Trail. Trailhead GPS: N34 38.261' / W84 11.710'

The Hike

This long trail begins at Springer Mountain with the Appalachian Trail. Although the trail crosses or runs along major roads in the mountains when necessary, it has many remote stretches and provides true wilderness hiking. The trail is blazed with white diamonds along its entire route.

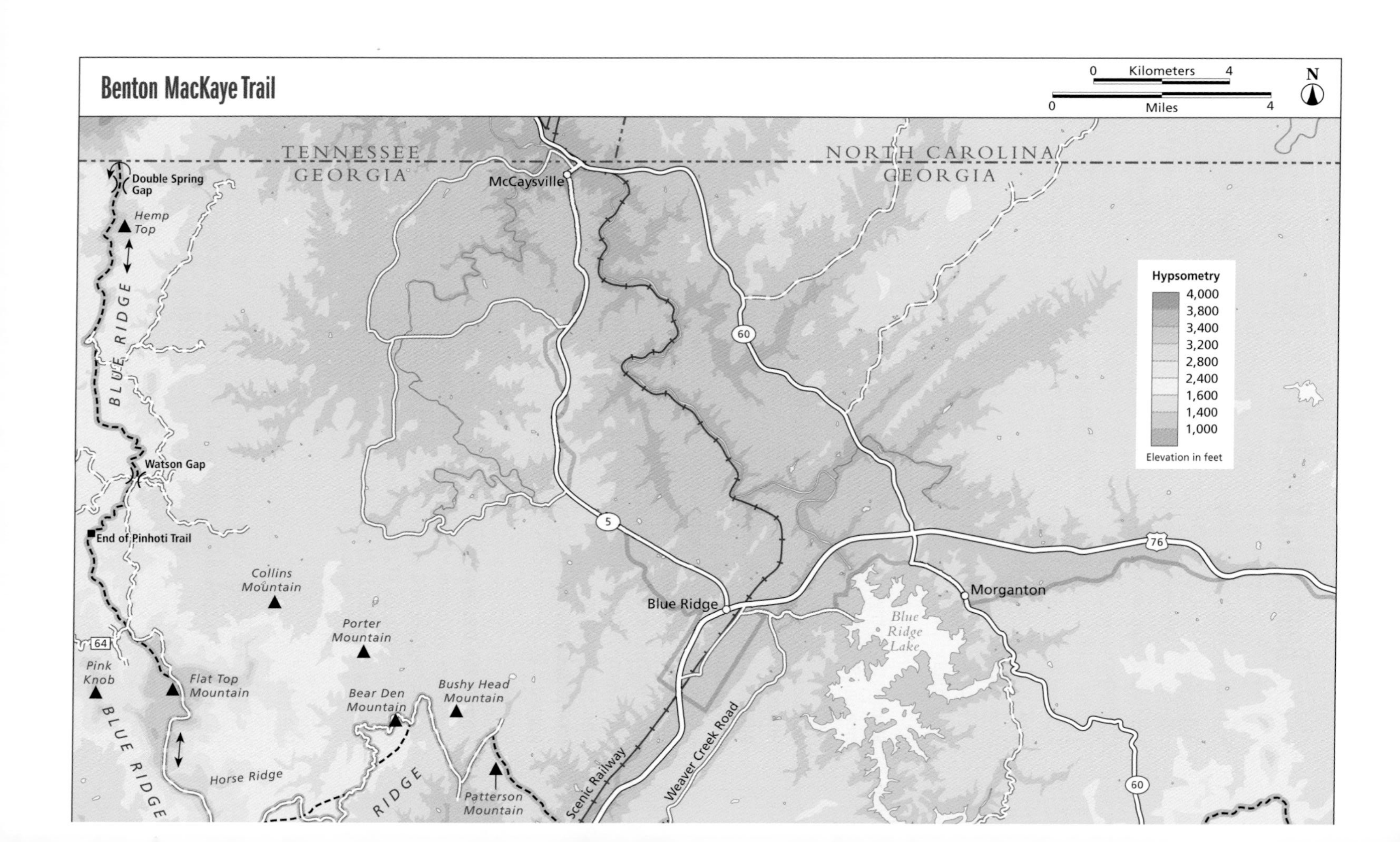
Benton MacKaye Trail
0 Kilometers 4
0 Miles 4
N
Hypsometry
4,000
3,800
3,400
3,200
2,800
2,400
1,600
1,400
1,000
Elevation in feet
TENNESSEE
GEORGIA
NORTH CAROLINA
GEORGIA
Double Spring Gap
Hemp Top
BLUE RIDGE
Watson Gap
End of Pinhoti Trail
McCaysville
60
5
76
Collins Mountain
Porter Mountain
Blue Ridge
Morganton
Blue Ridge Lake
64
Pink Knob
Flat Top Mountain
Bear Den Mountain
Bushy Head Mountain
Horse Ridge
RIDGE
Patterson Mountain
Scenic Railway
Weaver Creek Road

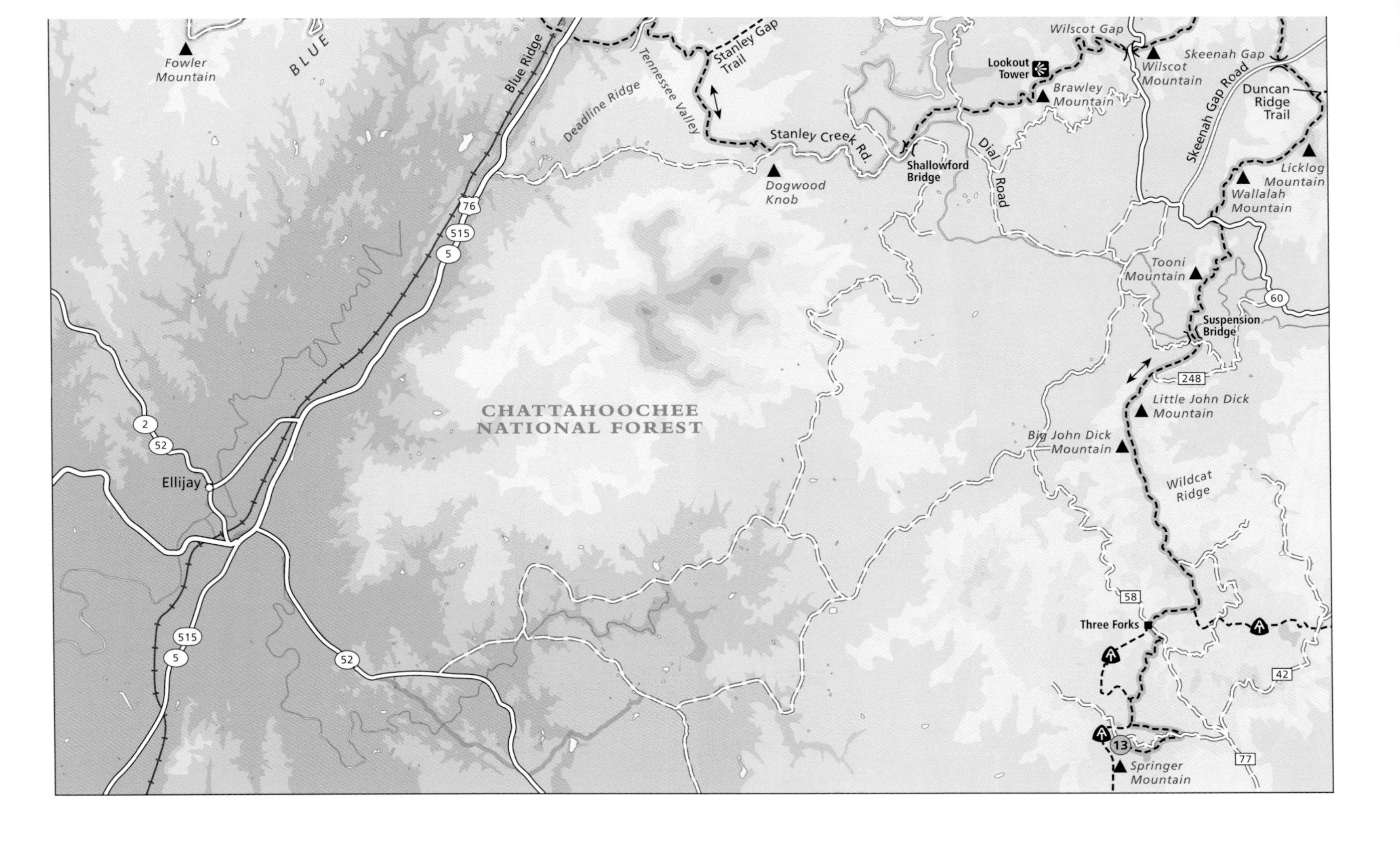

Fowler Mountain
BLUE
Blue Ridge
Deadline Ridge
Tennessee Valley
Stanley Gap Trail
Stanley Creek Rd.
Dogwood Knob
Shallowford Bridge
Dial Road
Lookout Tower
Brawley Mountain
Wilscot Gap
Wilscot Mountain
Skeenah Gap
Skeenah Gap Road
Duncan Ridge Trail
Licklog Mountain
Wallalah Mountain
Tooni Mountain
60
Suspension Bridge
248
Little John Dick Mountain
Big John Dick Mountain
Wildcat Ridge
58
Three Forks
42
13
77
Springer Mountain
76
515
5
2
52
Ellijay
CHATTAHOOCHEE NATIONAL FOREST

The Benton MacKaye Trail crosses the Toccoa River on the longest pedestrian suspension bridge east of the Mississippi River.

The hike follows rhododendron- and laurel-lined trout streams and crosses the longest pedestrian footbridge east of the Mississippi River. Mountains and ridges with scenic views, mature and regenerating forests, and paved and unpaved mountain roads are all part of the trail, with a variety of optional side trips of shorter loops along the route.

Miles and Directions

0.0 Follow the footpath carrying the Benton MacKaye and Appalachian Trails to the northwest from the summit of Springer Mountain.

0.2 The Appalachian Trail splits off to the left.

6.0 Reach Three Forks on Noontootla Creek and FS 58.

6.8 A side trail leads to the left to the foot of Long Creek Falls; the AT forks right, while the BMT is joined by the Duncan Ridge Trail running in to the left.

8.3 Cross the 265-foot suspension bridge over the Toccoa River.

11.4 Cross SR 60.

15.6 The Duncan Ridge Trail splits off to the right.

17.8 Cross paved Skeenah Gap Road.

24.1 Reach SR 60 in Wilscot Gap.

29.9 Cross the dirt surface of Dial Road.

31.7 Cross Shallowford Bridge and turn right on paved Aska Road.

32.0 Turn left on gravel Stanley Creek Road.

35.1 Turn right to leave the road and follow Falls Branch.

36.2 Join the path of the Stanley Gap Trail.

38.3 The Stanley Gap Trail splits off to the right.

41.2 Cross Weaver Creek Road.

43.7 Cross US 76.

44.2 Cross the Blue Ridge Scenic Railway track.

49.6 Reach Bush Head Gap and Fannin CR 14.

62.1 Cross FS 64 in Dyer Gap.

66.6 Pass through Watson Gap.

69.2 Intersect the Jacks River Trail at Dally Gap.

72.4 Pass the intersection with Penitentiary Branch Trail.

75.4 Reach Double Spring Gap and the Tennessee border.

The Benton MacKaye Trail is blazed with white diamonds.

Options

For hikers using the north to south route on the Benton MacKaye Trail, the last access before it leaves Georgia is in the Cohutta Wilderness Area.

That access is from Dally Gap, 8.5 miles before the trail enters Tennessee. To reach Dally Gap, take SR 5 north from SR 515 in Blue Ridge for 3.8 miles. Turn left on SR 2 and go 9.3 miles to the end of the pavement. Continue another 1.2 miles on gravel to Watson Gap. Turn right on FS 22 and drive 3.5 miles to Dally Gap. Trailhead GPS: N34 55.996' / W84 31.126'

Honorable Mentions

A Chickamauga Battlefield National Military Park Trails

The trails in this 8,000-plus-acre park provide a unique and enjoyable way to study Civil War history in a natural setting. At this site on September 19–20, 1863, 60,000 Union troops under Gen. William Rosecrans were defeated by 66,000 Confederates commanded by Gen. Braxton Bragg. The land remains almost as the soldiers saw it at the time of the battle.

The park's five trails vary in length from 5 to 14 miles, totaling about 40 miles of overlapping trails—70 miles if each trail is hiked separately. Each trail is color blazed to follow a specific theme of the historical battle. Roads parallel parts of the battlefield trails so that much can be viewed from a vehicle. Most visitors choose points of interest to hike amid the park's 1,400 monuments.

Spring wildflowers are abundant, and fall colors of the many hardwood trees can be spectacular.

The park is in the northwest corner of Georgia, about 5 miles south of the Tennessee-Georgia state line. The National Park Service headquarters and visitor center for Chickamauga Battlefield is located at the north entrance on US 27.

The park is open year-round. For more information: Superintendent, Chickamauga and Chattanooga National Military Park, PO Box 2128, Fort Oglethorpe 30742; (706) 866-9241; www.nps.gov/chch

DeLorme: Georgia Atlas and Gazetteer: Page 12 B4

B Cohutta Wilderness Area Trails

At 36,977 acres, this is the second largest wilderness area in Georgia. Steep, rugged, and heavily forested, the Cohutta Mountains are true wilderness today. But less than a century ago, this area on the Tennessee-Georgia border was intensively logged. Some of the old railroad beds used to haul the timber are still evident. There also were attempts at mining here, but these scars have healed and are not noticeable.

Fourteen backcountry trails totaling just shy of 89 miles of pathways lead to grand forests, scenic beauty, and multiple outdoor activities. Year-round hiking is possible.

One-lane dirt forest service roads define much of the boundary. These roads are pleasant to walk along and can be incorporated with the fourteen named trails into loop trails to get back to a parking area and trailhead.

More than forty species of rare and uncommon plants and a variety of game animals abound in the wilderness, and the many cold-water streams support fine trout populations. Birding, wildflower photography, fishing, and hunting for small and big game provide something for everyone.

For more information: Chattahoochee National Forest, Conasauga Ranger District, 3941 US 76, Chatsworth 30705; www.fs.usda.gov/conf

DeLorme: Georgia Atlas and Gazetteer: Page 13 B10

C Aska Adventure Area Trails

This group of five main trails and two connectors in the Aska Adventure Area total 17.4 miles of hiking and mountain-biking paths. All trails are interconnected, leaving only a few miles of backtracking to cover them all. Hikes are available along the clear waters of Lake Blue Ridge, climbing to mountains reaching to 3,000 feet with great views, passing through rich hardwood coves with trout streams, or tunneling through thickets of mountain laurel and rhododendron.

The trails are open year-round, with spring and fall best for wildflowers and spectacular leaf colors, respectively. All pathways are blazed with lime-green rectangles.

Three trails—Flat Creek Loop, Green Mountain Trail, and Stanley Gap Trail—can be started at Deep Gap on Aska Road, 4.4 miles south of Blue Ridge. Stanley Gap Trail can also be accessed at Stanley Gap, 8 miles farther south on Aska Road and then 4.1 miles west on Stanley Creek Road. The Long Branch Loop trailhead is at Shady Falls, 1.5 miles south of Deep Gap on Aska Road, then 0.2 mile to the left.

Bulletin boards at the Deep Gap and Long Branch Loop trailheads show maps of the trail system. Parking at these trailheads is free.

For more information: Chattahoochee National Forest, Blue Ridge Ranger District, 6050 Appalachian Hwy., Blue Ridge 30513; (706) 632-3031; www.fs.usda.gov/conf

DeLorme: Georgia Atlas and Gazetteer: Page 14 C4

Northeast Georgia

Northeast Georgia is the state's upland region, offering hikers many mountain vistas.

14 Amicalola Falls State Park, Appalachian Approach Trail

Amicalola, a Cherokee word meaning "tumbling waters," perfectly describes Amicalola Falls. Formed by Little Amicalola Creek plunging 729 feet in several cascades, it is the highest waterfall east of the Mississippi River and serves as the centerpiece of an 829-acre park.

The state park has seven short hiking trails totaling 4.5 miles and serves as the trailhead for two much longer hikes that leave the property and cross onto Chattahoochee National Forest lands.

The featured hike is a long trek on the Appalachian Approach Trail.

Start: At the Amicalola Falls Visitor Center
Distance: 8.3 miles one way from visitor center to Appalachian Trail at Springer Mountain
Hiking time: About 5 hours
Difficulty: Easy to strenuous
Trail surface: Compacted dirt and rocks
Best season: Mar–Dec
Other trail users: Hikers only in the park; hunters in season on national forest land
Canine compatibility: Dogs permitted in national forest; leashed dogs permitted in the state park
Land status: Georgia DNR, State Parks & Historic Sites Division; Chattahoochee National Forest
Nearest towns: Dahlonega, Ellijay
Fees and permits: Daily parking fee
Maps: USGS Amicalola and Nimblewill; detailed trail map available at visitor center; USDA Forest Service map of Chattahoochee National Forest and Georgia section of Appalachian Trail
Trail contacts: Amicalola Falls State Park and Lodge, 240 Amicalola Falls Park Rd., Dawsonville 30534; (706) 265-4703; www.gastateparks.org; www.georgia-atclub.org

Finding the trailhead: Amicalola Falls State Park Visitor Center is 20 miles east of Ellijay and 14 miles west of Dahlonega on SR 52. Trailhead for the Appalachian Approach Trail is behind the visitor center. Trailhead GPS: N34 33.465' / W84 14.957'

The Hike

The Appalachian Approach Trail begins as you walk through the attractive stone archway behind the visitor center. The blue-blazed trail climbs about 1,000 feet to the parking area above the falls. However, it starts with a gentle grade through a picnic area and along a boardwalk before crossing the road and passing through more picnic sites along Little Amicalola Creek. Upon reaching the Reflection Pool, the trail becomes a paved path.

Where the pavement ends, the trail beings the steep climb up 177 wooden steps to the observation bridge across the creek. At the end of the bridge the trail turns to the right to climb another 425 steps to the top of the falls. Here the trail follows a paved path back across the creek to the parking lot for the Len Foote Hike Inn.

Exiting the parking area, the trail now shares the path with the Hike Inn Trail and has both blue and green blazes. Shortly after crossing a road, the Hike Inn Trail splits off to the right, and the Approach Trail reverts to blue blazes only.

In the next 0.5 mile the trail crosses a footbridge, then another road, and exits the state park into the Chattahoochee National Forest. The trail climbs continuously until reaching a clearing on top of Frosty Mountain. Here the path leads between the concrete footings that are all that is left of the old fire tower that once stood on the peak.

Another 0.8 mile brings you to the junction with Len Foote Hike Inn Trail that approaches from the right. From here the trail begins to descend down to Old Bucktown Road in Nimblewill Gap. Next the trail climbs steeply for 1.5 miles to the junction with a side trail to the right leading to a trail shelter.

Enjoying the view from the observation bridge on the Foot of the Falls Trail

Continuing to climb, the path makes the final approach up the shoulder of Springer Mountain to an overlook at the point where the Appalachian National Scenic Trail begins at the crest. The spot is marked with a couple of plaques. Beneath one of these a compartment has been built into the side of the rock, and a notebook and pen are stored there. Be sure to sign your name and leave a note for other hikers reaching the point.

This is the turnaround point for heading back to the park. Or, if you have arranged a shuttle, you can continue on the Appalachian Trail for another mile to the parking lot on FS 42 (Alternate Trailhead GPS: N34 38.261' / W84 11.710'). That makes for a 9.2-mile hike. If you choose to head back to the park from Spring Mountain, the trek out and back covers 16.6 miles.

Miles and Directions

0.0 Start at the visitor center archway.

0.5 Pass the Reflection Pool.

0.7 Begin climbing the 602 steps to the top of the falls.

0.9 Cross the bridge over Little Amicalola Creek at the top of the falls.

1.0 Reach the parking area above the falls.

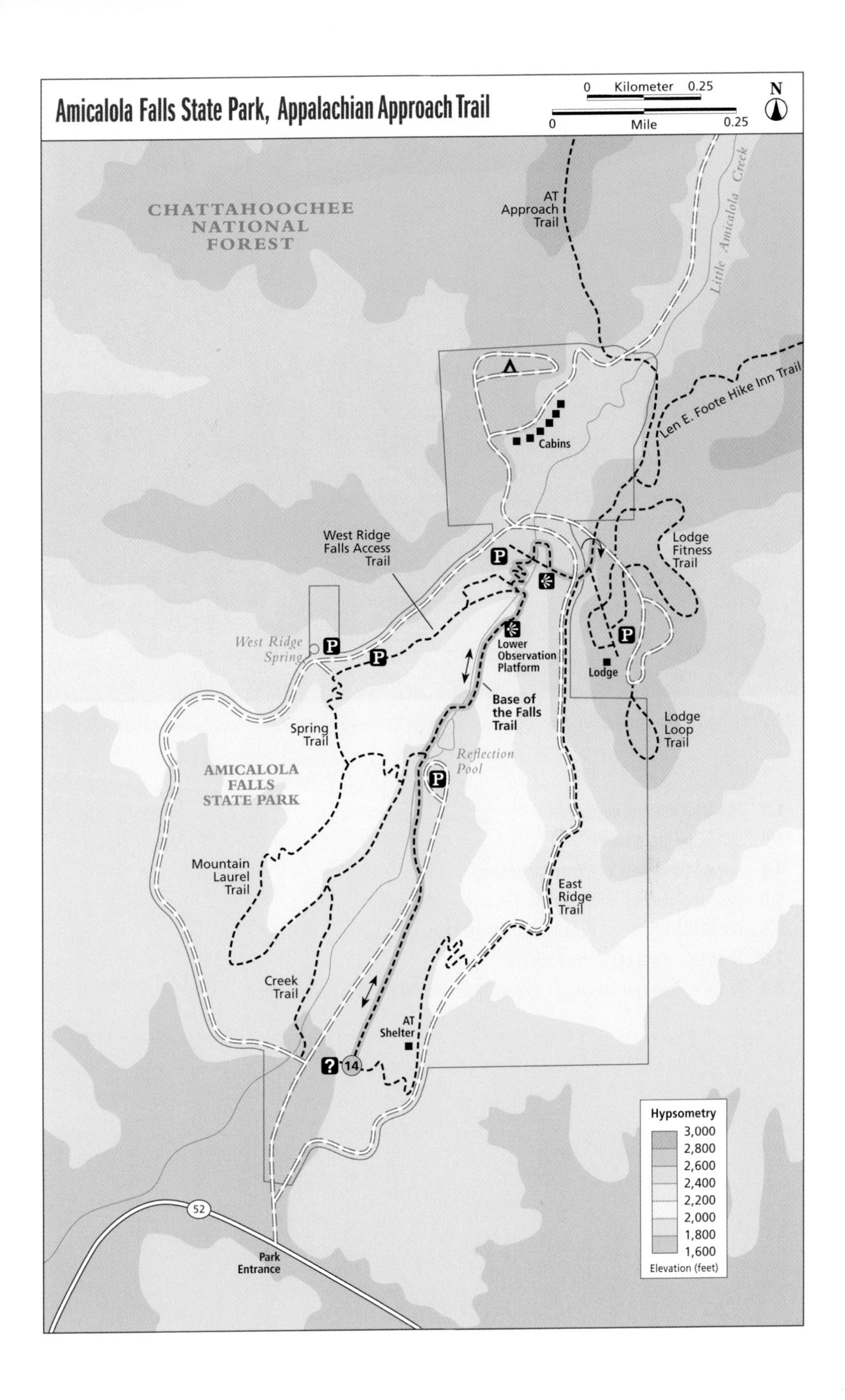
Amicalola Falls State Park, Appalachian Approach Trail
0 Kilometer 0.25
0 Mile 0.25
N
CHATTAHOOCHEE NATIONAL FOREST
AT Approach Trail
Little Amicalola Creek
Cabins
Len E. Foote Hike Inn Trail
Lodge Fitness Trail
West Ridge Falls Access Trail
West Ridge Spring
Lower Observation Platform
Lodge
Base of the Falls Trail
Lodge Loop Trail
Spring Trail
Reflection Pool
AMICALOLA FALLS STATE PARK
Mountain Laurel Trail
East Ridge Trail
Creek Trail
AT Shelter
14
52
Park Entrance
Hypsometry
3,000
2,800
2,600
2,400
2,200
2,000
1,800
1,600
Elevation (feet)

The panorama from the top of Springer Mountain at the beginning of the Appalachian Trail

1.2 The Hike Inn Trail separates to the right.

1.5 Leave the state park.

4.4 Arrive at the crest of Frosty Mountain.

5.0 Pass the junction with the Hike Inn Trail on the right.

5.6 Cross Old Bucktown Road in Nimblewill Gap.

7.0 Pass to the left of the trail shelter.

8.3 Arrive at Springer Mountain, the southern end of the Appalachian Trail.

15 Amicalola Falls State Park, Len Foote Hike Inn Trail

The Len Foote Hike Inn is located outside of Amicalola State Park on adjacent Chattahoochee National Forest property. However, the facility is managed and maintained by the Georgia State Parks and Historic Sites Division. Visitors can only reach the inn using the hiking trail that originates in the park.

The Len Foote Hike Inn Trail offers a leisurely morning or afternoon trek up to the inn. Once there visitors find soft beds, warm showers, and hot meals awaiting. A library and board games are provided, or one can simply lounge in a chair on the decks enjoying the mountain vista.

This featured hike is a long trek on the Len Foote Hike Inn Trail.

See map on page 86.
Start: At the top of the falls in the Hike Inn parking lot
Distance: 5.9 miles one way to the upper junction with the Appalachian Approach Trail
Hiking time: About 3–3.5 hours
Difficulty: Easy to strenuous
Trail surface: Compacted dirt and rocks
Best season: Mar–Dec
Other trail users: Hikers only in the park; hunters in season on national forest land
Canine compatibility: Dogs permitted in national forest; leashed dogs permitted in the state park
Land status: Georgia DNR, State Parks & Historic Sites Division; Chattahoochee National Forest
Nearest towns: Dahlonega, Ellijay
Fees and permits: Daily parking fee
Maps: USGS Amicalola and Nimblewill; detailed trail map available at visitor center; USDA Forest Service map of Chattahoochee National Forest and Georgia section of Appalachian Trail
Trail contacts: Hike Inn; (800) 581-8032; www.Hike-Inn.com

Finding the trailhead: Amicalola Falls State Park is 20 miles east of Ellijay and 14 miles west of Dahlonega on SR 52. The Len Foote Hike Inn Trail begins at the Hike Inn parking area at the top of the waterfall. Trailhead GPS: N34 34.035' / N84 14.610'

The Hike

Lime-green rectangular blazes mark the way for this trail to the Len Foote Hike Inn. The inn, a welcome sight after your hike, offers the opportunity to spend a night in the wilderness without the need for sleeping bag, tent, or other camping gear. If you're staying overnight at the inn, you must check in at the Amicalola State Park Visitor Center and receive your permit by 2 p.m. the day of your reservation to ensure that you complete the hike and return to the inn before dark.

The Hike Inn is named for Leonard E. Foote (1918–89), a consummate conservationist who spent his life in research and management of wildlife. For three decades he was the southeastern field representative of the Wildlife Management Institute.

Guests can only reach the Leonard Foote Hill Inn by walking.

In the evening, guests at the inn are treated to entertaining programs dealing with the natural history of the area, including illustrated discussions of birds and flowers. Visitors can also learn about the conservation techniques used to manage the facility efficiently.

From the parking area above the falls, follow along with the Appalachian Approach Trail across the paved road where the path at the stone wall directs you into the woods.

Where the Approach Trail splits off to the left, follow the green blazes to the right. It is a steady climb to the ridge crest on a well-maintained and easy-to-follow trail. You will cross four ridges, but none of them are very steep.

The forest floor has been relatively clear to this point, but now you encounter a thick growth of low vegetation in summer consisting of grasses, herbaceous plants, and many young sassafras trees. At the crest of this first ridge a couple of log benches provide a breather and a good vista in the winter, when leaves are off the trees.

Changes in vegetation will continue throughout the hike as you go from west- to east-facing and south- to north-facing ridge exposures. In spring look for the abundance of blooming wildflowers, including trailing arbutus, sessile and Vasey's trilliums, jack-in-the-pulpits, and pink lady's slippers. Among the trees and shrubs are silver bells, dogwoods, redbuds, buckeyes, yellow poplars, and mountain laurel. Along the trail are glades of New York ferns as well as marginal wood, lady, Christmas, and bracken ferns, along with some spleenworts.

You might be surprised at the number of seedling and sprouting American chestnuts along the trail. Unfortunately they will soon succumb to the chestnut blight that has been killing the trees since the 1930s.

Mammals in the area include black bears, white-tailed deer, foxes, squirrels, chipmunks, raccoons, and opossums along with smaller deer mice, shrews, and moles. Most are only seen as tracks in the soft ground or as signs of feeding.

This is an excellent birding trail in spring and fall for migrating warblers, grosbeaks, orioles, and others. Besides the migrant birds there are many resident species like warblers, towhees, wrens, hawks, owls and, at higher elevations, ravens.

On the crest of each ridge you get good fall and winter vistas to the southeast down the valley of Cochrans Creek. Just before you begin the final ascent to the lodge, the trail passes through a wet area with five boardwalks, finishing off by crossing another stream, Cochrans Falls Creek, on a footbridge.

At 4.9 miles you reach the front door of the Hike Inn.

If you are day hiking, be sure to walk the trail around the right side of the lodge to the fabulous overlook behind the building. You can then retrace your path back to the parking lot for a day hike of 9.9 miles. Another option is to continue another 1.0 mile past the inn up to the trail junction with the Appalachian Approach Trail. Turning left at that point creates a loop walk of 10.9 miles back to the parking lot.

Miles and Directions

0.0 Start at the designated parking area at top of the falls. The green-blazed Hike Inn and blue-blazed Appalachian Approach Trails share the path.

0.3 The Appalachian Approach Trail angles off to the left.

0.6 Exit the state park into the Chattahoochee National Forest.

0.9 Reach a bench rest, winter vista, and a section of trail with many sassafras trees.

2.6 Cross a footbridge over Cochrans Creek.

3.2 Arrive at a second bench rest with a winter view of the mountains to the south.

3.9 Pass through a rock outcrop with a vista to the south.

4.5 Cross five boardwalks over the creek bottom in the next 110 yards, then a bridge over Cochrans Falls Creek.

4.8 Reach the junction with the Fire Break Trail on the right.

4.9 Arrive at the Len Foote Hike Inn.

5.0 Pass the other end of the Fire Break Trail.

5.9 Arrive at the junction with Appalachian Approach Trail.

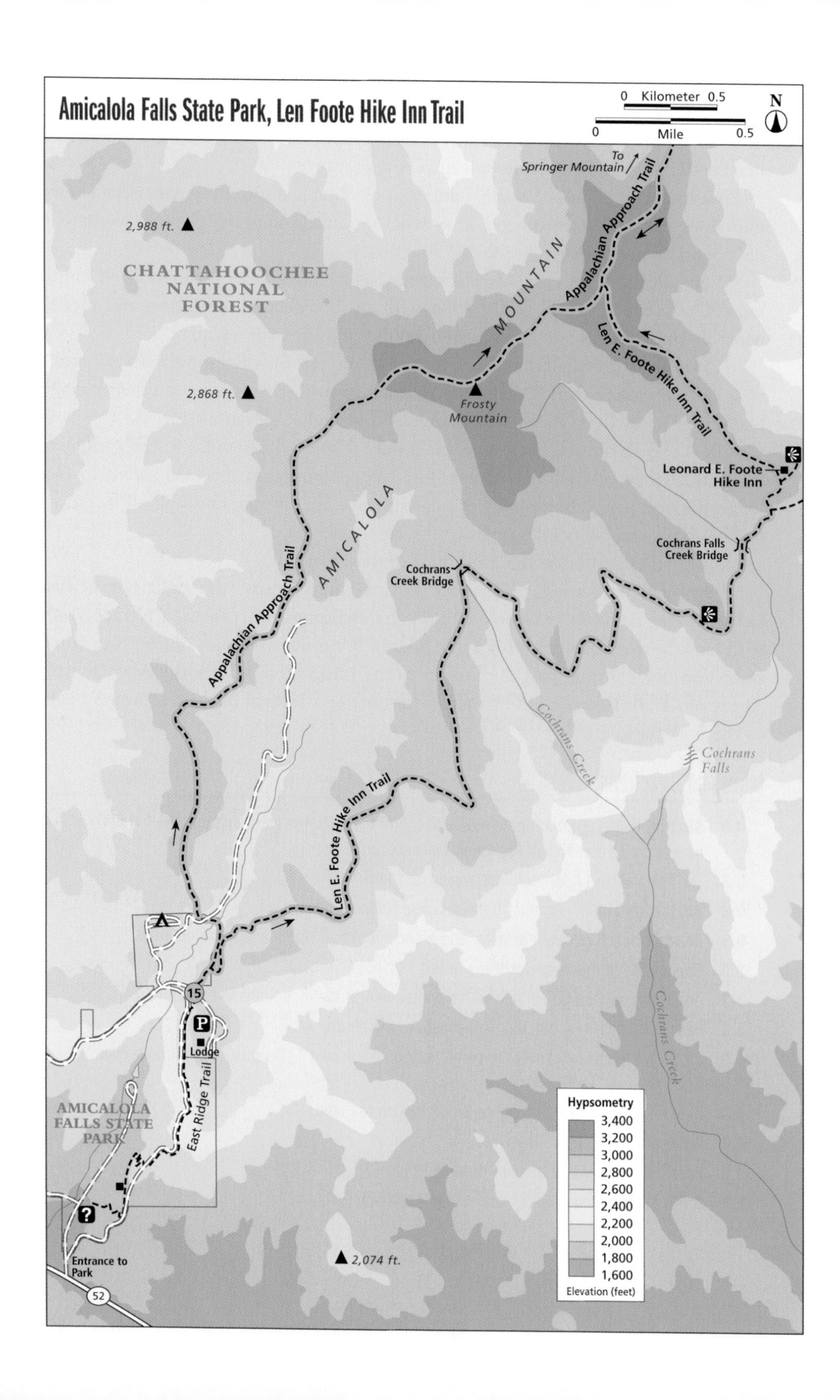

Amicalola Falls State Park, Len Foote Hike Inn Trail
0 Kilometer 0.5
0 Mile 0.5
N
To Springer Mountain
Appalachian Approach Trail
2,988 ft.
CHATTAHOOCHEE NATIONAL FOREST
MOUNTAIN
Len E. Foote Hike Inn Trail
2,868 ft.
Frosty Mountain
Leonard E. Foote Hike Inn
AMICALOLA
Cochrans Falls Creek Bridge
Cochrans Creek Bridge
Appalachian Approach Trail
Cochrans Creek
Cochrans Falls
Len E. Foote Hike Inn Trail
15
Lodge
East Ridge Trail
AMICALOLA FALLS STATE PARK
Cochrans Creek
Hypsometry
3,400
3,200
3,000
2,800
2,600
2,400
2,200
2,000
1,800
1,600
Elevation (feet)
Entrance to Park
52
2,074 ft.

Options

The **Creek Trail** follows the course of Little Amicalola Creek on the west, upstream to the reflection pool at the base of the waterfalls. The 0.6-mile trail has yellow blazes. It stays up on the ridge side for most of the way and is rated moderate to difficult.

The **Spring Trail** is a 0.4-mile path marked with orange blazes. Rated moderate, the path connects the West Ridge Falls Access Trail parking area to the Mountain Laurel Loop Trail.

The green-blazed **Mountain Laurel Loop Trail** is a 1.0-mile, moderate to difficult trail. The path runs along the top of the ridge to the west of Little Amicalola Creek. Access is from the Creek or Spring Trail.

The **West Ridge Falls Access Trail** is an easy 0.2-mile path running from the parking area on the drive to the top of the falls to the observation bridge over the creek halfway up the falls. The trail surface is made of recycled rubber tires and is wheelchair accessible.

The unblazed **East Ridge Trail** offers a 1.0-mile hike to the top of the falls on the eastern side. It begins at the visitor center, climbs through woodlands, and then follows a service road to the Hike Inn parking area. This was the original path of the Appalachian Approach Trail to the top of the falls.

The **Lodge Loop Trail** covers 0.25 mile of easy asphalt pathway to the south of the lodge's entrance. The loop is lighted and wheelchair accessible.

The **Lodge Fitness Trail** spans a 1.0-mile loop to the north of the lodge. There are twenty exercise stations spaced along the path.

Local Information

Accommodations

The Amicalola Falls Lodge offers 56 motel-style rooms, and its Maple Restaurant serves three meals daily. The state park also offers 14 fully equipped cottages and a 24-site campground; www.gastateparks.org/info/amicalola/.

The Len Foote Hike Inn has 20 guest rooms available by reservation only. Breakfast and dinner are served in the inn dining hall; www.hike-inn.com.

16 Appalachian Trail in Georgia

The Appalachian Trail (AT) is one of the longest continually marked trails in the world. Beginning at Springer Mountain in Georgia, the path ends at Mount Katahdin in Maine. Congress authorized the Appalachian Trail as the first National Scenic Trail in 1968. The Appalachian Trail Conference now has responsibility for the trail.

A long-trail concept along the Appalachian Mountains grew out of a 1921 proposal by forester and land-use planner Benton MacKaye. For sixteen years, Civilian Conservation Corps (CCC) members, hiking clubs, and other volunteers worked to see MacKaye's dream come true.

On August 14, 1937, the final 2 miles were opened in Maine, completing the 2,054-mile trail from Georgia to Maine. The original terminus in Georgia was Mount Oglethorpe, 20 miles farther south than today's Springer Mountain.

The trail has undergone many changes in the ensuing years. Storms, changes in land use, and other factors have made it necessary to reroute sections of the trail. This is an ongoing process.

Because of the multiple-approach paths on public land, this trail presents a many-faceted hiking opportunity for thousands of hikers each year. It is estimated that about 10 percent of them take four to six months to actually hike all the way to Maine. The rest discontinue the hike at varying distances up the Blue Ridge. Others hike only portions of the trail, and some hike only a few miles to some interesting point, usually using any one of the approach trails.

The beauty of the Appalachian Trail is that it seems to accommodate all. This concept is best described by the plaque on Springer Mountain that reads GEORGIA TO MAINE—A FOOTPATH FOR THOSE WHO SEEK FELLOWSHIP WITH THE WILDERNESS.

Start: From the visitor center in Amicalola State Park, take the 8.3-mile approach trail to Springer Mountain, the AT's official southern terminus.
Distance: 75.4 miles one way
Hiking time: About 4–5 days
Difficulty: Moderate to strenuous
Trail surface: Dirt and forest loam, with some rock portions
Best season: Mar–June; Oct–Dec
Other trail users: Hunters in season
Canine compatibility: Dogs permitted in national forest portions; leashed dogs permitted in wildlife management area portions
Land status: Primarily Chattahoochee National Forest
Nearest towns: Five paved highway crossings lead to Dahlonega, Cleveland, Blairsville, Helen, and Clayton.
Fees and permits: Daily parking fee at Amicalola State Park; arrangements can be made for longer term parking at the visitor center.
Schedule: The Georgia section of the trail can be hiked year-round.
Maps: USGS Amicalola, Nimblewill, Noontootla, Suches, Neels Gap, Cowrock, Jacks Gap, Tray Mountain, Macedonia, and Hightower Bald; *The Appalachian Trail in Georgia* (map and brochure), Georgia Appalachian Trail Club, Inc.; *The Guide to the Appalachian Trail in North Carolina and Georgia,* the Appalachian Trail Conservancy; Appalachian

Trail—Chattahoochee National Forest Georgia, USDA Forest Service

Trail contacts: Georgia Appalachian Trail Club Inc., PO Box 654, Atlanta 30301; (404) 494-0968; www.georgia-atclub.org

USDA Forest Service, Forest Supervisor, 1755 Cleveland Hwy., Gainesville 30501; (770) 297-3000; www.fs.usda.gov/conf (For specific Ranger Districts, see Appendix D.)

Georgia Department of Natural Resources (DNR); www.gadnr.org

Georgia State Parks and Historic Sites Division; www.gastateparks.org

Georgia Wildlife Resources Division, Game Management Section, 2150 Dawsonville Hwy., Gainesville 30501; (770) 535-5700; www.gohuntgeorgia.com (for hunting season information)

Special considerations: Anyone planning to hike long sections of the trail should first contact the Georgia Appalachian Trail Club for current information.

Because the route of the Appalachian Trail in Georgia is excellent black bear habitat, it is necessary to take precautions with food at campsites. Hang food from a tree limb at least 10 feet off the ground, and do not leave food in your tent if you are away from it for several hours. There is little physical danger from bears, which are usually only a nuisance at heavily used campsites.

Finding the trailhead: The southern terminus for the trail is remote Springer Mountain, near FS 42. Since this area is difficult to reach by automobile, the recommended start is at the Appalachian Approach Trailhead from the visitor center in Amicalola Falls State Park. To reach the park from Dahlonega, go 14 miles west on SR 52. Trailhead GPS: N34 33.465' / W84 14.957'

The Hike

A wilderness hike in rugged terrain along a clearly marked trail for many miles with appropriately spaced shelters, scenic vistas, wildlife, and a variety of hiking adventures and challenges on a world-famous trail makes the Appalachian one of the most popular of all hiking destinations.

Spring and early summer offers displays of azalea, mountain laurel, rhododendron, and many other wildflowers. October brings spectacular leaf color. Mountain scenery that is hidden from view by summer foliage is open in winter, with many eye-catching vistas.

The Georgia section of the trail runs from Springer Mountain to Bly Gap on the North Carolina state line. There are fourteen primitive shelters spaced about a day's hike apart on the trail. Most are three-sided and are close to water.

The oldest shelter, located atop Blood Mountain, was built by the CCC in the 1930s. This four-sided stone structure has a fireplace and a sleeping platform. Some of the shelters are well off the main trail. Whitly Gap shelter at Wildcat Mountain is 1.1 miles off the AT on a well-marked, blue-blazed trail. Other shelters are as much as 0.3 mile off the AT on side trails.

Trail relocation to prevent overuse causes variations in mileage from year to year.

From the visitor center, at an elevation about 1,800 feet, hike the blue-blazed trail past the waterfall. Continue to climb along old roads for about 3.5 miles to Frosty Mountain. Go through Nimblewill Gap, up to Black Mountain, and through another 3,200-foot-high

Appalachian Trail in Georgia

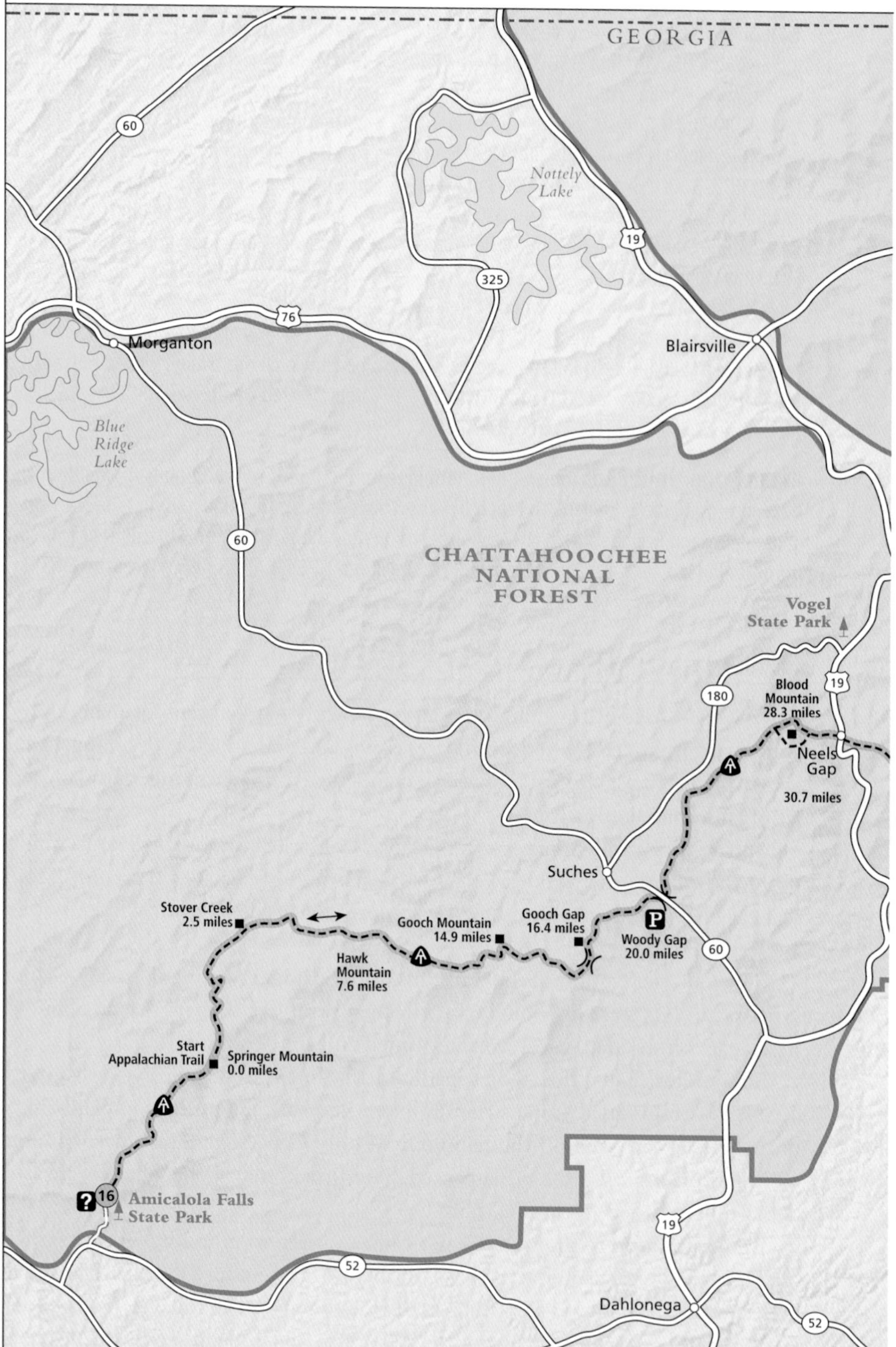

GEORGIA
60
Nottely Lake
19
325
76
Morganton
Blairsville
Blue Ridge Lake
60
CHATTAHOOCHEE NATIONAL FOREST
Vogel State Park
19
180
Blood Mountain 28.3 miles
Neels Gap
30.7 miles
Suches
Stover Creek 2.5 miles
Gooch Mountain 14.9 miles
Gooch Gap 16.4 miles
Woody Gap 20.0 miles
60
Hawk Mountain 7.6 miles
Start Appalachian Trail
Springer Mountain 0.0 miles
16
Amicalola Falls State Park
19
52
Dahlonega
52
To Ellijay

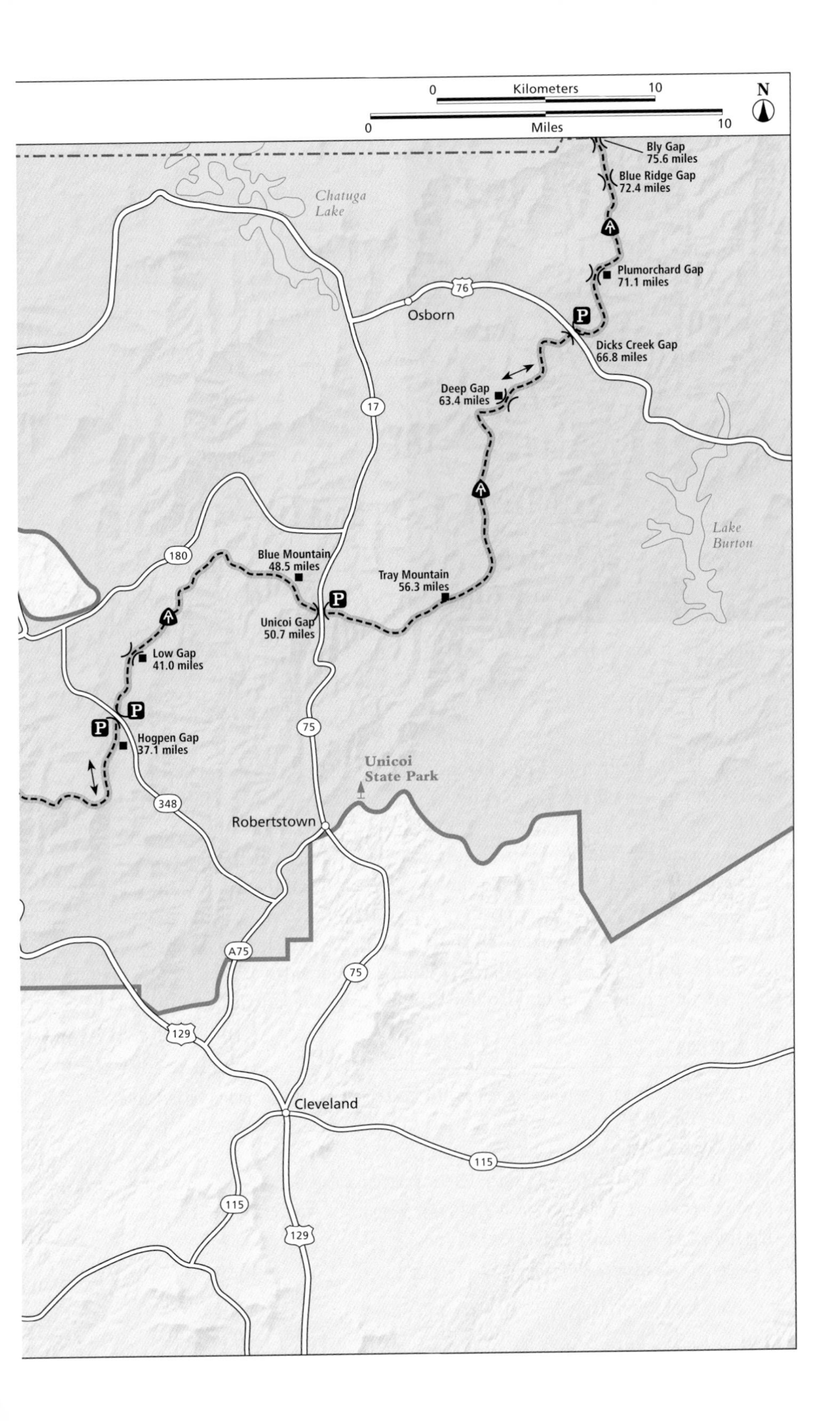

0
Kilometers
10
0
Miles
10
N
Bly Gap
75.6 miles
Blue Ridge Gap
72.4 miles
Chatuga
Lake
Plumorchard Gap
71.1 miles
76
Osborn
Dicks Creek Gap
66.8 miles
Deep Gap
63.4 miles
17
Lake
Burton
180
Blue Mountain
48.5 miles
Tray Mountain
56.3 miles
Unicoi Gap
50.7 miles
Low Gap
41.0 miles
75
Hogpen Gap
37.1 miles
Unicoi
State Park
348
Robertstown
A75
75
129
Cleveland
115
115
129

The view from the top of Springer Mountain at the start of the Appalachian Trail

gap where Gilmer, Fannin, and Dawson Counties join. The final uphill stretch to Springer Mountain is a 580-foot climb to an elevation of 3,782 feet. The trail then passes through a forest of the stunted oaks to the rock marking the beginning of the Appalachian Trail.

Jarrard Gap and Slaughter Gap Approach Trails begin at Lake Winfield Scott, 4.5 miles east of Suches on SR 180.

The Byron Herbert Reece Farm and Cultural Center Area is about 0.4 mile north on US 19/129 from Neels Gap. From this trailhead the Freeman Trail climbs 0.7 mile across the shoulder of Blood Mountain to the Appalachian Trail, a moderate 400-foot climb. To the right is a stiff climb to the top of Blood Mountain. To the left the trail drops down 1.0 mile to Neels Gap. This spur trail and parking area were designed to take pressure away from Neels Gap and the Walasi-Yi Center, where hiking and backpacking supplies are available.

Jacks Knob Trail provides access to the Appalachian Trail at Chattahoochee Gap.

Dockery Lake Trail is a 3.4-mile trail from the Dockery Lake Recreation Area. The recreation area is on SR 60, 12 miles north of Dahlonega. The trailhead is at the parking lot for the picnic area. This trail climbs about 400 feet to Millers Gap on the Appalachian Trail. This hike goes up Pigeon Roost Creek, a tributary of Waters Creek. The trail is moderate along the creek and becomes strenuous in the last climb to the gap.

Miles and Directions

0.0 Springer Mountain is the southern terminus of Appalachian Trail. Begin on the white-blazed trail to Bly Gap, NC.

2.5 Stover Creek Shelter; water.

4.1 Three Forks: elevation 2,500 feet; water; FS 58; limited parking.

7.6 Hawk Mountain trail shelter: elevation 3,380 feet; water.

8.1 Hightower Gap: elevation 2,854 feet; FS 69 and 42.

11.6 Cooper Gap: elevation 2,820 feet; FS 80, 42, and 15.

14.9 Gooch Mountain Shelter and a good spring are on a short side trail to the left.

16.3 Gooch Gap Shelter: elevation 2,784 feet; water; FS 42.

19.9 Woody Gap: elevation 3,160 feet; SR 60; first paved road, parking area, and trail information sign.

20.9 Big Cedar Mountain; good view from rock ledges.

22.9 Miller Gap: elevation 2,980 feet; Dockery Lake Trail on right.

25.5 Jarrard Gap: elevation 3,310 feet; water; Jarrard Gap Trail to Lake Winfield Scott.

27.2 Slaughter Gap: elevation 3,850 feet; end of Duncan Ridge Trail; Coosa Backcountry Trail to Vogel State Park; water nearby.

28.1 Blood Mountain: elevation 4,458 feet; no water; stone trail shelter; highest point on Appalachian Trail in Georgia.

29.5 Flatrock Gap: elevation 3,460 feet; spur trail to Byron Herbert Reece Trail; Freeman Trail.

30.5 Neels Gap: elevation 3,125 feet; Walasi-Yi Center with hostel for through-hikers only from March to Memorial Day. The center also has a hiking and camping outfitting store with books, maps, and snacks.

33.9 Wolf Laurel Top; campsite and views.

35.3 Cowrock Mountain: elevation 3,852 feet; vistas from rock outcrops.

36.0 Tesnatee Gap: elevation 3,120 feet; SR 348 (Russell Scenic Highway); Logan Turnpike Trail, parking.

36.7 Wildcat Mountain: elevation 3,730 feet; Whitly Gap trail shelter is about 1 mile south on a blue-blazed trail; water; good views; Raven Cliffs Wilderness.

36.9 Hog Pen Gap: elevation 3,480 feet; SR 348; parking, interpretive signs and markers.

41.1 Low Gap: elevation 3,032 feet; trail shelter; water.

46.1 Chattahoochee Gap: elevation 3,520 feet; water; beginning of the Chattahoochee River; Jacks Knob Trail to SR 180 and Brasstown Bald.

48.3 Blue Mountain: elevation 4,020 feet; trail shelter; water.

50.5 Unicoi Gap: elevation 2,949 feet; SR 17/75; parking.

53.3 Indian Grave Gap: elevation 3,120; FS 283; Andrews Cove Trail to Andrews Cove Recreation Area.

54.0 Junction with FS 79: elevation 3,400 feet; road leads down to Robertstown and Helen.

54.9 Tray Gap: elevation 3,841 feet; FR 79.

55.7 Tray Mountain: elevation 4,430 feet; trail shelter; water; rock outcrops and scenic views; only a few feet lower than Blood Mountain; Tray Mountain Wilderness.

61.3 Addis Gap: elevation 3,300 feet; FS 26; campsite; water.

63.1 Deep Gap Shelter and water in a piped spring are on a 0.3-mile trail to the right.

66.5 Dicks Creek Gap: elevation 2,675 feet, US 76; parking; picnic area.

70.9 Plumorchard Gap: elevation 3,100 feet; unique trail shelter put in place by helicopter; water.

72.4 Blue Ridge Gap: elevation 3,020 feet; FS 72.

75.4 Bly Gap: elevation 3,840 feet; North Carolina line; there is no road access to this gap as you leave Georgia.

17 Cooper Creek Wildlife Management Area Trails

The Cooper Creek Wildlife Management Area (WMA) covers 30,000 acres of forested mountain ridges within the Chattahoochee National Forest. The property is owned by the US Forest Service, but hunting and fishing are managed by the Georgia Department of Natural Resources. A portion of the WMA around the Cooper Creek Recreation Area campground is designated as the Cooper Creek Scenic Area.

Old timber stands remain untouched, except for a few trees removed many years ago. The 2,160-foot contour runs through the campground near the trailhead. From there, the highest elevation on the featured hike is at 2,963 feet on Yellow Mountain.

Trout fishing in Cooper Creek and its tributaries, wildflowers, wildlife, and camping add to the hiking experience.

The WMA contains a total of five trails offering a bit more than 9 miles of easy to moderate hiking. To a certain extent, confusion reigns on these pathways. All of them are marked with green blazes. Also, signs on the area show the lollipop path through the Cooper Creek Scenic Area as the Cooper Creek Trail. Additionally, the connector path between the Mill Shoals and Yellow Mountain Trails is marked as the Cooper Creek Trail. The latter is referred to here as the Cooper Creek Connector. The other path on the WMA is the Shope Gap Trail.

The featured hike is a Mill Shoals–Yellow Mountain Loop combination composed of all 3.0 miles of the Yellow Mountain Trail and the 0.4-mile Cooper Creek Connector, along with a portion of the 1.7-mile Mill Shoals Trail. This is an out-and-back trek that creates a loop near its beginning and ending point.

Start: At the steps going up the road bank on FS 236, 225 yards west of the Cooper Creek Scenic Area parking lot
Distance: 6.1-mile lollipop
Hiking time: About 2.5 hours
Difficulty: Easy to moderate; a few short, steep grades
Trail surface: Clean loamy dirt with leaf litter
Best season: Mar–June; Oct–Dec
Other trail users: Hunters in season
Canine compatibility: Leashed dogs permitted
Land status: Chattahoochee National Forest
Nearest town: Blairsville
Fees and permits: No fees or permits required for hiking; campsite fees charged mid-Mar to mid-Nov; free camping mid-Nov through Dec
Schedule: Open to year-round hiking; campground closed Jan to mid-Mar
Maps: USGS Mulky Gap; USDA Forest Service Chattahoochee National Forest map
Trail contacts: For marked trails in the Cooper Creek Scenic Area or camping in the Cooper Creek Recreation Area: USDA Forest Service, Blue Ridge Ranger District, 2042 SR 515 West, Blairsville 30512; (706) 745-6928, www.fs.usda.gov/conf

Finding the trailhead: From Blairsville travel west on US 76 to Old US 76; turn left on Old US 76 and go 2.9 miles to Mulky Gap Road. Turn left and follow this winding road 9.9 miles to the Cooper Creek Campground at FS 236; turn left and cross the bridge over Mulky Creek. At 0.5 mile cross the bridge over Cooper Creek and the parking area for the Cooper Creek Scenic Area is on the left. Walk 225 yards back toward the campground on FS 236 for the Mill Shoals Trailhead. Trailhead GPS: N34 45.502' / W84 04.043'

The Hike

The trails of this combination hike follow old logging roads and footpaths through a variety of hardwood, white pine, and hemlock forests, as well as through a variety of conditions, from old stands of large trees to tracts recovering from fire or storm damage.

From the Cooper Creek Scenic Area parking lot, walk west along gravel FS 236 for 225 yards to the Mill Shoals Trailhead. A wooden sign marks the trailhead on the right. Climbing the steps up the road embankment, you begin a steady climb following the green blazes.

The path runs through white pines and hardwoods, with small patches of trailing arbutus and galax at the path's edge. Old American chestnut logs and new sprouts from old stumps are reminders of this great tree that was once dominant on these ridges. The path switches back and forth up a steep ridge with patches of mountain laurel, white pines, chestnut oaks, and several species of ferns.

At the top of the ridge the trail forks; follow the directional sign to the right onto the Cooper Creek Connector for the combination hike. The left fork is the continuation of the Mill Shoals Trail as it follows an old logging road along Mill Shoals Creek for another 0.9 mile to FS 39.

The Cooper Creek Connector climbs over a low ridge and then levels out to a junction, where you turn left onto the Yellow Mountain Trail.

From here to the crest of Yellow Mountain, the hike is on a gentle rolling path for 0.7 mile. Along the way you pass the junction with the Shope Gap Trail entering from the left. At the high point of the trail on Yellow Mountain, you reach a campsite with an excellent vista to the southwest toward Horse Knob.

The Yellow Mountain Trail continues down the ridge crest into a stand of large hemlocks and white pines, switching back and forth until it reaches Bryant Creek and dense growths of rhododendron, dog-hobble, and mountain laurel. Bryant Creek is crossed on a log bridge. In a couple switchbacks you climb the next ridge and then drop into Addie Gap at FS 33A. Just before reaching the forest road, the trail crosses another gravel road running up the hillside.

Retrace your path back to Yellow Mountain and the junction with the Cooper Creek Connector. At the intersection, go left to continue on the Yellow Mountain Trail.

The trail follows the south face of the mountain along a path cut into the steep slope. Trailing arbutus and galax are abundant along this stretch. Next the path begins descending gently down through mountain laurel thickets with some large flame azalea shrubs that bloom April through May. As the trail drops into a hardwood cove, the canopy is composed of yellow poplar and white oaks, then gives way to a stand of white pines as the path reaches the trailhead on FS 236. Turn left and walk along the road back to the parking area.

Miles and Directions

0.0 Start at the Mill Shoals Trailhead sign.

0.7 Turn onto the Cooper Creek Connector that intersects on the right.

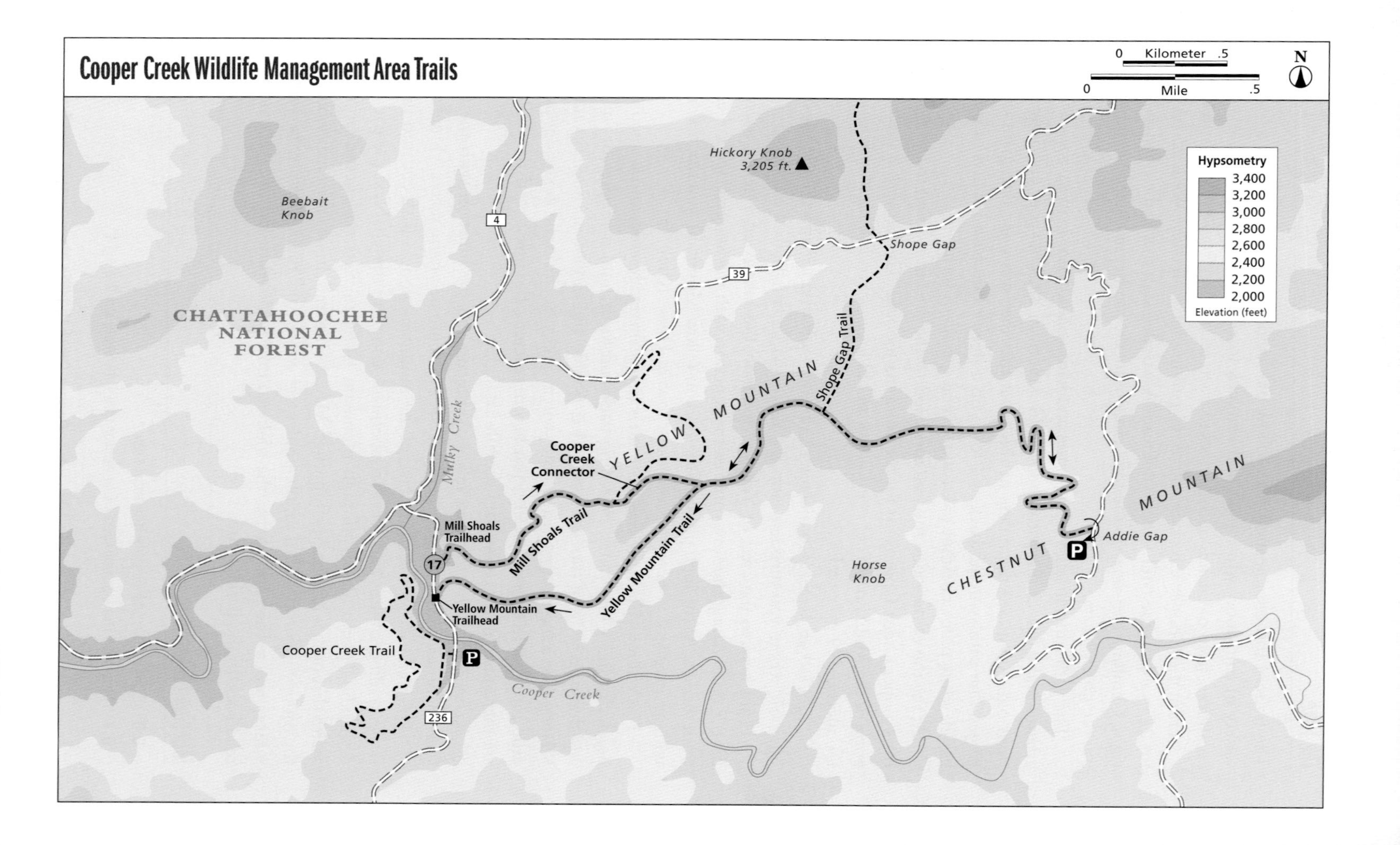
Cooper Creek Wildlife Management Area Trails
0 Kilometer .5
0 Mile .5
N
Hypsometry
3,400
3,200
3,000
2,800
2,600
2,400
2,200
2,000
Elevation (feet)
Hickory Knob
3,205 ft.
Beebait
Knob
4
39
Shope Gap
Shope Gap Trail
CHATTAHOOCHEE
NATIONAL
FOREST
YELLOW MOUNTAIN
Cooper
Creek
Connector
Mulky Creek
Mill Shoals
Trailhead
Mill Shoals Trail
Yellow Mountain Trail
17
Yellow Mountain
Trailhead
Cooper Creek Trail
P
Cooper Creek
236
Horse
Knob
CHESTNUT MOUNTAIN
Addie Gap
P

A log bridge carries the trail across Bryant Creek.

1.1 Reach the junction with the Yellow Mountain Trail and turn left.
1.7 The Shope Gap Trail intersects from the left.
1.8 Pass the campsite and overlook at the crest of Yellow Mountain.
2.6 Cross Bryant Creek on a log bridge.
3.1 Arrive at the turnaround point in Addie Gap.
5.0 Turn left at the junction with the Cooper Creek Connector.
6.1 Reach the Yellow Mountain Trailhead and turn left on FS 236 to the parking area.

Options

The **Cooper Creek Trail** has carsonite stakes with arrows at major directional turns in the trail. The trailhead is located across FS 236 from the Cooper Creek Scenic Area parking lot. You cross a small bridge over Tom Jones Branch. A granite stone provides the path's history and designates the trailhead. It is best to begin this walk to the left around the 1.7-mile loop.

The 2.4-mile **Shope Gap Trail** branches off the Yellow Mountain Trail, running north for 0.6 mile to a parking area on FS 39. The path then continues for 1.8 miles more to Mulky Gap and the Duncan Ridge Trail.

18 Lake Winfield Scott Recreation Area Trails

Like many other facilities in the Georgia highlands, Lake Winfield Scott and its recreation area were projects constructed by the Civilian Conservation Corps (CCC) in the 1930s. The clear 18-acre lake offers fishing, swimming, and camping. Wildflower and bird viewing are also exceptional here.

Many of the place names in this area hark back to an earlier history. Both Slaughter Creek and Gap, along with nearby Blood Mountain, got their gruesome names from a sixteenth-century battle between Native American tribes that supposedly occurred here. One version names the adversaries as the Cherokees and Creeks, with the Cherokee victory sealing their claim to the Georgia mountains. Unfortunately, with no written history from the period, that remains just one line of conjecture.

The recreation area contains one trail and the opening sections of two others. The Lake Loop Trail is an easy walk encircling Lake Winfield Scott. The Jarrard Gap Trail is a longer, moderate hike from the lake to Jarrard Gap on the Appalachian Trail (AT). The Slaughter Creek Trail, starting at the same trailhead as the Jarrard Gap Trail, also leads to the AT.

The featured trail combines the Slaughter Creek Trail with the Jarrard Gap Trail and up-and-back portion of the AT to Blood Mountain to form a loop.

Start: At the south end of the lake at the information and trailhead signs
Distance: 7.9 mile loop
Hiking time: About 5–5.5 hours
Difficulty: Moderate
Trail surface: Loamy with leaf litter; old roadbeds with dirt and loose rock
Best Season: Oct–June
Other trail users: Hikers only
Canine compatibility: Dogs permitted
Land status: Chattahoochee National Forest
Nearest towns: Blairsville, Dahlonega
Fees and permits: Daily parking fee and recreation area camping fees
Schedule: Open year-round for hiking; recreation area open 7 a.m.–10 p.m. daily.
Maps: USGS Neels Gap; Chattahoochee National Forest map
Trail contacts: USDA Forest Service, Blue Ridge Ranger District, 2042 SR 515 West, Blairsville 30512; (706) 745-6928; www.fs.usda.gov/conf

Finding the trailhead: The entrance to Lake Winfield Scott Recreation Area is 4.3 miles east of Suches on SR 180 and 6.7 miles west of US 129 near Vogel State Park. The trailhead for both Jarrard Gap and Slaughter Creek Trails is on the main entrance road at an information sign and across the road from the parking area on the southeast side of the lake. Trailhead GPS: N34 44.250' / W83 58.370'

The Hike

The Jarrard Gap and Slaughter Creek Trails share a wide path along Slaughter Creek as they leave the trailhead. The trail is marked with light blue blazes.

The Blood Mountain Trail Shelter is one of the most familiar sights along the Georgia portion of the Appalachian Trail.

At the junction with a side trail that goes straight across a footbridge over the creek, the trail turns sharply left and enters a wooded area. After a short stretch along the creek, the path crosses a bridge over the water and comes out onto a gravel road.

The Jarrard Gap Trail splits off, running up the road to the right. Continue straight across the road onto the 2.9-mile-long Slaughter Creek Trail.

The trail passes through a cove hardwood forest, now on the south side of Slaughter Creek. This is a good example of a regenerated hardwood forest that was heavily logged seventy years ago. The path follows blue blazes along an old logging road for much of its distance. As you near the gap, a side trail from the left leads down to the creek and several primitive campsites. Just after this a boundary sign for the Blood Mountain Wilderness Area is at trailside.

After crossing several small streams and springs that are the headwaters of Slaughter Creek, the trail makes the final approach to Slaughter Gap. Along the way the path cuts through a large boulder field to eventually reach the gap at 3,920 feet of elevation. This is 1,050 feet above Lake Winfield Scott. At the gap the Slaughter Creek Trail ends at its junction with the white-blazed Appalachian Trail.

Turn sharply uphill on the AT to the left to continue on to Blood Mountain. The first part of this trail is quite rocky and steep, but it quickly levels out again. You soon pass a pair of side trails to the right that lead to designated primitive campsites.

The overlook at the top of Blood Mountain is a good place to stop for lunch while enjoying the view.

Next, the junction with the Duncan Ridge Trail appears, approaching from the left. From that point the trail climbs through several switchbacks as it ascends Blood Mountain. When the trail crosses a large stretch of exposed rock, the crest is another 500 feet ahead.

At the top of the 4,461-foot peak, you find the Blood Mountain Trail Shelter. Another product of the CCC, this two-room stone building was built in 1934 and is one of the more elaborate trail shelters on the AT. Climbing to the top of the boulders surrounding the shelter affords sweeping panoramas of the surrounding mountains and valleys from the highest point on the Appalachian Trail in Georgia.

From the top of Blood Mountain, walk back down the AT to the junction with the Slaughter Creek Trail. At the intersection turn left to follow the white blazes of the AT. This trail to the southwest is a gently rolling path, staying on the ridge crest and skirting the mountaintops.

After 0.4 mile the Freeman Trail intersects from the left. The Freeman trail descends for 1.8 miles across the shoulder of Blood Mountain to Flatrock Gap. It also intersects with the 0.7-mile Byron Herbert Reece Trail leading down to the Byron Herbert Reece Farm and Cultural Center. Reece was a noted poet and novelist from Union County in the first half of the twentieth century. His family farm is now open to the public as a museum and arts center on SR 180, just north of Vogel State Park.

Just after the Freeman Trail, a 0.4-mile spur trail leads to the right to the Wood Hole Trail Shelter.

Continuing along on the AT, the path skirts to the west of Turkey Stamp Mountain and passes through Horseshoe Gap. The trail then goes west around Gaddis Mountain to reach Jarrard Gap.

From the gap, turn right on the gravel road and walk 50 yards, following the blue blazes of the 1.3-mile Jarrard Gap Trail to the point it turns left off the road and into the woods. Shortly you cross a wooden footbridge over Lance Branch and begin following that stream gently down its course.

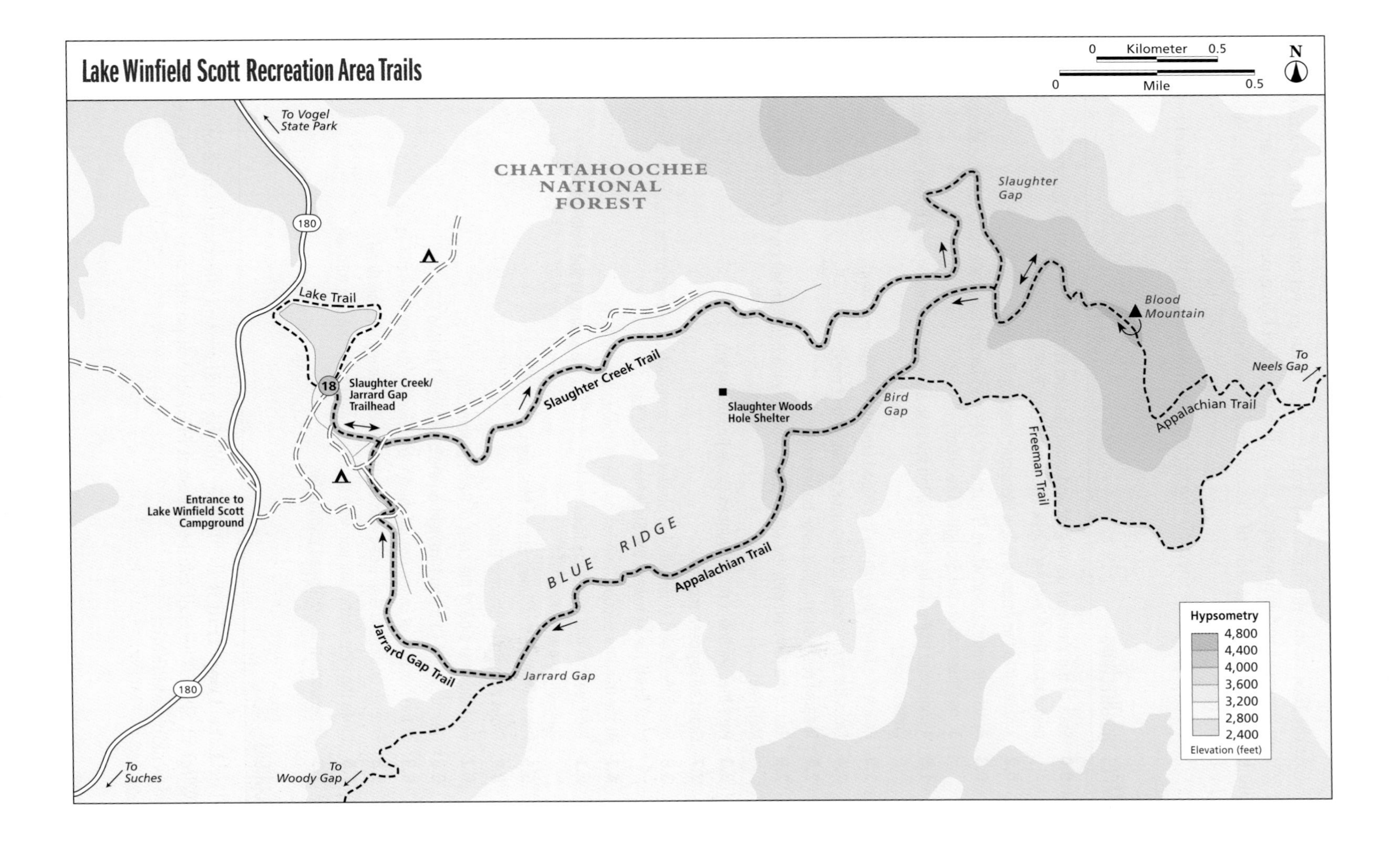
Lake Winfield Scott Recreation Area Trails
0 Kilometer 0.5
0 Mile 0.5
N
To Vogel State Park
180
CHATTAHOOCHEE NATIONAL FOREST
Slaughter Gap
Blood Mountain
To Neels Gap
Appalachian Trail
Lake Trail
18
Slaughter Creek/ Jarrard Gap Trailhead
Slaughter Creek Trail
Slaughter Woods Hole Shelter
Bird Gap
Freeman Trail
Entrance to Lake Winfield Scott Campground
BLUE RIDGE
Appalachian Trail
Jarrard Gap Trail
Jarrard Gap
180
To Suches
To Woody Gap
Hypsometry
4,800
4,400
4,000
3,600
3,200
2,800
2,400
Elevation (feet)

At the foot of the mountain the trail emerges onto gravel Jarrard Gap Road. Turn right on the road and immediately take a left on gravel Slaughter Creek Road. There are blue blazes along the side of the roadway, which takes you to the point at which the loop closes.

Turn left and follow the trail through the woods back to the trailhead and parking lot.

Miles and Directions

0.0 Start at the trailhead parking lot and cross the Lake Winfield Scott dam to the shared trailhead of the Slaughter Creek and Jarrard Gap Trails.

0.2 Turn left into the wood to follow Slaughter Creek upstream.

0.3 Reach the intersection where Slaughter Creek and Jarrard Gap Trails split; continue straight across the road on the Slaughter Creek Trail.

1.8 A connector trail entering from the left leads to a primitive camping area beside Slaughter Creek.

1.9 Reach the boundary sign for the Blood Mountain Wilderness Area.

2.4 Cross the springhead at the origins of Slaughter Creek.

2.7 The trail passes through a large boulder field.

2.9 Reach the junction with the white-blazed Appalachian Trail. Turn left on the AT toward Blood Mountain.

3.3 Pass the junction with the Duncan Ridge Trail on the left.

3.7 Cross an exposed rock face.

3.8 Reach the Blood Mountain Trail Shelter and overlook on the crest of the mountain. Return back down the AT toward the Slaughter Creek Trail.

4.7 At the trail intersection, turn left on the AT toward Jarrard Gap.

5.1 The Freeman Trail intersects from the left, and then the spur to Wood Hole Trail Shelter splits off to the right.

5.5 Pass to the west of Turkey Stamp Mountain.

5.9 Cross through Horseshoe Gap.

6.2 Skirt the west side of the crest of Gaddis Mountain.

6.6 Reach Jarrard Gap and turn right on the blue-blazed Jarrard Gap Trail.

6.9 At the crossing of Lance Branch, begin following the stream down the valley.

7.3 Emerge on Jarrard Gap Road and begin following Slaughter Gap Road.

7.5 Close the loop at the junction with the Slaughter Creek Trail and turn left.

7.9 Arrive back at the trailhead parking lot.

Options

The **Lake Loop Trail** is a 0.4-mile walking path around the clear waters of Lake Winfield Scott. The trail can be accessed from several points, providing good access to walking and fishing.

19 DeSoto Falls Scenic Area Trails

The name DeSoto Falls comes from a tale that a piece of armor found near the falls some decades ago belonged to Hernando de Soto or one of his men. Though that expedition traveled through this general area of Georgia in search of gold, the story had been dismissed by historians who doubted such a relic would have survived so long. However, in the late 1920s a portion of an iron Spanish sword was found in an Indian burial mound near Chatsworth to the west. Whatever the truth of the story, the falls have retained the conquistador's name.

To have a look at some of the gold de Soto never found, you can drop in at the nearby Dahlonega Gold Museum or visit Smithgall Woods State Park, where gold was discovered and mined in the 1830s.

There are two waterfalls on this hike, both of which are on tributaries of Frogtown Creek, which runs through the USDA Forest Service's DeSoto Falls Scenic Area. The upper of these two cascades is identified by the forest service as DeSoto Falls, while the other is called Lower Falls. Most visitors combine the hikes to the two falls into a single out-and-back trek.

Start: At the trailhead in the recreation area day-use parking lot
Distance: 2.3 miles out and back
Hiking time: About 1–1.5 hours
Difficulty: Easy
Trail surface: Loamy dirt
Best season: Mar–Dec
Other trail users: Hikers only
Canine compatibility: Dogs permitted; leashed dogs permitted in campground
Land status: Chattahoochee National Forest
Nearest town: Cleveland
Fees and permits: Daily parking and camping fees
Schedule: Trails and campground open year-round
Maps: USGS Neels Gap; USDA Forest Service map of Chattahoochee National Forest
Trail contacts: USDA Forest Service, Blue Ridge Ranger District, 2042 SR 515 West, Blairsville 30512; (706) 745-6928; www.fs.usda.gov/conf

Finding the trailhead: DeSoto Falls Scenic Area is 14.6 miles north of Cleveland on US 129. The trailhead is at the day-use parking lot. Trailhead GPS: N34 42.397' / W83 54.911'

The Hike

This trail takes you through a range of forest types, from the thick rhododendron, mountain laurel, and dog-hobble of the streamsides to a more open hardwood forest of oak, hickory, yellow poplar, maple, and buckeye. Fine spring flower displays begin as early as March and continue with colorful displays of shrubs and trees like silver bell, serviceberry, deciduous magnolias, mountain laurel, rhododendron, and sourwood from April through August. The mountainsides exhibit grand color in mid- to late October.

The Lower Falls Trail runs along Frogtown Creek after leaving the junction with the Upper Falls Trail.

The trail begins at the parking lot, first traversing the camping area to reach the banks of Frogtown Creek. Though small, this creek is stocked with rainbow trout but has some wild fish in it as well.

A picturesque footbridge provides access across Frogtown from the campground. After you cross the bridge, a large wooden sign welcomes you to DeSoto Falls Scenic Area. A smaller sign directs you to the left for the Lower Falls and to the right to DeSoto Falls.

Turn left and walk downstream on the west side of Frogtown Creek. After roughly 100 yards the trail turns away from the creek and begins climbing through a series of switchbacks to reach the unnamed feeder stream just below the Lower Falls. The trail gains about 100 feet of elevation in 0.1 mile as it runs up the cove on the southeast flank of Cedar Mountain. At the foot of the falls, an observation deck provides a good view of the 35-foot cascade.

Return back down the trail, and at the bridge over Frogtown, continue straight on the trail to DeSoto Falls. The path now follows Frogtown Creek upstream through a picturesque area that is abundantly rich in wildflowers during spring. Along the way it crosses one footbridge before turning uphill to the left, away from the stream.

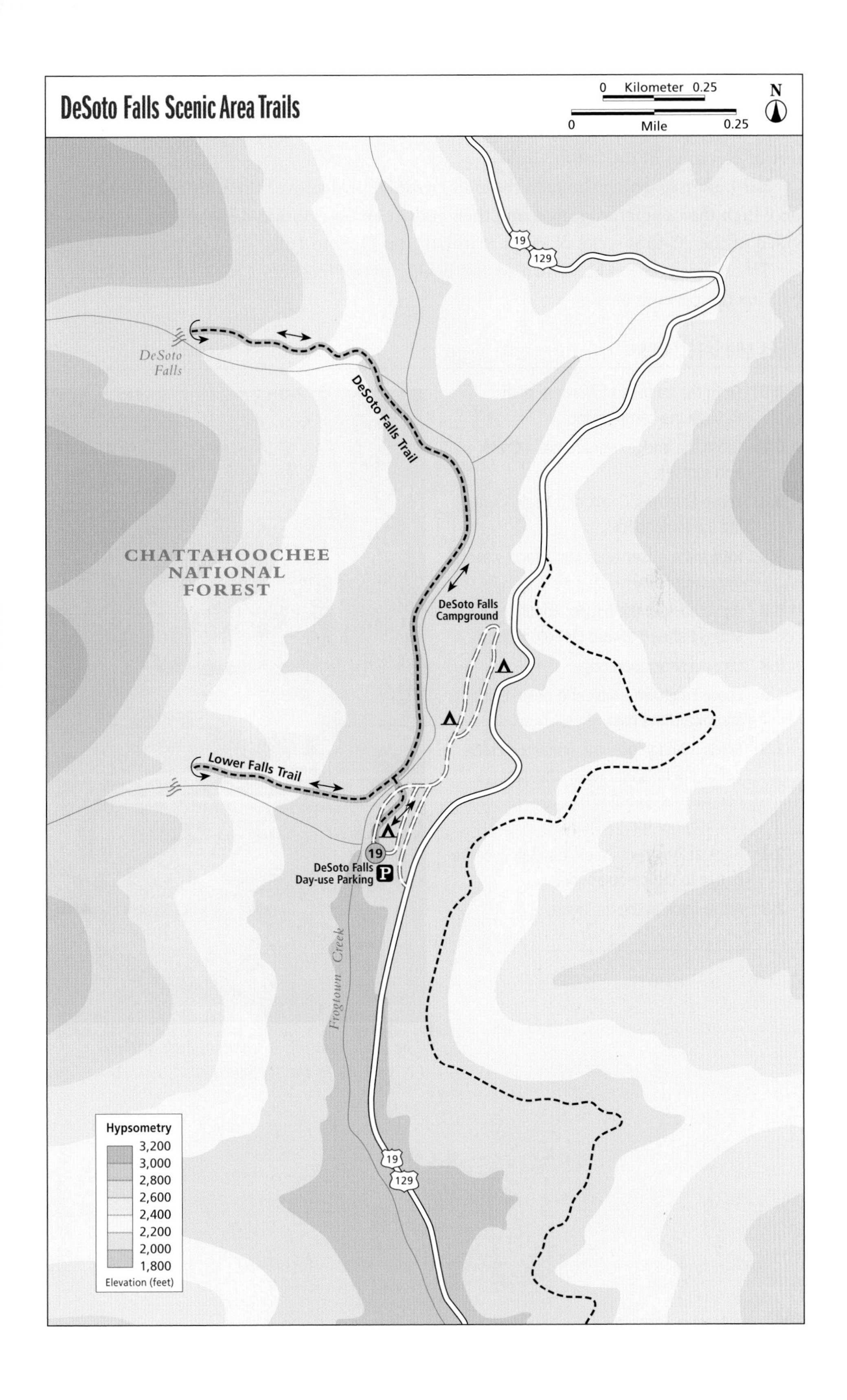
DeSoto Falls Scenic Area Trails
0 Kilometer 0.25
0 Mile 0.25
N
DeSoto Falls
DeSoto Falls Trail
CHATTAHOOCHEE
NATIONAL
FOREST
DeSoto Falls
Campground
Lower Falls Trail
19
129
DeSoto Falls
Day-use Parking
Frogtown Creek
Hypsometry
3,200
3,000
2,800
2,600
2,400
2,200
2,000
1,800
Elevation (feet)

From here to the waterfall the trail gently climbs up into the gap between Rocky Mountain on the north and Cedar Mountain on the south. The path gains almost 100 feet of elevation in the last 0.3 mile.

Just before reaching the falls, the trail crosses a bridge over the unnamed branch on which the cataract is located, and then ends at an observation deck. A vista is provided of the 90-foot series of drops that make up DeSoto Falls.

To complete the hike, return to the bridge over Frogtown Creek and turn left, back to the parking area.

Miles and Directions

- **0.0** From the trailhead follow the path through the campground.
- **0.2** Cross the bridge over Frogtown Creek and turn left.
- **0.3** Leave Frogtown Creek and begin climbing the switchbacks.
- **0.4** Reach the observation deck for a view of the Lower Falls.
- **0.6** Arrive back at the bridge; continue straight ahead toward DeSoto Falls.
- **0.8** Cross a short footbridge.
- **1.0** Leave Frogtown Creek and begin climbing toward the falls.
- **1.3** Cross a bridge over the unnamed creek below the falls and reach the observation deck at DeSoto Falls; reverse course back toward the trailhead.
- **2.1** Back at Frogtown Creek, turn left over the bridge to the campground.
- **2.3** Arrive back at the trailhead.

The view from the observation deck at the Lower Falls in the DeSoto Falls Scenic Area

20 Vogel State Park Trails

One of the oldest state parks in Georgia, Vogel is also one of the most scenic. The park is situated on land donated to the state by the Vogel Tanning Company.

Wolf Creek runs through the park and is impounded in the waters of Lake Trahlyta. The impoundment was constructed by the Civilian Conservation Corps (CCC) in the mid-1930s.

Park amenities include campgrounds, a playground, picnic areas, and rental cabins. There is also a minigolf course and paddleboats on the lake. A CCC museum is located on-site as well.

The park's four trails, along with nearby Sosebee Cove Trail, total more than 20 miles and cover a wide variety of conditions and habitats.

Be aware that the Bear Hair and Coosa Backcountry Trails begin at a joint trailhead; both have green blazes. Also, these trails start in the state park, but they also run through lands in the Chattahoochee National Forest. Portions of both trails traverse the Blood Mountain Wilderness Area as well.

The featured hike is on the Coosa Backcountry Trail.

Start: On the drive between the park office and the campground
Distance: 13.2-mile loop
Hiking time: About 2 days if camping, or 1 long, strenuous day hike
Difficulty: Moderate to strenuous
Trail surface: Dirt and old logging roads
Best season: Mar–June; Oct–Dec
Other trail users: Hunters in season
Canine compatibility: Leashed dogs permitted in the state park; dogs permitted on national forest trails
Land status: Georgia DNR, State Parks & Historic Sites Division; Chattahoochee National Forest
Nearest town: Blairsville
Fees and permits: Daily parking fee in the state park; free permit available at the park office for camping on Coosa Backcountry Trail
Schedule: Park hours 7 a.m.–10 p.m. daily, year-round.
Maps: USGS Coosa Bald and Neels Gap; page-size map of park available from the visitor center
Trail contacts: Vogel State Park, 7485 Vogel State Park Rd., Blairsville 30512; (706) 745-2628; www.gastateparks.org

USDA Forest Service, Blue Ridge Ranger District, 2042 SR 515 West, Blairsville 30512; (706) 745-6928; www.fs.usda.gov/conf

Finding the trailhead: Vogel State Park is 11 miles south of Blairsville on US 129. The Coosa Backcountry Trailhead is located about 100 yards from the visitor center on the drive toward the camping areas. Trailhead GPS: N34 45.825' / N83 55.586'

The Hike

The joint trail carrying the Bear Hair and Coosa Backcountry Trails begins with a steady climb along tumbling Burnett Branch. The pathway quickly passes an observation deck overlooking Burnett Branch, then the junction with the Byron Herbert

The footbridge over the West Fork of Wolf Creek on the Coosa Backcountry Trail

Reece Trail. After crossing the branch on a footbridge, you next reach the intersection where the Bear Hair and Coosa Backcountry Trails jointly complete their loops. There is a sign with trail information at this juncture.

Turn right, continuing to follow the path carrying the Bear Hair and Coosa Backcountry Trails. After 70 yards the Bear Hair Trail forks to the left. Turn right, immediately cross a footbridge over Burnett Branch, and climb up to Burnett Gap. In the gap the trail crosses SR 180. The path then runs down the old blocked road that is to the right of the entrance to FS 107. The trail stays on this abandoned road down to the West Fork of Wolf Creek and across it on a footbridge.

Just beyond the bridge the path crosses FS 107 and begins a steady climb. You pass through an impressive rock outcrop prior to reaching Locust Stake Gap. This gap is used frequently as a campsite.

The forest up to this point has been similar to that along the Bear Hair Trail. The forest now is more open, with oaks and hickories dominant. Virginia pines occur on the dry south and west slopes. From here you begin to experience the ridgetop hiking so common in the mountains.

The trail climbs one high, rounded knob after another, only to drop between each one to another gap. You reach Calf Stomp Gap, which is near 3,200 feet, as you cross FS 108. This is about halfway around the loop.

The next mile is a climb to the 4,150-foot contour and the junction with Duncan Ridge Trail, which is marked with blue blazes. The open and flat ridgetop here is another area used frequently as a campsite. If you turn sharply to the right and follow the blue blazes for about 0.25 mile along the Duncan Ridge Trail, you come to Coosa Bald at an elevation of 4,280 feet.

Off the trail to the southwest there is a large rock outcrop. In winter and early spring before the leaves have fully developed, you have an impressive view of the Cooper Creek Valley and the surrounding mountains. Backtracking to the Coosa Backcountry Trail, turn right to follow the green and blue blazes running together all the way to Slaughter Gap.

From Coosa Bald, the trail passes through Wildcat Gap, where it briefly touches FS 39 (Duncan Ridge Road) before climbing up Wildcat Knob. The elevation of the trail here is about 3,800 feet.

The path next drops steeply to Wolfpen Gap and crosses SR 180 again at an elevation of 3,320 feet. This is a good place to leave a shuttle vehicle for breaking the trail into a two-day hike.

From the gap, one of the steepest climbs on the trail winds up onto Duncan Ridge, eventually topping out at 4,145 feet of elevation. During the climb you pass through a boulder field and, as the trail levels out, reach a rock outcrop with a vista to the northeast.

Dropping only slightly into a high gap at more than 4,000 feet, the path then levels out as you go around the east side of Slaughter Mountain. The trail is on an old logging road and is very pleasant, with excellent conditions for spring and early-summer wildflowers. If you are hiking in April, this is also a good place to stop and watch for spring migrating birds. Ravens frequent this high ridge.

At a point due east of the peak of Slaughter Mountain, the trail passes through another boulder field with a good view to the east.

A gentle slope on a long switchback leads down near Slaughter Gap, where the Duncan Ridge Trail splits off to the right to end at the Appalachian Trail. The Coosa Backcountry Trail turns to the east on the left fork at this junction and descends rapidly for about a mile before the Bear Hair Trail enters from the left beside Wolf Creek. Continue along the joint pathway until closing the loop back in the state park. A right turn takes you back to the trailhead.

Miles and Directions

0.0 Start at the shared trailhead with the Bear Hair Trail.

0.1 Reach the observation deck over Burnett Branch; just beyond is the Byron Herbert Reece Trail on the right.

0.3 Cross the footbridge over Burnett Branch.

0.4 Reach the intersection where the loop closes from the left. Turn right; at 70 yards pass the junction where the Bear Hair Trail forks to the left. Follow the right fork across a footbridge over Burnett Branch.

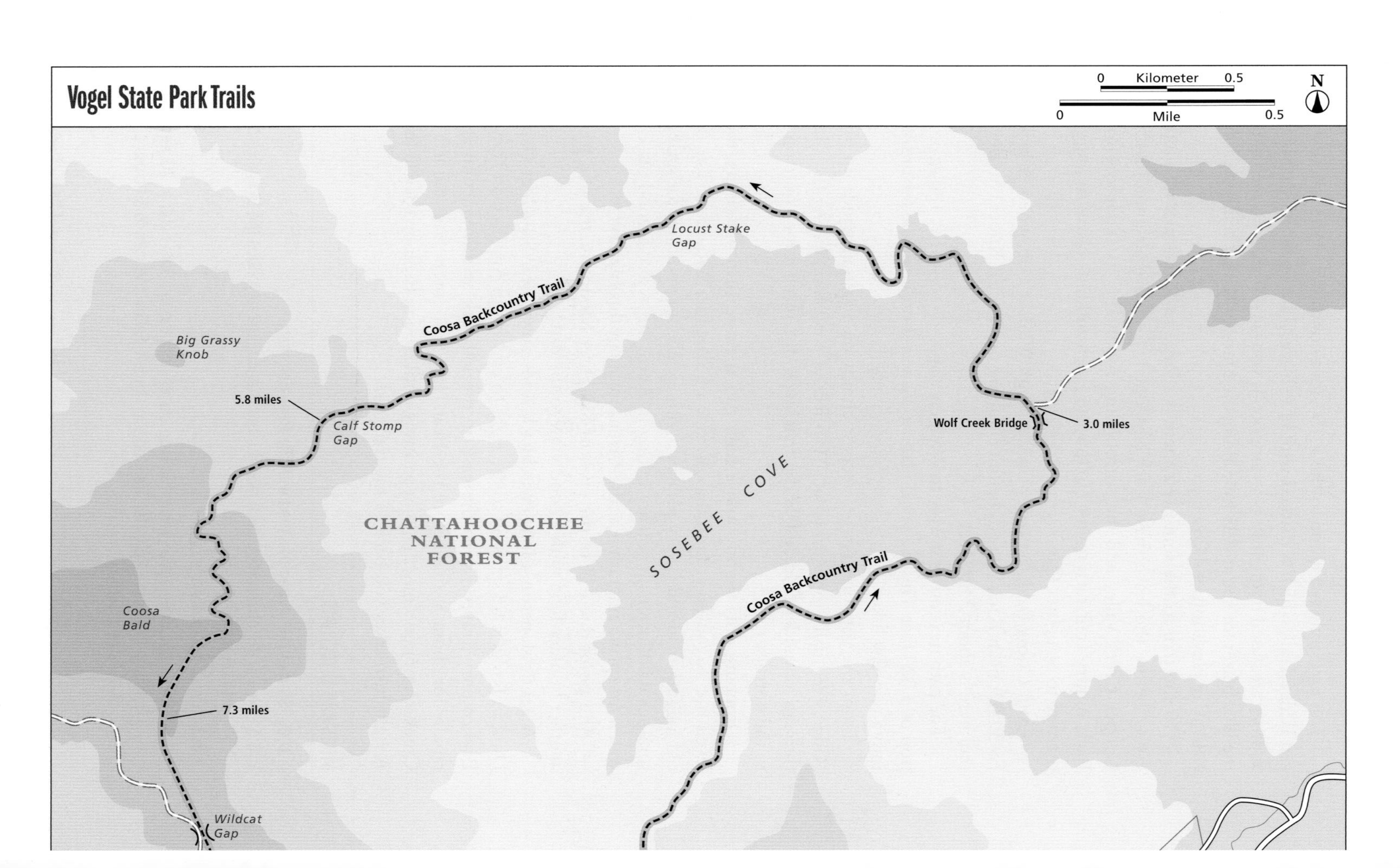
Vogel State Park Trails
0 Kilometer 0.5
0 Mile 0.5
N
Locust Stake Gap
Coosa Backcountry Trail
Big Grassy Knob
5.8 miles
Calf Stomp Gap
Wolf Creek Bridge
3.0 miles
SOSEBEE COVE
CHATTAHOOCHEE NATIONAL FOREST
Coosa Backcountry Trail
Coosa Bald
7.3 miles
Wildcat Gap

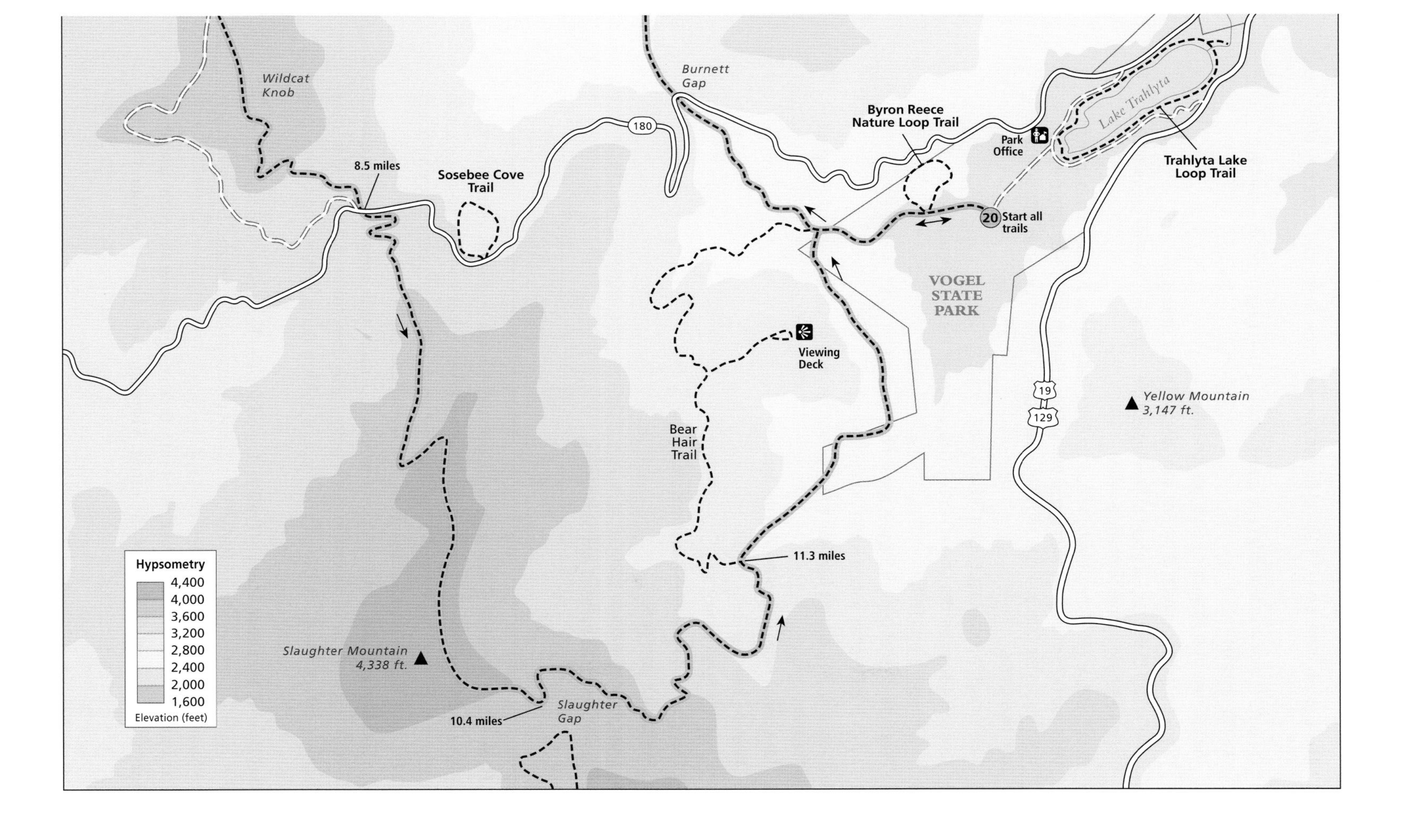
Wildcat Knob
Burnett Gap
180
8.5 miles
Sosebee Cove Trail
Byron Reece Nature Loop Trail
Park Office
Lake Trahlyta
Trahlyta Lake Loop Trail
20 Start all trails
VOGEL STATE PARK
Viewing Deck
Bear Hair Trail
19
129
Yellow Mountain 3,147 ft.
11.3 miles
Hypsometry
4,400
4,000
3,600
3,200
2,800
2,400
2,000
1,600
Elevation (feet)
Slaughter Mountain 4,338 ft.
10.4 miles
Slaughter Gap

1.0 After a steady climb, cross SR 180 at Burnett Gap and follow an old road to the right of FS 107.

3.3 Cross Wolf Creek on a footbridge and quickly cross FS 107; begin a steady ascent in a westerly direction.

4.0 The trail runs through an impressive rock formation.

4.7 Reach a popular campsite at the first ridge crest in Locust Stake Gap.

5.8 Arrive at Calf Stomp Gap at about halfway around the loop; there's another campsite here. Begin walking in a more southerly direction.

6.9 At this relatively level area, reach the Duncan Ridge Trail junction. A sharp turn to the right takes you 0.25 mile on the blue-blazed trail to Coosa Bald at 4,271 feet. Return to the main trail as the Duncan Ridge and Coosa Backcountry Trails run together, with both green and blue blazes.

7.3 Pass through Wildcat Gap, skirting Duncan Ridge Road.

8.5 Cross SR 180 again, this time at Wolfpen Gap, and begin the steepest climb on the loop.

8.6 Pass through a boulder field.

9.1 Reach the crest of Duncan Ridge in another boulder field.

9.2 A rock outcrop offers a good winter vista to the east.

9.8 Cross through a boulder field with a rock outcrop overlook on the east flank of Slaughter Mountain.

10.4 The Duncan Ridge Trail splits off to the right.

11.3 Meet the Bear Hair Trail.

11.6 Cross Wolf Creek on foot logs.

11.9 Leave the Blood Mountain Wilderness Area.

12.0 Reenter the state park.

12.8 Close the loop and turn right.

13.2 Arrive back at the trailhead and parking area.

Options

The **Bear Hair Trail** is a 4.4-mile lollipop that begins and ends using the same pathway as the Coosa Backcountry Trail. This trail then climbs a ridge to the west to reach a spur trail running to Vogel Overlook. From that vantage point an exceptional view of Lake Trahlyta is presented from 900 feet above the water.

The **Trahlyta Lake Trail** is a comfortable 1.0-mile walk around the lakeshore. A side trail leads to an observation deck below the dam spillway. The bridge over the spillway offers a vista of Blood and Slaughter Mountains that is one of the most photographed in North Georgia.

The **Byron Herbert Reece Trail** is named for the local poet and novelist who owned a farm near Vogel State Park. The farm is now operated by the Byron Herbert Reece Society as a heritage center.

The trail is a short 0.8-mile hike, with interpretive signs along the path describing the interesting natural features of the forest. More species of trees are found on this

The view of Trahlyta Lake from the Vogel Overlook on the Bear Hair Trail

trail than in all of Yellowstone National Park. The path begins 0.1 mile east of the trailhead along the Coosa Backcountry Trail.

The **Sosebee Cove Trail** is located outside of the state park on national forest property, but it's circled by the Coosa Backcountry Trail. This easy 0.5-mile double loop trail through the 175-acre Sosebee Cove Scenic Area is a memorial to Arthur Woody. Known as the "Barefoot Ranger" for his dislike of footwear, he served as the forest ranger for what is now the Chattahoochee National Forest from 1911 to 1945. He also negotiated the purchase of this area by the federal government.

Situated on the north-facing slope at the very headwaters of Wolf Creek, the cove often has twenty to thirty species of wildflowers in bloom on a single spring day. It also features some of the largest buckeye and yellow poplar trees in the region.

The trailhead and parking area are 3.0 miles west of Vogel State Park on SR 180.

21 Raven Cliffs Trail

This trail in the Raven Cliffs Wilderness Area is one of the more popular hikes in the Georgia mountains. If you want a solitary experience, it is best to walk it during the week or in winter. On weekends from spring through fall, it gets moderately heavy use.

The trail follows a relatively gentle grade along Dodd Creek to Raven Cliffs, which features a waterfall dropping down through a crevice in the tall stone wall.

This is a fine trail for family hiking.

Start: At the trailhead sign at the parking area
Distance: 5.0 miles out and back
Hiking time: About 2.5 hours
Difficulty: Moderate
Trail surface: Dirt with firm loam
Best season: Mar–Dec
Other trail users: Anglers
Canine compatibility: Dogs permitted
Land status: Chattahoochee National Forest
Nearest town: Helen
Fees and permits: None
Schedule: Year-round
Maps: USGS Cowrock; USDA Forest Service map for Chattahoochee National Forest in Georgia
Trail contact: USDA Forest Service, Chattooga River Ranger District, 9975 US 441 South, Lakemont 30552; (706) 754-6221; www.fs.usda.gov/conf

Finding the trailhead: Take SR 75 north out of Helen for 1.5 miles to SR 75 Alternate. Turn left and travel 2.3 miles to the Richard B. Russell Scenic Highway (SR 348). Turn right; after passing the Dukes Creek Recreation Area sign, continue another 0.9 mile and turn left on FS 244. The parking lot is on the left side, and the trailhead is across the gravel road. Trailhead GPS: N34 43.382' / W83 49.398'

The Hike

The trail starts across FS 244 from the parking lot, information kiosk, and restrooms. The path quickly climbs to a bluff overlooking the heavily used primitive camping area at the junction of Dukes and Dodd Creeks. It then drops down to a footbridge over Dodd Creek, just upstream of the creek junction.

The path leads upstream along cascading Dodd Creek in a northwesterly direction toward the cliffs. The creek is home to both wild rainbow and brown trout, so it is not unusual to encounter anglers in the creek or on the path.

The trail alternately brushes up against the stream or climbs 30 to 50 feet above the water level when the steep-sided valley makes it necessary. Although there are no blazes on the trail, it is very easy to follow.

You pass through rhododendron and mountain laurel thickets that form passageways with thick overhead cover. Spring seeps and small brooks cross the trail, making wet places, most of which can be crossed on foot logs.

The massive rock formation of Raven Cliffs towers above the path at the end of the trail.

As the trail climbs following the creek, three major waterfalls appear. The first of these has the creek leaping down a 10-foot drop. Shortly an even more impressive 30-foot cascade is encountered. The third and tallest waterfall before reaching Raven Cliffs is a 70-foot drop on the left of the trail. The hiking path squeezes between that cascade and a rock outcrop on the right.

Large hemlocks, white pines, yellow poplars, deciduous magnolias, hickories, oaks, maples, and buckeyes thrive along the moist valley sides and floor. Under this canopy, a resplendent array of flowering plants bloom throughout early spring, summer, and into late fall. Hepatica, dwarf iris, trout lily, jack-in-the-pulpit, Solomon's seal, various trilliums, foamflower, parasitic squawroot, and one-flowered cancer root start the show beginning in early March. Next come wild geranium, saxifrages, asters, white snakeroot, and mountain mint to finish out the show. Along with spleenworts, bunches of Christmas, New York, beech, maidenhair, and rockcap ferns grow in the valley near the cliffs.

The trail ends below the massive rock face through which Dodd Creek tumbles. That initial drop is 60 feet, plunging through a narrow cleft in the rock wall. From

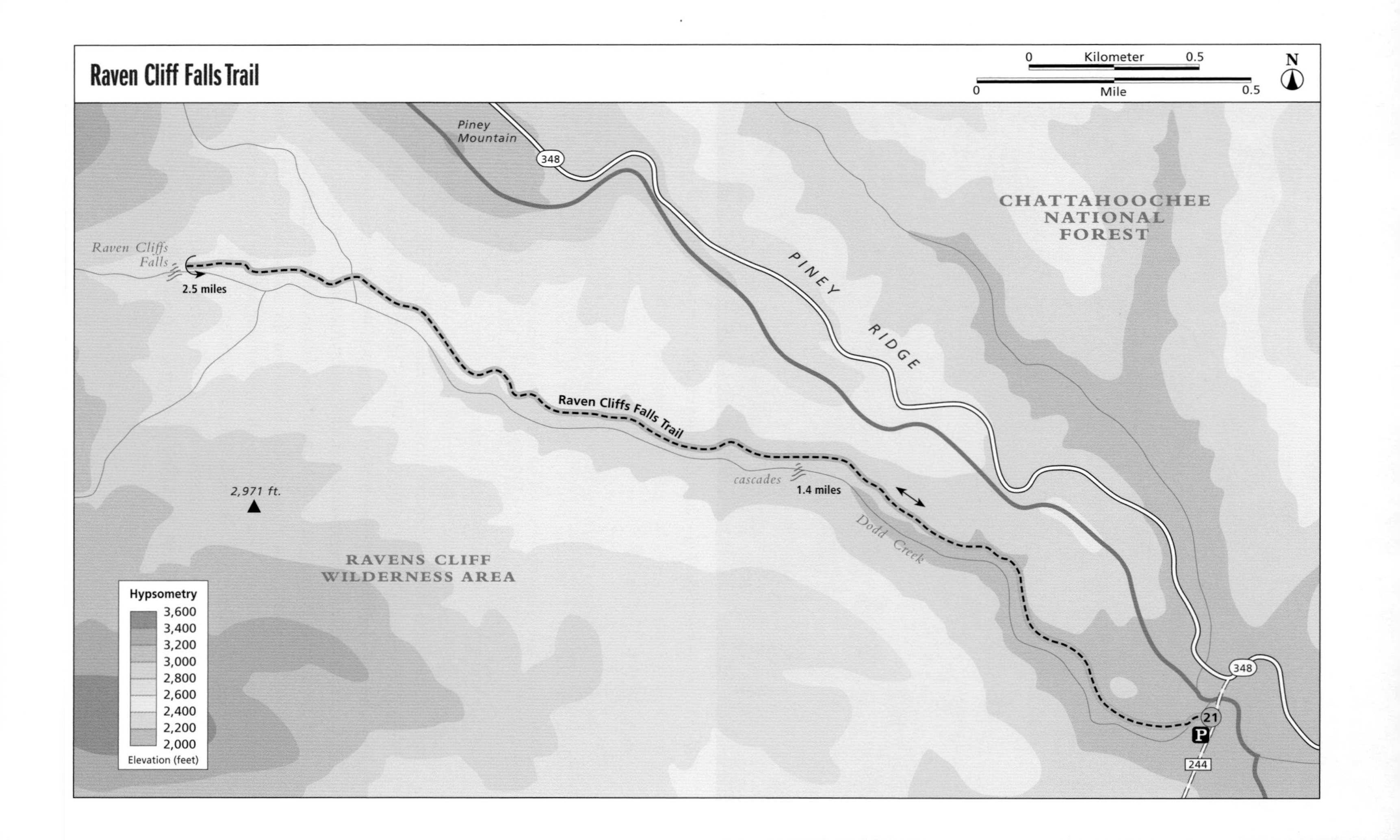
Raven Cliff Falls Trail
Kilometer
0
0.5
Mile
0
0.5
N
Piney Mountain
348
CHATTAHOOCHEE NATIONAL FOREST
PINEY RIDGE
Raven Cliffs Falls
2.5 miles
Raven Cliffs Falls Trail
cascades
1.4 miles
Dodd Creek
2,971 ft.
RAVENS CLIFF WILDERNESS AREA
Hypsometry
3,600
3,400
3,200
3,000
2,800
2,600
2,400
2,200
2,000
Elevation (feet)
348
21
P
244

The first bridge across Dodd Creek on the Raven Cliffs Trail

there the creek leaps over a pair of 20-foot drops to complete its passage through Raven Cliffs Falls.

An extension of the main trail climbs precipitously up the mountainside over rough terrain to allow access to the top of the cliffs and views of Dodd Creek valley, 3,620-foot Adams Bald, Wildcat Mountain, and Piney Ridge.

Miles and Directions

0.0 Start at the marked trailhead across FS 244 from the restrooms.

0.2 Cross the footbridge near the junction of Dukes and Dodd Creeks.

0.4 The trail passes close to a 10-foot waterfall on Dodd Creek.

1.2 To the left is an impressive view up toward a 30-foot waterfall on the creek.

1.4 The trail passes between a rock outcrop on the right and a shear drop down to a 70-foot waterfall on the left.

2.2 Cross a footbridge over a feeder creek joining Dodd Creek.

2.5 Reach the base of the massive rock face and Raven Cliffs. This is your turnaround point.

5.0 Arrive back at the trailhead.

22 Brasstown Bald, Arkaquah Trail

At 4,784 feet, Brasstown Bald Mountain is the highest point in Georgia. One short path to the top of the peak from the visitor center and three long trails down the sides of the mountain provide the hikes in this trail complex. The long trails are the featured hikes. The first of those is the Arkaquah Trail, which leads down the western slope.

Hiking down Brasstown Bald is fascinating because of the elevation change. Both plant and animal life are noticeably different from other areas in the mountains. Brasstown's flanks support species found at their southernmost geographic range. The trees of the north-facing coves produce an abundant supply of food for wildlife. You are apt to see deer, squirrels, and turkeys.

Start: At the Brasstown Bald parking area
Distance: 5.3 miles one way
Hiking time: About 3-4 hours
Difficulty: Moderate descent; strenuous when climbing back up.
Trail surface: Clean loamy earth
Best season: Mar-Dec
Other trail users: Hunters in season
Canine compatibility: Dogs permitted
Land status: Chattahoochee National Forest
Nearest town: Blairsville
Fees and permits: Parking fee charged
Schedule: Visitor center open daily from early May through mid-Nov, weather permitting; trails open year-round
Maps: USGS Jacks Gap, Hiawassee, and Blairsville; Chattahoochee National Forest map
Trail contacts: USDA Forest Service, Blue Ridge Ranger District, 1881 SR 515, Blairsville 30512; (706) 745-6928; www.fs.usda.gov/conf (Click on "Special Places.")

Brasstown Bald Visitor Center; (706) 896-2556

Brasstown Heritage Association Bookstore at the parking area; (706) 896-3471

Finding the trailhead: From Blairsville go south on US 19/129 for 8 miles to SR 180. Turn east on SR 180 and go 7 miles to Jacks Gap and the SR 180 Spur. Turn left (north) and travel 4.5 miles to the parking area. (This is a very steep drive, gaining almost 1,500 feet in 3 miles.) The Arkaquah Trailhead is at the northwest corner of the parking area. Trailhead GPS: N34 52.229' / W83 48.629'

The alternate trailhead for Arkaquah is the Track Rock Archeological Area parking lot. The road distance between the Brasstown Bald and Track Rock Trailheads is 23 miles. Trailhead GPS: N34 52.923' / W83 52.674'

The Hike

Starting at the trailhead sign at the northwest end of Brasstown Bald parking area, the Arkaquah Trail is a moderate 5.3 miles. You hike through the Brasstown Wilderness, providing spectacular views in a pristine setting.

The view from the observation deck on top of Brasstown Bald offers a spectacular panorama covering three states.

The trail is blazed in green, but there is only a single blaze at each end of the path. Fortunately it is well used and easily followed.

The trail passes through a thick canopy of rhododendron and laurel along a southwest-facing slope. Look for pink lady's slippers, bluets, and trilliums blooming beside the trail in May, along with many ferns. As you reach the crest of the ridge, gnarled and stunted yellow birch and dwarfed oak trees are festooned with "old man's beard," a lichen, giving the trees an elfin atmosphere. This is especially true on the many days when clouds shroud the mountain.

In the first portion of the hike there is relatively little change in elevation. Most of the ridge stays above 4,000 feet. This produces a climate that is quite like the southern latitudes of Canada. This is a northern hardwood "cloud forest" of striking old birches and dwarfed red oak and white oak trees. Rhododendron and mountain laurel are some of the few shrubs that can survive here. Wildflower displays are particularly outstanding in the north- and east-facing coves.

Along this stretch you pass an unmarked and easily missed trail running to the right up onto a rock outcrop. This offers your first panoramic view to the north.

Shortly afterward the trail crosses a large flat rock, again offering a spectacular view to the north. Just 0.1 mile farther another grand view back toward the visitor center is offered by looking to the northeast on the left side of the trail. When the path passes directly north of Chimney Top Mountain, yet another great vista opens to the north.

Next the trail squeezes between two rocks standing perpendicular on the sides of the trail. Stepping down between them reveals a large rock shelter on the right side of the path, creating one of the more interesting spots along the hike.

From this point the trail drops into a gap and then climbs over Locust Log Ridge, only to plunge into another gap. Finally reaching the peak of Buzzard Roost Ridge, which provides your last overlook to the north, the trail begins the steep climb down to Track Rock Gap. The trail goes through switchbacks and clings to the edge of shear drops as it descends 1,401 feet at a steep grade.

As you reach lower altitudes, watch for the elegant pink blossoms of the unusual Catesby's trillium as they droop beneath the leaves of the low-growing plant.

Miles and Directions

0.0 Start at the parking area trailhead.

0.9 Watch on the right for the poorly marked path to a rock outcrop and overlook.

1.2 Cross a large flat rock with great vistas to the north.

1.3 Look back to the northeast for a fine view of the visitor center on Brasstown Bald.

1.5 A large rock shelter is to the right of the trail.

3.7 Reach the crest of Buzzard Roost Ridge. (***Option:*** Go west out to Buzzard Roost and return without going down to Track Rock Gap for a round-trip hike of 7.4 miles.)

5.3 Come to the end of trail at Track Rock Gap Road. Unless you've arranged for a shuttle, this is your turnaround point for a 10.6-mile out-and-back hike.

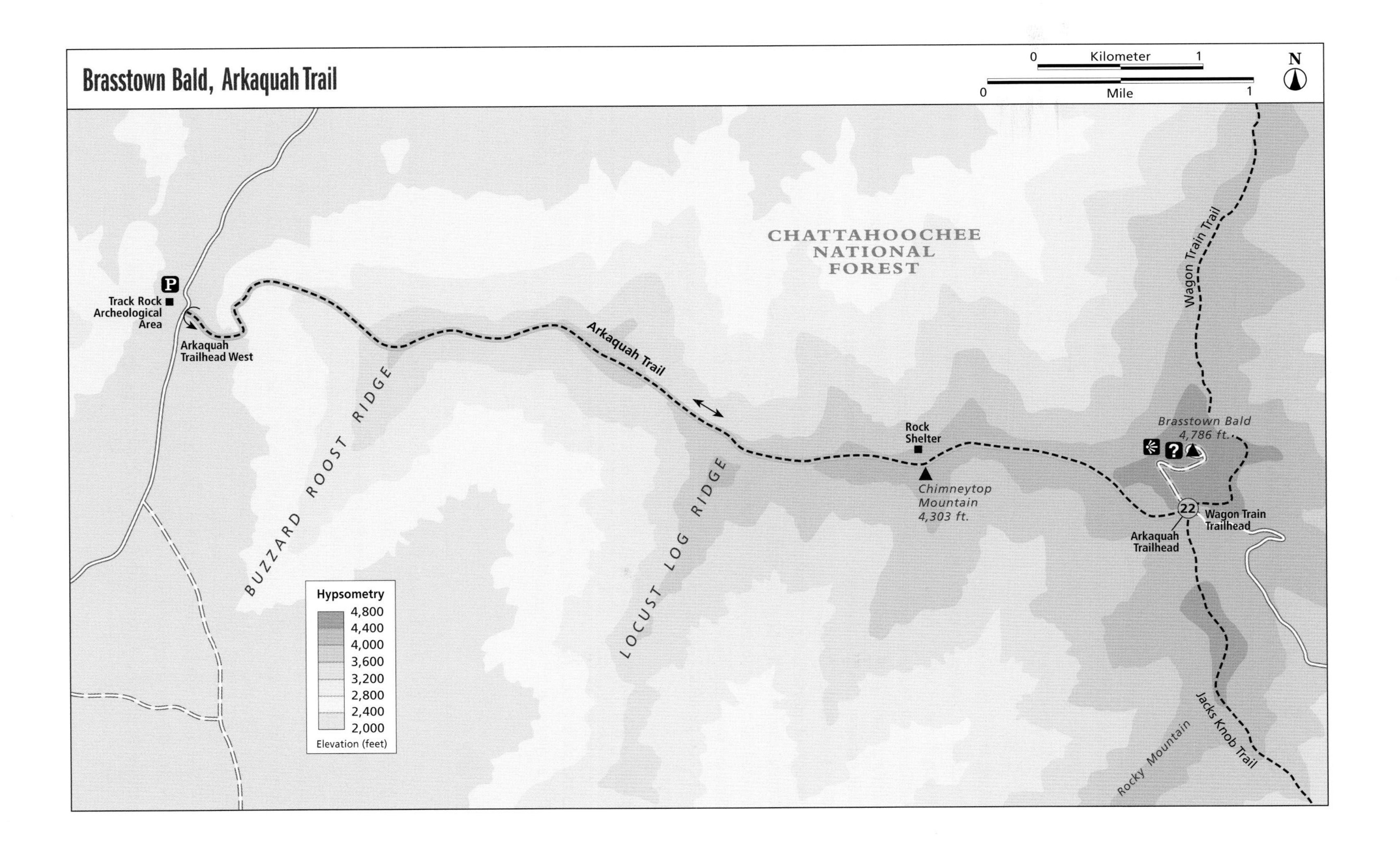
Brasstown Bald, Arkaquah Trail
0
Kilometer
1
0
Mile
1
N
Track Rock
Archeological
Area
P
Arkaquah
Trailhead West
Arkaquah Trail
CHATTAHOOCHEE
NATIONAL
FOREST
BUZZARD ROOST RIDGE
LOCUST LOG RIDGE
Rock
Shelter
Chimneytop
Mountain
4,303 ft.
Brasstown Bald
4,786 ft.
Wagon Train Trail
22
Wagon Train
Trailhead
Arkaquah
Trailhead
Jacks Knob Trail
Rocky Mountain
Hypsometry
4,800
4,400
4,000
3,600
3,200
2,800
2,400
2,000
Elevation (feet)

23 Brasstown Bald, Jacks Knob Trail

The Jacks Knob Trail travels south from the parking area on Brasstown Knob. From there it stretches to Chattahoochee Gap on the Appalachian Trail (AT), just below Jacks Bald.

Spring and fall migrations of warblers, tanagers, thrushes, and raptors make the Brasstown Bald area especially popular with birders. Also watch for ruffed grouse and ravens, the large crow of the high mountains. Any of these may be spotted during the walk down the south slope.

Start: At the Brasstown Bald parking area
Distance: 8.6 miles out and back
Hiking time: About 4–5 hours
Difficulty: Moderate descents; strenuous when climbing back up
Trail surface: Clean loamy earth
Best season: Mar–Dec
Other trail users: Hunters in season
Canine compatibility: Dogs permitted
Land status: Chattahoochee National Forest
Nearest town: Blairsville
Fees and permits: Parking fee charged
Schedule: Visitor center open daily from early May through mid-Nov, weather permitting; trails open year-round
Maps: USGS Jacks Gap, Hiawassee, and Blairsville; Chattahoochee National Forest map
Trail contacts: USDA Forest Service, Blue Ridge Ranger District, 1881 SR 515, Blairsville 30512; (706) 745-6928; www.fs.usda.gov/conf (Click on "Special Places.")

Brasstown Bald Visitor Center; (706) 896-2556

Brasstown Heritage Association Bookstore at the parking area; (706) 896-3471

Finding the trailhead: From Blairsville go south on US 19/129 for 8 miles to SR 180. Turn east on SR 180 and go 7 miles to Jacks Gap and the SR 180 Spur. Turn left (north) and travel 4.5 miles to the parking area. This is a very steep drive, gaining almost 1,500 feet in 3 miles. The Jacks Knob Trail originates at the south end of the parking area. Trailhead GPS: N34 52.060' / W83 48.631'

The Hike

The blue-blazed trail follows the ridge crest from Brasstown Bald to Chattahoochee Gap and the headwaters of Georgia's most famous stream, the Chattahoochee River. The trail begins at the south end of the parking area.

You enter a rhododendron thicket and continue south on Wolfpen Ridge, climbing steadily to the highest point on the trail: 4,552 feet. From here the trail leads down steadily and rather steeply, losing more than 1,500 feet to Jacks Gap and SR 180. In the spring you see bluets, pink lady's slippers, Catesby's trillium, and dwarf iris blooming along this part of the trail.

You cross the highway and immediately begin to climb up Hiwassee Ridge. You go around the southwest side of Henry Knob more or less on a contour through a mature hardwood forest with large rock outcrops above the trail. Passing through a

A Catesby's trillium bloom on the Arkaquah Trail in April

stand of white pines, you enter a sweeping north-facing cove of mature hardwoods. Stepping-stones have been placed across the only wet area on this trail. Red and large-flowered trilliums appear through here, along with beds of mayapple.

The trail continues around to the east side of Brookshire Top and drops down into another of several gaps. From here the path follows along the crest of Hiwassee Ridge and the Towns-Union County line. From the gap south of Eagle Knob to just before starting up Jacks Knob, the trail goes around the west side and drops down to Chattahoochee Gap and the Appalachian Trail. Chattahoochee Spring, headwater for the Chattahoochee River, is about 175 yards just below this gap.

From the south end of Jacks Knob Trail at the Appalachian Trail, you can return to SR 180. Or you can hike east on the Appalachian Trail to the Blue Mountain Shelter at 2.3 miles or to Unicoi Gap (SR 75), an additional 2.2 miles. If you choose to hike southwest on the Appalachian Trail, you go past the Low Gap Shelter at 5.0 miles or continue an additional 4.2 miles to Hog Pen Gap on the Richard B. Russell Scenic Highway (SR 348).

This trail offers spectacular views from the high points, and a challenging hike along the higher ridges and into the gaps makes this an interesting one-way trail. Wildflowers, from many spring herbaceous plants to the grand display of mountain laurel and rhododendron, add to the trail's beauty, and fall leaf colors can be dazzling. Birds of the higher mountains like ravens, hawks, and warblers make this a good birding and wildlife-watching trail.

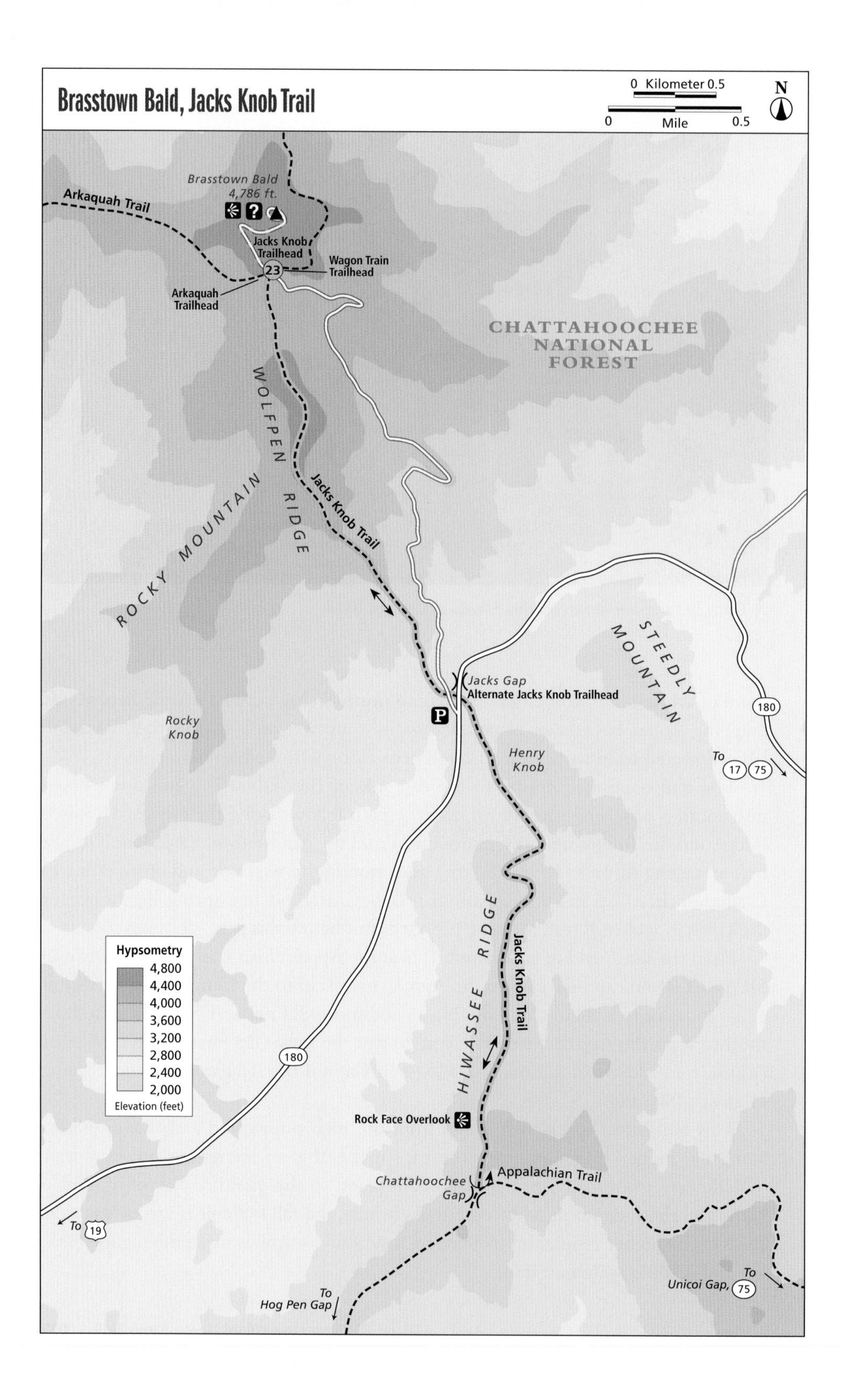

Brasstown Bald, Jacks Knob Trail
0 Kilometer 0.5
0 Mile 0.5
N
Brasstown Bald
4,786 ft.
Arkaquah Trail
Jacks Knob Trailhead
23
Wagon Train Trailhead
Arkaquah Trailhead
CHATTAHOOCHEE NATIONAL FOREST
WOLFPEN RIDGE
ROCKY MOUNTAIN
Jacks Knob Trail
Jacks Gap
Alternate Jacks Knob Trailhead
STEEDLY MOUNTAIN
180
Rocky Knob
Henry Knob
To 17 75
HIWASSEE RIDGE
Jacks Knob Trail
Hypsometry
4,800
4,400
4,000
3,600
3,200
2,800
2,400
2,000
Elevation (feet)
180
Rock Face Overlook
Appalachian Trail
Chattahoochee Gap
To 19
To Hog Pen Gap
To Unicoi Gap, 75

Miles and Directions

0.0 Start at the south end of the Brasstown Bald parking area.

0.3 Reach the Wolfpen Ridge high point (4,552 feet).

0.6 Begin the descent to Jacks Gap.

2.1 Arrive at SR 180. Cross the highway and begin the climb to Brookshire Top.

2.8 You have a sweeping view down into a north-facing cove, with many wildlife food-producing trees.

3.1 Reach Brookshire Top, with great views east and west at 3,533 feet.

3.7 Arrive at Eagle Knob.

4.2 Jacks Knob crest is on the left, fronted by a large rock outcrop. The view to the west is spectacular.

4.3 Reach the Appalachian Trail (AT); this is your turnaround point if you're not continuing on the AT.

8.6 Arrive back at the parking area.

24 Brasstown Bald, Wagon Train Trail

The final hike descending from Brasstown Bald is along the Wagon Train Trail. This path is the longest of the trails off the mountain. The pathway runs along old roadbeds to the north, ending in the town of Young Harris.

A mixture of common and northern plant species are found along the Wagon Train Trail. As you hike down the mountain, it is possible to pass through more than one season of growth. Near the crest it may be early spring, yet at the foot of the mountain early summer may be taking hold.

Start: At the Brasstown Bald parking area
Distance: 6.8 miles one way
Hiking time: About 4–5 hours
Difficulty: Moderate descent; strenuous when climbing back up
Trail surface: Clean loamy earth on most of the trails, but stretches of old gravel roads
Best season: Mar–Dec
Other trail users: Hunters in season
Canine compatibility: Dogs permitted
Land status: Chattahoochee National Forest
Nearest town: Blairsville
Fees and permits: Parking fee charged
Schedule: Visitor center open daily from early May through mid-Nov, weather permitting; trails open year-round
Maps: USGS Jacks Gap, Hiawassee, and Blairsville; Chattahoochee National Forest map
Trail contacts: USDA Forest Service, Blue Ridge Ranger District, 1881 SR 515, Blairsville 30512; (706) 745-6928; www.fs.usda.gov/conf (Click on "Special Places.")

Brasstown Bald Visitor Center; (706) 896-2556

Brasstown Heritage Association Bookstore at the parking area; (706) 896-3471

Finding the trailhead: From Blairsville go south on US 19/129 for 8 miles to SR 180. Turn east on SR 180 and go 7 miles to Jacks Gap and the SR 180 Spur. Turn left (north) and travel 4.5 miles to the parking area. This is a very steep drive, gaining almost 1,500 feet in 3 miles. The Wagon Train Trailhead is at the northeast corner of parking area at the concession building. Trailhead GPS: N34 52.233' / W83 48.598'

The Hike

There are no blazes on this trail, but the comfortably graded path is easy to follow. This trail has the greatest change in elevation of all the short trails in the state. You stay at or above the 4,000-foot level for almost a mile and then begin the gentle descent along the old roadbed until you reach the gated road at the national forest and wilderness boundary. From here on, you are on a former roadway (Bald Mountain Road) to Young Harris College and US 76.

Graduating students from the college and their families traditionally walk this trail on the evening prior to graduation. Once at the top of Brasstown Bald, they participate in a vesper service.

The entire path of the Wagon Train Trail follows the long-abandoned path of SR 66 from the town of Young Harris to the mountain's peak. The route was laid out in the 1950s, but the SR 180 Spur down the opposite side was the only portion of this roadway that was ever completed.

The best hike is from the top down to the gate at the national forest boundary and back up to the top. Primitive camping is permitted in the national forest and wilderness areas.

Beginning on the paved Summit Trail between the log cabin gift shop and concession building in the parking area, you walk about 100 yards up this trail to an opening in the dense rhododendron. Here is the two-track, grassy road that is the upper end of the Wagon Train Trail. Turn right and follow it to the gated section of the trail that enters the Brasstown Wilderness. Here the trail loses its two-track character.

The crest of Brasstown Bald is visible from the overlook at Chimney Top Mountain on the Wagon Train Trail.

The path follows under the bald as it winds along the most appropriate contour for a roadbed. You soon pass rock bluffs blasted out to make the road. Notice the narrow half-cylinder markings running down the rock faces. Those are drill marks from the holes bored down into the stone. The holes were then filled with blasting powder to break off the rocks.

These cliffs and boulder fields are now covered with rock tripe and other lichens. Sphagnum moss hanging on the rocks, old man's beard on the trees, and club moss flourish in the frequent cloud cover.

Steep slopes opposite the rock walls afford grand views of the mountains in winter and early spring on clear days. The trail passes along the north-facing slopes through quiet and majestic cove hardwood forests with large yellow poplars, hemlocks, silver bells, yellow birches, basswoods, buckeyes, and maples. On the points and western and southern slopes, the tree canopy becomes oaks, hickories, sourwoods, black gums, and pines, under which may be rhododendron and mountain laurel or one or more kinds of huckleberry.

Along the steep east and west slopes, there are excellent views during winter. This is especially true as you pass to the west and below Chimney Top and along Wolf Pen Ridge for the next mile. Even the untrained eye will see how the forest changes as you get lower and lower on the trail. At the higher elevations you will see the more open stands of oaks, yellow birch, and the less common red-berried mountain ash. As you go lower, sweet birch, large yellow poplars, and massive oaks dominate; still farther down, you see Virginia and shortleaf pines.

From early spring and throughout the warm months, you will be able to enjoy a wide variety of wildflowers, including four species of trilliums and flame azaleas. Near the top, these blooms are a full two months behind those found farther down the slope.

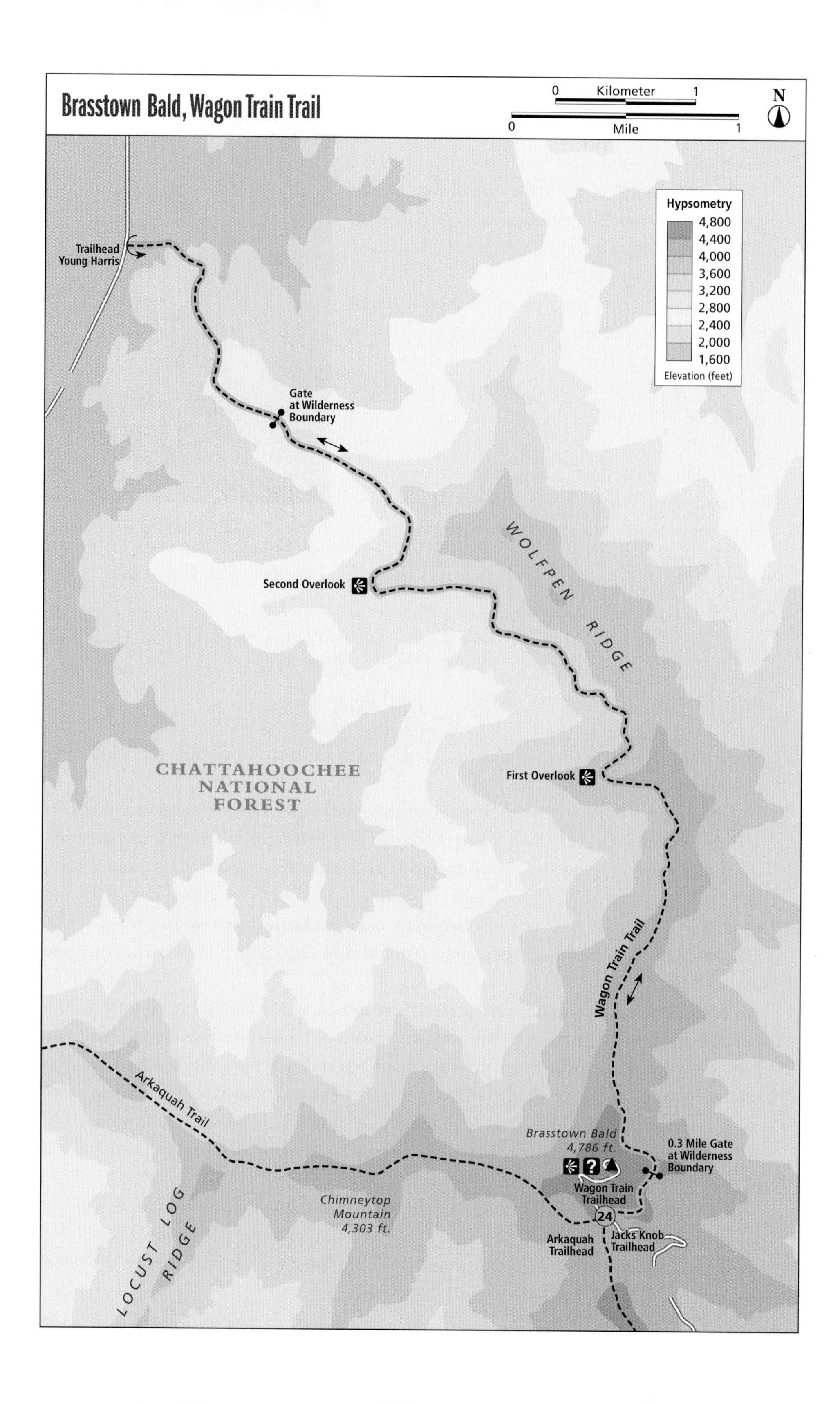
Brasstown Bald, Wagon Train Trail
0 Kilometer 1
0 Mile 1
N
Hypsometry
4,800
4,400
4,000
3,600
3,200
2,800
2,400
2,000
1,600
Elevation (feet)
Trailhead
Young Harris
Gate
at Wilderness
Boundary
Second Overlook
WOLFPEN RIDGE
CHATTAHOOCHEE
NATIONAL
FOREST
First Overlook
Wagon Train Trail
Arkaquah Trail
Brasstown Bald
4,786 ft.
0.3 Mile Gate
at Wilderness
Boundary
Wagon Train
Trailhead
24
Chimneytop
Mountain
4,303 ft.
LOCUST LOG RIDGE
Arkaquah
Trailhead
Jacks Knob
Trailhead

At Mile 6.1 you reach the gate that marks the forest and wilderness area boundary. If you have arranged for transportation at Young Harris College or at US 76, you have a bit more than a mile of rutted, littered road to follow down to the highway.

Miles and Directions

0.0 Start at the paved trail between the gift shop and concession building.

0.1 Turn right off the paved Summit Trail.

0.3 Reach the bar gate on the trail.

0.6 Pass the sign marking the edge of the Brasstown Wilderness Area.

1.0 Reach the beginning of the rock face on the right of the trail.

1.3 Arrive at an overlook to the left of the trail facing Big Bald Cove to the west.

2.4 Come to an overlook on the west side of Chimney Top Mountain, with a good view back to the north toward the Brasstown Bald Visitor Center.

4.5 Go around the west point of Double Knob and pass a gate to begin the descent on the north of Double Knob Ridge.

5.4 Reach Carrol Gap.

5.5 Skirt the southwest side of Granny Knob.

6.1 Pass the third gate on the trail.

6.3 Reach the forest service boundary line and edge of the Brasstown Wilderness Area. This roadway takes you down to private property and the end of the trail at US 76 and Young Harris.

6.8 Arrive at Young Harris College Campus. Unless you've arranged for a shuttle, this is your turnaround point for a 13.6-mile out-and-back trek.

Options

The **Summit Trail** to the top of the mountain and visitor center is paved. It is steep, climbing almost 500 feet in a 0.5-mile trek. Dogs must be on leashes on this trail.

The visitor center exhibits tell of "Man and the Mountain" and other features unique to this highest point in Georgia. The observation decks stand above the trees and afford a 360-degree view of the surrounding wilderness and distant villages. On a clear day, four states can be seen from here.

At the Young Harris College campus, a private road marked by a red gate is the beginning of the Wagon Train Trail on private property that leads to the national forest boundary. You must get permission in advance to leave a shuttle vehicle on the school property. There is no other access to the national forest boundary from this end of the trail. Trailhead GPS: N34 55.878' / W83 50.712'

Local Information

Food/Lodging

Brasstown Valley Resort, US 76, Young Harris, GA 30582; (800) 201-3205; brass townvalley.com

25 Dukes Creek Falls Trail

Located in the Dukes Creek Falls Recreation Area, this trail provides a trek down into the creek gorge to view several scenic waterfalls. From the trailhead elevation of 2,107 feet, the path drops 340 feet through a pair of long switchbacks. Along the way the trail descends on a broad path with very few steep spots.

The vegetation changes from the well-drained, drier ridgetop of pine and oak, through dense rhododendron and mountain laurel, to the stream edge with large yellow poplar and buckeye trees. An understory of silver bells and dogwoods add their masses of color from early spring into early summer.

Start: Beside the restrooms at the Dukes Creek Falls Recreation Area parking lot
Distance: 2.4 miles out and back
Hiking time: About 1.5 hours
Difficulty: Easy to moderate
Trail surface: Paved to the first observation deck, followed by a short expanse of fine gravel; the lower trail is mostly firm loam.
Best season: Mar–Dec
Other trail users: Hikers only
Canine compatibility: Leashed dogs permitted
Land status: Chattahoochee National Forest
Nearest town: Helen
Fees and permits: Daily parking fee
Schedule: Open year-round, sunrise to sunset
Maps: USGS Cowrock; Chattahoochee National Forest map
Trail contacts: USDA Forest Service, Chattooga River Ranger District, 9975 US 441 South, Lakemont 30552; (706) 754-6221; www.fs.usd.gov/conf

Finding the trailhead: From Helen, go north 1.5 miles on SR 75. Turn left on SR 75 Alternate and go 2.3 miles to Richard Russell Scenic Highway (SR 348). Turn right and go 2 miles; the Dukes Creek Falls parking area is on the left. The trail begins at the south end of the paved parking lot. Trailhead GPS: N34 42.100' / W83 47.347'

The Hike

Before starting down the Dukes Creek Falls Trail, take a moment to look to the southeast. A good view of the distinctively shaped Mount Yonah is afforded from this spot.

The trail begins to the west, traveling along a relatively flat, paved path that leads to an observation deck. This first portion is wheelchair accessible to the overlook. From the deck, a 300-foot cascade can be seen on the opposite side of the gorge. That waterfall is formed by Davis Creek crashing down the cliffs to join Dukes Creek in the creek bottom.

The remainder of the trail is an easy walk into the gorge. From the overlook the trail drops down a set of stairs to a path of fine gravel and loam soil. It is usable in most weather conditions, although rain, ice, or snow might make the footing slippery.

The trail passes through dense rhododendron thickets growing on the very steep gorge slope. About halfway down, the forest changes to the typical cove hardwood

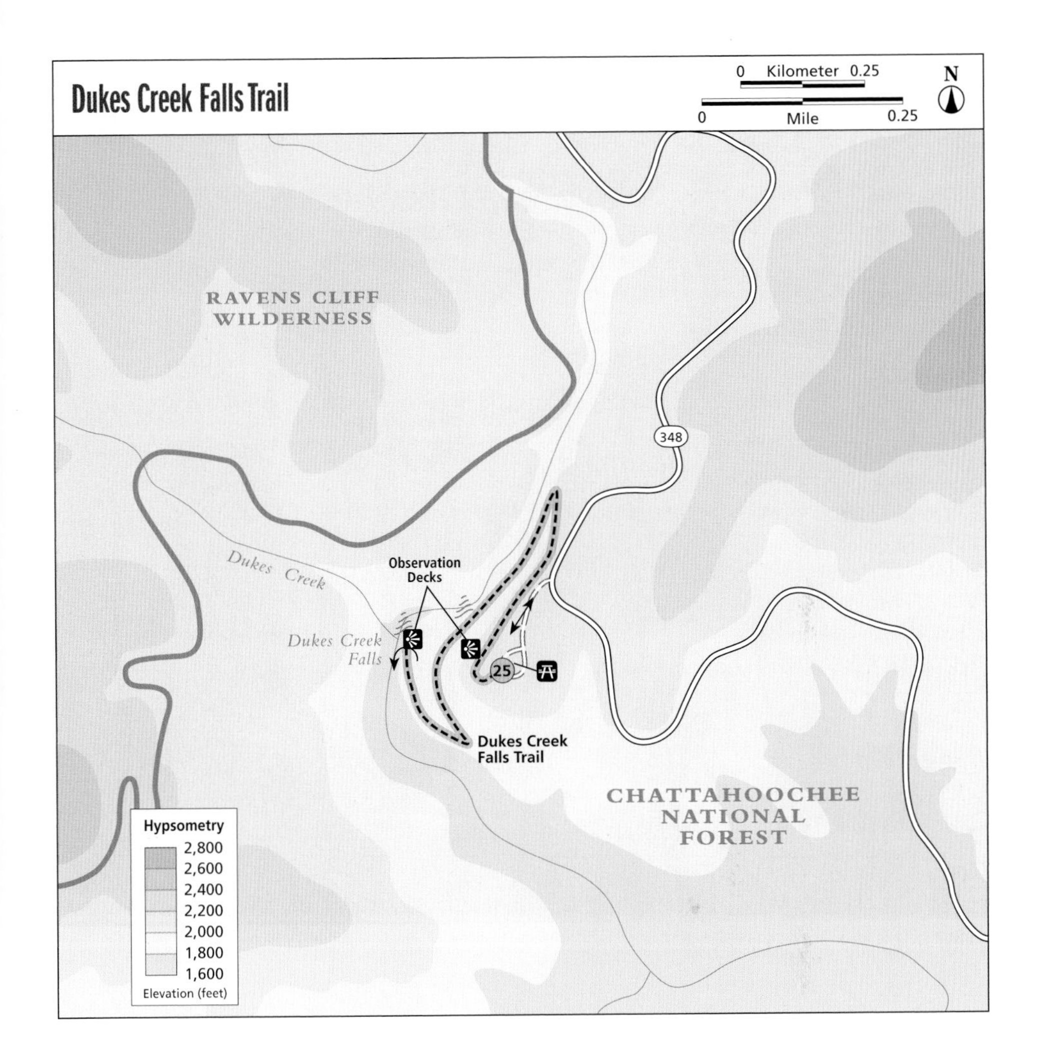

trees. On some of the drier sites, oaks, hickories, and Virginia pines dominate. As with many trails in the mountains, spring migrating warblers can be heard as they pass through on their northern flight.

During the descent you first pass a trail junction leading upstream to the Raven Cliffs Wilderness Area and later another for a trail going downstream to Smithgall Woods State Park.

Once at the bottom of the gorge, the trail ends on a set of three connected wooden observation decks. One is directly across the main creek from the foot of the waterfall on Davis Creek. The others provide views of the beautiful cascades, rapids, and pools on Dukes Creek. This stretch of the creek is home to populations of wild rainbow and brown trout.

View of the falls on Dukes Creek

Miles and Directions

0.0 Start at the trailhead beside the restrooms at the parking area.

0.1 Reach the observation deck at the end of the wheelchair-accessible trail.

0.4 At the hairpin curve of the first switchback, the trail to the right connects to the Raven Cliffs Wilderness Area; turn left for the main trail.

0.9 Reach the trail junction for Smithgall Woods State Park at the turn for the second switchback.

1.2 Reach the three observation decks at the end of the trail. The third one overlooks a waterfall on Dukes Creek; this is the turnaround point.

2.4 Arrive back at the trailhead.

26 Smithgall Woods State Park Trails

The 5,604 acres of mountain woodlands here were acquired in 1994 as a gift to the state from conservationist Charles A. Smithgall. The park is dedicated to the purpose of protecting existing landscape, maintaining wildlife diversity, providing environmental education, and permitting low-impact recreational activities.

The prime resource of the park is a stretch of Dukes Creek that runs through the property. This creek is a fine trout stream managed for catch-and-release angling. Trout fishing using artificial lures with barbless hooks is permitted on Wednesday, Saturday, and Sunday.

But it wasn't fish that originally brought people to Dukes Creek. The land along the stream was the site of a gold discovery in 1828 that set off a gold rush twenty-one years prior to the more famous one in California.

The visitor center is well worth the time spent here. It offers information on the natural and mining history of the property. Besides permits to fish the stream, you can pick up a map of the park and guides to interpretive stations on each of the hiking trails. In all, six relatively short marked trails are laid out to interpret the natural and cultural history of the area.

However, because no private vehicles are allowed beyond the visitor center, getting to the trailheads often involves long walks along the paved or gravel portions of Tsalaki Trail, the main drive through the property.

In addition to the hiking trails, more than 12 miles of paved and unpaved roads are available for walking and bike riding.

The Ash Creek Trail is the featured hike.

Start: At the park visitor center on Tsalaki Trail
Distance: 3.8-mile lollipop
Hiking time: About 1.5–2 hours
Difficulty: Easy to moderate
Trail surface: Dirt; bark chip in a few places; asphalt on Tsalaki Trail
Best season: Mar–Dec
Other trail users: Anglers, bikers, and vehicles on the Tsalaki Trail portion
Canine compatibility: Leashed dogs permitted.
Land status: Georgia DNR, State Parks & Historic Sites Division
Nearest town: Helen
Fees and permits: Daily parking fee
Schedule: Park hours 7 a.m.–10 p.m., year-round; Laurel Creek Trail open year-round; other trails closed during managed hunts
Maps: USGS Cowrock and Helen; page-size map of park with trails available from the visitor center
Trail contacts: Smithgall Woods State Park, 61 Tsalaki Trail, Helen 30545; (706) 878-3087 or (706) 878-3520; www.gastateparks.org/info/smithgall/
Special considerations: Near the end of the Ash Creek Trail, the path crosses Dukes Creek. There is no bridge, and the water usually runs knee deep. Wading is the only option for crossing.

Finding the trailhead: From Helen go north 1 mile on SR 75 to Robertstown. Turn left on SR 75A and go 2.5 miles to the state park entrance on the left.

The Ash Creek Trail begins at the east end of the visitor center parking lot. Trailhead GPS: N34 41.477' / W83 46.061'

The covered bridge on Tsalaki Trail in Smithgall Woods State Park

The Hike

The easiest way to hike the green-blazed Ash Creek Trail is to travel clockwise following the twenty markers for the interpretive sites along the path. The tops of these posts are painted lime green and constitute the only blazes along the trail.

Begin by following Tsalaki Trail over a steep ridge and past the Alder Picnic Shelter and Bay's Covered Bridge to the point where the road turns to gravel. The Ash Creek Trail runs off to the right along the gravel drive into the Bear Ridge Camp. Climbing steadily, the trail veers off the left onto a closed and overgrown road just before reaching the camp.

This portion of the path continues steeply through a hardwood forest featuring poplars, white and red oaks, hickories, and maples. Interspersed are some hemlocks and white pines. Watch for wild violets blooming in the spring, along with patches of mayapple.

On top of Bear Ridge the trail passes through one small and another large wildlife clearing. These feature grasses, clover, sedge, and blackberries. At the end of the second clearing, the trail turns sharply to the right and drops steeply down the ridge.

You next enter a spring bottom lined with New York and Christmas ferns. From there the path runs around the hillside through a tunnel of mountain laurel and rhododendron, before again dropping steeply down to ford Ash Creek.

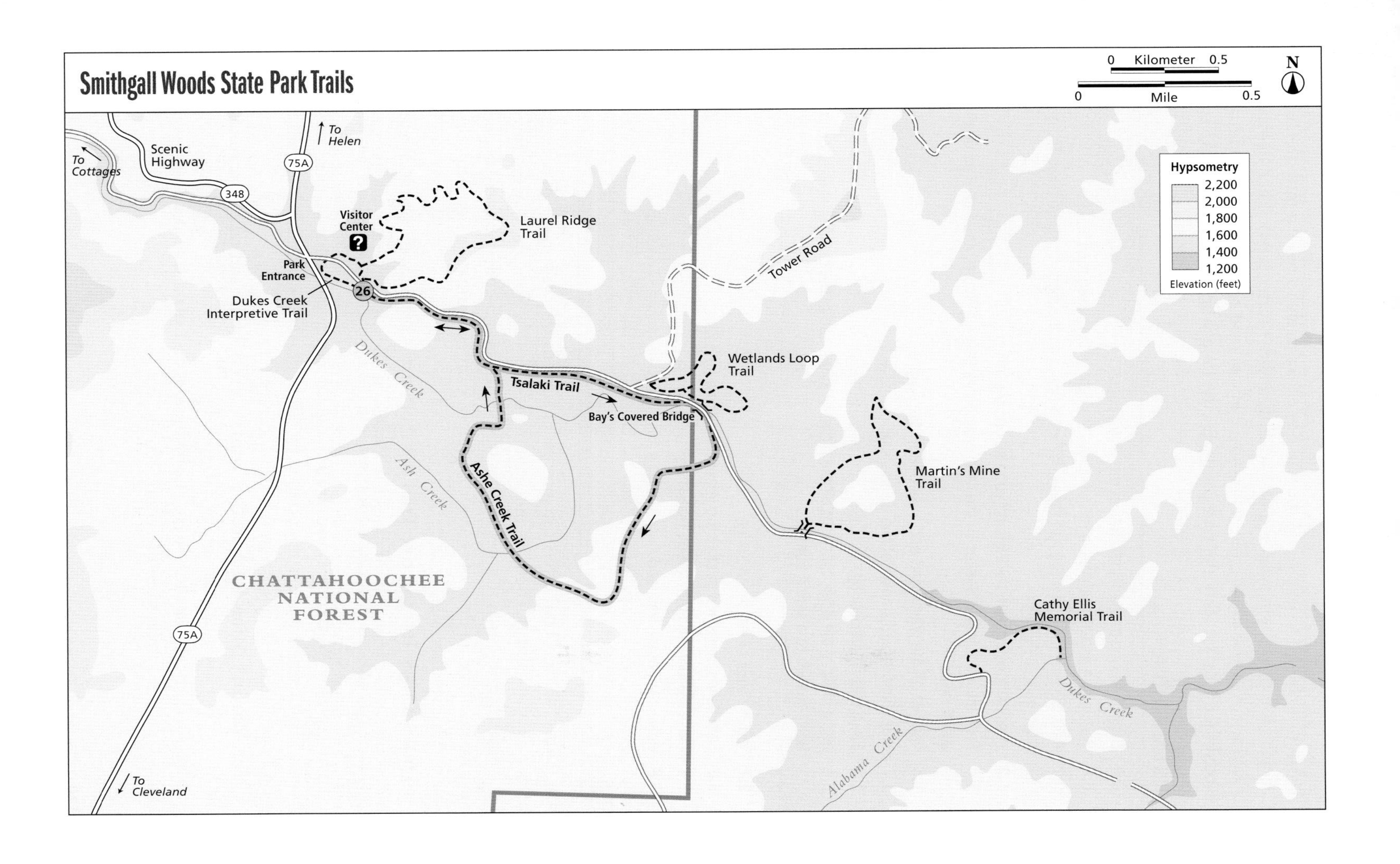

Smithgall Woods State Park Trails
0 Kilometer 0.5
0 Mile 0.5
N
Hypsometry
2,200
2,000
1,800
1,600
1,400
1,200
Elevation (feet)
To Cottages
Scenic Highway
348
75A
To Helen
Visitor Center
Park Entrance
26
Dukes Creek Interpretive Trail
Laurel Ridge Trail
Tower Road
Wetlands Loop Trail
Tsalaki Trail
Bay's Covered Bridge
Ashe Creek Trail
Dukes Creek
Ash Creek
Martin's Mine Trail
Cathy Ellis Memorial Trail
Alabama Creek
CHATTAHOOCHEE NATIONAL FOREST
To Cleveland

After climbing a second ridge, the trail descends sharply to reach a ford on Dukes Creek. This is the crossing that requires wading, and the water can be knee deep.

Once across the stream, the trail joins a gravel road around the left side of a planted food plot. Quickly the trail completes the loop when it reaches Tsalaki Trail.

Miles and Directions

0.0 Begin following paved Tsalaki Trail at the visitor center.

0.6 Watch for a line of beehives in the woods to the right of the paved road.

0.7 Pass the junction where the Ash Creek Trail loop closes on the right. Continue down Tsalaki Trail.

1.2 Pass the junction with the Wetland Loop Trail on the left.

1.4 Pass the Alder Picnic Shelter on the right, cross Bay's Covered Bridge, and turn right up the gravel road.

1.5 Veer left off the gravel road and pass Bear Ridge Camp.

1.7 Enter the first and smaller of two clearings on the ridge.

1.9 Reach the larger clearing.

2.1 At the crest of the ridge, turn right off the old road at the end of the clearing and descend sharply down to a spring bottom.

2.4 Ford Ash Creek.

2.7 Top the crest of the second ridge.

3.0 Ford Dukes Creek and pass to the left of the wildlife food plot.

3.1 Close the loop and turn left on Tsalaki Trail.

3.8 Arrive back at the trailhead.

Options

The **Laurel Ridge Trail** offers the most fascinating nature walk in the park because of its variety of habitats. There are nineteen marked stations along the way, interpreted by a leaflet that discusses features at each waypoint. The 1.5-mile loop trail begins at the paved walkway in front of the visitor center. A large information sign helps orient you to what you may see.

Dukes Creek Interpretive Trail is a short, flat 0.3-mile walk beside a typical mountain trout stream. The trailhead is located at the visitor center on the paved Tsalaki Trail.

The 0.6-mile **Wetlands Loop Trail** is a good example of what happens in this mountain area when water is impounded by either beavers or humans. The trailhead is on Tsalaki Trail, 1.3 miles from the visitor center.

The **Martin's Mine Interpretive Trail** covers 0.9 mile and takes you through the history of early gold mining. Special guided tours are available by advanced registration (check the website for dates). The trailhead is on Tsalaki Trail at a bridge across Dukes Creek, 2.1 miles from the visitor center

Near its end, the Ash Creek Trail requires wading across a ford on Dukes Creek.

The **Cathy Ellis Memorial Trail** is a pleasant 1.0-mile out-and-back walk to a small but beautiful cascading waterfall on Alabama Branch. This trail is also called the Chunanee Falls Trail. A plaque on the trail explains that this is where "gold mining began with the discovery of a gold nugget in 1828 by a slave of Major Franck Logano." The trailhead is on Tsalaki Trail, 2.8 miles from the visitor center on the left.

Local Information

Food/Lodging

Tucked away in a forested wilderness setting, the cottages at Smithgall Woods offer upscale, rustic accommodations. For information and reservations call (800) 864-7275 or visit www.gastateparks.org/info/smithgall.

27 Andrews Cove Recreation Area Trail

The Andrews Cove Recreation Area is situated in a picturesque cove hardwood forest, with developed campsites, just off SR 75 to the north of Helen. The valley upstream of the campground was inhabited by mountain homesteaders and hosted some gold mining in the late 1800s.

The Andrews Cove Trail leads from the camping area to Indian Grave Gap at an elevation of 3,090 feet, having climbed 1,057 feet. At this point the path intersects FS 238 and the Appalachian Trail. The hike traverses an old logging road for much of its length. The surrounding woodland is an excellent example of a cove hardwood forest, with large yellow poplars, maples, and oaks, along with streamside rhododendron and mountain laurel thickets.

Andrews Creek is visible from the path during the lower half of the hike. This flow is a rocky, tumbling, freestone stream, which is fed from rainwater or snowmelt runoff, as opposed to coming from an underground aquifer. It contains a population of wild rainbow trout.

Start: At the day-use parking area in the back of the campground at Campsite 6
Distance: 3.8 miles out and back
Hiking time: About 2.5–3 hours
Difficulty: Mostly easy to moderate; the last 0.4 mile turns steeply up to the gap.
Trail surface: Dirt, with occasional large weathered rocks and stony sections
Best season: Mar–Dec
Other trail users: Hunters in season
Canine compatibility: Dogs permitted; leashed dogs permitted in the campground
Land status: Chattahoochee National Forest
Nearest town: Helen
Fees and permits: Camping fee
Schedule: Open 7 a.m.–10 p.m. daily; campground closed Dec–Mar
Maps: USGS Tray Mountain; Chattahoochee National Forest map
Trail contacts: USDA Forest Service, Chattahoochee National Forest, Chattooga River Ranger District, 9975 US 441 South, Lakemont 305552; (706) 754-6221; www.fs.usda.gov/conf

Finding the trailhead: The campground entrance is 5 miles north of Helen on SR 75 from its junction with SR 75 Alternate. The trail begins at the wooden sign just beyond Campsite 6. Trailhead GPS: N34 46.731' / W83 44.146'

The Hike

Marked with blue blazes, the trail climbs easily but steadily through the forest of maples, oaks, yellow poplars, buckeyes, white pines, dogwoods, and hemlocks. Andrews Creek is on the left of the trail as you go up the cove. To the right the steep face of Tray Mountain towers over the path. That hillside hosts a variety of wildflowers and provides habitat for several species of less common small mammals, especially shrews and voles.

The upper portion of the trail becomes quite steep near Indian Grave Gap.

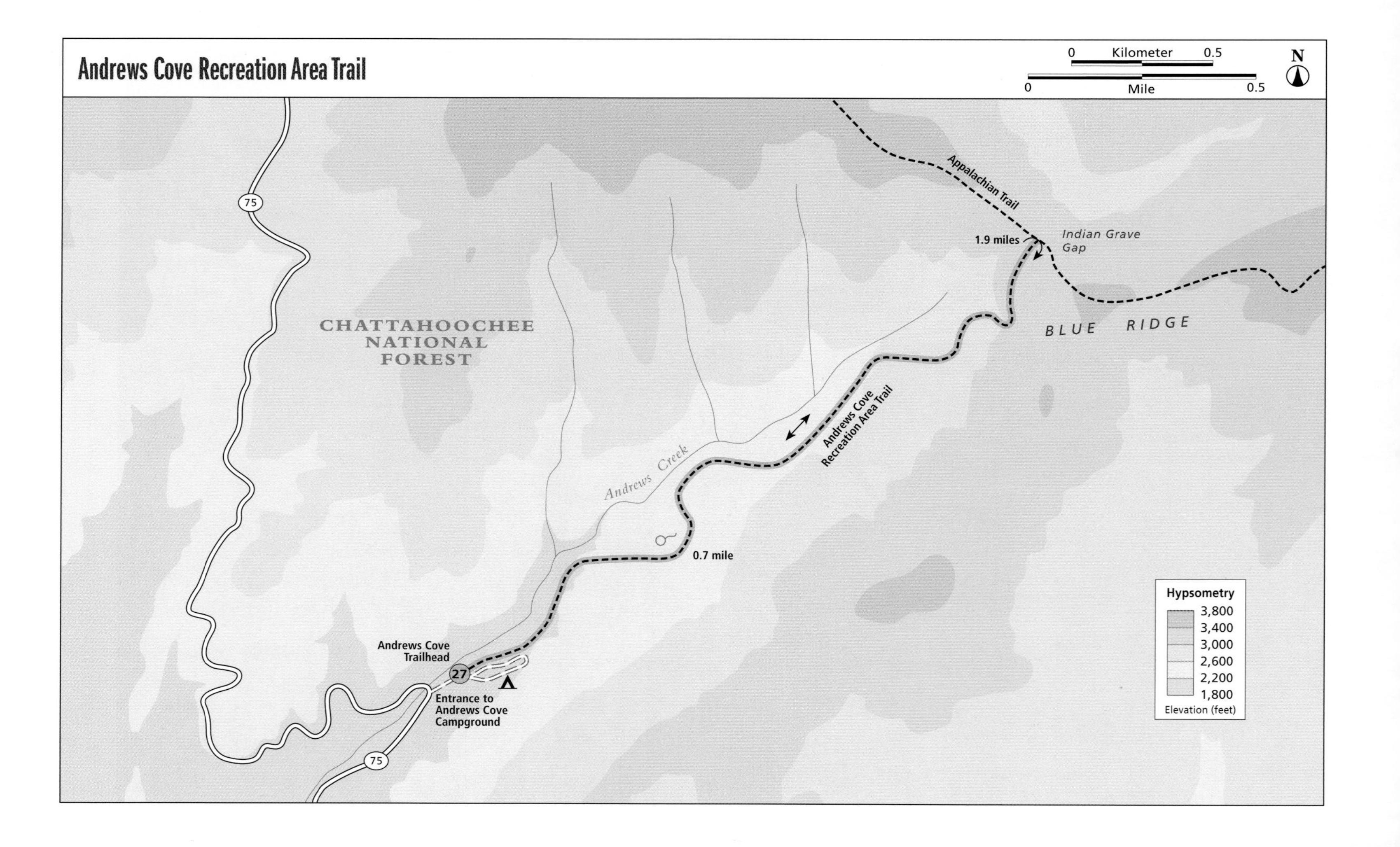
Andrews Cove Recreation Area Trail
0
Kilometer
0.5
0
Mile
0.5
N
75
CHATTAHOOCHEE
NATIONAL
FOREST
Appalachian Trail
1.9 miles
Indian Grave
Gap
BLUE RIDGE
Andrews Cove
Recreation Area Trail
Andrews Creek
0.7 mile
Andrews Cove
Trailhead
27
Entrance to
Andrews Cove
Campground
75
Hypsometry
3,800
3,400
3,000
2,600
2,200
1,800
Elevation (feet)

As you climb, watch for rock piles that indicate old homesites on the more level spots in the valley.

Soon after beginning the trail, the path fords a small feeder stream. Next the trail skirts right around a massive boulder. A spring surrounded by ferns emerges from beneath this rock to flow down to Andrews Creek.

Eventually the trail leaves the creek where the stream begins to splinter into a number of small branches. The path then becomes progressively steeper, particularly in the last 0.4 mile, as it ascends to the gap. The cove hardwood forest gives way to drier, better drained stands of chestnut, black, and southern red oaks.

The trail ends at FS 238 and the Appalachian Trail (AT). From here, the AT can be hiked in either direction. To the right (northeast) is Tray Mountain, which reaches to an elevation of 4,000 feet. The trail to the left (southwest) leads to Unicoi Gap and SR 75.

Miles and Directions

0.0 Start at the trailhead sign near Campsite 6.

0.3 Ford a feeder stream of Andrews Creek.

0.7 Pass the boulder on the left of the path with the spring flowing from beneath it.

1.2 The trail leaves the main branch of Andrews Creek.

1.5 Begin climbing the steep grade up to the gap.

1.9 Reach the trail's end at Indian Grave Gap, FS 238, the Appalachian Trail, and the turnaround point.

3.8 Arrive back at the trailhead.

28 High Shoals Scenic Area Trail

The High Shoals Scenic Area contains two impressive and picturesque waterfalls. High Shoals Creek originates on Tray Mountain, one of the summits on the Appalachian Trail that is more than 4,000 feet in elevation.

The first waterfall is called Blue Hole Falls. Downstream is 100-foot High Shoals Falls. Observation decks are at the foot of both of the cascades.

This area is a favorite with backpack campers. Upstream of High Shoals Falls the creek contains a wild population of native southern Appalachian brook trout. The presence of these fish also draws fishermen down the trail.

Start: At the parking area on FS 283
Distance: 2.6 miles out and back
Hiking time: About 1.5 hours
Difficulty: Easy to moderate
Trail surface: Dirt
Best season: Mar–Dec
Other trail users: Anglers; hunters in season
Canine compatibility: Dogs permitted
Land status: Chattahoochee National Forest
Nearest towns: Hiawassee, Helen
Fees and permits: None
Schedule: Open year-round
Maps: USGS Tray Mountain; Chattahoochee National Forest Map; *Trail Guide to the Chattahoochee-Oconee National Forests*
Trail contacts: Chattahoochee National Forest, Blue Ridge Ranger District, 2042 SR 515 West, Blairsville 30512; (706) 745-6928; www.fs.usda.gov/conf

Finding the trailhead: The trailhead is reached from SR 75, 11.4 miles north of Helen or 9.5 miles south of Hiawassee. Turn right from Helen or left from Hiawassee on FS 283 (Indian Grave Gap Road). A short distance after leaving the paved road, you ford the Hiawassee River, a small stream at this elevation. Continue for 1.5 miles up a steep grade to the High Shoals Scenic Area. The trailhead is near the sign at a small, unpaved parking area on the left of the road. Trailhead GPS: N34 48.973' / W83 43.623'

The Hike

The High Shoals Trail loses 515 feet in elevation on the way into the creek valley. On the climb out, all three steep sections are very short. During winter, freezing weather and high water can make the trail more difficult to reach and to hike. Green blazes mark the path throughout its length.

The trail begins with steps going down from the parking area. The trail drops down the steep-sided cove, but two sweeping switchbacks keep the grade moderate for the descent and climb back out. A big oak tree with cavities large enough to accommodate a hibernating bear stands beside the path before the first switchback.

As the trail descends, hardwood trees in the cove give way to large white pines and hemlocks as the trail nears High Shoals Creek. The cascading water of the creek can be heard well before you reach the stream. At the creek the trail abruptly flattens

High Shoals Falls is the taller cascade on High Shoals Creek.

out and follows an old roadbed to the first bridge on the trail. This span crosses High Shoals Creek in an open, level area in the cove that has been used for many seasons as a primitive campsite.

Downstream of the camping area the trail parallels the creek on the eastern side. Thick rhododendron covers the stream in much of this section. Two footbridges and a boardwalk span brooks and spring seeps that cross the path.

As you near the end of the trail, a side path leads off to the left to an observation deck at the bottom of Blue Hole Falls. This 30-foot waterfall spills into a deep catch pool in front of the wooden platform. A sign warns of the dangers of leaving the trail and climbing on the rocks. The smart hiker will heed these warnings.

Returning to the main trail, the path leaves the creek temporarily as you descend through two switchbacks. In the middle of these twists in the trail, a rock shelter appears on the left of the trail.

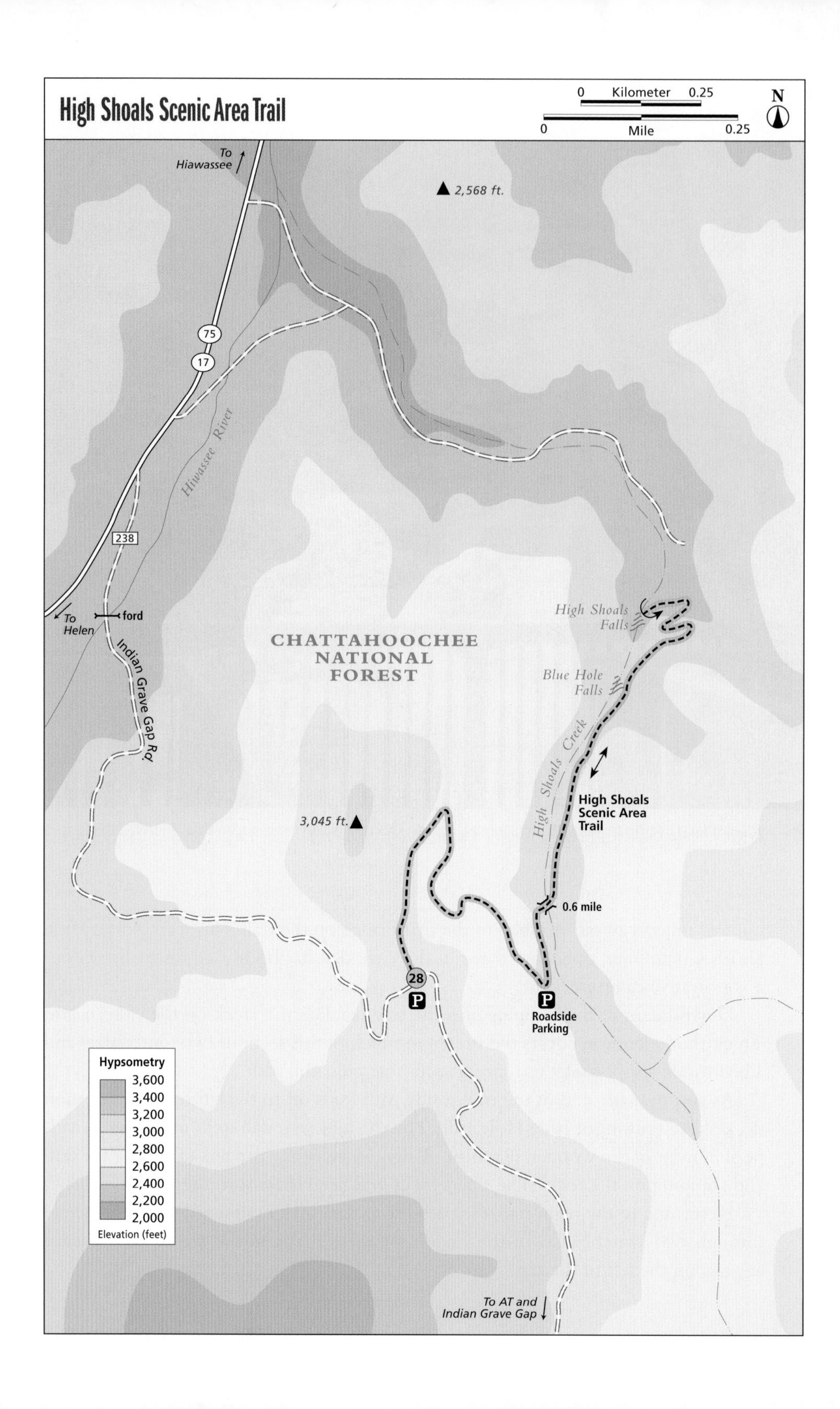
High Shoals Scenic Area Trail
0 Kilometer 0.25
0 Mile 0.25
N
To Hiawassee
2,568 ft.
75
17
Hiwassee River
238
To Helen
ford
Indian Grave Gap Rd.
CHATTAHOOCHEE NATIONAL FOREST
High Shoals Falls
Blue Hole Falls
High Shoals Creek
High Shoals Scenic Area Trail
3,045 ft.
0.6 mile
28
P
P
Roadside Parking
Hypsometry
3,600
3,400
3,200
3,000
2,800
2,600
2,400
2,200
2,000
Elevation (feet)
To AT and Indian Grave Gap

High Shoals Creek holds a population of native southern Appalachian brook trout.

At the end of the trail you are back at the creek and another observation deck below High Shoals Falls. Here the creek plunges more than 100 feet, splashing grandly down the steep rock face.

Many moisture-tolerant plants, including liverworts, mosses, and wildflowers, add to the beauty of the falls. The massive rhododendrons on either side of the stream, large hemlocks, white pines, and hardwood trees complete the enchantment of the site.

After admiring the falls, backtrack to the trailhead.

Miles and Directions

0.0 Start at the FS 238 parking area; walk down the timber steps, and after 60 yards pass the large hollow white oak tree on the right.

0.2 Round the first turn of the long switchbacks.

0.5 Round the second switchback and reach level ground.

0.6 Cross High Shoals Creek on a footbridge.

0.9 Arrive at the side trail to Blue Hole Falls viewing platform.

1.1 Pass the rock shelter on the left.

1.3 Reach the High Shoals Falls viewing platform and the turnaround at the end of the trail.

2.6 Arrive back at the trailhead.

29 Anna Ruby Falls Recreation Area Trails

Anna Ruby Falls Recreation Area is on USDA Forest Service property adjacent to Unicoi State Park. The roadway through the state park is the only access to this federal facility. The twin cascades of Anna Ruby Falls form the most visited waterfall in the North Georgia mountains.

The recreation area contains the paved pathway of 0.5-mile Anna Ruby Falls Trail that runs from the visitor center up to two viewing platforms at the base of the falls. Also originating at the visitor center is the Lion's Eye Nature Trail for sight-impaired hikers.

The Smith Creek Trail starts in the recreation area at the base of the waterfalls, runs through land in the Chattahoochee National Forest, and ends at the Little Brook Campground in Unicoi State Park.

The featured hike is the combination of the Anna Ruby Falls and Smith Creek Trails.

Start: To the left of the Anna Ruby Falls Visitor Center
Distance: 4.9 miles one way
Hiking time: About 3–3.5 hours one way
Difficulty: Moderate from the falls; strenuous starting from the state park
Trail surface: Asphalt to the falls; dirt and firm loam, with loose stones in short segments
Best season: Mar–Dec
Other trail users: Hikers only
Canine compatibility: Dogs permitted on the Smith Creek Trail; dogs must be leashed on the Anna Ruby Falls Trail.
Land status: Chattahoochee National Forest
Nearest town: Helen
Fees and permits: Daily user fee charged per person
Schedule: Anna Ruby Falls gates are open 9 a.m.–5 p.m. daily, except Christmas Day.
Maps: USGS Tray Mountain; Unicoi State Park Trails map
Trail contacts: USDA Forest Service, Chattooga Ranger District, 9975 US 441 South, Lakemont 30552; (706) 754-6221; www.fs.usda.gov/conf

Finding the trailhead: Take SR 75 north from Helen for 1 mile and turn right on SR 356. At 1.5 miles turn left on Anna Ruby Falls Road and travel 3.3 miles to the Anna Ruby Falls Visitor Center and parking area. The joint trailhead for the Anna Ruby Falls, Lion's Eye Nature, and Smith Creek Trails is at the visitor center. Trailhead GPS: N34 45.478' / W83 42.618'

The Hike

Begin the hike on the paved Falls Trail from the parking area and visitor center. Follow it upstream along Smith Creek to Anna Ruby Falls. The hike is easy to moderate, with benches along the way providing comfortable resting places for those who need to take it easy. An observation bridge and a deck at the end of the trail provide great

The twin cascades at Anna Ruby Falls ▶

views of the twin falls on Curtis and York Creeks, which join at the foot to form Smith Creek.

This part of the trail is good for taking children hiking. The pavement is safe, and the moderate grade is not too difficult, even with toddlers in strollers. A complete canopy of hardwood trees shades the trail during the warm months.

During April and May, thirty to forty species of wildflowers are likely to be in bloom at the same time along here. The large hornblende schist boulders along Smith Creek support some of the largest colonies of rockcap ferns in the state. These are also the type of rock sought by early gold miners: Quartz veins running through the schist often contained the precious metal.

From the junction with the falls pathway, the blue-blazed Smith Creek Trail climbs gradually up the side of Hickory Nut Ridge and then crosses a saddle to the southwest side. Eventually the trail reaches the crest at 2,645 feet, before descending to Little Brook Campground at 1,760 feet of elevation.

The first segment of the trail climbs beside a small branch through a hardwood cove and is canopied by dense patches of rhododendron and mountain laurel. As the forest becomes more open, wildflowers begin to appear. In the spring the path is fringed with blooming pink and white azaleas, as well as white blooms of foamflower and purple spiderwort. Also watch for bright red flowers of the fire pink.

During the winter and early spring, when the leaves are off the hickory, oak, poplar, dogwood, and red maple trees that compose the forest, there are excellent views of the surrounding mountains. A few white pines are also mixed into this forest.

After the path reaches the saddle, the trail crosses a small spring with timber steps installed to get you up the steep facing bank.

As the climb continues, very large boulders form a wall on the left of the trail. Spiderwort blooms here in the spring, and Virginia creepers spread amid the rocks. This area offers a sweeping view. American chestnut logs from trees that fell in the mid-1930s are still visible on this dry southwestern slope.

A mile farther the trail drops into a large spring bottom. The pathway is then lined with New York, hay-scented, and Christmas ferns in this damp area. Also some large cinnamon ferns are present.

Follow the spring downhill as it grows into a small brook, with four bridges at points where the trail crosses the flow. This part of the path also passes some patches of wild ginger.

Eventually the trail climbs out of the creek bottom on timber steps and crosses the face of the hillside, paralleling the paved park road to the right. Between the trail and road you can see the remains of the Sautee Ditch, which was used to channel water to hydraulic cannons used for gold mining in the nineteenth century.

The hike ends on the park road across from the Little Brook Campground entrance at a parking turnout and trailhead sign.

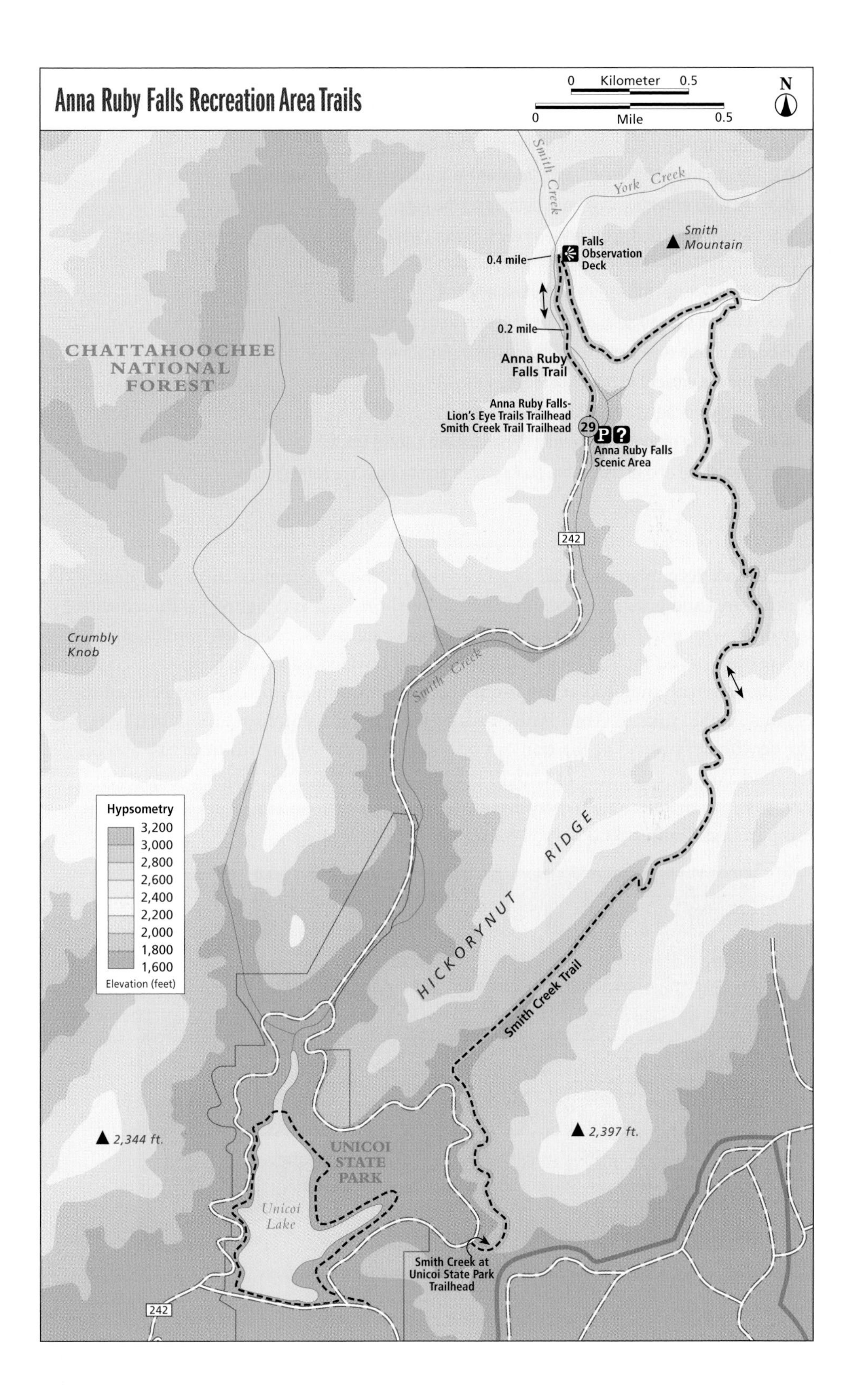
Anna Ruby Falls Recreation Area Trails
0 Kilometer 0.5
0 Mile 0.5
N
Smith Creek
York Creek
Smith Mountain
Falls Observation Deck
0.4 mile
0.2 mile
Anna Ruby Falls Trail
CHATTAHOOCHEE NATIONAL FOREST
Anna Ruby Falls-Lion's Eye Trails Trailhead
Smith Creek Trail Trailhead
29
P
?
Anna Ruby Falls Scenic Area
242
Crumbly Knob
Smith Creek
HICKORYNUT RIDGE
Hypsometry
3,200
3,000
2,800
2,600
2,400
2,200
2,000
1,800
1,600
Elevation (feet)
Smith Creek Trail
2,344 ft.
2,397 ft.
UNICOI STATE PARK
Unicoi Lake
Smith Creek at Unicoi State Park Trailhead
242

Miles and Directions

0.0 Start on the trail to the left of the visitor center.

0.2 Reach the bridge over Smith Creek where a trailside bench is located.

0.3 Pass an extremely large rock outcrop on the right.

0.5 Arrive at the bridge observation deck, Smith Creek Trail junction, and upper observation deck; continue onto the Smith Creek Trail.

1.4 Pass through the saddle and cross a spring.

1.5 Cross a second spring with timber steps in its bank.

2.1 Reach the rock formation with a sweeping southwest view.

2.2 Top the crest of Hickory Nut Ridge.

3.1 Drop into the spring bottom.

4.3 Climb out of the creek bottom to parallel the Sautee Ditch.

4.9 Reach the end of trail at the parking area across from the campground.

Options

The **Lion's Eye Nature Trail** begins at the northeast corner of the visitor center parking area and goes along Smith Creek. This short loop is designed for the visually impaired, with guide rails and Braille interpretive signs describing the sounds, smells, and texture of the forest. The paved trail is easily traveled by wheelchair.

The alternate trailhead at the south end of the Smith Creek Trail can be used to begin an uphill hike to Anna Ruby Falls or for leaving a shuttle vehicle when walking downhill. This end of the trail can be reached by turning north from SR 356 on the road along the east side of Unicoi Lake leading to the Little Brook Campground. Just past the park cabins, a gravel parking area appears on the right, opposite the campground. Trailhead GPS: N34 43.604' / W83 42.954'

The spring bottom along Smith Creek Trail, lined with large ferns

30 Unicoi State Park Trails

Unicoi State Park is the gateway to the higher mountains of the southern Appalachians and is one of the most popular parks in Georgia. Four well-marked trails in Unicoi State Park provide hikers with diverse habitat and degree of difficulty. Unicoi Lake Trail is an almost level walk around Unicoi Lake. The Bottoms Loop and Frog Pond Trails explore the natural history and ecology of the park.

The featured Unicoi to Helen Trail skirts Smith Creek on the way to the Alpine Bavarian–themed resort town of Helen.

Start: At Unicoi Lodge rear parking area
Distance: 2.5 miles one way
Hiking time: About 1-1.5 hours
Difficulty: Easy to moderate
Trail surface: Mostly dirt; a few short segments on paved and unpaved roads
Best season: Mar–Dec
Other trail users: Mountain bikers
Canine compatibility: Leashed dogs permitted
Land status: Georgia DNR, State Parks & Historic Sites Division
Nearest town: Helen
Fees and permits: Daily parking fee
Schedule: Park hours 7 a.m.–10 p.m., year-round
Maps: USGS Helen and Tray Mountain; page-size Unicoi State Park trail maps available at the lodge
Trail contacts: Unicoi State Park, 943 Anna Ruby Falls Rd., Helen 30545; (706) 878-2201; www.gastateparks.org

Finding the trailhead: For the state park, follow SR 356 to the east across the dam at Unicoi Lake. The entrance drive for Unicoi Lodge and Conference Center is then on the right. The common trailhead for the paths is in the conference center's rear parking area. Trailhead GPS: N34 43.379' / W83 43.317'

The Hike

The Unicoi to Helen Trail is marked with orange blazes and takes you to the resort town of Helen. It begins at the common trailhead behind the lodge, descending a series of step landings down to the junction where the Unicoi Lake Trail turns off to the left. As you turn right, the Frog Pond Loop also splits off to the left. The trail continues to descend, sharing the path with the Bottoms Loop Trail. The trail has both orange and yellow blazes.

Arriving at the park's tennis court on the right of the path, the other end of the Frog Pond Loop intersects from the left. Continue straight, crossing a footbridge over a feeder stream, turning downstream, and passing the tennis courts.

From here the trail crosses paved Unicoi Bottom Road, climbs a low ridge, and arrives at the first junction with the Bottoms Loop Trail. That path forks off to the left.

The trail again begins descending and enters a large open grass field in which deer are often seen. The path runs along the edge of the opening for 230 yards, before

A vein of quartz running through a hornblende schist boulder along Smith Creek

again entering woodlands. At the point the trail crosses a footbridge over a small feeder stream, Smith Creek comes into view on the right. Smith Creek contains rainbow and brown trout and is managed under special delayed-harvest fishing regulations. Signs along the stream explain the rules.

The junction where the Bottoms Loop Trail splits off is 70 yards farther along. That path turns to the left across a footbridge over a small feeder stream. The main Unicoi to Helen Trail turns right, crossing a footbridge over Smith Creek. It then continues to follow downstream.

Just before crossing back over the creek on another bridge, the trail intersects the park's white-blazed Bike Trail. Both trails follow the path across the bridge and run together for 70 yards before the Bike Trail turns off to the right.

The Unicoi to Helen Trail turns sharply left and begins climbing steeply up the side of the ridge. It runs through a series of switchbacks until meeting the Bike Trail on the top of the ridge at the highest point of the hike. Dropping off the other side of the ridge, the trail next begins following a small mountain brook to the south.

The path leaves the valley of the small stream to climb up to a junction where the Bike Trail crosses the hiking trail. Almost immediately the trail then crosses a footbridge over another small creek and turns sharply left to follow that flow downstream. After 125 yards the stream drops over a rock ledge, forming a small waterfall as the flow runs down into a steep-sided gorge on the left of the trail.

Next the trail comes out on the shoulder of paved White Strasse. Up to the right you see a large water tower as you break out on the roadside. The trail then reenters the woods 25 yards along on the same side of the road and quickly reaches the Unicoi Hill Park trailhead and parking lot. For a 5.0-mile round-trip, reverse course and walk back to the park lodge.

To go into the town of Helen, follow White Strasse 0.2 mile down to Main Street (SR 75). Turn left to visit the downtown shopping and entertainment area before your return hike.

Miles and Directions

0.0 Start at the common trailhead at the lodge and convention center parking lot; turn right at the end of the step landings, past the junctions with the Lake Trail and Frog Pond Loop.

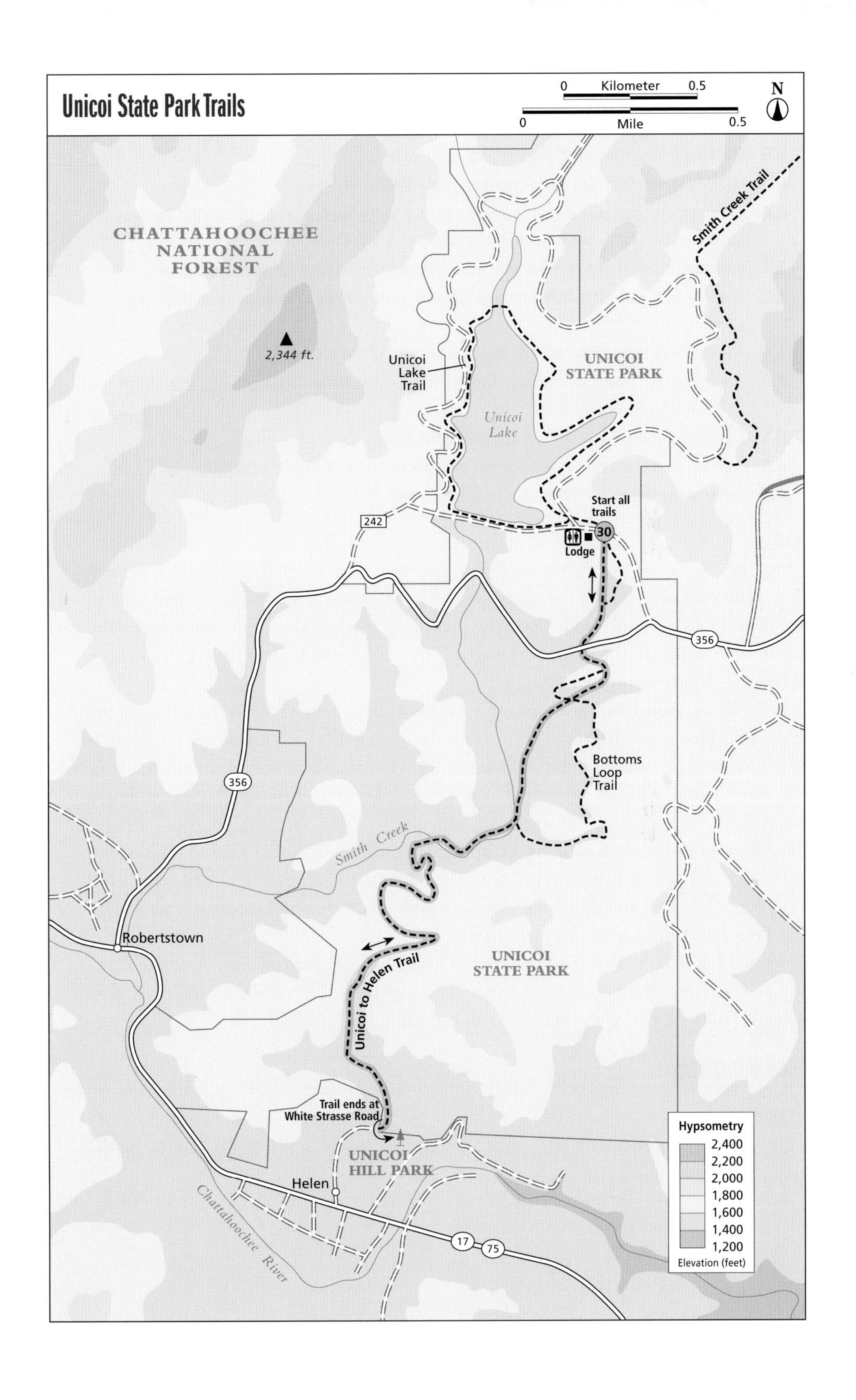

Unicoi State Park Trails
0 Kilometer 0.5
0 Mile 0.5
N
CHATTAHOOCHEE NATIONAL FOREST
2,344 ft.
Smith Creek Trail
Unicoi Lake Trail
UNICOI STATE PARK
Unicoi Lake
242
Start all trails
30
Lodge
356
Bottoms Loop Trail
Smith Creek
Robertstown
Unicoi to Helen Trail
UNICOI STATE PARK
Trail ends at White Strasse Road
UNICOI HILL PARK
Helen
Chattahoochee River
17
75
Hypsometry
2,400
2,200
2,000
1,800
1,600
1,400
1,200
Elevation (feet)

0.2 Reach another junction with the Frog Pond Loop at the park tennis courts; next cross a footbridge and paved Unicoi Bottoms Road.

0.5 Pass the first junction with the Bottoms Loop Trail.

0.6 Walk along the left edge of a large open grass field.

0.8 Cross a footbridge over a small brook and arrive at the second junction with the Bottoms Loop Trail; turn right, crossing the footbridge over Smith Creek.

1.1 Intersect the white-blazed Bike Trail; cross the footbridge to the left over Smith Creek.

1.2 The Bike Trail runs off to the right: turn left and begin climbing the ridge away from Smith Creek.

1.6 The Bike Trail crosses the path at the highest point of the hike.

2.0 The Bike Trail crosses the trail again; immediately cross a footbridge and turn sharply left to follow a small stream.

2.1 The small waterfall and creek gorge are on the left.

2.4 Walk on the shoulder of White Strasse, with the water tower uphill to the right.

2.5 Arrive at the alternate trailhead in Unicoi Hill Park.

Options

The **Unicoi Lake Trail** a 2.4-mile loop and the easiest and most accessible hike in the park. The yellow-blazed path can be picked up at several locations, but it shares the common trailhead at the lodge parking lot. The path circles Unicoi Lake, coming back across the dam to complete the loop.

The **Frog Pond Loop** is an easy 0.5-mile walk that splits off to the left from the Unicoi to Helen and Bottoms Loop Trails soon after that path leaves the trailhead. It is a good trail to walk first for anyone interested in the surrounding forest. Many of the more common trees in the park are labeled. The trail runs clockwise, circling a small pond.

The yellow-blazed **Bottoms Loop Trail** is an easy 2.4-mile hike that takes you through a variety of habitat types, including hardwood forests, dry pine stands, old homesites, wetland areas, and meadows. A portion of this trail shares the path with the Frog Pond and Unicoi to Helen Trails.

The Unicoi to Helen Trail also can be hiked from Helen, or there is ample parking at the alternate trailhead to leave a shuttle vehicle. The southern trailhead is in Unicoi Hill Park on White Strasse. Trailhead GPS: N34 42.182' / W83 43.892'

Local Information

Accommodations

Unicoi State Park offers 82 RV and tent campsites, a 100-room lodge and 30 cabins; (800) 573-9659; www.gastateparks.org.

31 Moccasin Creek Trails

There are two trails along Moccasin Creek, both of which are located on Chattahoochee National Forest property. The Wildlife Trail is a 1.1-mile loop, while the Hemlock Falls Trail is 2.0 miles out and back. But due to their close proximity, the trails can be hiked together as a single trek. The featured hike is the combined loop, beginning at the trailhead for the Wildlife Trail.

Lake Burton, Moccasin Creek State Park, and Lake Burton Fish Hatchery are a few yards away, across SR 197 from those trails. Aside from RV and tent camping at Moccasin Creek State Park, there is trout fishing in a section of the creek reserved for children under age 12 and senior citizens. At the hatchery there is a family fishing pond open to the public. Lake Burton also offers boating, sightseeing, and quality fishing.

Start: At the fenced parking area as you turn onto Andersonville Lane from SR 197
Distance: 3.3 miles out and back with a loop on the beginning portion
Hiking time: About 1–1.5 hours
Difficulty: Easy
Trail surface: Dirt; some gravel road
Best season: Mar–June; Oct–Dec
Other trail users: Anglers and hunters in season
Canine compatibility: Dogs permitted
Land status: Chattahoochee National Forest
Nearest town: Clayton
Fees and permits: None
Schedule: Year-round
Maps: USGS Lake Burton; page-size hand-drawn map of the trails available at the Moccasin Creek State Park Office
Trail contacts: USDA Forest Service, Chattooga River Ranger District, 9975 US 441S, Lakemont 30552; www.fs.usda.gov/conf
Moccasin Creek State Park, 3655 SR 197, Clarksville 30523; (706) 947-3194; www.gastateparks.org

Finding the trailhead: From Clayton go west 11.5 miles on US 76 to SR 197. Turn left and go 3.8 miles to the Moccasin Creek State Park sign; turn right into the parking area beside Andersonville Lane. The trailhead for the Wildlife Trail is at this parking lot. Trailhead GPS: N34 50.678' / W83 35.407'

The Hike

To begin a combined hike on the Wildlife and Hemlock Creek Trails, start at the parking area and trailhead for the Wildlife Trail. This pathway is designed to show some of the wildlife management principles and structures that are beneficial to both game and nongame animals. Along the path are interpretive signs describing practices or some of the devices used to monitor habitat and wildlife populations.

The trail begins on the bank of Moccasin Creek at the water-control dam that supplies the flow for the fish hatchery. An information board describes the trail and its purpose. Stakes with arrows within a circle direct you around the loop. As you

walk this trail, you cross small streams feeding into Moccasin Creek on a number of footbridges.

Interpretive signs and markers provide information and are placed strategically along the trail. This is an exceptionally good trail for children to see and learn more about plants and wildlife and how they relate.

Shortly you reach the beginning of the loop portion of the pathway. Turning right in a counterclockwise direction, the trail reaches an open wildlife-viewing area. Roughly 40 feet before the clearing, a connector trail runs to the right to an observation tower overlooking the opening. This is a good place for watching deer in the late afternoon.

Where the trail crosses Andersonville Lane, turn right and follow the gravel roadway for 0.1 mile to the trailhead for the Hemlock Falls Trail. Along the road, the driveway for Camp Winfield, a children's summer retreat, is on the right. A large rock with the trail name engraved upon it marks the beginning of the trail at a parking area.

Hemlock Falls Trail goes through a typical hardwood forest with Moccasin Creek in sight most of the way. This is an easy walk that features multiple waterfalls before ending at the impressive Hemlock Falls cascade. The pathway is blazed with small metal diamonds attached to trees along the way.

For the first 200 to 300 yards, the trail follows an old roadbed that at one time was also a railroad bed for hauling sawlogs out of the forest. Along the streamside and well up the bank along the trail, rosebay rhododendron is the most obvious cover. Trilliums, jack-in-the-pulpits, dog-hobble, silver bells, sweet shrub, bear huckleberry, and anemones are at trailside. New York and Christmas ferns predominate along the path. Dogwoods, yellow poplars, buckeyes, white pine, hemlock, oak, maple, deciduous magnolia, birch, and beech make up the forest canopy.

The first waterfall encountered is not actually on Moccasin Creek. At 1.0 mile, look across the creek to the right for a small cascade on a tributary branch of Moccasin Creek. It may not be flowing during very dry weather.

Just a few yards farther you will see a large rock overhang on the left side of the trail. Should you get caught in one of the frequent spring or summer rainshowers, the structure provides a good rain shelter.

From this point to where a wooden footbridge crosses Moccasin Creek, you pass three waterfalls on the stream, the first of which rushes around a huge boulder on the opposite shore. The last one is immediately below the footbridge. Any of these would merit walking to on most creeks.

Across the bridge the trail continues up the right side of the stream. The valley is narrower, the ridges are higher, the stream is more turbulent, and you are in shade even at midday. The path narrows as it skirts a long cascade composed of small falls and slides.

A footbridge crosses Moccasin Creek just above the fourth waterfall.

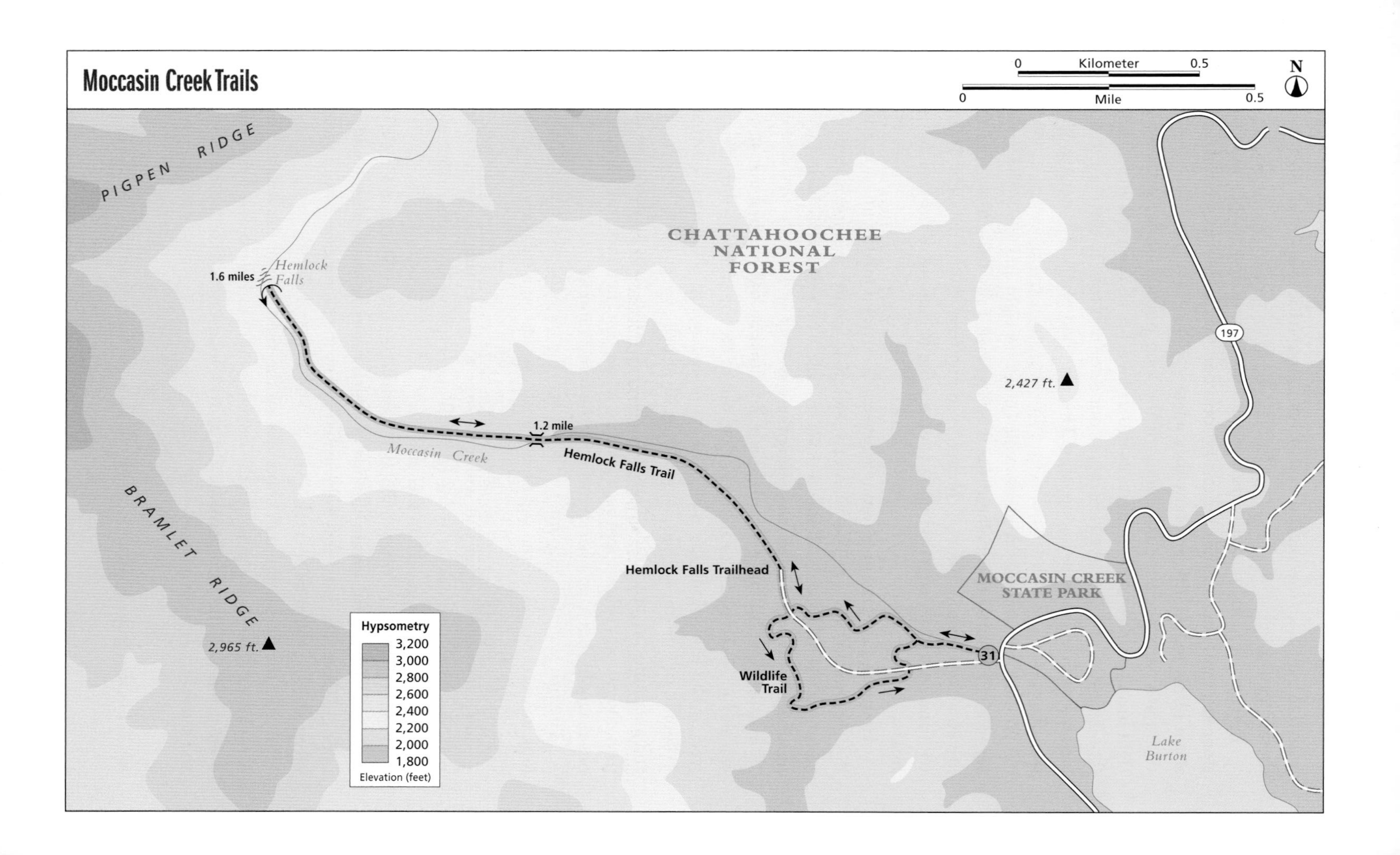
Moccasin Creek Trails
0
Kilometer
0.5
0
Mile
0.5
N
PIGPEN RIDGE
1.6 miles
Hemlock Falls
CHATTAHOOCHEE NATIONAL FOREST
197
2,427 ft.
1.2 mile
Moccasin Creek
Hemlock Falls Trail
BRAMLET RIDGE
Hemlock Falls Trailhead
MOCCASIN CREEK STATE PARK
31
Wildlife Trail
2,965 ft.
Hypsometry
3,200
3,000
2,800
2,600
2,400
2,200
2,000
1,800
Elevation (feet)
Lake Burton

At the trail's end you reach Hemlock Falls. The attractive 30-foot fall plunges into a large pool. In warmer months this spot is a favorite with trout fishermen and swimmers. The large broken boulders alongside the pool make rustic benches.

This is the turnaround point for the trail. However, a poorly marked trail does continue above the falls, leading up Moccasin Creek and its South Fork. This path climbs the highland ridge that includes Tray Mountain, eventually reaching Addis Gap and the Appalachian Trail.

Retracing your steps back to the junction with the Wildlife Trail, turn right off Andersonville Road to complete that loop.

On this return side of the loop you pass a waterfowl pond and another wildlife opening. After again crossing Andersonville Lane, the trail completes the loop. A right turn takes you back to the trailhead.

Hemlock Falls empties into a large, deep plunge pool at the end of the trail.

Miles and Directions

0.0 Start at the trailhead at the parking lot and dam on Moccasin Creek.

0.1 Reach the beginning of the Wildlife Trail loop and turn right.

0.2 Cross the first wildlife clearing.

0.5 Turn right onto gravel Andersonville Lane and pass the entrance to Camp Winfield.

0.6 Pass the engraved stone at the trailhead for the Hemlock Falls Trail.

1.0 Look for a small but picturesque waterfall on the opposite side of Moccasin Creek.

1.1 Reach the waterfall rushing around the boulder on the opposite shore.

1.2 Pass two more falls and cross a footbridge over Moccasin Creek.

1.3 The cascade of falls and slides is on the left.

1.6 Arrive at Hemlock Falls, your turnaround point.

2.7 Arrive back at the junction with the Wildlife Trail.

2.8 Pass the waterfowl pond with wood duck nesting boxes on the left.

2.9 Cross a second wildlife clearing.

3.1 Cross Andersonville Lane.

3.2 Close the loop and turn right.

3.3 Arrive back at the trailhead.

32 Lake Rabun Beach Recreation Area Trail

The Lake Rabun Beach Recreation Area is a USDA Forest Service facility located on the shores of Lake Rabun. This is another of the areas originally constructed during the Great Depression by the Civilian Conservation Corps (CCC). The area contains an 80-site campground, boat launch, and swimming beach.

The only hike in the recreation area is provided by the Angel Falls Trail. This pathway follows the tumbling course of Joe Creek upstream past Panther Falls to end in a short loop beneath Angel Falls at an observation bridge.

Start: At the north end of Rabun Beach Campground Loop 2
Distance: 1.8 miles out and back
Hiking time: About 1 hour
Difficulty: Easy to moderate
Trail surface: Loamy dirt; some loose stones at upper end; rock hopping over narrow stream
Best season: Waterfall conditions are best in Dec–Mar
Other trail users: Hikers only
Canine compatibility: Dogs permitted; must be leashed in the campground
Land status: Chattahoochee National Forest
Nearest towns: Tallulah Falls, Clayton
Fees and permits: Daily parking fee
Schedule: Open to hiking year-round; campground closed Nov–Apr
Maps: USGS Tiger; Chattahoochee National Forest map
Trail contacts: USDA Forest Service, Chattooga River Ranger District, 9975 US 441 South, Lakemont 30552; (706) 754-6221; www.fs. usda.gov/conf

Finding the trailhead: On US 441, go 3.6 miles north of Tallulah Falls or 8 miles south of Clayton and turn west on Joy Bridge Road. At 0.1 mile, turn right on Old US 441 (Terrora Circle). Go 1.4 miles and turn left onto Lake Rabun Road; proceed another 5.5 miles and turn right into Rabun Beach Campground Loop 2. In the campground turn right and go to the parking area at the trailhead near Campsite 53. Trailhead GPS: N34 45.681' / W83 28.369'

The Hike

From the parking area, cross Joe Creek on a footbridge and continue upstream on the left side of the creek. The trail is marked with white diamond and lime-green metal blazes along the way.

On the right at 60 yards, you pass the junction with the path leading to Lake Rabun Road.

The beginning of the trail is in a corridor of dog-hobble, rhododendron, and mountain laurel under the shade of white pines and hemlocks. Farther up, the trail is covered by a more open canopy of yellow poplars, maples, buckeyes, deciduous magnolias, and oaks. The final stretch of the path passes through a dense laurel and rhododendron thicket.

On the opening phase of the hike, you pass a spring box on the left with a sign explaining its use. Built by the CCC, this rock enclosure provided a way to keep

Panther Falls is the smaller of the two cascades on the Angel Falls Trail.

perishables like eggs and milk fresh prior to the era when refrigeration units were common.

Panther Falls is the first of the two cascades on the trail. Prior to reaching the falls you cross the creek on a boardwalk, two bridges, and a ford. Joe Creek here drops about 40 feet in a series of steps down a stratified rock formation. During normal flows, the streambed of exposed rock is visible. The switchbacks around Panther Falls have metal-cable handrails along their steep edges.

Angel Falls is another 600 yards upstream. However, the trail to reach the falls is 0.4 mile, and it climbs more steeply, crossing the creek on another footbridge before creating a loop near its end. Keep to the right at the loop junction to reach the observation platform and bridge. These offer a good view of Angel Falls as it cascades 60 feet over rock formations.

The moist rocks alongside and at the foot of the falls support a wide variety of plants specific to this habitat type, including Michaux's (mountain) saxifrage, ragwort, alumroot, ferns, mosses, and liverworts.

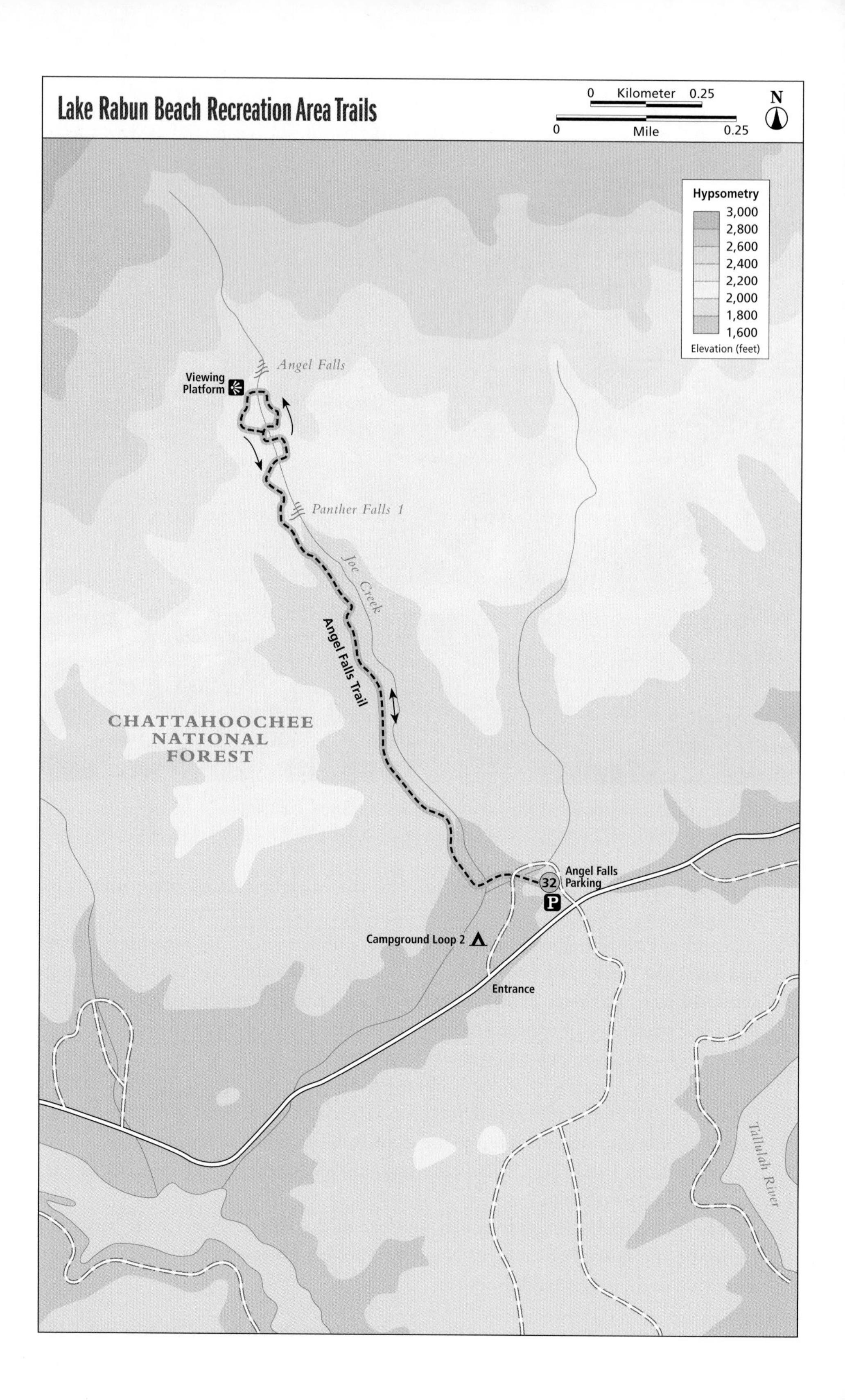
Lake Rabun Beach Recreation Area Trails
0 Kilometer 0.25
0 Mile 0.25
N
Hypsometry
3,000
2,800
2,600
2,400
2,200
2,000
1,800
1,600
Elevation (feet)
Angel Falls
Viewing Platform
Panther Falls 1
Joe Creek
Angel Falls Trail
CHATTAHOOCHEE NATIONAL FOREST
Angel Falls Parking
32
P
Campground Loop 2
Entrance
Tallulah River

The trail crosses Joe Creek at the platform, turns downstream, and closes the loop. At this point it again crosses the creek on a large flat rock. Continue back downstream to the trailhead.

Miles and Directions

0.0 Start at the parking area at the north end of Campground Loop 2, cross the footbridge, and turn upstream.

0.3 The CCC spring box is on the left of the trail.

0.6 Panther Falls comes into sight.

0.8 Cross the last bridge going upstream.

0.9 Stay to the right at the loop junction and, in 100 yards, reach the observation bridge below Angel Falls. Continue around to close the loop and turn right back to the trailhead.

1.8 Arrive back at the parking area.

Much of the trail is through a tunnel of rhododendron and mountain laurel.

33 Lake Russell Recreation Area Trails

The Lake Russell Recreation Area is a USDA Forest Service facility in the eastern section of the Chattahoochee National Forest. The area contains 100-acre Lake Russell and 3-acre Nancy Town Lake. The facility has a 42-site seasonal campground as well.

The Lady Slipper, Lake Russell Foot, Rhododendron, and Sourwood Trails are in the complex, totaling 15 miles in length, plus a partial-loop walking trail around Nancy Town Lake. The featured hike consists of a portion of the Nancy Town Lake walking trail and the Sourwood Trail, forming a 3.7-mile lollipop.

The official Sourwood Trailhead is in the camping area at the north end of the lake, but the road to it is closed from the end of October to the first of April. The parking area at the dam on the south end of Nancy Town Lake is open year-round, providing access to the Sourwood Trail.

Start: At the Nancy Town Lake parking area at the dam
Distance: 3.7-mile lollipop
Hiking time: About 1.5–2 hours
Difficulty: Easy
Trail surface: Dirt and unpaved roadway
Best season: Mar–June; Oct–Dec
Other trail users: Mountain bikes on the Sourwood Trail from the campground to the Nancy Town Road crossing; vehicles and mountain bikes on Nancy Town Lake Road
Canine compatibility: Dogs permitted; must be leashed in the campground
Land status: Chattahoochee National Forest
Nearest town: Mount Airy
Fees and permits: Daily parking fee
Schedule: Trails open year-round; campground and some roads closed Nov–Apr
Maps: USGS Ayersville; page-size maps available from the Chattooga River Ranger District office in Clarksville
Trail contacts: USDA Forest Service, Chattooga River Ranger District, 9975 US 441 South, Lakemont 30552; (706) 754-6221; www.fs.usda.gov/conf

Finding the trailhead: From SR 105 (South Main Street) in Cornelia, take Wyley Street toward Mount Airy for 1.8 miles. Turn right (south) on Lake Russell Road (FS 59) at the Lake Russell Recreation Area sign. Go 1.9 miles and turn left on FS 591, and then right on FS 59H. The parking area and trailhead is at the Nancy Town Lake dam. Trailhead GPS: N34 29.938' / W83 29.026'

The Hike

This is an easy walk past Nancy Town Lake to a small waterfall and beaver pond. The loop portion takes you through a variety of forest habitats, from clear-cuts and new pine plantations to maturing hardwood coves with large yellow poplars, oaks, hickories, and pines. This is an ideal trail for introducing children to a wide variety of plants and animals.

Start at the marker for Trail 152 beside Nancy Town Lake dam. The path drops down to cross Nancy Town Creek immediately below the dam and then climbs up the other side. From this point it skirts the east side of the lake past a large group

The view back across Nancy Town Lake dam to the Sourwood Trailhead

picnic pavilion. After crossing a footbridge over Nancy Town Creek at the head of the lake, the path reaches a junction at the trailhead for the Lady Slipper Trail.

Stay to the left through the campground and across the bridge at the other end. Turn right onto gravel Nancy Town Lake Road (also called Red Root Road on some maps) and walk 100 yards to the sign marking the beginning of Sourwood Trail loop on the left.

Follow the footpath into the woods as it runs on an old roadbed for about 200 yards along a steep hillside with a noticeable stand of Christmas ferns and mountain laurel. The trail parallels a small branch to the right at the bottom of the hill.

After crossing the branch on a footbridge, the path leads up a gentle slope through loblolly pines before entering a more mature forest. The trail next crosses Nancy Town Road at the highest point on this hike. Mountain bikes are no longer allowed on the trail on the other side of the road.

Beyond the roadway a very open hardwood forest begins, composed of white, chestnut, black, and southern red oaks along with scattered hickories. Look for places in the leaves where turkeys have been scratching in search of acorns and other food. Deer tracks almost always are present in the exposed clay soil of the path.

The path next reaches the junction for a side trail running to the left to Nancy Town Falls. The falls are actually on a small feeder stream of Nancy Town Creek and roughly 100 yards up this trail. Shrouded in dog-hobble and mountain laurel, the water cascades over rock ledges for a total drop of 20 feet.

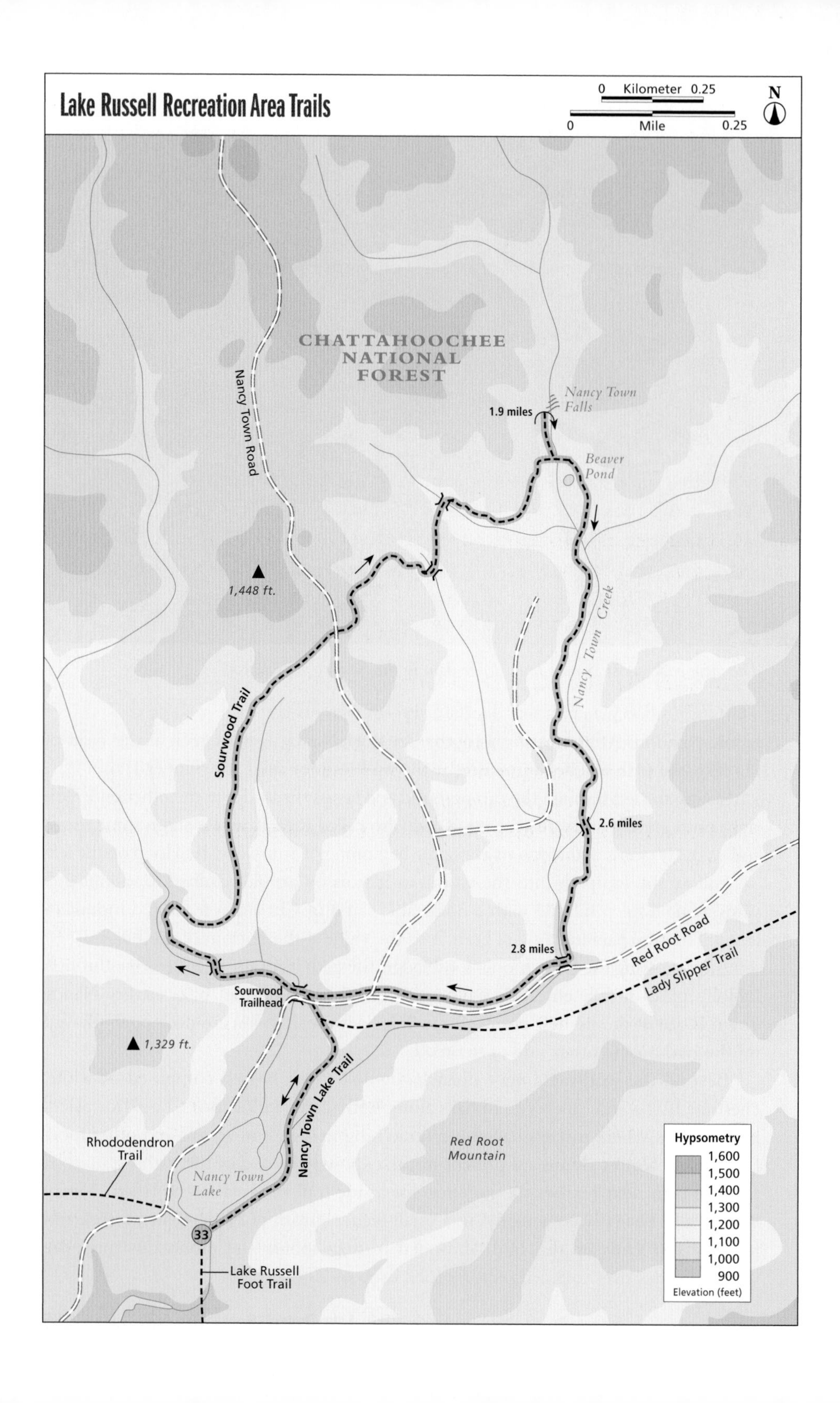

Lake Russell Recreation Area Trails
0 Kilometer 0.25
0 Mile 0.25
N
CHATTAHOOCHEE NATIONAL FOREST
Nancy Town Road
Nancy Town Falls
1.9 miles
Beaver Pond
1,448 ft.
Nancy Town Creek
Sourwood Trail
2.6 miles
2.8 miles
Red Root Road
Lady Slipper Trail
Sourwood Trailhead
1,329 ft.
Nancy Town Lake Trail
Red Root Mountain
Rhododendron Trail
Nancy Town Lake
33
Lake Russell Foot Trail
Hypsometry
1,600
1,500
1,400
1,300
1,200
1,100
1,000
900
Elevation (feet)

Returning to the main trail, turn left and follow the small creek downstream past a shallow beaver pond. In late November look for the blue soapwort gentian blooming at the water's edge. Grape ferns, Christmas ferns, and brown-stemmed spleenwort grow along the trail where it passes near the shore.

The pathway continues down the branch past its confluence with Nancy Town Creek, crosses a metal footbridge, and goes down the left bank through laurel and rhododendron. The trail crosses the creek on another bridge, and passes an area where the water cascades over rock ledges just before reaching Nancy Town Lake Road. Turn right on the gravel track, crossing Nancy Town Creek again, and continue along the road. Stay to the left in passing the junction with Nancy Town Road and again when closing the loop.

Miles and Directions

0.0 Start at the trailhead at the Nancy Town Lake parking area.

0.1 Pass the picnic pavilion on the right.

0.3 Cross a bridge over Nancy Town Creek and reach the junction with the Lady Slipper Trail.

0.4 Cross the bridge and turn right on Nancy Town Lake Road; 100 yards farther turn left off the road at the beginning of the loop.

0.7 Leave the creek valley to climb up the ridge to the east.

1.3 Cross Nancy Town Road.

1.8 Reach the junction with the side trail to Nancy Town Falls.

2.1 Cross Nancy Town Creek on a metal bridge and pass a beaver pond on the right.

2.6 Cross Nancy Town Creek on a second metal bridge.

2.8 Come to Nancy Town Road; turn right and cross the creek again.

3.1 Stay to the left at the junction with Nancy Town Road.

3.2 Cross a bridge, close the loop, and retrace the path to the left to return to the trailhead.

3.7 Arrive back at the trailhead and parking lot.

Options

The **Lady Slipper Trail** is a 6.2-mile loop beginning in the campground at the northern end of Nancy Town Lake. This multiuse path is maintained for hiking, mountain biking, and equestrian use. Mostly following old logging roads, the trail is rated as moderately difficult.

The **Lake Russell Foot Trail** begins at the dam parking area on Nancy Town Lake. Running to the southwest, the 4.6-mile loop skirts the shore of Lake Russell and climbs through the surrounding hillsides. The trail is rated easy to moderate.

The 1.5-mile **Rhododendron Trail** was created as an Eagle Scout project. The one-way path begins near the Nancy Town Lake parking area at the dam and runs to the town of Cornelia. It follows an old roadbed for about 200 yards along a steep hillside with a noticeable stand of Christmas ferns and mountain laurel. The trail is rated as easy.

34 Panther Creek Trail

A tributary of the Tugaloo River, Panther Creek originates in the foothills on the fringe of the Blue Ridge Mountains. Flowing through USDA Forest Service land in the Chattahoochee National Forest, the creek tumbles and cascades through a steep-sided valley with rocky cliffs. Along the way it rushes through Mill Shoals and over Panther Creek Falls.

Beginning at the Panther Creek Recreation Area, the path runs through sites the USDA Forest Service has designated as a Protected Botanical Area. Sections of both sides of the stream below Panther Creek Falls have that designation because of the richness and diversity of plant life. This area lies in the Brevard Fault Zone, characterized by a narrow band of limestone that supports vegetation not commonly found in northeast Georgia. Regionally rare gay-wings bloom along the Panther Creek Gorge.

The creek is stocked with rainbow trout each spring by the Georgia Department of Natural Resources, adding the option for some fishing to a day on the trail.

This path is marked with green metal blaze signs and offers an excellent one-way day hike with arrangements for transportation at the end. Due to the length and difficulty, hiking the trail both ways in a single day makes for a long and strenuous trek.

Start: At the Panther Creek Day-Use Area
Distance: 5.7 miles one way
Hiking time: About 2.5–3 hours
Difficulty: Moderate to strenuous from either direction
Trail surface: Dirt, bare rock surface, and firm loam
Best season: Mar–June; Oct–Dec
Other trail users: Anglers in the spring; hunters in season
Canine compatibility: Dogs permitted
Land status: Chattahoochee National Forest
Nearest towns: Tallulah Falls, Toccoa
Fees and permits: Daily parking fee at Panther Creek Day-Use Area
Schedule: Trail open year-round
Maps: USGS Tallulah Falls and Tugaloo Lake; USDA Forest Service map of the Chattahoochee National Forest
Trail contacts: USDA Forest Service, Chattooga River Ranger District, 9975 US 441 South, Lakemont 30552; (706) 754-6221; www.fs.usda.gov/conf

Finding the trailhead: Take US 23/441 2.2 miles south from Tallulah Falls. Turn right on US 441 Historical and go 1.5 miles to the Panther Creek Recreation Area on the right. The trailhead is across the highway from the recreation area. Trailhead GPS: N34 41.935' / W83 25.167'

The Hike

The trail begins on the opposite side of US 441 Historical from the Panther Creek Day-Use Area and paved parking lot. The trailhead is on the north side of the creek, and the path is marked with green metal blazes.

The trail quickly goes under the US 23/441 bridge that crosses Panther Creek and then passes through the right-of-way of a power line. From there it enters a mixed

The final drop of Panther Creek Falls forms the background of a favorite spot for picnics and swimming in warmer months.

forest of oaks, hickories, yellow poplars, and pines. Trailing arbutus grows abundantly along the first 0.5 mile. One patch is close to the trailhead, and large patches of the earth-hugging, sweet-smelling plant occur regularly along the south- and west-facing sections of the trail. Mountain laurel thickets border the pathway and bloom en masse in May, followed in June and July by the white rosebay rhododendron growing along the stream.

The trail continues down the northeast side of Panther Creek. Cascading water can be seen or heard throughout much of the hike, sometimes forming small waterfalls.

Two rock overhangs only a few feet apart are encountered at 0.9 mile. Look for a green blaze beneath the second of these shelters. The path goes under the rock ledge and sharply turns left around the end of the rocks. It then climbs for several yards to gain access to the earth path above the thick laurel and rhododendron. A false trail, created by anglers getting to the water and hikers missing the turn, is visible going below the rock shelters. You need to be alert at this point to get on the correct path.

Following this relatively easy-grade section of the trail, you return to the creek at a stand of hemlocks and white pines at a level area with a primitive campsite and fire ring. A footbridge carries the trail over the creek.

The path now is in a level area rich in wildflowers, ferns, ground pine, and other plants thriving in the rich alluvial soil. Along here you pass the mouth of Little Panther Creek entering the main stream from the opposite side.

Once the creek makes an abrupt turn to the east, Horse Creek's mouth is on the opposite side. You now enter an area of more steep-sided rock cliffs, where the first of several steel-wire guardrails have been installed to prevent mishaps. The forest service recommends that hikers with heavy packs use extra caution walking under the rocky overhangs.

Panther Creek picks up speed here and dashes over several beautiful cascades forming Mill Shoals. This is a former gristmill site.

The main show is still 0.3 mile along the trail. Panther Creek Falls are composed of three separate cascades, each with its own plunge pool. The trail leads out onto a large rock overlook for the upper and middle section of the falls. At the foot of the final drop, the trail opens into a flat area beside the large plunge pool.

From the falls, the trail remains on the southeast side of the creek, but it is much less used and at times hard to follow. There are few blazes downstream of the falls.

After passing through a gorge, at 0.4 mile below the cascades, the trail turns sharply uphill to the right and gains 300 feet of elevation as it quickly climbs to the flat top of a pine ridge at the highest point on this hike.

The trail then drops sharply down to the other side the ridge as you return to a forest of large oaks and yellow poplars along the creek. The rest of the pathway is relatively level until it crosses a final bridge spanning Panther Creek and reaches the eastern trailhead.

Miles and Directions

0.0 Start at the day-use area across US 441 Historical.

0.1 Pass under the US 23/441 highway bridge.

0.2 Enter the cleared right-of-way under a power line.

0.9 Reach the two rock shelters and the sharp left turn up the hillside.

1.4 Cross Panther Creek on a footbridge at a primitive camping area.

1.5 Pass the mouth of Little Panther Creek on the opposite shore.

2.6 Horse Creek enters the main flow from the opposite side.

2.8 The rock ledges now become the valley side as the first cable guardrail begins.

3.2 Reach Mill Shoals on the left of the trail.

3.5 The overlook at the head of Panther Creek Falls provides a view of the upper cataracts, and the plunge pool at the foot of the last drop is just beyond.

3.9 Leave the creek and start to climb up the ridge to the right.

4.3 Enter more open woods as you crest the high point on the trail at 1,300 feet.

4.8 Come back to the stream again in a much flatter area.

5.7 Cross Panther Creek on a footbridge and arrive at the alternate eastern trailhead and parking area.

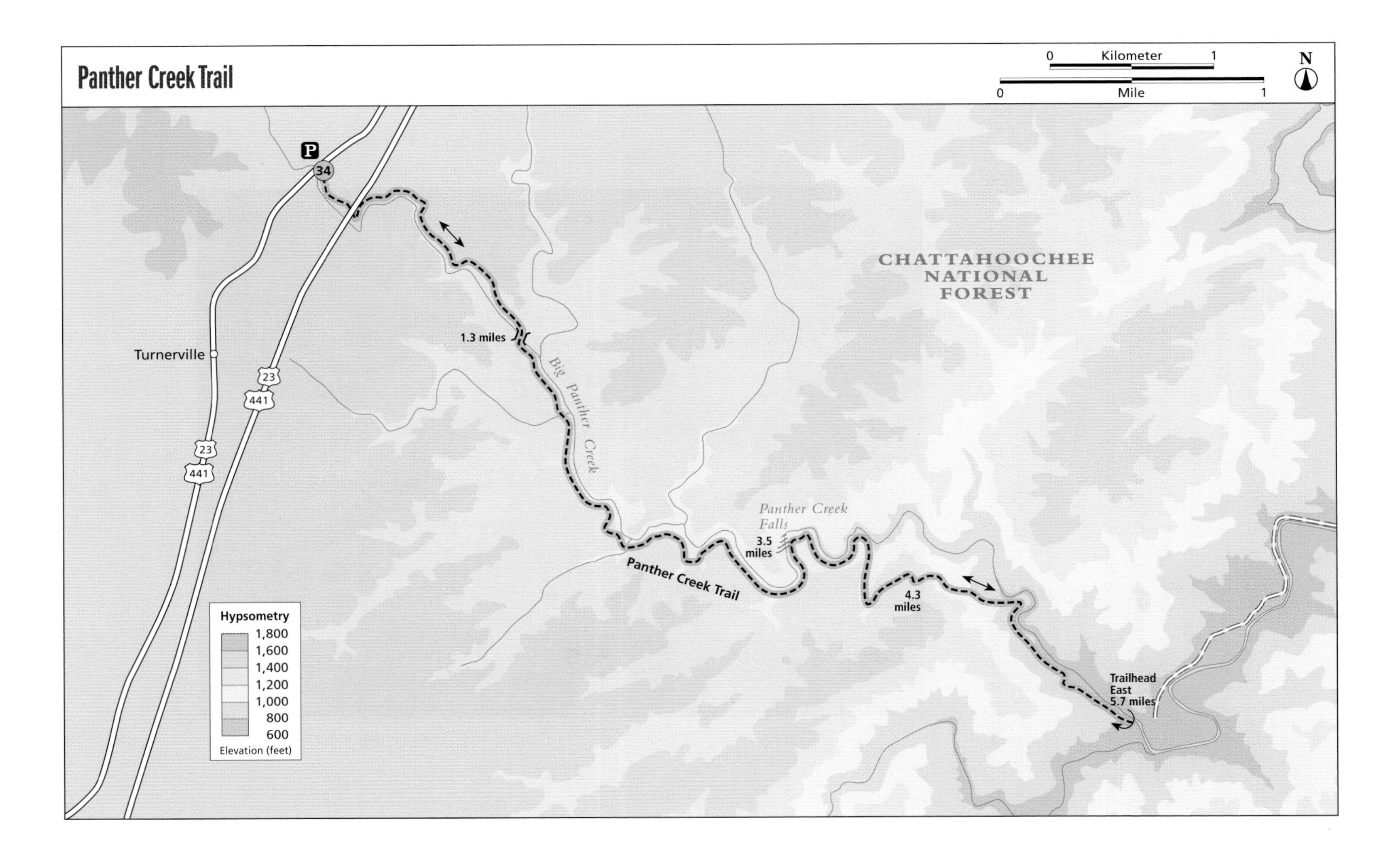

Panther Creek Trail
0
Kilometer
1
0
Mile
1
N
P
34
Turnerville
23
441
23
441
1.3 miles
Big Panther Creek
CHATTAHOOCHEE
NATIONAL
FOREST
Panther Creek
Falls
3.5
miles
Panther Creek Trail
4.3
miles
Trailhead
East
5.7 miles
Hypsometry
1,800
1,600
1,400
1,200
1,000
800
600
Elevation (feet)

Options

Due to the length and rugged terrain on the Panther Creek Trail, an out-and-back day hike only is practical for extremely fit and energetic trekkers. Fortunately, there is an alternative trailhead at the eastern end of the path, where a shuttle vehicle can be parked. To reach that site, take SR 184 (Prather Bridge Road) for 5.1 miles east from Toccoa. At this point SR 184 turns to the right. Continue straight onto Yonah Dam Road for 4.4 miles to the junction with Panther Creek Road. The intersection is 0.6 mile past the bridge over Panther Creek. Panther Creek Road is on the left but is marked only with a small sign with the word CHURCH on it. Follow Panther Creek Road past Old Union Baptist Church on the right; the parking area and alternate trailhead is at the end of the road. Alternate trailhead GPS: N34 40.035' / W83 21.854'

The trail makes a sharp left turn around the end of the second outcrop after going under the rock shelter.

35 Lake Russell State Wildlife Management Area Trail

The Broad River Trail follows beautiful, cascading Dicks Creek and Middle Fork of the Broad River as they flow through the Lake Russell State Wildlife Management Area (WMA). The path was originally laid out in 1939 by the Depression-era Resettlement Administration. It was refurbished to its present form by the Youth Conservation Corps in 1980.

Today the trail and the unpaved roads in the WMA are quiet places to walk, and they offer good opportunities to see wildlife.

This trail can be hiked in either direction, but it is easier to walk down from Dicks Creek rather than up from the parking area in Farmers Bottom.

Start: At the Dicks Creek Trailhead, on the west side of the road, 120 yards from the FS 87 bridge over the creek
Distance: 4.0 miles one way
Hiking time: About 2 hours
Difficulty: Easy to moderate
Trail surface: Compacted loamy dirt
Best season: Mar–June; Oct–Dec
Other trail users: Hunters in season
Canine compatibility: Leashed dogs permitted
Land status: Chattahoochee National Forest
Nearest town: Cornelia
Fees and permits: None
Schedule: Open year-round
Maps: USGS Ayersville; Chattahoochee National Forest map
Trail contacts: USDA Forest Service, Chattooga Ranger District, 9975 US 441 South, Lakemont 30552; (706) 754-6221; www.fs.usda.gov/conf

Georgia Wildlife Resources Division, Game Management, 2150 Dawsonville Hwy., Gainesville 30501; (770) 535-5700; for hunting seasons: www.gohuntgeorgia.com

Special considerations: The Ayersville USGS quadrangle map does not list the forest service roads. On that map, FS 87 is identified as Sellers Road. The wildlife management area map and the sign at the intersection with Ayersville Road identify it as Guard Camp Road.

Finding the trailhead: From Cornelia take Wyley Street east from the junction with SR 105 (South Main Street). This road becomes Dicks Hill Parkway. At 12.8 miles, turn right onto Ayersville Road. Go 1.8 miles to the intersection with FS 87 and turn left. There is a check station sign at this junction. Continue 0.6 mile to pass the check station. At 2.1 miles reach the bridge over Dicks Creek. The trailhead is on the right, just past the bridge. Trailhead GPS: N34 31.726' / W83 25.232'

The Hike

After dropping down from the roadbed, the path begins with a lime-green plastic blaze and a wooden sign with trail information. The rest of the trail has infrequent blazes but is easily followed.

Throughout the hike a wide variety of spring wildflowers are present before the leaves are on the trees. Closer to Dicks Creek you can hear cascading water more

Much of the Broad River Trail weaves along the hillsides overlooking the water of the West Fork of the Broad River.

often than seeing it. The vegetation is typical of stream banks, with mountain laurel and dog-hobble thickets.

The pathway at first skirts the hillsides south of Dicks Creek. In the first 0.5 mile, the path crosses two footbridges over small tributaries of the main stream. It then goes through a flat area shaded by white pines, hemlocks, and yellow poplars before reaching an overlook above a set of shoals on the creek.

At the junction of Dicks Creek with the Middle Fork, the trail turns south. For the rest of the trek, until reaching Farmers Bottom, the path stays on the hill slope to the south or east of the river. The trail constantly changes elevations as it passes over one small ridge after another that run down toward the water.

Three wooden footbridges cross wet areas along this route. You also pass two rock shelters that are very close together and a third one farther into the hike.

At 3.7 miles you reach the trickiest point on the trail. The path turns sharply to the left uphill through what appears to be a washout or drainage ditch. After about 50 feet the trail turns back to the right, onto a normal path. These turns are not well marked.

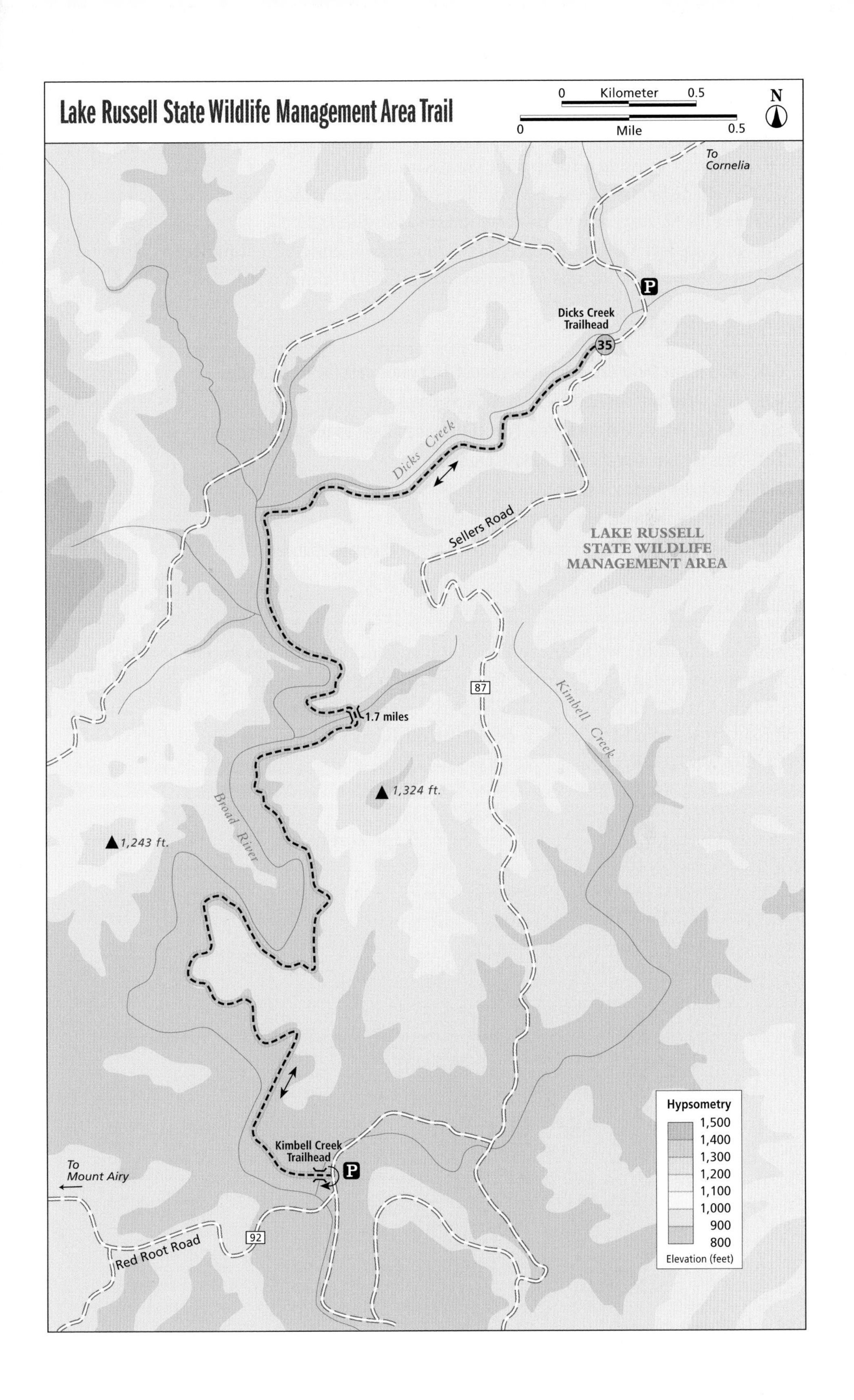
Lake Russell State Wildlife Management Area Trail
0
Kilometer
0.5
0
Mile
0.5
N
To
Cornelia
P
Dicks Creek
Trailhead
35
Dicks Creek
Sellers Road
LAKE RUSSELL
STATE WILDLIFE
MANAGEMENT AREA
87
Kimbell Creek
1.7 miles
1,324 ft.
Broad River
1,243 ft.
Kimbell Creek
Trailhead
P
To
Mount Airy
92
Red Root Road
Hypsometry
1,500
1,400
1,300
1,200
1,100
1,000
900
800
Elevation (feet)

As you drop down into the flatter area along the river at Farmers Bottom, an unusual number of American holly trees are present along the path. The trail ends at FS 87, just after crossing a footbridge over Kimbell Creek.

The vehicle bridge across the Middle Fork and the parking area at the junction of FS 87 and FS 92 are a few yards down the road to the right.

If you have left a shuttle vehicle here, your hike is ended. To complete a 7.0-mile loop back to the parking area at Dicks Creek, walk 3.0 miles north (left) on FS 87.

Miles and Directions

0.0 Start at the Dicks Creek Trailhead, about 100 yards past the FS 87 bridge.

0.8 Reach the overlook at the shoals on Dicks Creek.

1.1 Get the first view of the Middle Fork of the Broad River as the trail turns south.

1.8 Pass the two rock shelters in close proximity.

2.9 Reach the third rock shelter.

3.7 Negotiate the tricky turn uphill in the washout.

4.0 Cross the Kimbell Creek bridge and arrive at the alternate trailhead.

Options

A shuttle vehicle for walking the Broad River Trail one way can be left at an alternate trailhead in Farmers Bottom. To get to the trailhead continue 3.0 miles on past the Dicks Creek bridge on FS 87. The parking area is located beside a bridge where the road crosses the Middle Fork of the Broad River. Alternate trailhead GPS: N34 30.076' / W83 25.903'

36 Black Rock Mountain State Park Trails

At 3,640 feet, Black Rock Mountain is the highest state park in Georgia. Located in the northeast corner of the state, the park's 1,502 acres lie along the ridgeline of the Eastern Continental Divide, 2,700 feet above the valley at Clayton. Many scenic overlooks provide views of the surrounding southern Appalachian Mountains.

The park offers a variety of activities for visitors, including wildflower programs, nature walks, and overnight backpacking trips.

The park has a total of five main trails, but three of those are quite short. Together they provide a variety of mountain environments and unusual plant diversity. The James E. Edmonds Backcountry Trail is the featured hike. Rounding out the hiking opportunities are the Tennessee Rock, Ada-Hi Falls, Norma Campbell Cove, and Black Rock Lake Trails, plus a couple of connector paths. In all, the park contains just shy of 11.5 miles of trails.

Start: At the day-use area near the springhouse on Black Rock Road
Distance: 7.0-mile lollipop
Hiking time: About 4 hours
Difficulty: Moderate to strenuous
Trail surface: Dirt and firm loam
Best Season: Mar–June; Oct–Nov
Other trail users: Foot travel only
Canine compatibility: Leashed dogs permitted
Land status: Georgia DNR; State Parks & Historic Sites Division
Nearest towns: Mountain City, Clayton
Fees and permits: Daily parking fee
Schedule: State park and trails open Mar 16–Nov 30, 7 a.m.–10 p.m. daily
Maps: USGS Dillard; detailed page-size map available from visitor center
Trail contacts: Black Rock Mountain State Park, Mountain City 30562; (706) 746-2141; www.gastateparks.org

Finding the trailhead: From Clayton go north 3 miles on US 441 to Mountain City. Turn left (west) onto Black Rock Mountain Parkway and go 2.5 miles into the park. The trailhead for the James E. Edmonds Backcountry Trails is at the graveled day-use parking and picnic area on the main access road near the large free-flowing spring and springhouse. Trailhead GPS: N34 54.441' / W83 24.724'

The Hike

The James E. Edmonds Backcountry Trail was named to honor one of Black Rock Mountain State Park's first rangers. The path shares a trailhead with the Tennessee Rock Trail and is marked with orange blazes.

From the point it splits off to the right from the Tennessee Rock Trail, the path begins down a gradual descent that is moderately steep in some places until it reaches a fork. The right fork takes you in a counterclockwise direction around a loop.

The overlook on Lookoff Mountain offers a panoramic view of the valley of the Little Tennessee River.

As the trail breaks out of evergreen rhododendrons into hardwood coves, you can look down on Black Rock Lake through the trees. Great patches of galax grow all along the trail. Galax sometimes emits an odor resembling the scent of skunk. Other spring wildflowers are abundant all along the trail. You cross a tributary of Greasy Creek in another of the frequent rhododendron thickets that are beautiful when in bloom.

Following along an old roadbed, the path comes out in a gap and crosses North Germany Road that runs from Mountain City to Germany Valley. Crossing the road into another rhododendron tunnel, the trail alternates from open hardwoods to streamside rhododendron. The path now crosses a bridge spanning a tributary stream with another view of the lake; the trail then begins to follow Taylor Creek upstream. The trail crosses this creek on a footbridge and bends back, climbing to gravel Taylor Chapel Road that runs past Black Rock Lake.

Across the road the path begins the long, steady 600-foot climb up to the north shoulder of Scrugg Knob, and then along the watershed divide down to Scrugg Gap. It then goes along an old roadbed on the west flank of Marsen Knob into Gibson Gap.

At the trail junction in the gap, turn right to begin the climb up Lookoff Mountain. Stay to the right at 0.2 mile as the trail splits to form a loop on top of the peak. The trail then goes to the granite outcrop that gives the mountain its name. The view from here is spectacular. A cable fence with stone-masonry pillars protects the edge of the sheer drop. The north-by-northwest view looks down more than 1,000 feet to the headwater valley of the Little Tennessee River and the attractive farms on its floodplain.

Complete the loop through a primitive camping area (free permits from the park office are required for backcountry camping) and then return to Gibson Gap. Turn right at the trail junction and drop back down to recross Taylor Chapel Road and Taylor Creek on a footbridge.

The trail next skirts the south side of Black Rock Lake, crossing a footbridge over a small feeder brook and a second bridge over Greasy Creek. Greasy Creek is a small, very pretty mountain stream that literally slides down the mountain over the exposed granite that is covered in places with algae. The algae gives the stream a slick appearance, hence the name.

Just past the bridge the stream tumbles down a 20-foot waterfall. Just beyond, the side trail on the right leads to the Creek Ridge Campsite No. 4.

Continue uphill on the main trail following Greasy Creek until you reach a final bridge over the stream. Immediately the path climbs up to cross North Germany Road again. The next 0.3 mile climbs about 700 feet and crosses one more feeder stream bridge before closing the loop. Turn right to head back to the trailhead.

Miles and Directions

0.0 Start at the common trailhead with the Tennessee Rock Trail.

0.7 Meet the fork in the trail that starts the loop. Go right.

0.8 Cross a small tributary of Greasy Creek.

1.4 Cross North Germany Road.

1.9 Reach a bridge over a feeder stream with a view to the left toward Black Rock Lake.

2.3 Cross Taylor Creek and Taylor Chapel Road.

2.8 Pass on the north side of Scrugg Knob and continue on a ridge to Scrugg Gap.

3.1 Reach Scrugg Gap and begin walking north on an old logging road.

3.3 On the west side of Marsen Knob, come to the spur path leading to Lookoff Mountain.

3.5 Begin the loop to the granite outcrop edge of the mountain.

3.7 Reach the "lookoff" at about 3,100 feet elevation.

3.9 Complete the Lookoff Mountain loop and backtrack to the main trail. Turn right, heading down to Black Rock Lake.

5.1 Cross Taylor Chapel Road and Taylor Creek again.

5.4 Cross a small feeder stream of Greasy Creek and begin to regain all the elevation lost from the trailhead.

5.5 Reach a footbridge over Greasy Creak.

5.6 Pass the waterfall on the left and campsite trail junction on the right.

5.9 Recross Greasy Creek on a footbridge.

6.0 Cross North Germany Road.

6.2 Reach a footbridge across a small feeder stream.

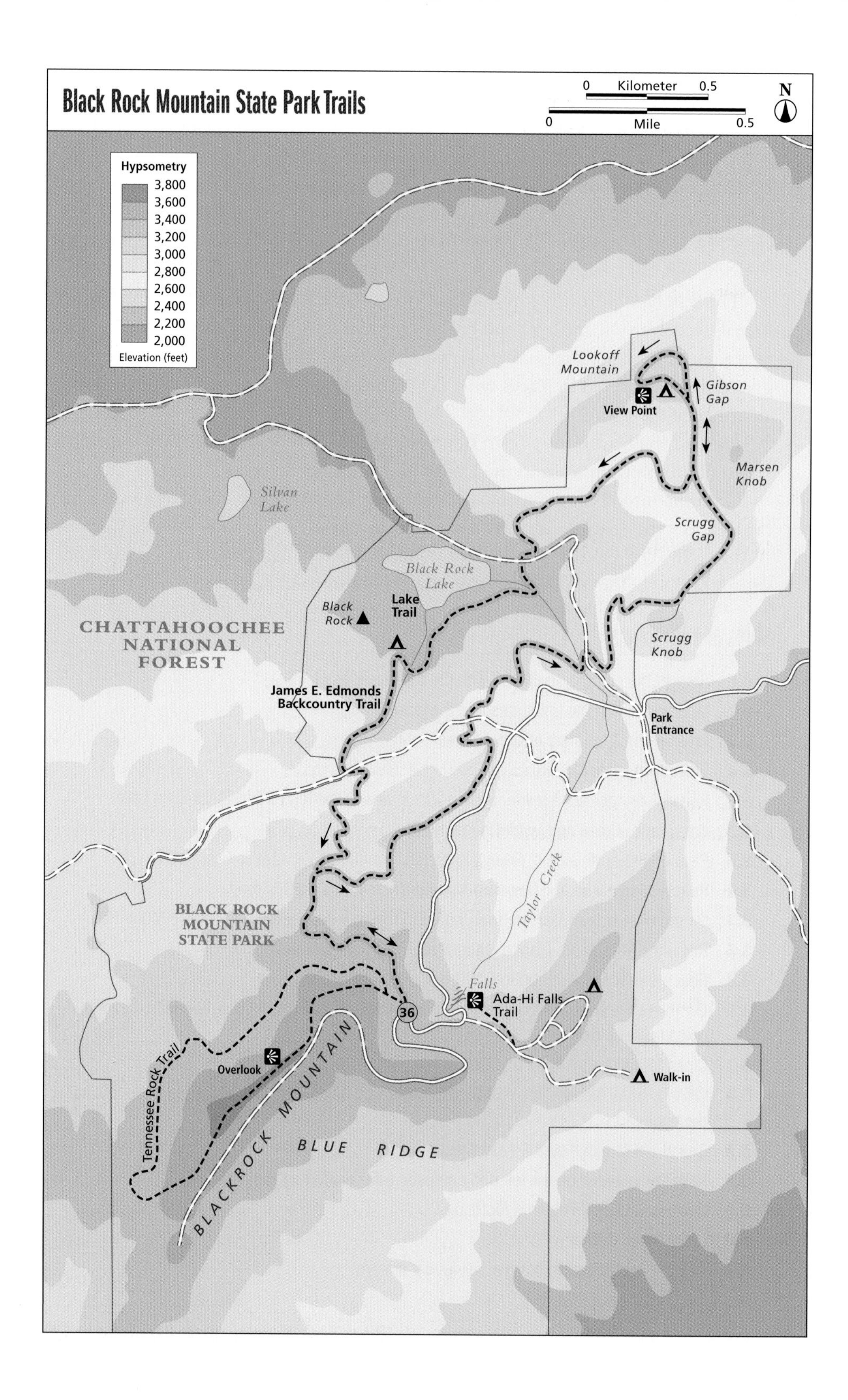
Black Rock Mountain State Park Trails
0 Kilometer 0.5
0 Mile 0.5
N
Hypsometry
3,800
3,600
3,400
3,200
3,000
2,800
2,600
2,400
2,200
2,000
Elevation (feet)
Lookoff Mountain
View Point
Gibson Gap
Marsen Knob
Scrugg Gap
Silvan Lake
Black Rock Lake
Black Rock
Lake Trail
CHATTAHOOCHEE NATIONAL FOREST
James E. Edmonds Backcountry Trail
Scrugg Knob
Park Entrance
Taylor Creek
BLACK ROCK MOUNTAIN STATE PARK
Falls
Ada-Hi Falls Trail
36
Tennessee Rock Trail
Overlook
Walk-in
BLACKROCK MOUNTAIN
BLUE RIDGE

6.3 Close the loop and turn right.

7.0 Arrive back at the trailhead.

Options

The yellow-blazed **Tennessee Rock Trail** loops along a north-facing mountain slope that supports a wide variety of wildflowers and breaks out on top of Black Rock Mountain at an elevation of 3,280 feet, following the Eastern Continental Divide.

This trail is designed as a self-guided nature trail. The booklet *An Interpretive Guide to the Tennessee Rock Trail* is available at the park office for a nominal fee. It explains conditions and species at the twenty-five stations along the way.

At the high point of the trail an engraved granite slab marks the peak of Black Rock Mountain. On clear days the nearby Tennessee Rock Overlook offers a panoramic view all the way to North Carolina's Great Smoky Mountains.

The **Ada-Hi Falls Trail** is a very short, very strenuous 0.5-mile round-trip walk into a north-slope Appalachian cove. The trail drops 220 feet on a series of steps down to an observation deck that provides a good view of the falls. The stream cascades and slides down about 80 feet of sheer granite. The Ada-Hi Falls Trailhead is at the concession and trading post area near the campground. Due to the climb back out of the cove, allot an hour to enjoy this walk.

A waterfall drops 20 feet over the rocks on Greasy Creek on the James E. Edmonds Backcountry Trail.

The **Norma Campbell Cove Trail** is rated as moderate to difficult, though it is only 0.1 mile long. Named for the late Norma Campbell, a popular park naturalist, the path runs down the southern edge of the Eastern Continental Divide to the headwater springs of Stekoa Creek. Beginning at the trailhead at the park trading post, this walk takes about half an hour.

The **Black Rock Lake Trail** is a 0.85-mile walk around the 17-acre lake. Rated easy, the path circles the pond, crossing bridges over Greasy and Taylor Creeks as well as an 80-foot span across Cricket Cove at the southwest corner. This hike takes about half an hour from its trailhead on Taylor Chapel Road on the north side of the lake.

37 Tallulah Gorge State Park Trails

Tallulah Gorge State Park is a bit of a hybrid facility, containing not only the park but also a wildlife management area (WMA). The site was developed under a lease agreement between the Georgia Power Company and the Department of Natural Resources.

The word *Tallulah* has its origin in the Cherokee language but cannot be translated. The gorge is described as one of the oldest natural geologic features on the North American continent.

The Tallulah Gorge area has a long history as a scenic area and summer resort, beginning in the mid-1880s. The park's Jane Hurt Yarn Interpretive Center exhibits the rich history of the nearby Victorian town of Tallulah Falls, along with the rugged terrain and fragile ecosystem of the area.

There are more than 20 miles of pathways in the park, composed of nine hiking and biking trails, plus several short connectors.

The Stoneplace Trail is the longest at 10 miles as it winds through the WMA property above the gorge and down to a boat landing on Tugaloo Lake. High Bluff Trail is 1.4 miles long, forming a loop off the Stoneplace Trail. If walked as a complete loop from the interpretive center, High Bluff covers 2.6 miles.

These two trails are combined with portions of the Hurricane Falls, Inspiration Loop, and North Rim Trails to form the featured 10.5-mile hike. Walked together, these provide a sample of all the scenic and habitat features offered by the park.

Start: At Jane Hurt Yarn Interpretive Center parking area
Distance: 10.5 miles out and back
Hiking time: About 6–7 hours
Difficulty: Moderate to strenuous
Trail surface: Shredded auto-tire composition, asphalt paved, rocks, and dirt
Best seasons: Mar–June; Oct–Dec
Other trail users: Mountain bikers; hunters in season
Canine compatibility: Leashed dogs permitted on gorge rim trails; dogs not permitted on gorge floor trails
Land status: Georgia DNR, State Parks & Historic Sites Division
Nearest towns: Clayton, Clarkesville
Fees and permits: Daily parking fee; free permits required for hiking Stoneplace, High Bluff, Inspiration Loop, and gorge floor trails
Schedule: Park hours 8 a.m. to dark; interpretive center open 8 a.m.–5 p.m.
Maps: USGS Tallulah Falls and Tugaloo Lake; page-size maps of trails available at the Jane Hurt Yarn Interpretive Center
Trail contacts: Tallulah Gorge State Park, PO Box 248, Tallulah Falls 30573; (706) 754-7970; www.gastateparks.org

Finding the trailhead: From Clayton go 12 miles south on US 441 to the Tallulah Gorge State Park sign. Turn left on Jane Hurt Yarn Drive and go 0.8 mile to the Jane Hurt Yarn Interpretive Center. The trailhead for the High Bluff–Stoneplace combination hike is at the center's front entrance. Trailhead GPS: N34 44.386' / W83 23.455'

The view into the gorge from Overlook No. 3 toward L'Eau d'Or and Tempesta Falls

The Hike

Begin the hike at the front door of the Jane Hurt Yarn Interpretive Center. Upon entering you are on the top floor. At the desk, pick up the free permit that is required for the Inspiration Loop, High Bluff, and Stoneplace Trails, and then descend the ramps to the first floor. Exhibits along the ramps describe how the geology, flora, and fauna change as one climbs down into Tallulah Gorge.

Exiting the back door, walk across the patio and take the stone pathway down to the junction with the blue-blazed North Rim Trail. This pathway is paved with a recycled-rubber surface. Turn right and walk 80 yards to Overlook No. 3, which provides a view of L'Eau d'Or (pronounced La-DORE) Falls below in the gorge. From this point, follow the Hurricane Falls Trail for 60 yards to Overlook No. 2 and an equally spectacular panorama of L'Eau d'Or and the top of Tempesta Falls.

Retracing your steps back past the interpretive center, walk east on the North Rim Trail as it skirts the gorge. You pass the junction where the white-blazed Inspiration Loop Trail enters on the left and then reach a set of forty-five step landings that take you down to a bridge over a small brook.

This path along the canyon rim is shaded by white and chestnut oaks, maples, and Virginia pines, with dogwoods and sassafras common along the trail.

The North Rim Trail then takes you to Overlook No. 1, where the North Wallenda Tower is lying on its side. This structure held the northern end of the high wire on which aerialist Karl Wallenda walked across the gorge on July 18, 1970. Along the way, he stopped to do two headstands on the cable!

Continuing east the path is now on the Inspiration Loop Trail. Follow the white blazes on this path 0.2 mile farther, gaining 200 feet of elevation to reach Inspiration Point. A bench on the overlook provides an awesome view of the lower gorge area. At the trail junction just beyond the point, turn right onto the blue-blazed High Bluff Trail.

This trail goes through a shaded, moist cove with rhododendron, galax, and spring flowers along with white oak, yellow poplar, dogwood, black gum, and maple trees.

When you hike under a high power line, look to the southwest for a view of the electric-generation plant on the opposite side of the gorge.

The trail follows a more exposed, western slope, where bracken ferns grow, as it crosses a dry ridge to the moister cove areas with rhododendron, yellow poplar, hemlock, and white pine. The low vegetation includes galax, partridgeberry, and ferns.

After a trek of 1.4 miles, the High Bluff Trail intersects the yellow-blazed Stoneplace Trail. Turn right and follow the Stoneplace Trail along an old, rutted roadbed. This pathway is open to both hiking and mountain biking. The surface of the trail is sandy clay.

The surrounding forest is more open through here. Yellow poplars, pines, sourwoods, and oaks are present in the canopy, while grapevines, high-bush huckleberries, and an abundance of seedling sourwood trees line the trail. In spring there are many flowering plants in bloom, especially in the coves where the hillside is steep above and below the trail.

The Stoneplace Trail descends almost 800 feet in the next 3.5 miles. Just prior to reaching the turnaround point at Tugaloo Lake, you pass the Adirondack shelter of Backcountry Campsite No. 3 on the right. Overnight camping reservations for the shelters along the trail are available by calling (800) 864-7275. Backcountry campers must arrive before 3 p.m. to register and complete a required permit before hiking to the sites.

The trail ends at a gate and the gravel four-wheel-drive road leading to a boat landing. Walk 120 yards downhill to the right on the road to reach the Henry Ezzard Memorial Boat Ramp on the Chattooga River arm of Tugaloo Lake.

After a break, retrace your hike back up to the junction with High Bluff Trail. Stay to the right at this intersection. The Inspiration Loop and Stoneplace Trails are now sharing the path. At 0.1 mile farther, a gate and sign-in board are at the edge of the Northern WMA. A boulder field stretches uphill to the right of the gate.

Another 0.5 mile brings you to the junction where the Stoneplace Trail continues to the right to its trailhead at the interpretive center parking lot. Turn left here to follow the combined Inspiration Loop and High Bluff Trails back toward the gorge. This path quickly passes Backcountry Campsites No. 2 and 3 on the right.

When the High Bluff Trail splits off to the left, go to the right to follow the Inspiration Loop back toward the interpretive center. As you reach that building, a trail enters from the right. Climb the thirty steps up to the parking lot and reach the trailhead at the center's front door.

Miles and Directions

0.0 Start at the interpretive center's front entrance, passing through the building's lobby exhibit hall.

0.1 Turn right onto the North Rim Trail and reach Overlook No. 3 with a view of L'Eau d'Or Falls and Hawthorne Pool.

0.2 Overlook No. 3 provides a view of L'Eau d'Or Falls, Hawthorne Pool, and the top of Tempesta Falls.

0.4 Descend the forty-five step landings and cross the footbridge.

0.5 Pass the North Wallenda Tower at Overlook No. 1 and the view of Oceana Falls.

0.8 Reach Inspiration Point.

0.9 Turn right onto the blue-blazed High Bluff Trail.

2.0 Cross under the power line with a view of the power station.

2.3 Turn right onto the yellow-blazed Stoneplace Trail.

4.8 Pass Backcountry Campsite No. 1 on the right.

5.7 Turn right on the gravel road.

5.8 Reach the Henry Ezzard Memorial Boat Ramp on Tugaloo Lake; retrace your path back uphill on the Stoneplace Trail.

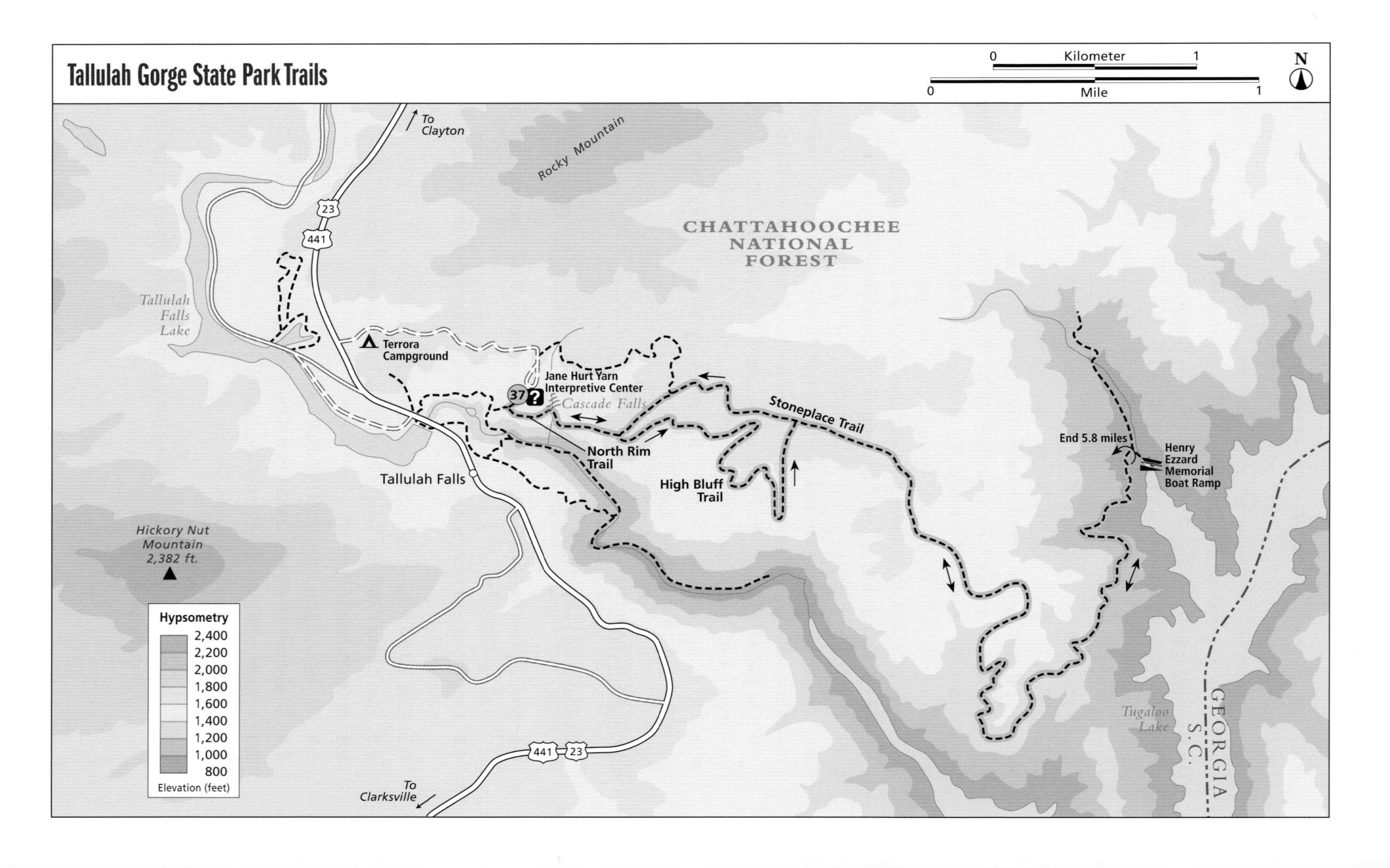
Tallulah Gorge State Park Trails
0
Kilometer
1
0
Mile
1
N
To Clayton
Rocky Mountain
23
441
CHATTAHOOCHEE NATIONAL FOREST
Tallulah Falls Lake
Terrora Campground
Jane Hurt Yarn Interpretive Center
37
Cascade Falls
Stoneplace Trail
North Rim Trail
High Bluff Trail
Tallulah Falls
End 5.8 miles
Henry Ezzard Memorial Boat Ramp
Hickory Nut Mountain 2,382 ft.
Hypsometry
2,400
2,200
2,000
1,800
1,600
1,400
1,200
1,000
800
Elevation (feet)
441
23
To Clarksville
Tugaloo Lake
GEORGIA
S.C.

9.2 At the junction with the High Bluff Trail, follow the yellow blazes of the Stoneplace Trail to the right.

9.4 Pass the gate, sign, and boulder field at the boundary of the WMA.

9.9 Turn left onto the High Bluff Trail and pass Backcountry Campsites No. 2 and 3.

10.0 Follow the white blazes of the Inspiration Loop to the right.

10.3 Turn right up the 30 steps to the interpretive center.

10.5 Arrive back at the trailhead.

Options

The **North Rim and South Rim Trails** combine for a moderate 3.0-mile out-and-back hike that takes about 2 hours. Following the gorge escarpment, these offer the best views of the chasm from eleven overlooks.

Hurricane Falls Trail Loop is rated as a difficult 2.0-mile hike as it drops down and climbs back up from a 600-foot suspension bridge that is 80 feet about the river. There's also a connector path to the gorge floor. You descend and climb a total of 1,099 steps on this hike. No permit is required for this trail.

The **Gorge Floor Trail** is a very difficult 3.0-mile out-and-back trek over rocks and boulders to the bottom of the gorge. This trail requires a free gorge floor permit. Only one hundred gorge floor permits are issued per day.

Sliding Rock Trail offers only a 0.5-mile out-and-back hike, but it descends and climbs back up more than 500 feet at a 45-degree angle over boulders. Rated as very difficult, it requires a free gorge floor permit. At the gorge floor you reach Bridal Veil Falls, where swimming is permitted.

The **Inspiration Loop** covers 1.5 miles as it passes Inspiration Point and circles around the interpretive center. Mostly on an old, rutted roadbed, it is open to mountain biking and requires a free permit.

The **Shortline Trail** is a 3.0-mile out-and-back paved hiking and biking trail that follows the old roadbed of the Tallulah Falls Railroad. Rated as easy, this path is located on the west side of US 441, across from the main park. It is accessed from Terrora Circle Road.

38 Chattooga National Wild and Scenic River Trail

The Chattooga Wild and Scenic River lives up to its name as a great rafting and kayaking stream, but there is so much more to enjoy in the river corridor, including good primitive campsites and excellent trout fishing. Originating in North Carolina's Nantahala National Forest, the river flows through the Ellicott Wilderness Area and ends in Tugaloo Lake, 50 miles downstream and 2,000 feet lower in elevation.

The area supports excellent wildflower displays in spring and summer. Wildlife includes wild turkeys, deer, raccoons, squirrels, and other small mammals. A variety of forest types—from old forest habitat to second-growth hardwoods and evergreens—make this a fine birding area.

There are more than 50 miles of trails in the Chattooga National Wild and Scenic River corridor in Georgia and North and South Carolina. This hike covers only the Georgia section of the Chattooga River Trail.

This path follows the Chattooga River, which forms the state boundary between Georgia and South Carolina.

Start: At the parking area at the US 76 bridge
Distance: The Georgia section of the trail is 16.8 miles one way.
Hiking time: About 2–3 days
Difficulty: Easy to moderate
Trail surface: Mostly sandy loam, with some wet areas
Best season: Mar–Dec
Other trail users: Anglers; hunters in season
Canine compatibility: Dogs permitted
Land status: Chattahoochee National Forest in Georgia; Sumter National Forest in South Carolina
Nearest town: Clayton, GA; Westminster, SC
Fees and permits: None
Maps: USGS Satolah, Whetstone, and Rainy Mountain; excellent large-scale detailed map of the Chattooga National Wild and Scenic River with trails available from the forest service
Trail contacts: USDA Forest Service, Chattooga River Ranger District, 9975 US 441 South, Lakemont 30552; (706) 754-6221; www.fs.usda.gov/conf

Finding the trailhead: The lower trailhead can be reached by driving 8.4 miles east from Clayton on US 76 to the Chattooga River. The parking area is on the left just as you enter South Carolina. Trailhead GPS: N34 48.882' / W83 18.309'

To access the upper trailhead go east from Clayton for 14.4 miles on Warwoman Road to SR 28. Turn right and go 2.2 miles to the parking area on the left just before reaching Russell Bridge. Trailhead GPS: N34 55.211' / W83 10.150'

The Hike

The hike begins at the lower trailhead at US 76. Once the trail reaches Sandy Ford, the pathway joins with the Bartram Trail for the final 8.1 miles to SR 28. The Bartram Trail is

The trail begins by descending stairs, before turning right and crossing a walkway over the Chattooga River.

marked throughout with a yellow paint blaze; the Chattooga River Trail is marked with a white metal diamond blaze. Where the trails travel together, both blaze marks are used.

This hike can be covered in two days but takes three days at a more leisurely pace. Since this trail is most often hiked in one direction only, it is necessary to arrange for transportation at the end, whether you walk from the north or south trailhead.

Water is available all along the trail; however, you should drink it only after careful boiling, filtering, or chemically purifying it. The streams are highly vulnerable to giardia and other bacteria causing intestinal diseases.

From the parking area, descend the stairway to US 76. Cross the river on the walkway attached to the highway bridge. Once on the Georgia side, turn north to walk upstream along the river, quickly crossing the first of a number of small streams.

This is a good example of regenerated forest. Because the river was used to float logs to points to be transferred to land travel, the Chattooga River corridor forest was intensely cut during the late 1800s to early 1900s. There has been a remarkable recovery of the mixed-hardwood stands since it became a national forest. Today you are able to see a wide variety of trees and other plants on this hike, including great yellow poplars as straight as flagpoles, hemlocks, the deciduous Fraser magnolia, bigleaf magnolia, hickories, oaks, maples, green and white ash, buckeyes, basswood, and Carolina silver bells. The coves away from the river are resplendent with many spring flowers that bloom before the leaves are on the trees.

When the trail is close to the river, you have great views of this renowned world-class rafting, kayaking, and canoeing river. This is especially true with your first good view of the river at the Class IV rapids of Paint Rock.

After that shoal, you leave the river for a while until you are again looking through the trees at the constricted river for about a mile. Then, after turning with the river, you are looking down at the Class III Eye of the Needle rapids.

Crossing Rock Creek, you are at the first road, the unpaved gravel track of Sandy Ford Road. Sandy Ford is popular because of the view of the river and because the width of the river and shallow water make it great for wade fishing.

Coming back to the road, the Bartram Trail joins from the left. The two trails travel together until they cross into South Carolina at Russell Bridge on SR 28.

Sandy Ford is an excellent primitive camping area. Stop here; take the time to walk the 100 or so yards down to the river and enjoy the view of 60-foot Dicks Creek Falls and the grand vista of the Chattooga. A submerged band of rocks across the river called Dicks Creek Ledge creates a Class IV rapid, as well as a great place to wade fish for the stream's native Bartram's bass, sunfish, or even rainbow or brown trout that have strayed downriver. There is a smooth sandy shore here. During summer, the river loses some of its trout water coolness and is warm enough for swimming and wading.

A large, round river stone at this junction of the Bartram and Chattooga River Trails is engraved with direction arrows for both trails. The joint trail now continues upstream with and crosses Sandy Ford Road.

When the path reaches Warwoman Creek, it follows the stream's meandering course around to Earls Ford Road and the bridge over the creek. This next section to Laurel Branch goes into one cove and over one ridge after another and is an outstanding wildflower path.

After crossing Laurel Branch and then Bynum Branch, you should see several paths off to the left. Keep a sharp eye out for the yellow and white blazes so you stay on the main trail.

Very shortly you cross Adline Branch and walk beside Long Bottom, the only large, flat area that was suitable for farming along the river. This area was in agriculture until the federal river corridor was established. It is a pine plantation now.

After crossing Holden Branch, the trail next reaches the West Fork of the Chattooga River and the bridge across it.

Once across, turn back downstream along the West Fork. At SR 28, climb up the roadway embankment and cross the highway to the parking area.

Miles and Directions

0.0 Start by descending the stairway from the parking area down to US 76 and then across the river on the walkway attached to the highway bridge.

0.1 At the west end of the bridge, follow the path running upriver to the right.

0.7 Cross Pole Creek and turn right, going in and out of hardwood coves.

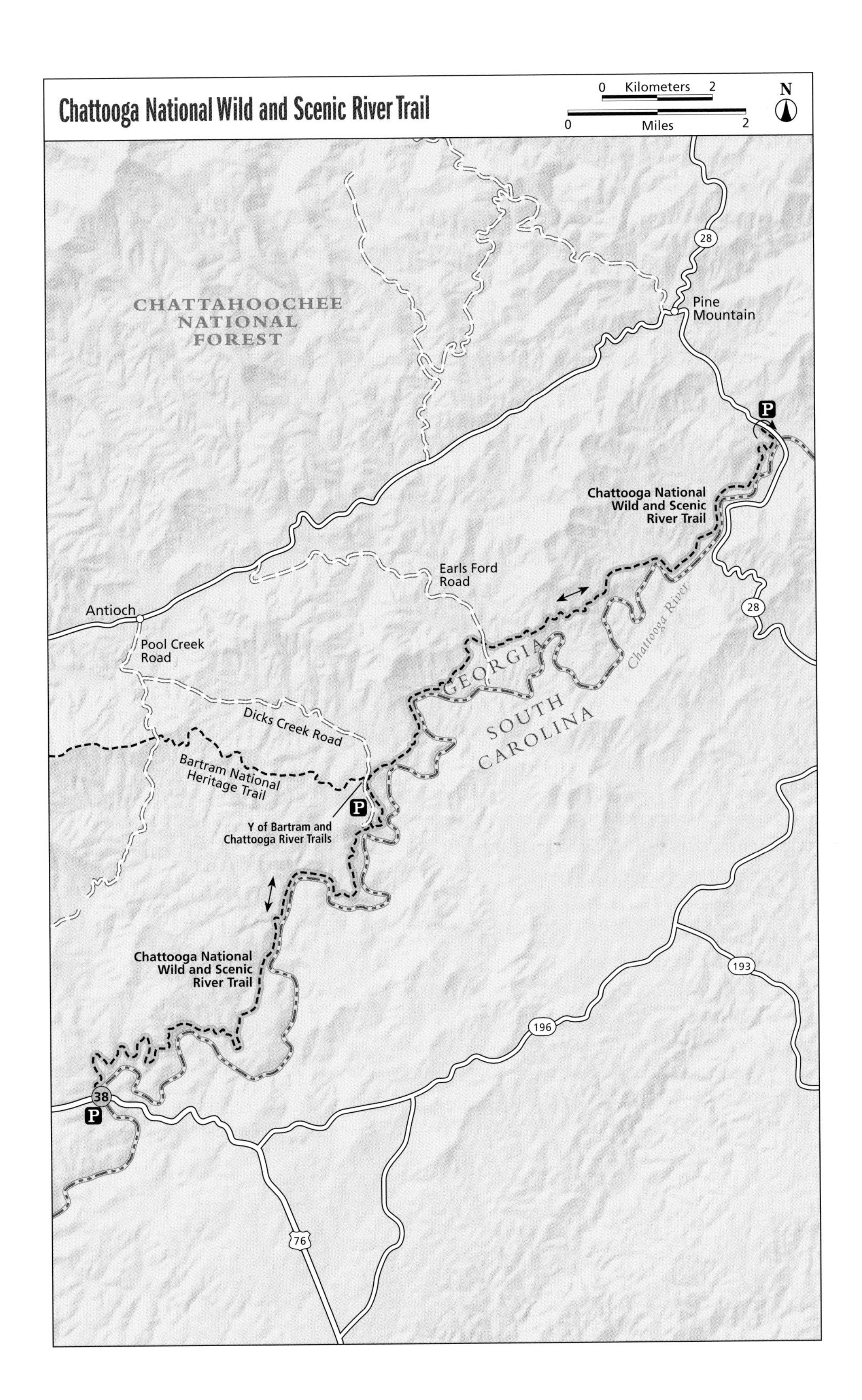
Chattooga National Wild and Scenic River Trail
0 Kilometers 2
0 Miles 2
N
CHATTAHOOCHEE NATIONAL FOREST
28
Pine Mountain
P
Chattooga National Wild and Scenic River Trail
Earls Ford Road
Chattooga River
28
Antioch
Pool Creek Road
GEORGIA
SOUTH CAROLINA
Dicks Creek Road
Bartram National Heritage Trail
P
Y of Bartram and Chattooga River Trails
Chattooga National Wild and Scenic River Trail
193
196
38
P
76

1.1 Cross the next small tributary and go through more coves and ridge points.

3.0 Come down closer to the river under a steep slope for a view of Paint Rock's Class IV rapids; the path then leaves the river.

3.4 Cross a small brook.

3.5 Cross another brook, now hiking in a southern direction.

3.7 Turn left and go north along this same stream, leaving the river that now flows in a steep-sided valley.

4.9 The trail comes back to the river, but up a steep slope; the Chattooga is visible through the trees.

5.4 Cross Licklog Creek on a bridge only about 150 yards from the river.

6.1 Turn right after crossing Buckeye Branch, walking close to the river with a steep, south-facing slope on the left.

6.6 Go up a steep slope and away from the river.

6.9 A path turns off to the right down to a sharp bend in the river, a popular place to fish or swim. You stay about 250 feet above the river.

7.7 Come back to an overlook close to the river and move away again.

8.1 Cross Rock Creek and the end of Dicks Creek Road at Sandy Ford. (***Note:*** This is one of only two places on the Georgia side where you can drive to the river.)

8.6 Reach Dicks Creek Road.

8.7 The Bartram National Recreation Trail comes in from the left. The trail now has both yellow and white blazes.

9.4 The trail offers a level walk to Dicks Creek and a footbridge across the stream.

9.9 Return to the river under a steep bluff on the left as you follow around a bend with the river in sight.

10.3 Leave the river along an old jeep road, with Warwoman Creek on the right.

11.3 Arrive at Earls Ford and cross Earls Ford Road.

11.5 After traversing a low knoll, cross Warwoman Creek on a bridge.

13.0 Cross Laurel Branch on a bridge.

13.7 Cross Bynum Branch. There are several paths off the trail; keep your eyes on the white and yellow blazes.

14.0 Cross Adline Branch on a bridge as you turn with the river and walk on the ridge side of Long Bottom.

15.3 Cross Holden Branch and continue on up the river.

16.3 Cross the West Fork of the Chattooga, a major tributary of the main river on a bridge. The trail comes back down the West Fork before you reach SR 28.

16.8 Cross SR 28 to the parking area, the northern trailhead of Chattooga National Wild and Scenic River and the southern terminus of the Georgia section of the Bartram National Recreation Trail.

39 Bartram National Recreation Trail

William Bartram, for whom this trail is named, collected seeds and plants in northeast Georgia in the spring of 1776. He was traveling alone, after his Indian guide failed to return, on a trip across the Blue Ridge Mountains to the Overhill towns, where he visited the heart of the Cherokee Nation in Tennessee on the Little Tennessee River. That site is now covered by the waters of Tellico Lake.

Today very little of the actual path that Bartram followed is on public land. But the great expanse of the Chattahoochee National Forest has made it possible to preserve this 34.2-mile section of his travels. The trail continues into the Nantahala National Forest in North Carolina. The Bartram Trail was dedicated as a National Recreation Trail in 1978. This Georgia mountain section is a part of a much longer 115-mile path running through the Carolinas.

Virtually all the forests that Bartram saw have been logged over time and again in the nearly 240 years since he rode his horse through the mountains. Although the great cove hardwood forests of yesteryear are gone, the high ridges that separate the Tennessee River Valley from the Savannah River Valley, supporting only stunted oaks and rhododendron thickets, may still look much the same. With the recovery of the forests under management of the USDA Forest Service, it is easy to imagine the magnificence of the original southern Blue Ridge Mountains as you look out from the truncated tower on Rabun Bald or over the valleys down to Martin Creek toward Warwoman Dell.

A good preparatory step before hiking this trail is to read chapters three and four of Part III in *The Travels of William Bartram*. That gives you a feel for how the naturalist viewed this area in its pristine state.

Start: The northern terminus of the Georgia portion of the trail begins at the crossing on Hale Ridge Road (FS 7) in Rabun County, about 400 yards from the North Carolina border.
Distance: 34.2 miles one way
Hiking time: About a minimum of 3 days; 4 days would be more comfortable.
Difficulty: Moderate to strenuous in the northern section; moderate to easy the rest of the way
Trail surface: Dirt and forest loam, with some rocky stretches
Best season: Mar–Dec
Other trail users: Hunters in season; anglers along the Chattooga River
Canine compatibility: Dogs permitted
Land status: Chattahoochee National Forest
Nearest town: Clayton
Fees and permits: None
Maps: USGS Rabun Bald, Rainy Mountain, Whetstone, and Satolah; Chattahoochee National Forest map; page-size map available at the Chattooga River Ranger District office in Clayton
Trail contacts: USDA Forest Service, Chattooga River Ranger District, 9975 US 441 South, Lakemont 30552; (706) 754-6221; www.fs.usda.gov/conf
Bartram Trail Society; www.bartramtrail.org

Finding the trailhead: From Clayton go 6.5 miles north on US 441 to Dillard. Continue 0.8 mile to SR 246; turn right (east) to North Carolina, where the road becomes NC SR 106. Go 7 miles to Hale Ridge Road in the Scaly Mountain community. Go 2 miles to the forks, and stay on paved Hale Ridge Road. Where the pavement ends, continue to the Georgia state line. The north end of the Bartram Trail crosses Hale Ridge Road (FS 7), about 400 yards from the North Carolina line. Limited parking space is available at this crossing. Trailhead GPS: N34 59.738' / W83 16.909'

The southern end of the trail is at Russell Bridge on the Chattooga River. Take Warwoman Road east from Clayton for 14.4 miles. Turn right on SR 28 and follow it 2.2 miles to the parking area on the left, just before the road cross the Chattooga River into South Carolina. Trailhead GPS: N34 55.211' / W83 10.150'

The Hike

The Georgia section of this long trail goes through a variety of habitat types, from high mountain ridges to the banks of the Chattooga National Wild and Scenic River. The Bartram Trail enters Georgia from North Carolina near Commissioner's Rock and follows the ridge crest that forms the Tennessee Valley Divide down to Warwoman Dell. It crosses the second-highest mountain in the state, Rabun Bald, at 4,696 feet. From there it drops down to the Chattooga River and joins the Chattooga River Trail for 8.1 miles.

Begin the hike where the trail crosses Hale Ridge Road (FS 7), 0.2 mile west of Commissioner's Rock on the Chattooga River at the North Carolina state line. This trail is marked by a rectangular yellow-paint blaze. The elevation here is 3,280 feet, and the trail remains very near the same elevation to the crossing of Holcomb Creek before the climb to Beegum Gap and the top of Rabun Bald.

The last 1.5 miles of this climb are through a rhododendron thicket on a well-used rocky trail. The old forest service fire lookout was converted into a large observation deck by the Youth Conservation Corps. The 360-degree view from the stone-based deck offers a full, spectacular panorama of the many rounded knobs of these ancient mountains.

From Rabun Bald, the trail leads to the southwest, dropping rapidly to Flint Gap and to Saltrock Gap. Go to the east and south of 4,142-foot Flat Top. The trail drops quickly through a gap and up again to Wilson Knob and then, in more moderate ascents and descents, past Double Knob and Wilson Gap.

Here the trail intersects a four-wheel-drive road. The trail stays on the road for about 0.5 mile and turns to the left and down to Windy Gap. After going around the east of Raven Knob, the path reaches Courthouse Gap. For the next 3.5 miles, the trail turns to the southeast into the Martin Creek drainage. Through here the trail heads back into thick rhododendron tunnels. The sound of falling water leads you to Martin Creek Falls, which cascades about 50 feet beside the trail before turning back to the west and to Becky Branch. Next the trail crosses Warwoman Road and enters the Warwoman Dell Recreation Area.

The Bartram Trail passes through Warwoman Dell Picnic Area east of Clayton.

You now leave the higher mountains and meander over lower and gentler hills and dells to Sandy Ford Road at the Chattooga River at Sandy Ford. This is an area of more open mixed hardwoods and pines along the higher, drier ridges and yellow poplar, beech, hemlock, and rhododendron along the shaded streams. This is a fine wildflower area in spring and, like the mountainous section, makes an interesting birding hike. Wildlife you might see includes deer, turkeys, gray squirrels and the less common fox squirrel, ruffed grouse, woodchucks, and chipmunks. Black bears, foxes, raccoons, and skunks are present but seldom seen.

At Sandy Ford the Bartram Trail joins the Chattooga River Trail about 100 yards beyond Sandy Ford Road. At this junction, look for the 2-foot-diameter rock with trail names and direction arrows carved in the stone.

The trail from here to SR 28 is described in the Chattooga National Wild and Scenic River Trail chapter.

Miles and Directions

0.0 Start where the Bartram Trail enters Georgia at the North Carolina line.

0.1 Cross Hale Ridge Road (FS 7).

1.4 Pass through Webster Gap.

1.8 At Beegum Gap pay close attention to the yellow blaze markers. A four-wheel-drive road leaves here that you will meet again.

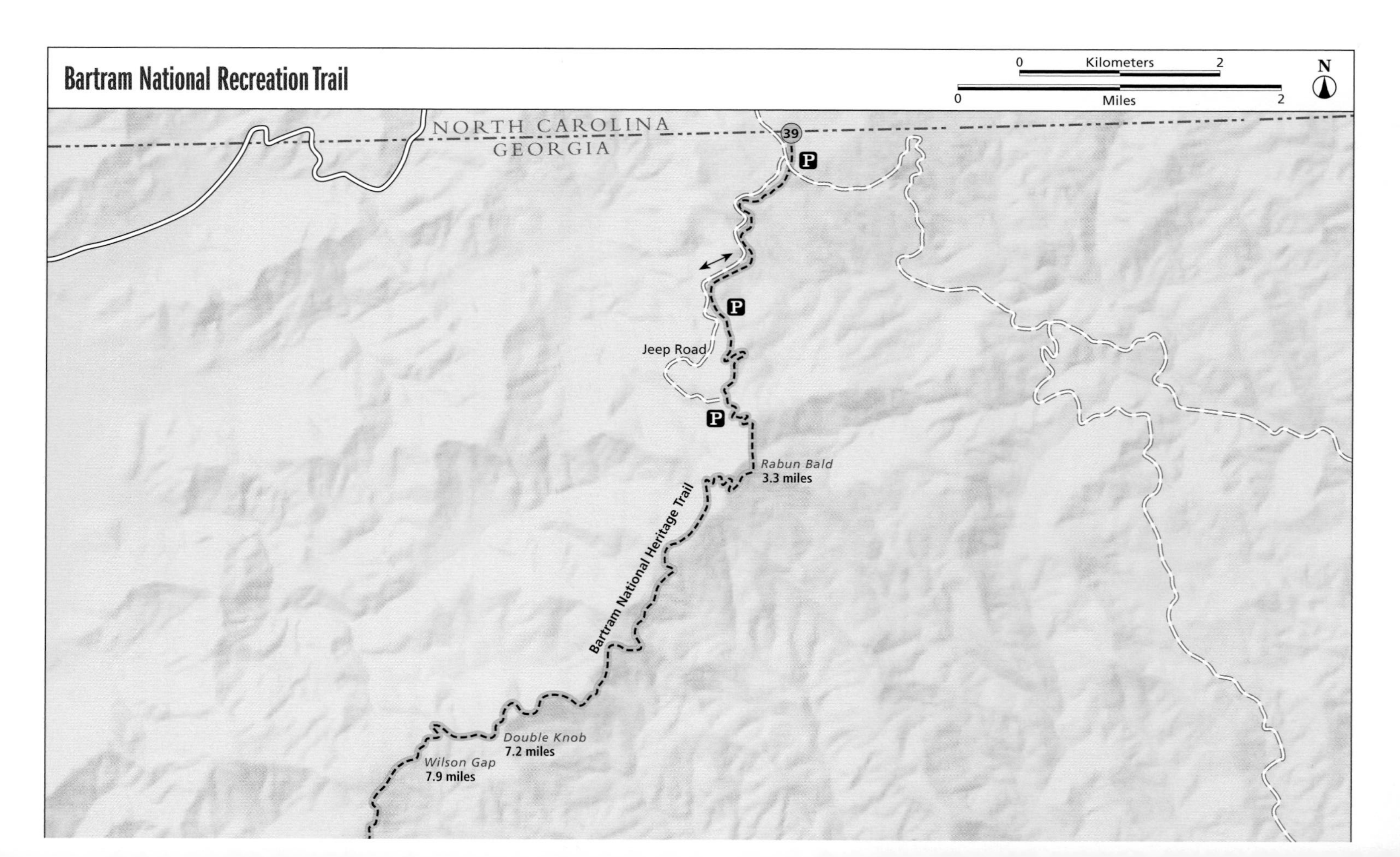

Bartram National Recreation Trail
0
Kilometers
2
0
Miles
2
N
NORTH CAROLINA
GEORGIA
39
P
P
Jeep Road
P
Rabun Bald
3.3 miles
Bartram National Heritage Trail
Double Knob
7.2 miles
Wilson Gap
7.9 miles

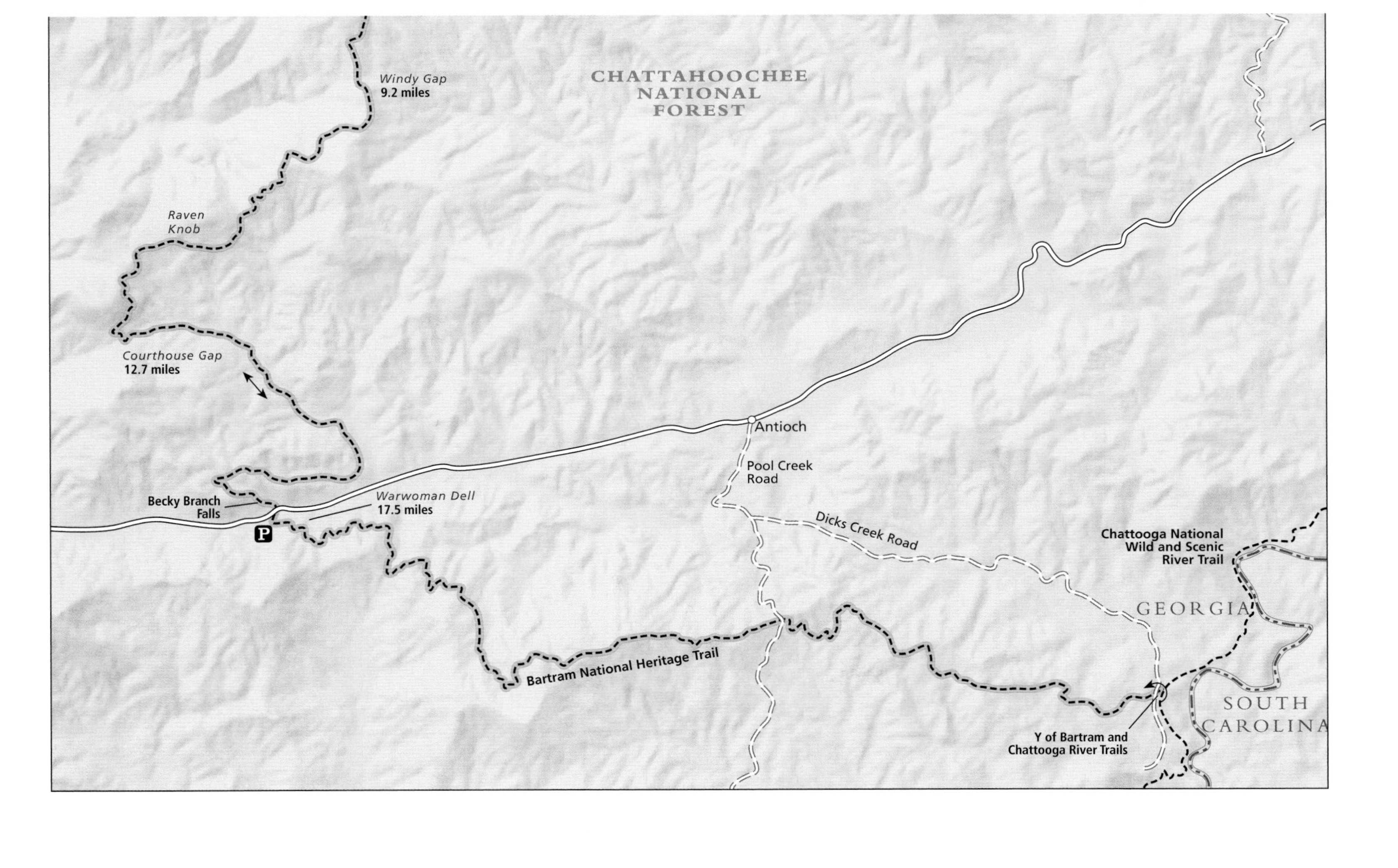
Windy Gap
9.2 miles
CHATTAHOOCHEE
NATIONAL
FOREST
Raven
Knob
Courthouse Gap
12.7 miles
Antioch
Pool Creek
Road
Becky Branch
Falls
Warwoman Dell
17.5 miles
P
Dicks Creek Road
Chattooga National
Wild and Scenic
River Trail
GEORGIA
Bartram National Heritage Trail
SOUTH
CAROLINA
Y of Bartram and
Chattooga River Trails

2.2 Begin the ascent to Rabun Bald.

2.6 You are in the switchback path, with dense rhododendron on either side. The four-wheel-drive road from Beegum Gap ends here at a limited parking area.

3.3 Reach Rabun Bald and the sturdy observation deck. The elevation here is 4,696 feet.

3.6 At the edge of the Rabun Bald crest, a trail turns off to the left as you begin rapidly descending down the switchbacks.

5.1 At Saltrock Gap, you are on the Tennessee Valley Divide, which crosses Rabun Bald. You will follow on one side and then the other for about 6 more miles.

5.3 Skirt to the east of Flat Top without going to its 4,114-foot elevation.

5.8 Switchbacks begin your descent down to Wilson Gap.

6.4 Reach Wilson Knob (3,480 feet) and a beautiful view down the southeast over Indian Grave Hill and all the way to Warwoman Road.

7.2 You are east of and going around the two domes of Double Knob on a 3,470-foot contour.

7.9 Pass through Wilson Gap.

9.2 Pass through Windy Gap.

9.5 The trail on the left down Beck Ridge ends at Antioch on Warwoman Road.

10.6 Switchbacks head down toward Raven Knob on the right, after which you will leave the Tennessee Valley Divide.

12.7 Reach Courthouse Gap and begin hiking east and southeast down Martin Creek watershed.

14.0 Listen for Martin Creek Falls on the left.

14.8 Turn toward the west now, almost paralleling Warwoman Road just below the trail.

15.5 Cross Becky Branch and the junction with a side trail down to Becky Branch Falls.

16.2 Arrive at the end of the north, mountainous section of the Bartram Trail at Warwoman Road.

17.5 Enter Warwoman Dell Day-Use Area.

17.6 Leave Warwoman Dell and continue on the yellow-blazed trail, heading southeast.

18.9 Hike up to Green Gap and turn left. Keep your eye on the yellow blazes. Avoid the several branching, unmarked trails on either side as you go toward the Chattooga River.

21.0 Turn toward the east; you are north of Rainey Mountain.

22.7 Reach Pool Creek Road after hiking almost due east. Cross the road, but stay on the right at the forks, following the yellow blazes.

24.3 Cross an unnamed, old road. The trail turns to the left off the road and goes mostly downhill toward the river.

26.1 The Bartram Trail crosses Sandy Ford Road. About 100 yards beyond is the junction of the Bartram and Chattooga River Trails, you reach a rock with the trail names carved on its surface. Turn north on the joint Bartram and Chattooga River Trails.

26.5 The trail offers a level walk to Dicks Creek and a footbridge across the stream.

26.3 Return to the river under a steep bluff on the left as you follow around a bend with the river in sight.

27.7 Leave the river along an old four-wheel-drive road, with Warwoman Creek on the right.

28.7 Arrive at Earls Ford and cross Earls Ford Road.

The Bartram National Recreation Trail begins at the North Carolina border.

28.9 After traversing a low knoll, cross Warwoman Creek on a bridge.

30.4 Cross Laurel Branch on a bridge.

31.1 Cross Bynum Branch. There are several paths off the trail; keep your eyes on the white and yellow blazes.

31.4 Cross Adline Branch on a bridge as you turn with the river and walk on the ridge side of Long Bottom.

32.7 Cross Holden Branch and continue on up the river.

33.7 Cross the West Fork of the Chattooga, a major tributary of the main river on a bridge. The trail comes back down the West Fork before you reach SR 28.

34.2 Reach the trailhead at the Russell Bridge on SR 28.

40 Victoria Bryant State Park Trails

This 475-acre park is located in the foothills of the Blue Ridge Mountain chain, which provides only moderate changes of elevation. The facility has the 18-hole Highland Walk Golf Course, a swimming pool, tent and trailer camping, and two fishing ponds, one of which is wheelchair accessible.

The entire Victoria Bryant State Park trail system is interconnected, providing a wide variety of hiking options. All trails except Victoria's Path are for both hiking and biking.

The Perimeter Trail goes around the park boundary for 3.0 miles. The Broad River Trail is a 3.4-mile double loop off the Perimeter Trail.

The featured hike is a combination of the Perimeter and Broad River Trails that stretches for 6.4 miles.

Start: At Fishpond No. 1 near the park entrance
Distance: 6.2 miles out and back, with multiple loops
Hiking time: About 2.5–3 hours
Difficulty: Moderate
Trail surface: Dirt; some paved roadway
Best season: Mar–Dec
Other trail users: Mountain bikers, anglers around the ponds
Canine compatibility: Leashed dogs permitted
Land status: Georgia DNR, State Parks & Historic Sites Division
Nearest town: Royston
Fees and permits: Daily parking fee
Schedule: Park hours 7 a.m.–10 p.m., year-round
Maps: USGS Carnesville; page-size map available at the park office
Trail contacts: Victoria Bryant State Park, 1105 Bryant Park Rd., Royston 30662; (706) 245-6270; www.gastateparks.org

Finding the trailhead: From exit 166 off I-85, go right (south) 1.5 miles on SR 145 to Carnesville. Continue 8.1 miles to US 29. Turn left and go about 100 yards; turn left on SR 327 and go 0.7 mile to the park entrance on the left.

The trailhead for the Perimeter–Broad River Trails is at Fishpond No. 1, only a few yards from the park entrance. Trailhead GPS: N34 17.930' / W83 09.563'

The Hike

The Perimeter Trail begins at Fishpond No. 1 on the entrance road. It is paved and barrier free for about 100 yards, offering wheelchair access to an observation deck that overlooks the 2-acre pond. This is an excellent place for viewing wildlife or fishing. Canada geese nest on a small island near the deck. At the end of the pavement, the wide path climbs the side of the small valley.

The forest here is a second-growth stand of typical Piedmont hardwoods—oaks and hickories—with dogwoods, redbuds, and other smaller trees growing underneath. The flowering trees put on a great show in spring.

The North Fork of the Broad River in the overlook clearing

Through the entire first half of the hike, the golf course parallels the right side of the trail. In the first 0.5 mile the trail twice crosses the course's paved cart paths. The second crossing can be confusing: It appears the trail goes straight across, but that path actually leads down to one of the park's picnic pavilions. Rather, turn right and walk roughly 30 yards uphill on the cart path to where the trail splits off to the left.

The Inner Loop Trail forks off to the left about 100 yards past the second cart-path crossing. Stands of switch cane grow in the bottoms of the sharp valleys with intermittent streams for the next 0.5 mile to the junction with the Broad River Trail. Turn right and follow this path across Rice Mill Road.

From here the trail descends roughly 150 feet in elevation as it drops for 0.7 mile into the valley of a small, unnamed feeder stream of the North Fork of the Broad River. The surrounding woodland continues to be composed of second-growth Piedmont species of trees. After passing to the right at the trail junction for the beginning of the beaver-pond loop portion of the path, the forest floor is heavily covered by jack-in-the-pulpit plants. The green with purple- or brown-striped blooms appear in mid-spring, and by late summer the plants are festooned with clumps of bright red berries. Midway through the loop you cross a footbridge over the small creek.

After passing the other end of the beaver-pond loop, the main trail climbs a ridge onto drier terrain and follows a power line right-of-way for a short distance.

Turning to the right at the beginning of the Broad River loop, the trail next makes a wide semicircle around a steep hollow, followed by a long switchback through the bottom of the ravine.

Just prior to closing this loop of the trail, the North Fork of the Broad River appears on the right of the trail. This clearing offers a good view up- and downstream on the stream.

Retracing your path toward the beaver-pond loop, stay to the right at the first junction. On this side of the loop the trail passes an observation tower overlooking the old beaver pond that now is mostly a bog and provides a good birding area. Kingfishers, blue herons, and ducks are possible sightings.

The loop ends just after crossing another footbridge over the stream. Turn right and head back uphill to the Perimeter Trail junction.

At the intersection, turn right again onto the Perimeter Trail. Erosion gullies, now healed, indicate past farming in the area. You pass an impressive stand of American holly and mountain laurel interspersed with switch cane. This evergreen area merges with the vegetation of Rice Creek as you steadily descend for 0.4 mile to a sturdy footbridge across the stream. Just prior to reaching the span, a trail to the primitive camping area runs to the left, and just past the bridge another red-blazed path to the left connects to Victoria's Path nature walk.

In early spring look for silver bell trees blooming here. The trail follows downstream to the corner of the park property line. This is a fine birding area, which passes through a wide variety of habitats. Many spring wildflowers grow along the trail.

The path now winds uphill to an open wildlife planting with an elevated observation platform on the crest of the hill. This is a great place to sit quietly and watch for birds and mammals, especially in early morning or at twilight. Deer and turkeys use the clearing along with other wildlife; watch for their tracks in the soft ground along the trail.

From the observation platform, you go through a moist depression with an especially large patch of ground pine (or club moss), a fern relative.

You pass the junction with the yellow-blazed Inner Loop to the left, a second wildlife clearing to the right, and another connector to the nature walk before reaching Fish Pond No.2. This small lake offers another good wildlife-watching area. The official end of the Perimeter Trail is at the end of the pond dam at the parking lot.

To complete the loop back to the trailhead, from the pond make your way across the paved parking area to the platform step-way down to the level of Rice Creek; cross the creek on a footbridge and walk through a couple more parking lots back to the trailhead.

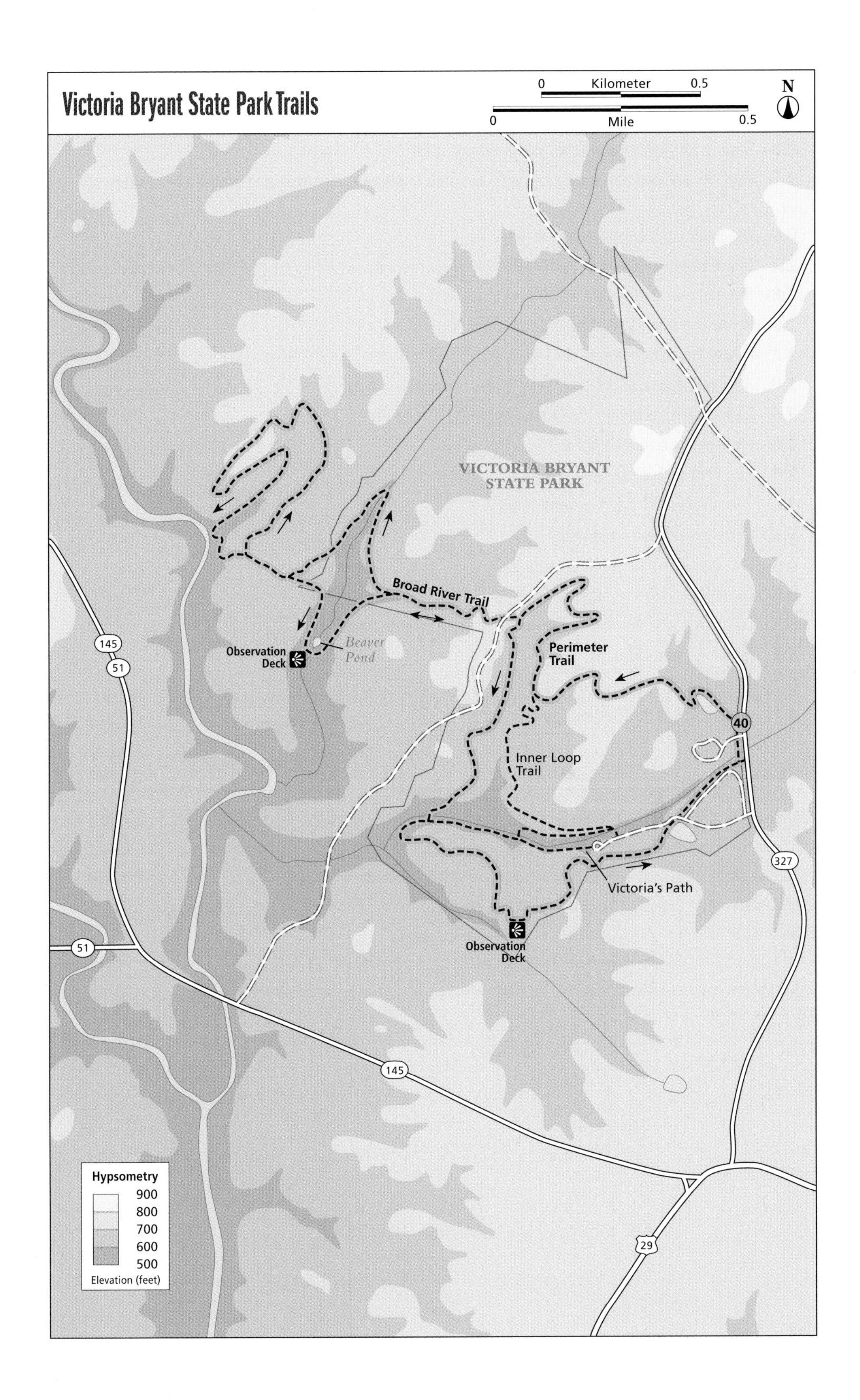

Victoria Bryant State Park Trails
0
Kilometer
0.5
0
Mile
0.5
N
VICTORIA BRYANT
STATE PARK
Broad River Trail
Beaver
Pond
Observation
Deck
Perimeter
Trail
Inner Loop
Trail
Victoria's Path
Observation
Deck
145
51
51
145
40
327
29
Hypsometry
900
800
700
600
500
Elevation (feet)

Miles and Directions

0.0 Start at the fishpond on the park entrance road.

0.5 Pass the second cart path crossing. Take care to follow the correct trail up the path to the right.

0.6 The Inner Loop takes off to the left.

1.2 Broad River Trail begins on the right.

1.6 Turn right on the beaver-pond loop.

2.0 Rejoin the main trail at the end of the loop.

2.1 Follow the power line.

2.2 Stay to the right at the beginning of the Broad River loop.

3.5 Reach the clearing on the North Fork of the Broad River.

3.6 Close the Broad River loop.

3.9 Turn right on the beaver-pond loop.

4.0 Pass the beaver-pond viewing tower.

4.1 Close the beaver-pond loop.

4.5 Turn right to rejoin the Perimeter Trail.

5.0 Cross Rice Creek on a footbridge.

5.3 Come to a wildlife observation platform with wildlife planting.

5.9 Reach Fishpond No. 2.

6.1 Cross Rice Creek on a footbridge.

6.2 Arrive back at the fishpond and trailhead.

Options

Victoria's Path is a 0.5-mile walk with interpretive signs and an overlook, taking you along both sides of Rice Creek. The north-facing slope features galax, Christmas ferns, Robin's plantain, and a number of other shade-tolerant plants. Also present are mountain laurel and dog-hobble that bloom from late April into May. The south-facing side is drier and has more open forest floor.

The yellow-blazed **Inner Loop** runs for 1.5 miles past the park's camping areas. Walking it in combination with portions of the Perimeter Trail creates a 2.8-mile loop.

41 Three Forks Trail

This trail originates at John Teague Gap and runs into the Chattooga National Wild and Scenic River area. Although named for the point at which Big, Holcomb, and Overflow Creeks meet to form the West Fork of the Chattooga River, the main trail does not actually reach that spot. Rather, it ends at the top of a chasm carrying Holcomb Creek over a waterfall and down to Three Forks.

The trailhead is marked with a large boulder engraved with the trail name and a trail marker bearing a green diamond blaze. The rest of the path has very few blazes, but is easy to follow.

Start: At John Teague Gap on Overflow Creek Road
Distance: 2.4 miles out and back
Hiking time: About 1 hour
Difficulty: Easy
Trail surface: Firm loam
Best season: Mar–June; Oct–Dec
Other trail users: Anglers; hunters in season
Canine compatibility: Dogs permitted
Land status: Chattahoochee National Forest
Nearest town: Clayton
Fees and permits: None
Schedule: Year-round
Maps: USGS Satolah; Chattooga National Wild and Scenic River map available from the USDA Forest Service
Trail contacts: USDA Forest Service, Chattooga River Ranger District, 9975 US 441 South, Lakemont 30552; (706) 754-6221; www.fs.usda.gov/conf

Finding the trailhead: From US 441 in Clayton, take Rickman Street east to the dead end at Warwoman Road. Turn right and follow Warwoman Road for 13.2 miles to the bridge across the West Fork of the Chattooga River. Immediately after the bridge, turn left (north) on the gravel Overflow Creek Road (FS 86). Continue on Overflow Creek Road 4 miles to the John Teague Gap trail sign. The trailhead is at the small, unpaved parking area on the right that accommodates 3 or 4 vehicles. Trailhead GPS: N34 57.735' / W83 13.725'

The Hike

From the parking area and trailhead sign, follow the north face of the ridge along the well-beaten but mostly unmarked path. The trail inclines slightly uphill at the beginning as it goes through a pine-oak-hickory forest and an occasional thicket of Catawba or rosebay rhododendron. Quickly the path then begins descending gently toward the river corridor.

At 0.7 mile a single blue blaze designates the boundary of the Chattooga National Wild and Scenic River area, which encompasses much of the watersheds of the three creeks that form the West Fork. From here the trail turns more steeply downhill, losing more than 300 feet of elevation in the last 0.5 mile.

Upon reaching the point where the trail intersects an old jeep road, the main path turns left on that track. The trail to the right also has a green diamond blaze and leads a few yards to a flat, open, primitive campsite.

The trail turnaround is at the waterfall overlook on Holcomb Creek.

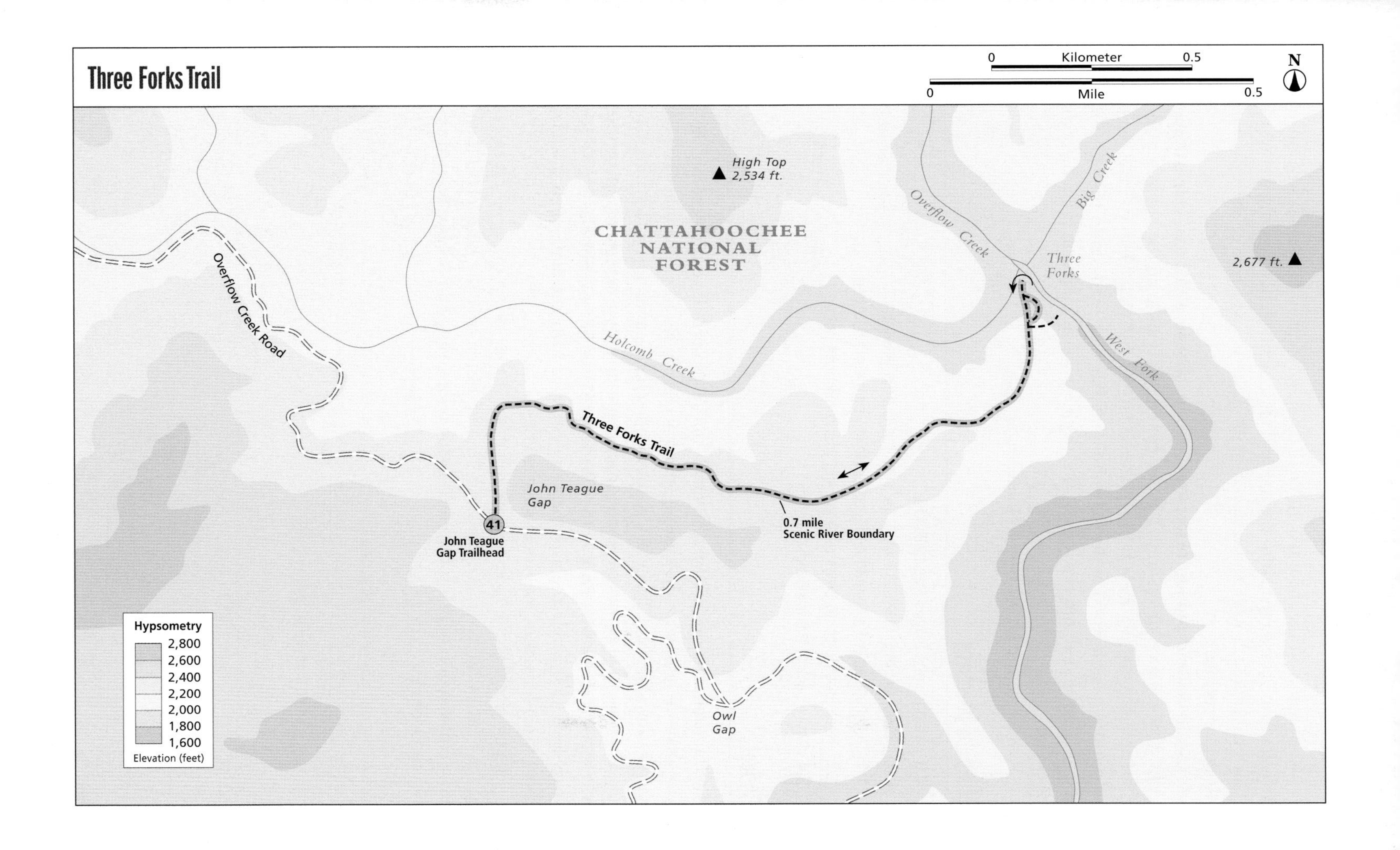
Three Forks Trail
0
Kilometer
0.5
0
Mile
0.5
N
High Top
2,534 ft.
CHATTAHOOCHEE
NATIONAL
FOREST
Overflow Creek
Big Creek
Three
Forks
2,677 ft.
West Fork
Holcomb Creek
Overflow Creek Road
Three Forks Trail
John Teague
Gap
41
John Teague
Gap Trailhead
0.7 mile
Scenic River Boundary
Owl
Gap
Hypsometry
2,800
2,600
2,400
2,200
2,000
1,800
1,600
Elevation (feet)

Continuing on the main trail to the left, several earthen barriers to stop off-road vehicles have been scraped into the trail and must be sidestepped during wet weather. This final approach to the turnaround point is the steepest part of the trek, with a 40-degree incline.

As you descend and just before reaching the bottom, a side trail enters from the right. This connects the main trail to the primitive campsite on the old jeep road.

The hike ends at a wide bedrock area at Holcomb Creek. Here you can see one of nature's greatest works as the full volume of the creek swirls down through a narrow crevice eroded into the rock. If the creek is swollen by recent rains, the sight is awesome.

Retrace your path back up to John Teague Gap.

Miles and Directions

0.0 Start at John Teague Gap trailhead.

0.7 Reach the blue blaze indicating the scenic river area boundary.

1.1 Intercept an old jeep road and turn left, following the old roadbed.

1.2 Reach the Holcomb Creek overlook and your turnaround point.

2.4 Arrive back at the trailhead.

Options

Two unnamed or unblazed trails branch out of the primitive campsite on the old jeep road. As you enter the clearing, the trail directly ahead on the other side drops sharply downhill for 0.2 mile before intersecting the main trail near Holcomb Creek.

The other trail runs for 0.4 mile to the right in a southwest direction, providing access down to the West Fork of the Chattooga River, but it is not easy access! Relatively level for 0.2 mile, the path then drops sharply down the bluff, often at angles of more than 45 degrees, over loose rocks and soil.

Upon reaching the river you are roughly 0.3 mile downstream of Three Forks at the head of the river. Anglers' trails lead upstream, over the boulders and under the rhododendron to that spot, which is one of the truly wild and beautiful places in North Georgia.

42 Ellicott Rock Wilderness Trail

On this hike you follow the Chattooga River from Burrells Ford Bridge to the North Carolina state line and Ellicott Rock. You are in sight of the river all the way as you walk through the Chattooga National Wild and Scenic River corridor. For most of the distance the path also is in the federal Ellicott Rock Wilderness Area.

Along the way excellent birding for warblers, thrushes, nuthatches, woodpeckers, and belted kingfishers is available. Some of the more unusual plants along the way are Dutchman's pipe vine, rough-leaf dogwood, running ground pine, shining club moss, and Clinton's lily.

This portion of the Chattooga is a famed trout stream, predominately supporting wild, stream-bred brown trout.

Start: In South Carolina on FS 646 near Burrells Ford Bridge
Distance: 7.1 miles out and back
Hiking time: About 4 hours
Difficulty: Moderate
Trail surface: Hard loam; a few rocky areas
Best season: Mar–Dec
Other trail users: Anglers
Canine compatibility: Leashed dogs permitted
Land status: Sumter National Forest, SC
Nearest towns: Clayton, GA; Walhalla, SC
Fees and permits: None
Schedule: Open year-round
Maps: USGS Tamassee; USDA Forest Service map of the Chattooga National Wild and Scenic River
Trail contacts: USDA Forest Service, Chattooga River Ranger District, 9975 US 441 South, Lakemont 30552; (706) 754-6221; www.fs.usda.gov/conf

USDA Forest Service, Andrew Pickens Ranger District, 112 Andrew Pickens Circle, Mountain Rest, SC 29664; (864) 638-9568; www.fs.fed.us

Finding the trailhead: From Clayton go 23 miles from US 441 on Warwoman Road to SR 28. Turn right and go 1.7 miles to FS 646. Turn left and follow this winding gravel road for 7 miles to the Chattooga River and Burrells Ford Bridge. The trailhead is 50 yards past the bridge on the left. Trailhead GPS: N34 58.492' / W83 06.884'

The Hike

The Ellicott Rock Wilderness Trail is included, even though it is in South Carolina. The Georgia Department of Natural Resources (DNR) and South Carolina DNR share jurisdiction on the river.

The trail begins on the South Carolina side, running north from the road. At first the path is wide and relatively flat through a pleasant stand of hemlock, white pine, yellow poplar, and a few white oak trees. You quickly pass a wooden sign marking the boundary of the Ellicott Rock Wilderness Area.

As the trail begins to narrow, you come to the first small stream crossing. On the other side a trail runs to the right, uphill to picturesque Spoon Auger Falls. The walk

The sandy beach and campsite are situated near the midpoint of the hike.

up is quite steep, with the up-and-back trek a total of 0.3 mile. Several switchbacks help you negotiate the steep slope.

Returning to the main path, turn right as the trail now hugs the riverbank, departing from it only where steep rock walls make it impossible to stay close to the water. You frequently go through tunnels of rhododendron, mountain laurel, and dog-hobble. Where the trailside vegetation is more open, spring wildflowers are more numerous.

After another 0.3 mile, the Foothills Trail joins the path from the right. That trail offers a 77-mile trek through the high country of western South Carolina and shares this path upstream to the East Fork of the Chattooga River. A forest service campground is located on the Foothills Trail where it crosses FS 646.

At 1.4 miles you reach a sandy beach on the trail side of the river. This spot is often used by campers and offers a good place to stop for a picnic.

Next the trail reaches the East Fork of the river that flows down from the South Carolina side of the stream. Here you can camp under a great stand of hemlocks, white pines, and yellow poplars. A uniquely constructed footbridge made entirely of large and small logs crosses the East Fork. Even the footings are large logs fitted together.

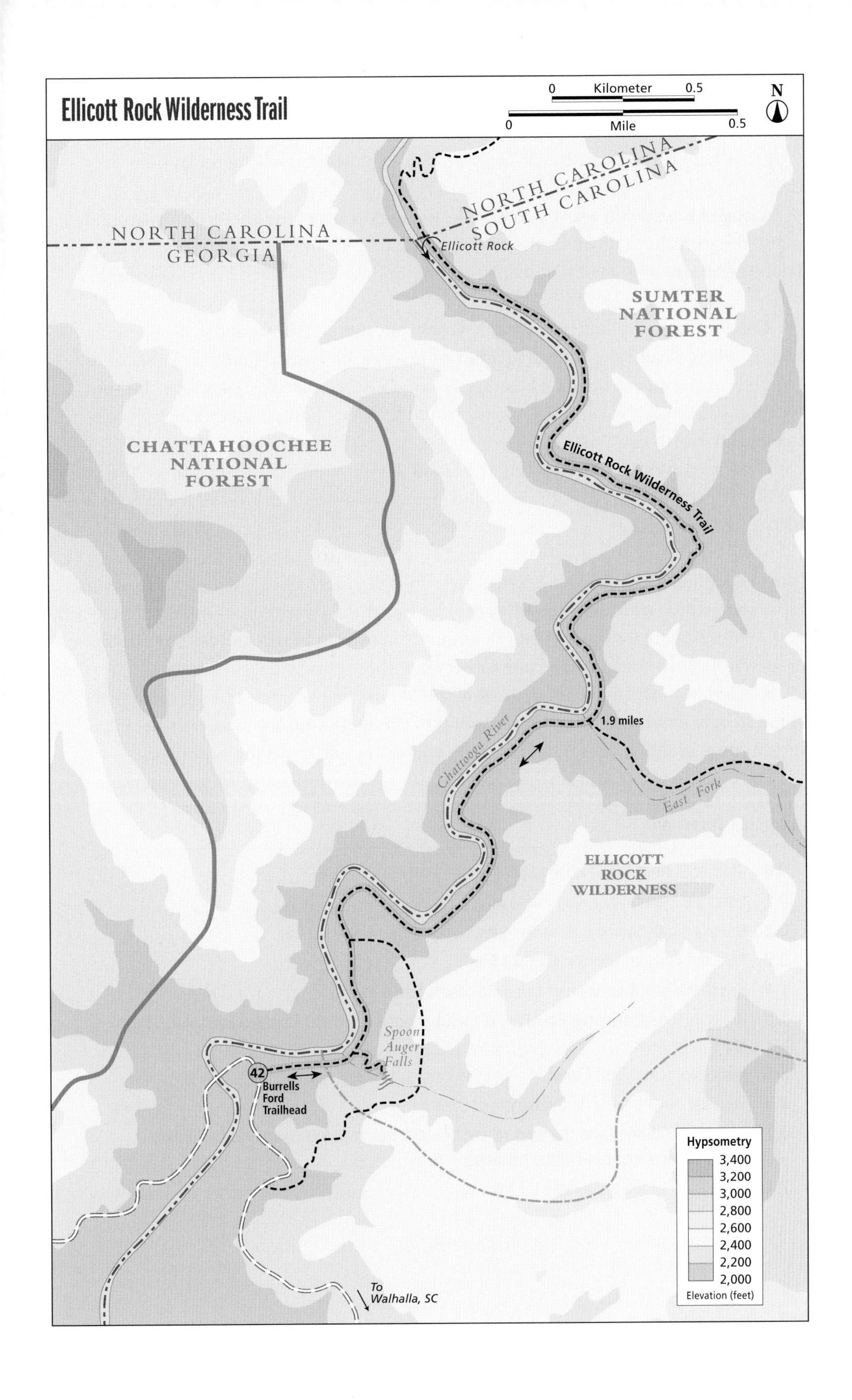

Ellicott Rock Wilderness Trail
0
Kilometer
0.5
0
Mile
0.5
N
NORTH CAROLINA
SOUTH CAROLINA
NORTH CAROLINA
GEORGIA
Ellicott Rock
SUMTER
NATIONAL
FOREST
CHATTAHOOCHEE
NATIONAL
FOREST
Ellicott Rock Wilderness Trail
1.9 miles
Chattooga River
East Fork
ELLICOTT
ROCK
WILDERNESS
Spoon
Auger
Falls
42
Burrells
Ford
Trailhead
To
Walhalla, SC
Hypsometry
3,400
3,200
3,000
2,800
2,600
2,400
2,200
2,000
Elevation (feet)

Across the bridge, the Foothills Trail splits off to the right for the 2.5-mile trek up the East Fork to South Carolina's Walhalla Fish Hatchery and beyond.

From here the Ellicott Rock Trail is much less used and changes elevation very little.

Along the way you cross Bad Creek. Just before reaching the trail turnaround point, the path drops down to the river shore and an opening in the foliage. A huge boulder, the size of a small building, sits in the middle of the river, towering over the water.

The turnaround point is at Ellicott Rock, but it is not easily apparent. The only hint is when small signs appear marking the edge of North Carolina game lands (wildlife management areas). These are about 20 yards past the rock and the spot where the Georgia, North Carolina, and South Carolina borders meet. The trail continues into North Carolina.

What is commonly referred to as Ellicott Rock is on the stream bank 20 feet below the path. Engraved on the rock and facing out toward the river near the water's surface is a carving: LAT 35 AD 1813 NC + SC.

Andrew Ellicott was a surveyor hired by Georgia to delineate the border with North Carolina in 1811. He marked a rock with the carving N–G, which is supposed to be somewhere near this point. But the carving at the river shore is more correctly on Commissioners Rock. A team of commissioners from North and South Carolina created it in 1813 to define the border between those two states.

Regardless of the name used, to view the old carving requires leaving the trail to climb steeply down the bank. Once on top of the rock, you can hang over the edge, or get down in the water for a look at the engraving just above the waterline.

Once up on the trail again, head back south for the return trip to the trailhead.

Miles and Directions

0.0 Start at Burrells Ford Bridge parking area.

0.1 Enter the Ellicott Rock Wilderness Area.

0.2 Cross a small branch and come to the Spoon Auger Falls side trail.

0.9 Pass the junction with the Foothills Trail.

1.4 Reach the sandy beach and campsite on the left.

1.9 Cross the bridge over the East Fork of the Chattooga River; the Foothills Trail splits off to follow that stream.

2.6 Rock hop across Bad Creek.

3.5 Pass the huge boulder in the middle of the river.

3.7 Reach Ellicott Rock and the point where Georgia, South Carolina, and North Carolina meet. Retrace your path to the trailhead.

7.1 Arrive back at the trailhead.

Honorable Mentions

D Duncan Ridge National Recreation Trail

This 35-mile trail is a challenging hike covering a wide variety of conditions from easy to strenuous. Many hikers consider it the toughest of Georgia's hiking trails.

At its eastern end it connects with the Benton MacKaye and Appalachian Trails at Long Creek. The trail quickly leaves the Appalachian Trail (AT), continuing with the Benton MacKaye Trail across the Toccoa River and soon heading east on ridgetops to join the Coosa Backcountry Trail. These two trails travel together to Slaughter Gap and connect with the AT at the end of the Duncan Ridge Trail. From here you can go back west to Springer Mountain on the AT and close a 60-mile backpacking loop.

There are good wilderness campsites all along the trail, except for long stretches with very little water. In addition to the scenic features along this trail, you cross the 260-foot suspension bridge over the Toccoa River, one of the longest swinging bridges just for foot travel in the eastern United States.

For more information: Chattahoochee National Forest, Blue Ridge Ranger District, 6050 Appalachian Hwy., Blue Ridge 30531; (706) 632-3031; www.fs.usda.gov/conf; www.georgia-atclub.org; www.bmta.org

DeLorme: Georgia Atlas and Gazetteer: Page 14 D6

E Holcomb Creek Trail

This year-round trail is a pleasant 3.0 miles of easy to moderate hiking to waterfalls. Holcomb Creek falls in a succession of drops for about 120 feet. Standing at the bottom where a bridge crosses the creek, it is hard to see the entire cascade. An observation deck at Ammons Creek Falls affords a good view of the falls as the creek plummets under the deck through narrow rock crevices. The best waterfall conditions are in winter and spring.

The trail starts at the junction of Overflow Road and Hales Ridge Road (FS 7). The Holcomb Creek Falls sign marks the trailhead. The trail goes through a steep cove lined with hemlock, white pine, large yellow poplars, and buckeyes forming a canopy over smaller silver bells, dogwoods, rhododendron, and mountain laurel.

Switchbacks keep the grade at a moderate rate of descent. In places, the trail is completely covered over by white rosebay rhododendron, which blooms from late May through the summer after the mountain laurel. These two large shrubs add much color and pleasant shade to the walk during the warm months.

The noise of the water can be heard well before the cascade is in sight. The trail ends at Hales Ridge Road where it crosses Holcomb Creek. An easy 0.6-mile walk on the road back to the starting point completes the loop.

For more information: Chattahoochee National Forest, Chattooga River Ranger District, 9975 US 441 South, Lakemont 30552; (706) 754-6221; www.fs.usda.gov/conf

DeLorme: Georgia Atlas and Gazetteer: Page 16 A4

F Tugaloo State Park

On a peninsula tucked away on 55,590-acre Lake Hartwell, 393-acre Tugaloo State Park has delightful hiking trails. Another of Georgia's well-kept secrets, the park is surrounded by water on all but about 110 yards over which the park road passes.

Located on the northern edge of the Piedmont Plateau, the area supports an interesting range of plants and animals found in both the mountains and plateau.

The four interconnected trails total 4.2 miles. Crow Tree and Muscadine Nature Trails take you through woods of oak, walnut, mulberry, and cherry trees, along with many low shrubs. The north and south sections of the loop trails combine for 3.2 miles of wooded, gently rolling topography. Lake Hartwell is noted for its fine fishing for largemouth and striped bass.

For more information: Tugaloo State Park, 1763 Tugaloo State Park Rd., Lavonia 30553; (706) 356-4362; www.gastateparks.org

DeLorme: Georgia Atlas and Gazetteer: Page 17 H6

Central Georgia

Central Georgia trails in the Piedmont often are associated with the region's river systems.

43 Chattahoochee Bend State Park Trails

One of Georgia's newest state parks, Chattahoochee Bend opened on 2,910 acres of land in northwest Coweta County in 2011. It also is Georgia's fifth-largest state park. Most of the land has been left in a wilderness setting as it stretches along 5 miles of river shore in a bend of the Chattahoochee.

The park has a visitor center, campground, picnic area, playgrounds, and a boat ramp. Visitors can fish or paddle on the river as well.

Chattahoochee Bend has three trails providing roughly 7 miles of hiking. The East-West (or Tower) Trail runs from the visitor center to the observation deck on the river. The Campground Loop connects with the Riverside Trail. The featured Riverside Trail runs from the boat ramp on the river, upstream to the north paddle-in campground.

Start: At the parking area for the boat ramp on the river
Distance: 9.2 miles out and back
Hiking time: About 2.5–3 hours
Difficulty: Easy
Trail surface: Sandy and forest loam
Best season: Mar–Dec
Other trail users: Hikers only
Canine compatibility: Leashed dogs permitted
Land status: Georgia DNR, State Parks & Historic Sites Division
Nearest town: Newnan
Fees and permits: Daily parking fee
Schedule: Park hours 7 a.m.–10 p.m., year-round
Maps: USGS Whitesburg; full-page map of trails available at the visitor center
Trail contacts: Chattahoochee Bend State Park, 425 Bobwhite Way, Newnan 30263; (770) 254-7271; www.gastateparks.org/chattahoocheebend

Finding the trailhead: From exit 47 near Newnan on I-85, go west 0.6 mile on SR 34 (Bullsboro Boulevard). Turn right onto SR 34 Bypass (Millard Farmer Industrial Boulevard) and drive 6 miles. Turn right at the four-way stop onto SR 34 (Franklin Road). After 8.2 miles, turn right onto Thomas Powers Road. Continue straight for 5.5 miles on this road, which changes names at a couple of intersections. Turn right on Flat Rock Road, which changes to Bobwhite Way and runs into the park. The Riverside Trailhead is at the boat ramp at the end of Bobwhite Way. Trailhead GPS: N33 25.792' / W85 00.671'

The Hike

The Riverside Trail begins at the east side of the boat ramp parking lot, immediately dropping down to cross a small feeder stream. The white-blazed path then turns left toward the riverbank.

As the trail begins following the river upstream, the Chattahoochee is always in sight for the first couple of miles. The trail passes through a forest of beech, water oak, and sweet gum trees. There are a number dead tree snags standing in the river bottom, so the sound of woodpeckers hammering on them is common. Along the

Large patches of mayapples cover the ground along several portions of the Riverside Trail in the early spring.

edges of the sandy path, large and abundant patches of mayapples can be seen in the early spring months.

The trail soon intersects the first of two blue-blazed trails that connect to the campgrounds. A bit farther along, the path reaches a creek crossing, which is the first of seven feeder streams that are encountered along the trail.

Just past the second blue-blazed campground connector entering from the right, another creek crossing immediately appears.

The next landmark that comes into sight is the observation tower and streamside picnic tables. Take a moment to climb the steps up to the top platform of the tower for a view of the river. Along here the Chattahoochee runs deep and several hundred feet wide. One striking feature of the river valley along the Riverside Trail is the quiet. Out of earshot of any roads, you can walk for long stretches without hearing any man-made sound.

After continuing another 150 yards, the blue-diamond-blazed East-West Trail intersects from the right, then 0.4 mile farther the largest of the tributary streams crossed is encountered. Upstream of the bridge, that creek bottom opens into a wide, swampy floodplain.

Beyond this creek the foliage along the trail begins to change. Heavy privet thickets appear along the path, along with yellow poplar trees and loblolly pines. Three more creek crossings are required, and just prior to the last, the trail passes to the right of one of largest beech trees you are ever likely to see. Next the trail reaches a pair of benches at an overlook on the riverbank.

From here the trail turns sharply right and begins climbing up the ridge and parallel to another feeder stream. As the path winds higher, redbuds, hickories, and pines become more common, while beneath there is an understory of buckeye, Christmas ferns, and heartleaf. Meandering around several hardwood coves, the path passes two large rocks jutting out like shelves.

Dropping back down to the river, a side trail leads off to the left and down to a picnic table beside the mouth of a feeder stream. Then the main trail again turns up the ridge side to leave the river. During this climb an old deer stand appears on the right of the trail. Constructed of lumber and mounted with an old boat seat, the contraption is now hanging at an angle from the tree.

Next the trail turns left to run along the edge of a thick, planted pine plantation. The path continues to skirt these evenly spaced rows of trees until reaching a wildlife clearing. After running through the edge of the opening for a short way, the trail reenters the woods to circle all around the rest of the clearing.

When the trail crosses another narrow clearing, it plunges into a pine plantation on the far side. As the path meanders through the rows of trees, it has a mazelike feeling. Pay careful attention to follow the white blazes in this area so you don't miss any and wander off the trail. At the far side of the plantation, the trail ends at the gravel road running down to the paddle-in campground.

This is the turnaround point. Reverse course at the trail-end sign and walk back to the downstream trailhead.

Miles and Directions

0.0 Leave the trailhead, cross the small creek, and turn left toward the river.

0.1 Pass the first connector trail to the campground.

0.4 Reach the second campground connector trail.

0.8 Come to the observation tower.

0.9 The East-West Trail enters from the right.

1.2 Cross the bridge over the largest tributary, with its floodplain to the right.

1.8 Pass the huge beech tree on the left of the path.

1.9 Reach the benches and overlook on the riverbank; the trail turns right up the ridge side.

2.3 Traverse the cove with the rock shelves.

2.5 The trail to the left leads to a picnic table on the riverbank.

2.7 The old deer stand is in a tree to the right of the path.

3.2 Begin skirting the pine plantation on the right side of the trail.

3.4 Pass through the edge of the wildlife clearing.

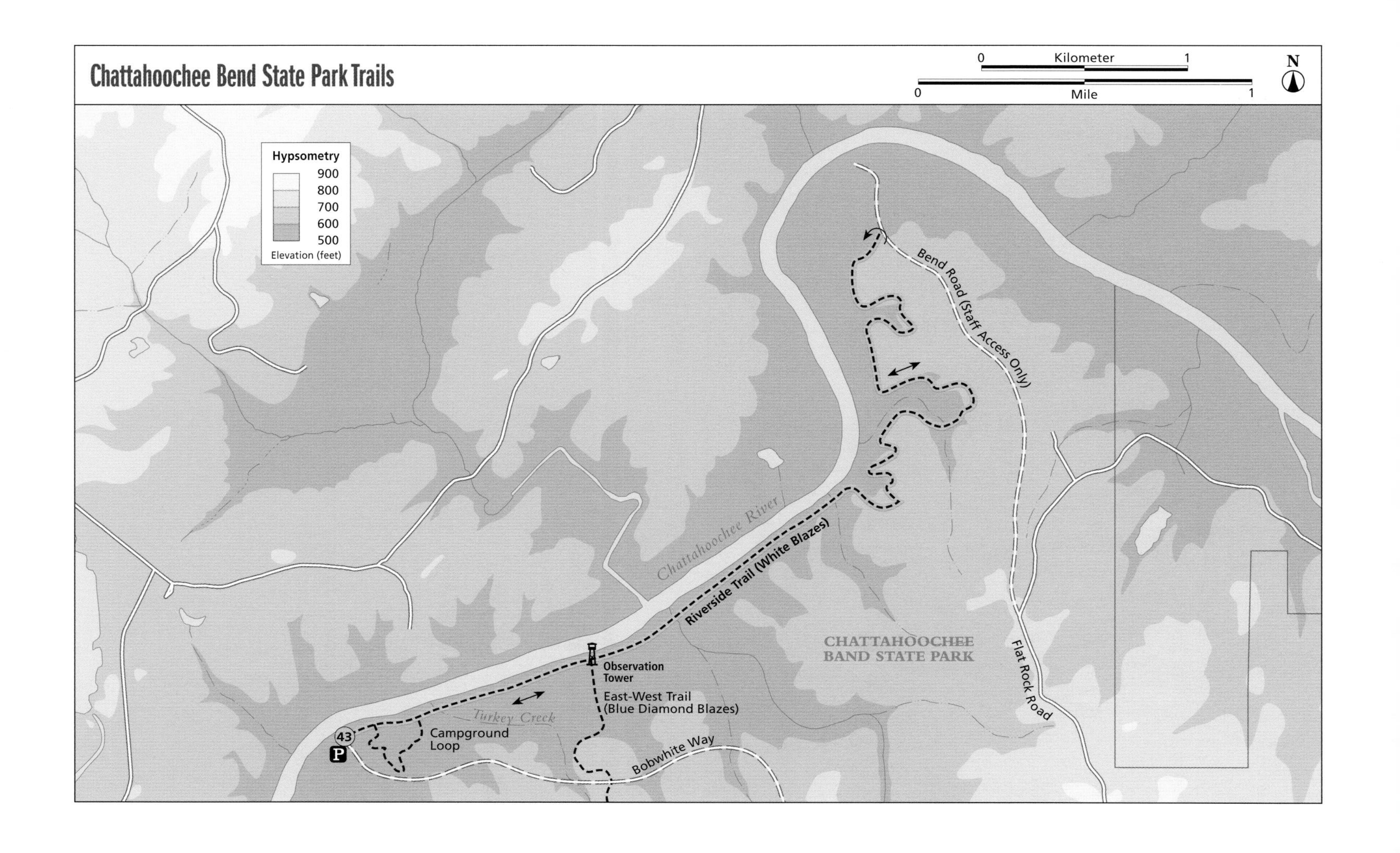
Chattahoochee Bend State Park Trails
0
Kilometer
1
0
Mile
1
N
Hypsometry
900
800
700
600
500
Elevation (feet)
Bend Road (Staff Access Only)
Chattahoochee River
Riverside Trail (White Blazes)
CHATTAHOOCHEE
BAND STATE PARK
Flat Rock Road
Observation
Tower
East-West Trail
(Blue Diamond Blazes)
Turkey Creek
Campground
Loop
Bobwhite Way
43
P

The observation tower on the Riverside Trail offers a view of the Chattahoochee River.

4.3 Cross the second wildlife clearing and enter the pine plantation.
4.6 Reach the turnaround point.
9.2 Arrive back at the trailhead.

Options

The 1.5-mile **East-West (or Tower) Trail** begins at the visitor center. It twice crosses Bobwhite Way, as well as touching the road again at an alternate trailhead near the path's midpoint. The trail climbs down into the river valley to intersect the Riverside Trail 150 yards east of the observation tower.

The **Campground Loop** covers 0.8 mile connecting the RV and walk-in tent campgrounds to the Riverside Trail.

44 F. D. Roosevelt State Park, Pine Mountain Trail

F. D. Roosevelt State Park is located on Pine Mountain in the central part of the state, about 25 miles northwest of Columbus. The long, narrow ridge composed of quartzite rock formations is the southernmost mountain in Georgia.

Covering 9,049 acres, the tract is Georgia's largest state park and is steeped in the legacy of the thirty-second president. President Roosevelt's Little White House retreat is near the western end of this elongated park, his favorite picnic area on Dowdell Knob is near the midpoint, and the entire park is dotted with facilities built by the Civilian Conservation Corps (CCC) during his administration.

Park amenities are picnic areas, campgrounds, rental cabins, 16 backcountry campsites, equestrian stables, a fishing lake, and swimming pool.

The park contains a total of 47.7 miles of interconnected trails. They are composed of the 23-mile Pine Mountain Trail (PMT), seven connected loops, and half a dozen connectors. The PMT is the centerpiece of trekking in the park, running the entire length from west to east.

Start: At the parking lot on the west end, across US 27 from the Callaway Gardens Country Store
Distance: 23 miles one way
Hiking time: 3 days hiking comfortably at 2–2.5 miles per hour
Trail surface: Dirt and rocky in places; some short sections on paved road
Best season: Mar–June; Oct–Dec
Other trail users: Hikers and backpackers only
Canine compatibility: Leashed dogs permitted
Land status: Georgia DNR, State Parks & Historic Sites Division
Nearest towns: Pine Mountain, Warm Springs
Schedule: Park hours 7 a.m.–10 p.m., year-round
Fees and permits: Daily parking fee
Maps: USGS Pine Mountain and Warm Springs; detailed map of the trails for sale by the Pine Mountain Trail Association (all funds from map sales are used to maintain the Pine Mountain Trail); page-size map of the park including the trail available from the park office
Trail contacts: F. D. Roosevelt State Park, 2970 SR 190, Pine Mountain 31822; (706) 663-4858; www.gastateparks.org

Pine Mountain Trail Association Inc., PO Box 5, Columbus 31902; www.pinemountaintrail.org

Finding the trailhead: The eastern trailhead for the PMT is at the paved parking lot and picnic area at the WJSP-TV tower, on US 27 / SR 85, just south of Warm Springs. Trailhead GPS: N32 51.173' / W84 42.064'

The western trailhead is at the parking lot at the junction of US 27 and SR 190 across the highway from the Callaway Gardens Country Store. Trailhead GPS: N32 48.650' / W84 51.325'

The Hike

The PMT is the longest single trail in Middle Georgia. The path stretches 23 miles along the crest of the mountain from the towns of Warm Springs in the east to Pine Mountain in the west.

F. D. Roosevelt State Park, Pine Mountain Trail and Dowdell Knob Loop

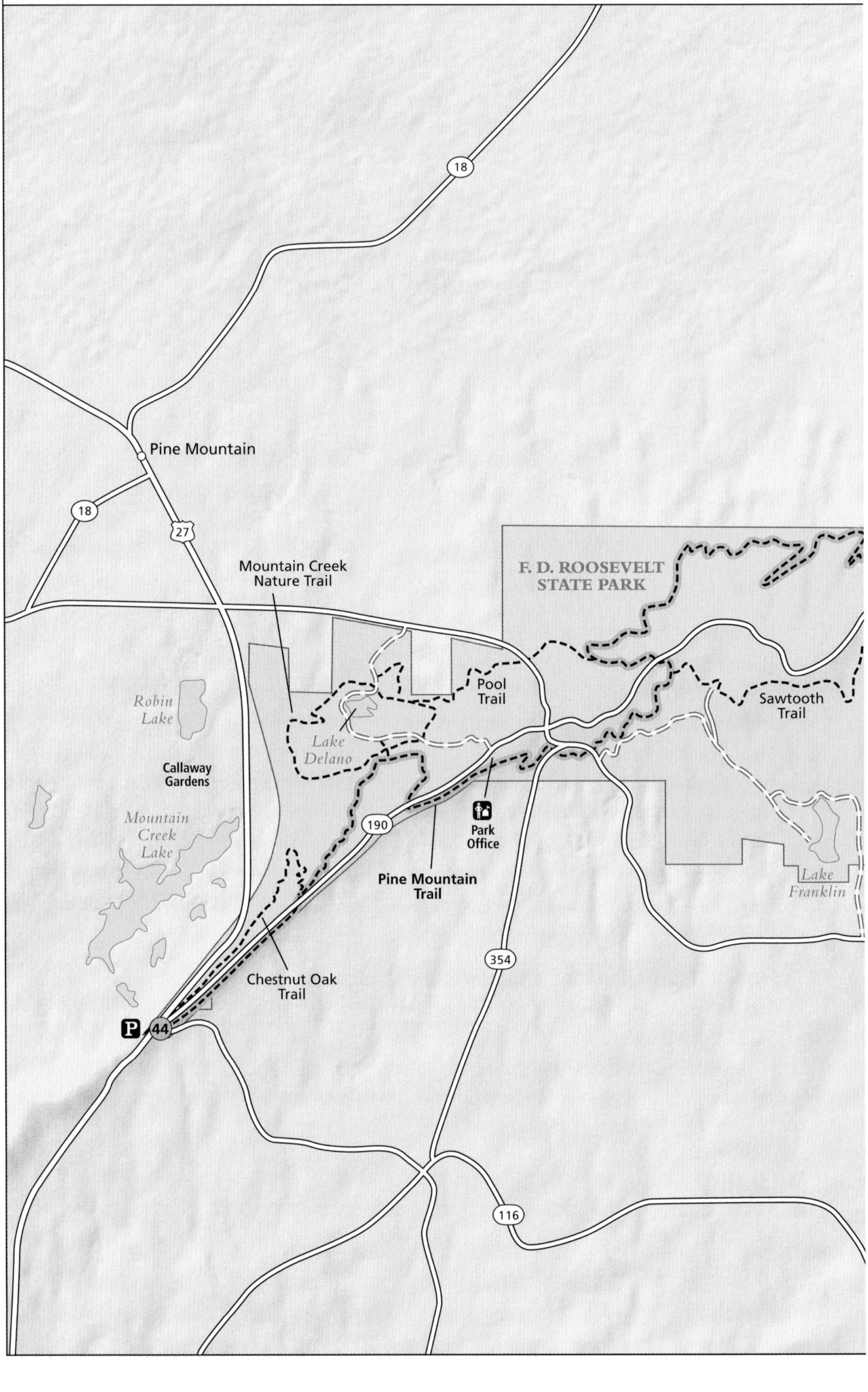

18
Pine Mountain
18
27
Mountain Creek
Nature Trail
F. D. ROOSEVELT
STATE PARK
Pool
Trail
Sawtooth
Trail
Robin
Lake
Lake
Delano
Callaway
Gardens
Mountain
Creek
Lake
190
Park
Office
Pine Mountain
Trail
Lake
Franklin
Chestnut Oak
Trail
354
P
44
116

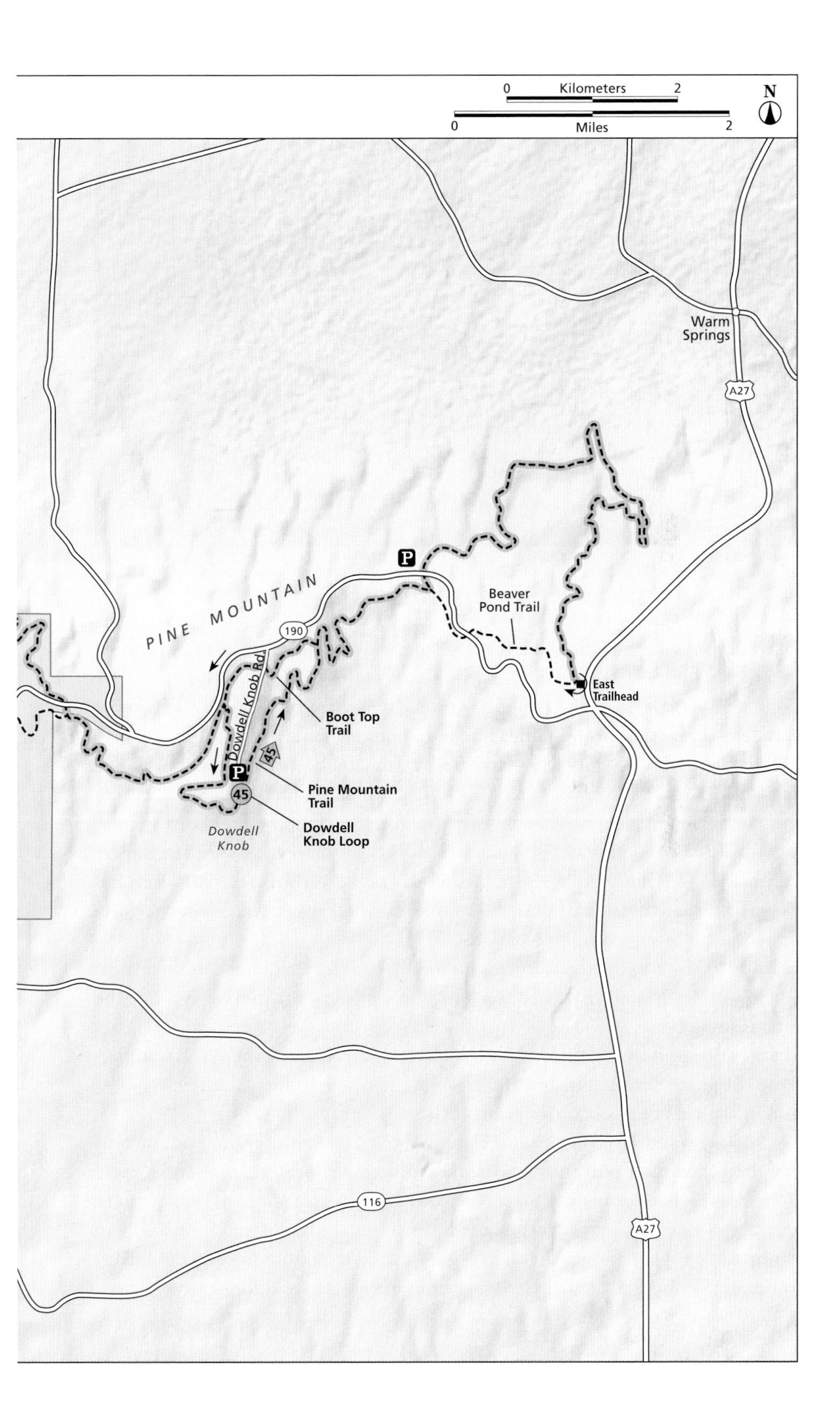

0 Kilometers 2
0 Miles 2
N
Warm Springs
A27
PINE MOUNTAIN
190
Dowdell Knob Rd.
P
45
Beaver Pond Trail
East Trailhead
Boot Top Trail
Pine Mountain Trail
Dowdell Knob Loop
Dowdell Knob
116
A27

Several sections of the PMT pass through stretches of tornado damage that devastated the forest.

Much of the land through which the PMT passes was originally on a farm owned by President Franklin D. Roosevelt. Today it is part of the state park property.

Combined with its loop and connector trails, 70 miles of treks are possible on the PMT system. These vary from multiday hikes to leisurely family strolls.

Although the trails on Pine Mountain are very much like many of the trails in the highlands of North Georgia, the views seem to be much more panoramic because everything surrounding the mountain is flat. The forest is composed of shortleaf pine, hickory, blackjack oak, chestnut oak, and black oak on the drier ridgetops. The undergrowth includes red buckeye, pawpaw, piedmont azalea, sparkleberry, blueberry, and huckleberry. In the coves and moister sites, you can find sweet gum, yellow poplar, beech, and maple along with loblolly pines.

In April 2011 a massive tornado crossed the PMT at several points. In these areas the forest was completely flattened, opening up some panoramic views from the mountain crest.

There are 16 primitive campsites for backpacking hikers along the PMT. Campers must use designated campsites, and campfires are permitted unless otherwise noted. Overnight campers must obtain a permit at the park office.

The trail is well marked with blue blazes. About 100 yards on the trail, there is a green metal box on a post that houses the trail register sheets. It is always a good idea to register when starting the hike. A register is also located at park headquarters. These registers give park personnel and the Pine Mountain Trail Association a tally of the number of people who use the trail. It is estimated that more than 60,000 hikers use some parts of the trail annually, coming from many states and foreign countries.

The trail is measured from west to east with stone cairns and signs at each mile. The trail crosses SR 190 at multiple places, which makes it possible to park and walk sections of the trail from one crossing to another. The Pine Mountain Trail Association has scouted and marked the connector trails with white blazes. The single exception is the Mountain Creek Nature Trail Loop, which is blazed with red marks.

These connectors add greatly to the variety of the long trail. These loop sections make nice day hikes. All the loops have campsites, providing flexibility for an overnight hike and camping in secluded forest areas. Most of the sites are near ample water sources; however, it is necessary to use standard backpacking purification techniques for stream or standing water.

Miles and Directions

0.0 Begin walking west from the parking lot and trailhead on US 27.

1.3 Cross SR 190 at the Garden Overlook Parking Area; the junction with the Chestnut Oak Trail is just across the road.

2.4 Pass the Dead Pine Campsite.

3.2 Reach the Buzzard Roost parking area and cross SR 190.

4.5 Cross SR 354.

4.8 Cross Kings Gap Road.

5.4 Reach the Broken Tree Campsite.

6.0 The white-blazed Sawtooth Trail intersects from the right.

6.2 Cross SR 190 at the Fox Den Cove Parking Area.

6.6 Pass the Turtle Hollow Campsite.

8.0 Reach the connector trail on the right for the Big Knot Campsite.

8.3 Pass the Jenkins Spring Campsite on the left.

9.0 The Beech Bottom Campsite is on the left of the PMT.

11.1 At the Mollyhugger Hill parking lot, cross to the south side of SR 190; the east end of the Sawtooth Trail is on the right just across the road.

11.5 Pass a large rock and a sign for the Whiskey Still Campsite on the right.

13.2 Reach the junction with the west end of the Boot Top Trail on the left.

14.5 Pass the airplane crash monument on the left of the trail.

14.6 The connector trail from the Dowdell Knob parking area enters from the left.

15.9 The Brown Dog Campsite is up a connector trail to the left.

16.3 Pass the east end of the Boot Top Trail.

16.9 The connector trail to the Sparks Creek Campsite is on the right.

17.2 Reach trail on the right to the Big Oak Springs Campsite.

18.0 Cross SR 190 at the Rocky Point parking area.

18.4 Pass the Sassafrass Hill Campsite on the right.

20.3 Reach the Old Sawmill Campsite.

21.5 Pass the Bumblebee Ridge Campsite.

23.0 Reach the eastern trailhead parking lot at the WJSP-TV tower and SR 85 Alternate.

45 F. D. Roosevelt State Park, Dowdell Knob Loop

The Dowdell Knob Loop is a 4.4-mile microcosm of what the loop hikes along the PMT have to offer. Besides being one of the most scenic, it also passes through a couple of the historic locations on Pine Mountain.

The Dowdell Knob overlook affords an impressive panorama. This was one of President Roosevelt's favorite places to go for a cookout. Information plaques tell of his visits.

See map page 222–23.
Start: In the parking lot at the end of Dowdell Knob Road
Distance: 4.4-mile loop
Hiking time: About 2 hours
Trail surface: Dirt and rocky in places; some short sections on paved road
Best season: Mar–June; Oct–Dec
Other trail users: Hikers and backpackers only
Canine compatibility: Leashed dogs permitted
Land status: Georgia DNR, State Parks & Historic Sites Division
Nearest towns: Pine Mountain, Warm Springs
Fees and permits: Daily parking fee
Maps: USGS Pine Mountain and Warm Springs; detailed map of the trails for sale by the Pine Mountain Trail Association (all funds from map sales are used to maintain the Pine Mountain Trail); page-size map of the park including the trail available from the park office
Trail contacts: F. D. Roosevelt State Park, 2970 SR 190, Pine Mountain 31822; (706) 663-4858; www.gastateparks.org

Pine Mountain Trail Association Inc., PO Box 5, Columbus 31902; www.pinemountaintrail.org

Finding the trailhead: The Dowdell Knob Loop trailhead is 5.6 miles east of the park office. Turn south off SR 190 onto Dowdell Knob Road and drive 1.3 miles to the parking lot at the end of the road. Trailhead GPS: N32 50.434' / W84 44.748'

The Hike

The Dowdell Knob Loop combines the short parking-lot approach trail, a 3.0-mile section of the PMT, and 1.3 miles of the Boot Top Trail. The last trail earns its name from its placement on the loop. The PMT portion of the path creates the outline of a boot, with Dowdell Knob overlook at its southern heel. The Boot Top Trail cuts across the other end, or top of the boot.

There is one campsite along the path, near Mile 16.0 at Brown Dog Bluff.

The hike begins at the Dowdell Knob parking area. Take a few minutes to read the historic markers and see the life-size statue of President Roosevelt that's seated on one of the benches. Also, the barbecue pit he had built on the knob is out on the overlook. The view across King Gap to the south from the overlook is spectacular.

Walk south roughly 90 yards on the connector path leading down to the PMT and turn left to begin the loop along that blue-blazed trail. The pathway passes around the hillside, beneath the overlook. The hike continues to drop down across the mountain

The plaque memorializing the crew of the US Air Force bomber that crashed at Dowdell Knob in 1953

side through a forest of hickory, chestnut oak, and sourwood trees, mixed with a few pines.

The trail then emerges into a large area where the forest is no longer standing but lies twisted and broken on the ground. An F-2 level tornado swept across Pine Mountain around midnight on April 27, 2011. The storm damaged some facilities in FDR State Park and leveled the forests along 4.5 miles of the PMT and its connectors.

The next 0.7 mile of trail is through this huge blowdown. New growth is apparent everywhere as the understory is regenerating with early succession plant life. With the trees downed, views off the mountainside have opened up impressively.

Just after the tornado damage ends, a natural rock wall parallels the left of the trail as the path climbs into a hardwood cove. At the back of the cove the trail fords a small creek beneath a stand of beech and white oak trees with an understory of switch cane. Just past the ford, a side trail leads up the hill on the left to the Brown Dog Bluff campsite.

The path next climbs across the hillside to the junction with the Boot Top Trail. At the intersection, turn left onto the white-blazed pathway. This portion of the hike is on the ridgetop, through an area dominated by oak and pignut hickory trees. Soon a damp springhead bottom full of switch cane is on the left. From here a single, long switchback carries the path up the ridge to cross Dowdell Knob Road.

Once on the west side of the ridge, the trail parallels the headwaters of tiny Bethel Creek to the junction with the PMT. Turn left onto the blue-blazed trail and cross the branch before entering another 0.3-mile stretch of tornado damage. One of the best panoramic views on the hike is provided to the west near the midpoint of this storm clearing.

Once back in the undamaged woodlands, the path begins a steep descent for more than 0.5 mile. Along the way it again passes through 0.3 mile of storm-flattened forests. That damage ends just after the trail starts its final climb back up onto Pine Mountain.

After passing an overlook above private Concharty Lake in King Gap to the south, a plaque appears on the left side of the trail. Near this spot on October 1, 1953, a US Air Force TB-25J twin-engine bomber crashed into the mountain. Flying through rain and fog, the plane had left Eglin Air Force Base (AFB) in Florida, headed to Andrews AFB in Maryland. Only one of the six passengers and crew survived the disaster. The Pine Mountain Trail Association placed the plaque at trailside in a ceremony in November 2012.

Walking another 250 yards completes the loop at the junction with the parking lot connector trail. Turn left to reach the trailhead.

Miles and Directions

0.0 Begin walking south from the trailhead and turn left onto the PMT.

0.2 Pass beneath the Dowdell Knob overlook.

0.5 Enter the area of tornado damage.

1.2 Exit the tornado damage.

1.3 A natural-rock wall parallels the left of the trail up to the creek ford and Brown Dog Bluff connector trail.

1.8 Turn left onto the Boot Top Trail.

2.1 Pass the springhead bottom on the left.

2.4 Cross Dowdell Knob Road.

3.0 Turn left onto the PMT.

3.2 Enter the second storm-damaged area.

3.3 Reach the panoramic view to the west.

3.5 Leave the tornado damage and begin a sharp descent.

3.7 Enter the third storm-damaged area.

4.0 Exit the tornado damage and begin climbing.

4.1 A good view of Lake Concharty in Kings Gap is to the right.

4.2 Pass the plane-crash plaque.

4.3 Close the loop and turn left.

4.4 Arrive back at the trailhead.

Options

The **Mountain Creek Nature Trail** provides a 3.0-mile hike at the foot of the mountain ridge around the park campground, past Lake Delano, and through the vestiges of an old Civilian Conservation Corps fish hatchery. The path also climbs to join a short stretch of the PMT.

The **East End Loop** is the newest of the side trails off the PMT. This 3.4-mile trek is composed of 2.4 miles of the White Candle Trail and parts of the Beaver Pond Trail and PMT. Access is available at the eastern trailhead of the PMT near Warm Springs.

The 6.7-mile **Wolfden Loop** is composed of 1.7 miles of the Beaver Pond Trail and 5.0 miles on the PMT. The trek starts at the WJSP-TV tower at the east end of the PMT. The plant life, rock formations, streams, and waterfalls along the trail make it particularly interesting, and it is considered one of the most beautiful trails in the Southeast. Three primitive campsites—Sassafras Hill, Old Sawmill, and Bumblebee Ridge—are on this loop.

The longest of the loops is the 7.8-mile **Big Poplar Loop,** formed by the 2.7-mile Sawtooth Trail and 5.1 miles of the PMT. Named for a huge yellow poplar located at Mile Marker 10, it runs between Mile Markers 6 and 11 south of SR 190. Big Knot, Beech Bottom, and Grindstone Gap campsites are located on this loop. Access points are at Fox Den Cove and Mollyhugger Hill parking areas.

The **Longleaf Loop** is 6.9 miles long and can be the most confusing of the loops. There are many trail connections, along with seven paved road crossings. It may be started at the Fox Den Cove parking area or at the FDR park office.

The **Overlook Loop** lies at the western end of the PMT. It is a 3.4-mile path formed by 2.1 miles of Chestnut Oak Trail and 1.3 miles of the PMT. Starting points are at the Callaway Country Store and the Gardens Overlook parking areas.

46 Red Top Mountain State Park Trails

Red Top Mountain State Park covers 1,776 acres of land on the shores of Allatoona Lake, just a short distance northwest of Atlanta. The US Army Corps of Engineers reservoir has almost 12,000 acres of water and is a popular destination for boaters and anglers from the metro Atlanta region.

The park features boat ramps, a swimming beach, picnic areas, and historic pioneer and mining areas. Abundant deer, squirrels, wild turkeys, and other wildlife are present, along with birding opportunities. The Piedmont forest of oak, hickory, and pine, combined with many wildflowers, make this a fascinating day-hike area.

A total of 16.5 miles of hiking and multiuse trails wind through the park, offering short walks in the forest or longer day treks. The featured hike is on the Homestead Trail.

Start: At the porch of the park office
Distance: 5.6-mile lollipop
Hiking time: About 2.5 hours
Difficulty: Easy to moderate
Trail surface: Dirt; some paved road sections
Best Season: Mar–Dec
Other trail users: Hikers only
Canine compatibility: Leashed dogs permitted
Land status: Georgia DNR, State Parks & Historic Sites Division
Nearest town: Cartersville
Fees and permits: Daily parking fee
Schedule: Park hours, 7 a.m.–10 p.m., year-round
Maps: USGS Allatoona Dam; page-size map of the trails available at the park office
Trail contacts: Red Top Mountain State Park, 50 Lodge Rd. SE, Cartersville 30120; (770) 975-0055; www.gastateparks.org

Finding the trailhead: From Atlanta go north on I-75 to exit 285. Go east on Red Top Mountain Road 1.5 miles; the Homestead Trail starts at the park office. Trailhead GPS: N34 08.883' / W84 42.440'

The Hike

The trailhead for the Homestead Trail is at the park office building. This yellow-blazed trail is the most varied and interesting of all the trails in the park. It leads you through a wide variety of habitats. Mile-marker posts have been placed along the path, a handy reference for the beginning hiker.

The trail begins by alternately descending into hollows with wet-weather streams and climbing onto and over ridgelines. The bottoms have loblolly pines and tulip poplar trees with frequent Christmas ferns in the understory. Scattered throughout the trail are dogwoods and muscadine vines. On the ridges the tree canopy turns to an oak and hickory mix.

Before reaching the 1.1-mile mark, the trail twice shares the path with stretches of the red-blazed Sweet Gum Trail, passes over a boardwalk, and crosses the paved lodge entrance road. Just across the road the Sweet Gum Trail splits off a final time.

The Homestead Trail loops around several coves on Allatoona Lake.

Roughly 100 yards beyond the pavement, the loop starts and goes around to the right (counterclockwise). The path drops down to one of the arms of Allatoona Lake, which comes into view at 0.4 mile beyond the loop junction. From there you climb to a higher ridge providing scenic views of the lake.

Now skirting the lake, you reach a trailside bench that offers an overlook of the reservoir, and then you come to a trail junction. An obvious path leads downhill to the right, but the blue blazes on it are poorly marked. This trail extends down to a point overlooking the lake. From this spot you have a panoramic view of the reservoir and can see Allatoona Dam to the west. The out-and-back walk on the side trail adds 0.4 mile to the hike, while dropping and regaining 70 feet of elevation along the way.

Returning to the yellow-blazed trail, you pass near one of the old homesites that were occupied when iron ore and clay were mined from Red Top Mountain.

You can expect to see deer along any portion of the trail; the wild turkeys are much more wary and difficult to spot. You're sure to see squirrels and many species of birds.

The path loops back around the crest of Red Top Mountain before completing the loop, crossing the paved road, and returning to the park office.

Be aware that the path from the road back to the next junction where the Sweet Gum Trail joins from the left is only blazed in red, despite also carrying the Homestead Trail.

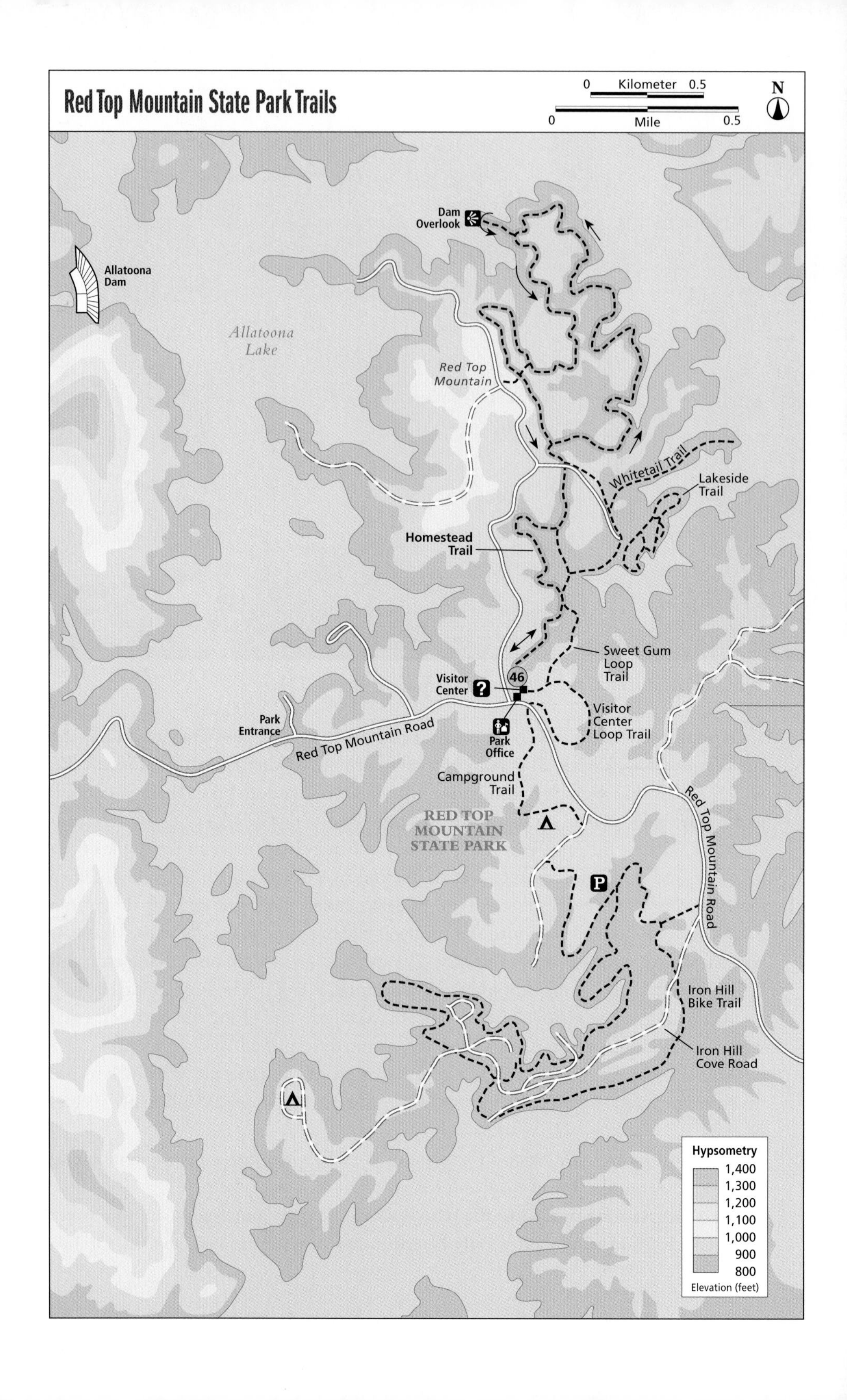
Red Top Mountain State Park Trails
0 Kilometer 0.5
0 Mile 0.5
N
Dam Overlook
Allatoona Dam
Allatoona Lake
Red Top Mountain
Whitetail Trail
Lakeside Trail
Homestead Trail
Sweet Gum Loop Trail
Visitor Center
46
Visitor Center Loop Trail
Park Entrance
Red Top Mountain Road
Park Office
Campground Trail
RED TOP MOUNTAIN STATE PARK
Red Top Mountain Road
P
Iron Hill Bike Trail
Iron Hill Cove Road
Hypsometry
1,400
1,300
1,200
1,100
1,000
900
800
Elevation (feet)

Miles and Directions

0.0 Start at the visitor center.

0.4 Join the red-blazed Sweet Gum Trail until it angles off to the right in about 90 yards. Where they join, a patch of mayapple hugs the ground on the right side of the trail.

0.9 Rejoin the Sweet Gum Trail.

1.0 Pass over a boardwalk.

1.1 Cross the paved road that leads to the lodge. The Sweet Gum Trail turns off to the right; continue straight ahead on the yellow-blazed Homestead Trail for 125 yards to where the trail divides; take the right fork to follow the loop counterclockwise.

1.4 Get your first view of Allatoona Lake, with more to follow in the next 1.5 miles. Good views of the lake are especially available in winter and early spring.

1.8 An overlook with a bench provides a very good view of a cove on the reservoir.

2.7 A short trail takes off to the right. (**Option:** Take this 0.4-mile trail out and back for a good view of the lake and Allatoona Dam.)

3.9 The trail makes a U-turn after circling the crest of Red Top Mountain.

4.5 Close the loop and head back to the visitor center.

5.6 Arrive back at the visitor center.

Options

The **Lakeside Trail** is 0.6 mile long, completely barrier free and wheelchair accessible. It is a good trail for anyone interested in wildlife. Bird feeders and bird and mammal nest boxes are placed at appropriate places along the trail. White-tailed deer come right to the trail. They are well conditioned to people and easily seen if you remain quiet. Many birds, including hummingbirds and a variety of songbirds, are attracted to the area. Lake Allatoona is visible throughout most of the walk.

The Vaughn Cabin, a pioneer structure dating from 1869, is on this trail, along with exhibits of vintage farm equipment. The path also passes a boat dock.

Two cross paths make it possible to return to the trailhead without making the entire loop or backtracking. A small field, mixed hardwood-pine forest, and lake edge give the walk an interesting mixture of habitat types.

The green-blazed **Visitor Center Loop Trail** begins at the north end of the park office parking lot on the same path as the Sweet Gum Trail (red blazes). At 165 yards the Sweet Gum Trail forks to the left. The undulating Visitor Center Trail, a 0.6-mile loop, takes you through stands of almost pure loblolly pine and into a forest of large hardwood trees and beside a small stream. There are two observation platforms along the path. The trail ends beside the tennis courts at the south end of the visitor center parking lot.

The **Whitetail Trail** bears white blazes and originates at the visitor center area. This path leads down a ridge and then follows a short hollow toward the lake. From that it climbs to the top of a point running out into Allatoona Lake. The 0.5-mile trail ends at the rocky tip of the point, where you have a view of the lake.

A short side trail leads to a panoramic view of the lake, including a view of Allatoona Dam.

The **Sweet Gum Loop Trail,** marked with red blazes, travels along a dry ridge of white, chestnut, and red oaks, with dogwoods, huckleberries, and other shrubs growing underneath. This is a good place to look for spring wildflowers. The trail overlooks a small, quiet valley. Two observation decks allow you to sit and watch for wildlife.

The very interesting gold-blazed 0.5-mile **Campground Trail** leads from the campground to the park office. It passes an opening in the woods where deer are likely to be seen, crosses three bridges, and passes the stone ruins of an old homestead. The trailhead is located in the campground near comfort station No. 2.

The **Iron Hill Bike Trail** is a multi-use biking and hiking gravel path. This trail makes a 3.9-mile loop through an area that hosted an iron mining community in the nineteenth century. The path follows the shoreline of the lake, passing amid a profusion of native wildlife and plants.

The parking lot for this trail is located off Red Top Mountain Road, on the right 0.5 mile past the campground as you travel to the southeast.

Local Information

Accommodations

Red Top Mountain State Park has a 92-site RV and tent campground, a yurt, and 18 rental cottages.

Organizations

Friends of Red Top Mountain State Park; FriendsOfRedTop.org

47 High Falls State Park Trails

High Falls State Park covers 1,050 acres in Monroe County on the shores of High Falls Lake. The impoundment is formed by an old rock dam on the Towaliga River. The river derives its name from the Creek Indian language and translates as "roasted scalps." Those Native Americans were known to scalp their enemies and used the area around High Falls on the river to dry and preserve those trophies.

Waterfalls below the lake drop almost 100 feet in multiple cascades over granite outcrops. These shoals give the area and the state park their names. This is an area of remarkable natural beauty and historic significance, with something of interest throughout the year, including spring wildflowers, fishing, fall colors, and bird migrations.

The rockwork below the river dam is a remnant of the hydropower operation that continued in operation until the mid-twentieth century. Previously there had been a gristmill at the site that was burned during the Civil War and rebuilt in 1866. The park office has excellent historical information on the many businesses that once flourished on the power supplied by the falling water.

The park features picnic and camping areas, boat ramps, playgrounds, miniature golf, a swimming pool, and fishing areas on the lake and river. Three hiking trails varying in length and difficulty provide access to the falls, as well as to historical and natural areas of the park.

The featured hike is a combination trek on the 0.7-mile Historic and 1.9-mile Tranquil Trails.

Start: At a parking area on the left side of Towaliga River Drive on the southwest side of the river
Distance: 2.6-mile double loop
Hiking time: About 1–1.5 hours
Difficulty: Easy to moderate
Trail surface: Loam with leaf litter; occasional rocky areas
Best season: Mar–Dec
Other trail users: Hikers only
Canine compatibility: Leashed dogs permitted
Land status: Georgia DNR, State Parks & Historic Sites Division
Nearest town: Forsyth
Fees and permits: Daily parking fee
Schedule: Park hours, 7 a.m.–10 p.m., year-round
Maps: USGS High Falls; detailed maps of the park and trails available from the park office
Trail contacts: High Falls State Park, 76 High Falls Park Dr., Jackson 30233; (478) 993-3053; www.gastateparks.org

Finding the trailhead: From exit 198 on I-75, go east 1.5 miles on High Falls Road to the park entrance. To reach the trailhead for the Historic and Tranquil Trails, turn right on Towaliga River Drive at the park entrance sign. The parking area is at 0.2 mile on the left. The Historic Trail is on the north side of the road, and the Tranquil Trail runs to the south. Trailhead GPS: N33 10.602' / W84 00.968'

The old millstones and dam on the Towaliga River at the turnaround point on the Historic Trail

The Hike

The Historic and Tranquil Trails provide samples of all the habitats, history, and scenic views that the park has to offer. The hardwood forests of the yellow-blazed Tranquil Trail are home to deer, turkeys, squirrels, foxes, skunks, and many songbirds. The Historic Trail provides views of the shoals on the river and passes amid the ruins of the old canal and hydroelectric powerhouse that were used in conjunction with the rock dam.

Start the hike at the parking area on the left side of Towaliga River Drive. Begin by walking north across the Canal Dam on the Historic Trail. There are no blazes on this path, but it is easily followed.

As you walk with the canal on the left, the opposite side is covered with a thick stand of bamboo cane. To the right the hillside drops sharply toward the river. After passing the junction where the loop turns down the hillside, continue straight ahead. Next, cross High Falls Road to a millstone at the old mill site. The stub of the old Alabama Bridge extends out over the river, offering a good view upstream toward the rock dam.

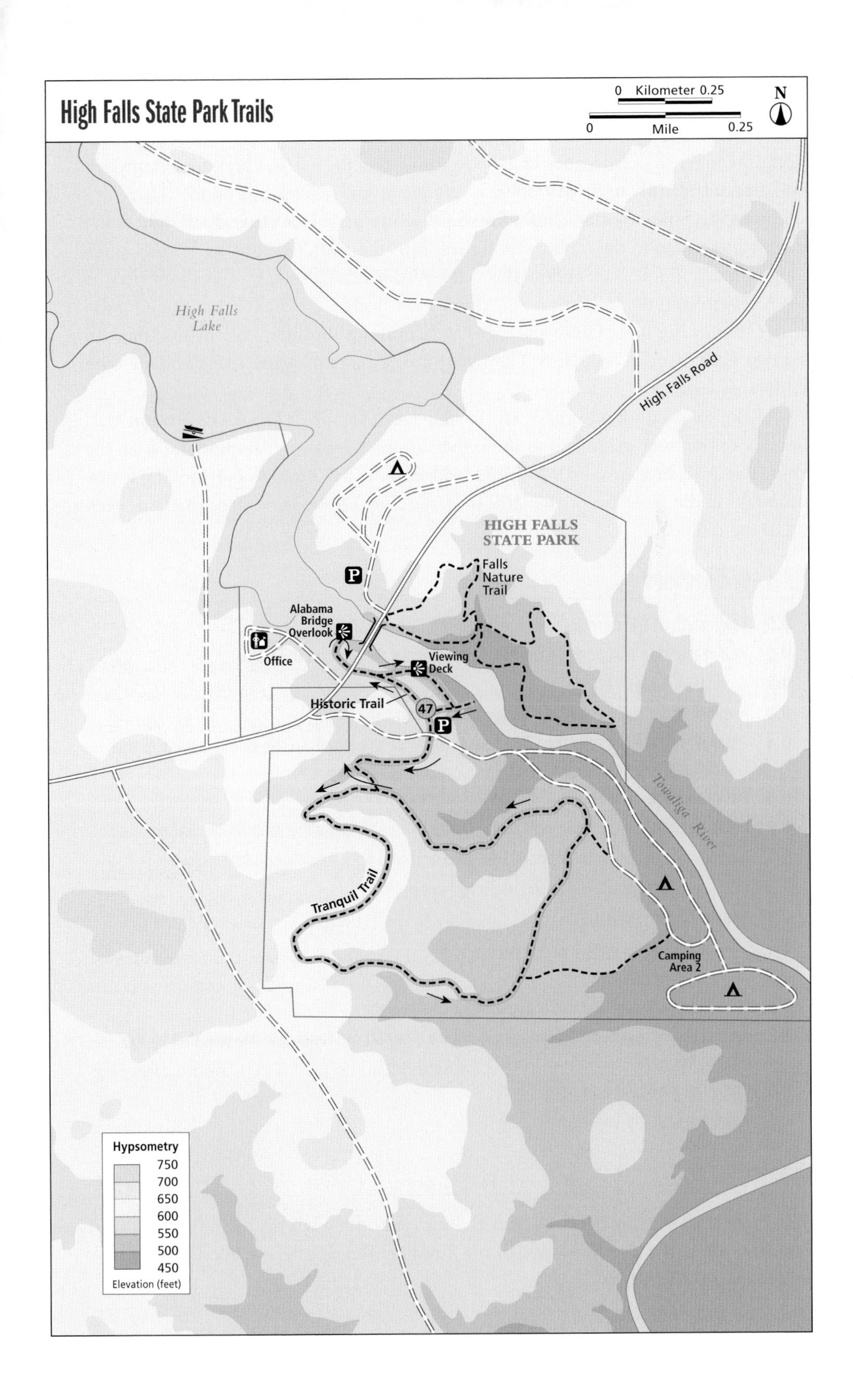
High Falls State Park Trails
0 Kilometer 0.25
0 Mile 0.25
N
High Falls Lake
High Falls Road
HIGH FALLS STATE PARK
Falls Nature Trail
Alabama Bridge Overlook
Office
Viewing Deck
Historic Trail
47
Towaliga River
Tranquil Trail
Camping Area 2
Hypsometry
750
700
650
600
550
500
450
Elevation (feet)

Retrace your route back to the loop junction and turn left down the hill. Two observation decks on this portion of the path offer views of Towaliga Falls. A bit farther along, the trail reaches the ruins of the powerhouse on the left. Just beyond, a connector trail descends sharply to the left down to the picnic and fishing area on the river.

From this point the trail climbs back up to Towaliga River Drive. Turn right along the road to return to the trailhead and then cross the road. You now are at the beginning of the Tranquil Trail. Follow this yellow-blazed trail down to a small stream.

After crossing the stream on a small wooden bridge, you next reach the junction at the start of the loop. Go to the right and climb up through a hardwood forest to a ridge with a more level area. Then start a descent into a gully resplendent with Christmas ferns.

As the loop continues, cross two footbridges over small brooks or erosion gullies before reaching a side trail to the right. This path leads to Campground 2 on the river. The path then crosses four more bridges to reach a bench overlooking a tiny waterfall on the right. Soon after this spot, the loop closes. Turn right to climb back up to the trailhead.

Miles and Directions

0.0 Start north at the parking area and cross the Canal Dam.

0.1 Reach the loop trail junction on the right. Continue straight on the trail.

0.2 Cross High Falls Road.

0.3 Arrive at the millstone and old bridge observation site.

0.4 Retrace your steps to the loop junction and turn to the left down the wooden stairs to the two observation decks.

0.6 Pass the powerhouse ruins and junction with the connector trail to the fishing area.

0.7 Arrive back at the trailhead on Towaliga River Drive and cross the road on the Tranquil Trail.

0.9 Reach the junction of the Tranquil Trail loop and turn right to walk counterclockwise.

1.2 Hike along the ridge crest at the trail's highest point.

1.3 Reach the fern gullies.

1.4 Cross a footbridge over a fern gully.

1.7 Reach another footbridge.

1.9 Pass the connector trail to Campground 2 on the right.

2.3 After crossing four more footbridges, come to a bench overlooking a tiny waterfall on the right of the path.

2.4 Close the loop and turn right.

2.6 Arrive back at the trailhead.

Options

The **Falls Trail** forms a figure eight with loops at both ends. This 1.2-mile red-blazed trail runs along the northeast side of the Towaliga River, offering good, close views of Towaliga Falls.

48 Charlie Elliott Wildlife Center Trails

The 6,400-acre Charlie Elliott Wildlife Center encompasses the Marben Public Fishing Area (PFA), the Clybel Wildlife Management Area (WMA), and the Charlie Elliott Visitor Center and Conference Center. This is a must-visit area for hiking, birding, fishing, and family outings.

Before being purchased by the Georgia Department of Natural Resources, the tract was used as a private hunting and fishing retreat.

Today the wildlife center is a museum of the history of modern conservation in Georgia, demonstrated in the life of conservationist, wildlife administrator, and outdoors writer Charlie Elliott. The WMA and PFA provide public access to hunting and fishing. The property contains twenty man-made lakes that are open to fishing under varying regulations. It is worth noting that one of those, Margery Lake, has produced the No. 2 and No. 5 biggest largemouth bass ever caught in Georgia. Those lunkers respectively weighed 18 pounds, 1 ounce, and 17 pounds, 4 ounces.

Five short trails within the no-hunting safety zone of the wildlife center total 5.4 miles and provide easy walking as they pass through a variety of habitats from dense woodlands, open fields, and lakeshores to granite outcrops with unique fauna and flora. Additionally, there is a 5.7-mile multiuse trail that meanders through the WMA grounds.

The featured hike is the Clubhouse Trail.

Start: At a shared trailhead at the visitor center
Distance: 1.9-mile lollipop
Hiking time: About 1–1.5 hours
Difficulty: Easy
Trail surface: Soil and loam
Best season: Apr–June; Sept–Nov
Other trail users: Hikers only
Canine compatibility: Leashed dogs permitted
Land status: Georgia DNR, Wildlife Resources Division
Nearest towns: Mansfield, Monticello
Fees and permits: No fees or permits to use the hiking trails
Schedule: Trails open year-round; visitor center open 9 a.m.–4:30 p.m. Tues–Sat, except on state holidays
Maps: USGS Farrar; trail map available at the visitor center or online
Trail contacts: Charlie Elliott Wildlife Center, 543 Elliott Trail, Mansfield 30055; (770) 784-3059; www.georgiawildlife.com/node/694

Finding the trailhead: From Mansfield travel 3 miles south, or 14 miles north from Monticello, on SR 11 and turn southwest on Marben Farm Road. At 0.8 mile turn right on Elliott Trail and proceed to the visitor center parking area. The trailhead is at the walkway leading to the visitor center. Trailhead GPS: N33 27.760' / W83 44.028'

The Hike

Starting at the trailhead, the path turns sharply left at the wooden direction sign 50 yards into the hike. This also is the junction where the Granite Outcrop Trail splits

A view of Clubhouse Lake from the western shore

off to the right. The blazes on the trail now are red. From here the path curves back to the left around and behind the visitor center, where it crosses two short bridges while dropping into a creek valley full of granite boulders. At the bottom the trail crosses the creek on a third bridge and reaches the junction with the white-blazed Pigeonhouse Trail on the left.

Next the path climbs quickly up the opposite side of the creek bottom to run for a short distance on the ridge crest. Upon reaching the next trail junction, turn right to walk the loop in a counterclockwise direction. At this point the trail drops sharply downhill, ending the descent on some wooden steps that bring you to the shore of Clubhouse Lake.

The trail now crosses one of the feeder creeks at the head of the lake and begins skirting along the steep hillside between the water and the conference center buildings. Through here the trail has some wild ginger, or heartleaf, along the path and passes close to several very large beech trees.

Upon reaching the lake dam, the yellow-blazed Murder Creek Trail approaches from the right. Continue to follow the red blazes across the dam, past the fishing pier, to the opposite side.

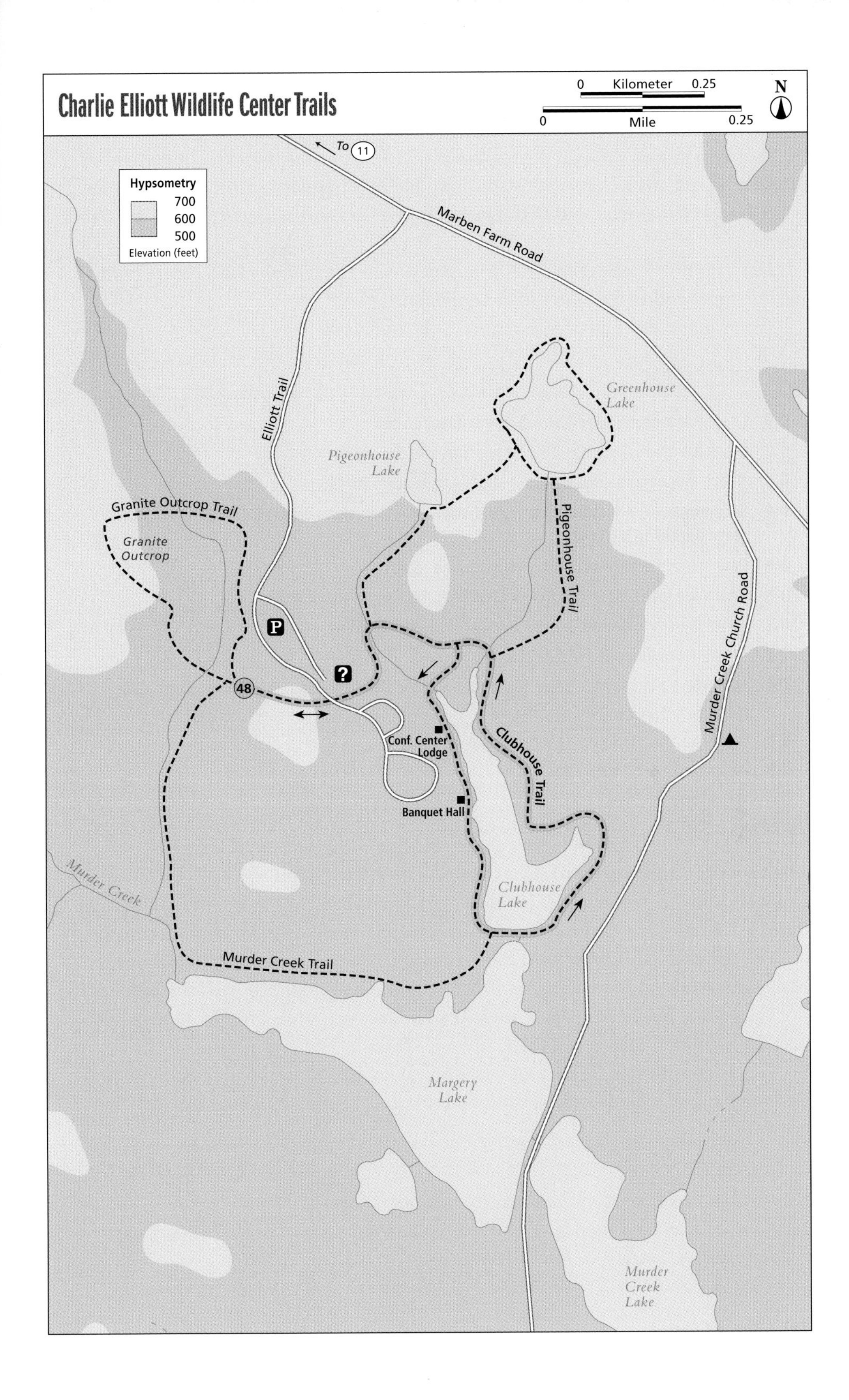

Charlie Elliott Wildlife Center Trails
0
Kilometer
0.25
0
Mile
0.25
N
Hypsometry
700
600
500
Elevation (feet)
To
11
Marben Farm Road
Elliott Trail
Greenhouse Lake
Pigeonhouse Lake
Granite Outcrop Trail
Granite Outcrop
Pigeonhouse Trail
Murder Creek Church Road
P
?
48
Conf. Center Lodge
Banquet Hall
Clubhouse Trail
Murder Creek
Clubhouse Lake
Murder Creek Trail
Margery Lake
Murder Creek Lake

Climb the set of stairs beside the Brooke Ager Discovery Building and turn left, following the lakeshore.

Shortly you pass through a large boulder field and then, near the upper end of the lake, an old abandoned deer stand is visible in a tree just off the trail. Soon the white blazes of the other end of the Pigeonhouse Trail are seen on the right at a trail junction.

The path now crosses the other tributary stream entering the lake, before rounding the upper end of the water to close the loop.

Turn right at this junction to return to the trailhead.

Miles and Directions

0.0 Leave the trailhead and turn left at the direction sign.

0.2 Cross the creek and pass the first junction with the Pigeonhouse Trail.

0.3 Reach the loop junction and turn sharply right down the hill.

0.4 Descend a set of wooden steps to the lakeshore, then cross the bridge over the feeder stream entering the lake.

0.5 Pass the conference center buildings on the right.

0.8 Reach the lake's dam and the junction with the Murder Creek Trail.

0.9 Climb the steps beside the Brooke Ager Discovery Building.

1.1 Pass the boulder pile on the right.

1.4 Just before reaching the second junction with the Pigeonhouse Trail, an abandoned deer stand is in a tree overlooking the trail.

1.5 Close the loop and turn right for the trailhead.

1.9 Arrive back at the trailhead.

Options

The **Granite Outcrop Trail** shares the path with the Clubhouse Trail for 50 yards to a wooden orientation sign. This blue-blazed trail then runs to the right. The path forms a 1.1-mile loop that runs over two ridges and circles a large granite formation.

The 5.7-mile **Multiuse Trail** forms a loop through the more open areas of the hunting grounds on Marben Farms WMA. It is open to hiking, horses, and bicycles.

The yellow-blazed **Murder Creek Trail** follows that stream for 0.9 mile to connect the Granite Outcrop and the Clubhouse Trails.

The **Pigeonhouse Trail** loops northward to pass close by Pigeonhouse and Greenhouse Lakes. Both ends of this white-blazed, 1.2-mile trail intersect the Clubhouse Trail.

49 Piedmont National Wildlife Refuge Trails

The Piedmont National Wildlife Refuge was established in 1939 to manage the wildlife potential of the exhausted farmland. Walking these paths provides a window into the natural and human history of the region.

The area also features a visitor center, the Little Rock Wildlife Drive, and several ponds. An information kiosk provides basic details about the red-cockaded woodpecker and other wildlife on the refuge.

Another sign cautions about ticks, which can transmit Lyme disease and other ailments. Even in cooler weather it is wise to wear protective clothing, tuck pants into footwear, use a strong insect repellent, and check for ticks both during and after the hike.

Three trails are located on the refuge, totaling 4.7 miles of paths. The Red-cockaded Woodpecker, Pine & Creek, and Allison Lake Trails are located near the visitor center.

The featured hike is the Red-cockaded Woodpecker Trail.

Start: At the information kiosk in the parking lot at the end of CR 262
Distance: 2.9-mile lollipop
Hiking time: About 1.5 hours
Difficulty: Easy
Trail surface: Clay loam
Best season: Mar–June; Oct–Dec
Other trail users: Hikers only
Canine compatibility: Leashed dogs permitted
Land status: US Fish and Wildlife Service
Nearest towns: Forsyth, Monticello
Fees and permits: None
Schedule: Open year-round during daylight hours
Maps: USGS Dames Ferry and Hillsboro; trail maps available at the visitor center; Oconee National Forest map
Trail contacts: Refuge Manager, Piedmont National Wildlife Refuge, 718 Juliette Rd., Round Oak 31038; (478) 986-5441; www.fws.gov/piedmont/

Finding the trailhead: From I-75 at exit 186 in Forsyth, travel east on Juliette Road. Go 9.4 miles to a bridge across the Ocmulgee River. Continue on Round Oak Juliette Road 8.2 miles to the refuge visitor center; turn left onto CR 262. The visitor center is 0.5 mile on the right. Continue to the end of the road for the Red-cockaded Woodpecker Trail. Trailhead GPS: N33 06.857' / W83 41.076'

The Hike

The featured Red-cockaded Woodpecker Trail goes through typical pine-hardwood forest to an active nesting site of this small, endangered bird. Benches have been placed so that you can sit quietly to watch for the birds at their nest cavities in live pine trees.

The trail begins at the information kiosk at the end of CR 262. The path quickly passes the start of the Allison Lake Trail on the right and then follows the paved drive

The trail passes the boat landing and fishing pier on Allison Lake.

downhill to Allison Lake. A left turn next puts you on an unpaved service road across the lake's dam.

Nest boxes for wood ducks are placed about the lake and are easily seen from the trail. This area was one of the pioneer places for experimentation with wood duck boxes to improve the population of this most beautiful of our native ducks.

Across the dam the trail continues on the service road for another few yards before turning left into a pine forest on a wide path. Fiberglass posts with hiker symbols mark the path throughout the loop. There also are interpretive signs located along the course of the hike.

As the trail enters wetter sites, oak, yellow poplar, and sweet gum trees replace the pines. The undergrowth of dogwood and occasional redbud trees bloom profusely in early spring. Wildlife along the trail includes deer, foxes, gray squirrels, turkeys, and songbirds.

After crossing a footbridge, reach a bench at the point where the loop portion of the trail begins. The right prong leads to the red-cockaded woodpecker colony; the left prong is the return path to complete the loop.

At 250 yards into the loop the trail crosses a footbridge. Through here watch for erosion gullies that indicate the extent to which this area was farmed during the early 1930s, before it became a national wildlife refuge.

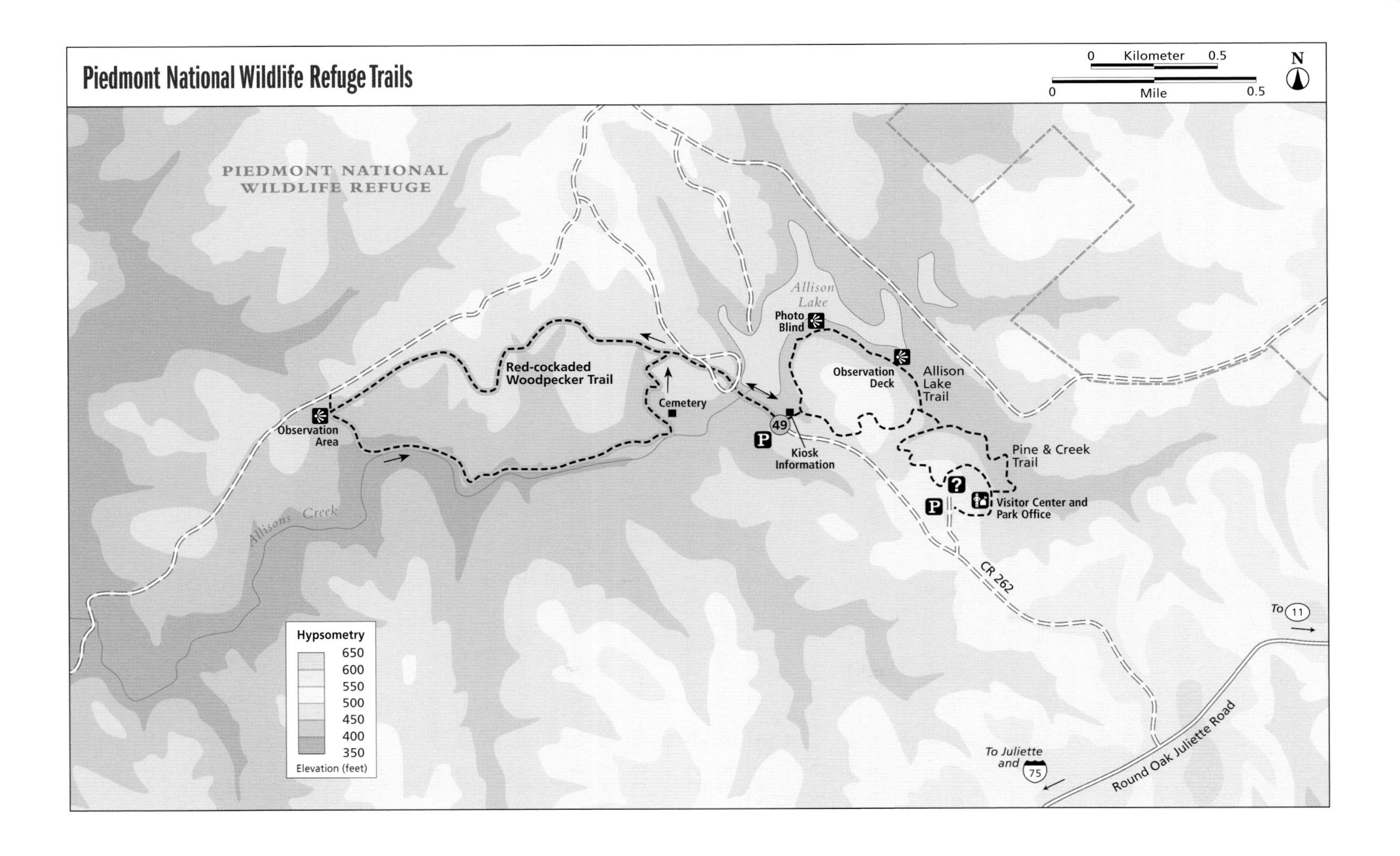
Piedmont National Wildlife Refuge Trails
0 Kilometer 0.5
0 Mile 0.5
N
PIEDMONT NATIONAL
WILDLIFE REFUGE
Allison Lake
Photo Blind
Observation Deck
Allison Lake Trail
Red-cockaded Woodpecker Trail
Cemetery
Observation Area
49
Kiosk Information
Pine & Creek Trail
Visitor Center and Park Office
Allisons Creek
CR 262
To 11
To Juliette and 75
Round Oak Juliette Road
Hypsometry
650
600
550
500
450
400
350
Elevation (feet)

At slightly more than a mile, where the path parallels a dirt road on the right, you reach the mature, towering loblolly pines that are the focal point of the trail. A white ring is painted about 8 feet up on selected trees. These designate the nest trees of the endangered red-cockaded woodpecker. The birds excavate nest cavities in old, live pines that have a fungus disease called red-heart. The small woodpeckers chip away at the bark around the nest cavity, causing the resin to flow down around the tree. The cavities are 15 to 20 feet and higher above the ground.

A bench has been provided for watching the trees for a glimpse of these rare birds. Quiet observation often results in seeing the 8.5-inch woodpeckers, described as zebra-backed with a black cap and a white cheek. They live in family colonies and use the same nest cavity for several years.

The trail next leads away from the nesting colony down to Allison Creek. Wildflowers, ferns, and other plants that prefer moist soils are abundant along the floodplain. The beautiful piedmont azalea grows here, blooming in April and May.

After crossing another footbridge, keep an eye out for a rock wall off the trail to the right. This is an old cemetery. The graves are marked with stones that are so weathered that no detail is visible.

Upon closing the loop, turn right to walk back to the trailhead.

Miles and Directions

0.0 Start the hike at the information kiosk.

0.3 Leave the service road to follow the trail marked by the fiberglass posts with hiker symbols.

0.6 The trail forks; take the right fork.

0.8 Cross the footbridge.

1.1 Arrive at the benches near the red-cockaded woodpecker nest site. Then follow the trail marker posts, continuing around the loop.

1.6 Reach Allison Creek and walk to the left, upstream along the flow.

1.9 Veer left, leaving the creek, crossing a footbridge, and heading uphill.

2.3 Close the loop and turn right to return to the trailhead.

2.9 Arrive back at the parking area and information kiosk.

Options

The **Pine & Creek Trail** forms a loop beginning at the visitor center and running toward Allison Lake. It is interesting because of the variety of habitats through which it passes.

The 0.9-mile hike begins at a concrete-paved, wheelchair-accessible section 500 feet long. A backyard wildlife habitat demonstration area with a small pool and plantings attracts birds, butterflies, and other animals.

Red-cockaded woodpecker nest trees along the trail are marked with white rings.

The path then drops down the slope to the creek. The forest changes from a mostly pine canopy to deciduous hardwoods. A bench at a spring invites you to stop and take in the quietness of this pleasant microhabitat.

The Pine & Creek Trail connects to the Allison Lake Trail at an observation deck, before looping back to the trailhead.

The **Allison Lake Trail** begins at the shared trailhead with the Red-cockaded Woodpecker Trail. The 0.9-mile path creates a loop through loblolly pine and bottomland hardwood forests beside attractive Allison Lake. A completely covered photo blind provides an excellent observation point and should be approached quietly.

50 Hard Labor Creek State Park Trails

Hard Labor Creek State Park is a 5,864-acre facility situated to the north of I-20, between Covington and Madison in eastern Georgia. Local lore offers two sources for the park's name. One ascribes the name's origin to antebellum slaves who worked in the summer sun in surrounding plantation fields, while the other attributes it to Native Americans that found the stream hard to cross.

The park is best known for its golf course, fishing lakes, swimming beach, and rental cabins. There also are two interconnecting hiking trails that pass through farmland abandoned in the mid-1930s. Additionally, 22 miles of equestrian trails wind through the park.

The featured trail is a joint trek on the Brantley Nature and Beaverpond Nature Trails.

Start: About 100 yards in front of the office/trading post
Distance: 2.2-mile loop
Hiking time: About 1.5 hours
Difficulty: Easy
Trail surface: Dirt with leaf litter
Best season: Year-round
Other trail users: Hikers only
Canine compatibility: Leashed dogs permitted
Land status: Georgia DNR, State Parks & Historic Sites Division
Nearest town: Rutledge
Fees and permits: Daily parking fee
Schedule: Park hours 7 a.m.–10 p.m., year-round
Maps: USGS Rutledge North; trail maps available at the office/trading post
Trail contacts: Hard Labor Creek State Park, 5 Hard Labor Creek Rd., Rutledge 30663; (706) 557-3001; www.gastateparks.org

Finding the trailhead: From I-20 at exit 105, go north on Newborn Road 2.8 miles to Rutledge and continue 2.5 miles on Fairplay Road to Knox Chapel Road. Turn left and go 0.4 mile to Campground Road. Turn right; the office/trading post is 0.1 mile on the right. The trailhead for Brantley Nature Trail is about 100 yards in front of the office on the left of the road to the campground. Trailhead GPS: N33 39.889' / W83 36.354'

The Hike

The 1.0-mile Brantley Nature and 1.1-mile Beaverpond Nature Trails are most practically walked as a single hike. Both are loop trails that are joined by a 70-yard connector. Also, the Beaverpond Nature Trail does not have a separate trailhead of its own.

The trails meander through a mature, second-growth mainly pine-oak forest. However, bridges across small, eroded ravines and terraces in the woods are reminders that this was farmland until abandoned in the mid-1930s.

Wildlife you may encounter includes deer, turkeys, armadillos, and squirrels. Waterfowl and beavers can be found around the park's ponds and lakes.

The Brantley Nature Trail begins by descending a ridge from the trailhead. Along the way it passes through an exposed rock formation and then drops steeply to the bottom along a tributary of Hard Labor Creek.

Loblolly pine, several oak species, hickories, dogwood, sourwood, yellow poplar, and beech are all present. Undergrowth plants include redbud, gooseberry, muscadine, Christmas ferns, wood ferns, and pickerel weeds.

The rare piedmont barren strawberry grows along this trail as well. This low plant spreads by subsurface stems like the cultivated strawberry. The five-petaled white flowers bloom from April to June.

A giant poplar tree stands on the left of the path just after the start of the Beaverpond Nature Trail loop.

At the junction where the loop begins on the Brantley Trail, take the right fork. The trail next crosses a footbridge, just before reaching the connector path to the Beaverpond Trail. At this intersection turn right, walk 70 yards, and turn right again at the beginning of the Beaverpond loop.

The Beaverpond Nature Trail is much like the Brantley Nature Trail, except that it includes areas of older trees and the beaver pond. Roughly 50 yards past the beginning of the loop, a very large yellow poplar is on the left, about 20 yards from the trail. The tree is well over 5 feet in diameter.

Next, the beaver pond appears on the right of the trail. The path crosses three bridges over gullies as it runs long the pond.

Standing water in the pond killed a number of trees that have become excellent habitat for cavity-nesting birds, including the colorful wood duck. The pond is almost completely covered with vegetation and is a favorite place for quiet birding. Pileated and other species of woodpeckers, wading birds, and flycatchers often are observed.

Beyond the pond the trail continues to parallel the creek bottom, which is full of pickerel weed.

Once the trail veers up out of the bottom, it crosses two more bridges and then reaches a sharp left turn. A bent tree at this location forms a perfect natural bench for taking a break.

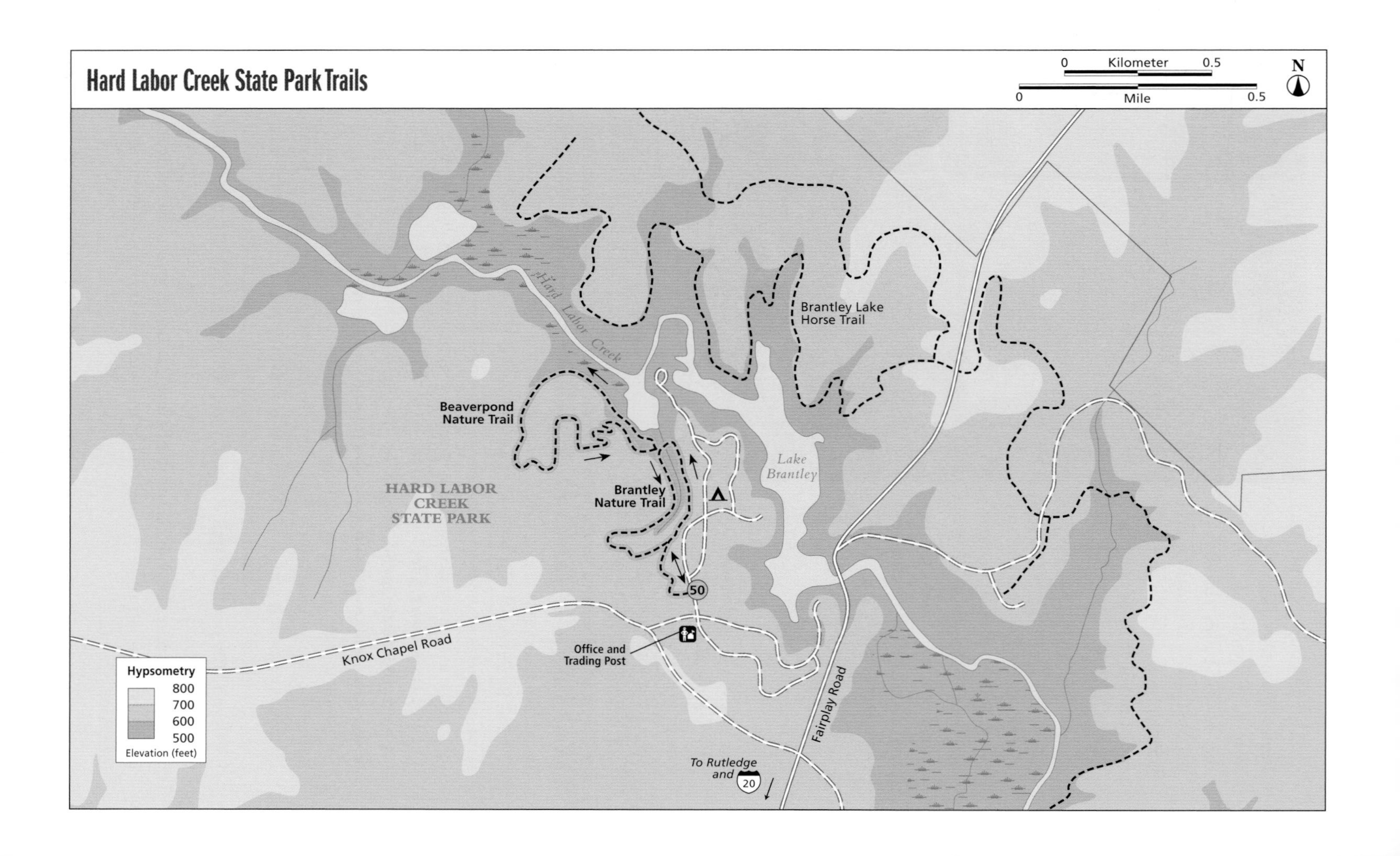
Hard Labor Creek State Park Trails
0
Kilometer
0.5
0
Mile
0.5
N
Hard Labor Creek
Beaverpond Nature Trail
Brantley Nature Trail
Brantley Lake Horse Trail
Lake Brantley
HARD LABOR CREEK STATE PARK
50
Office and Trading Post
Knox Chapel Road
Fairplay Road
To Rutledge and
20
Hypsometry
800
700
600
500
Elevation (feet)

The rest of the Beaverpond loop stays up on the ridge side, crossing three more bridges. Just prior to closing the loop, the path skirts a rock pile that was the foundation of an old building.

At the close of the loop turn right, and back at the Brantley Trail, take another right turn.

This portion of the hike also is up on the ridge side. After crossing another bridge, the path arrives at the close of this loop. Turn right and walk back to the trailhead.

Armadillos are just one of the species that may be spied on the Brantley Nature Trail.

Miles and Directions

0.0 Start at the Brantley Nature Trail trailhead.

0.1 Pass through the rock outcrop and descend to the creek bottom.

0.2 Take the right fork at the beginning of the loop.

0.4 Cross the bridge over the small branch and turn right to reach the Beaverpond Nature Trail.

0.5 Turn right onto the Beaverpond Nature Trail and at 50 yards pass the huge poplar tree.

0.6 Reach the beaver pond on the right and the creek bottom beyond.

0.7 Leave the wetland area and start to climb a well-forested hillside.

0.8 Turn sharply left at the natural bench tree.

1.4 Pass the old building foundation.

1.6 Close the loop on the Beaverpond Nature Trail; follow the connector back to the Brantley Nature Trail and turn right.

1.9 Cross the last footbridge on the trails.

2.0 Close the loop on the Brantley Nature Trail; turn sharply right.

2.2 Arrive back at the trailhead.

Local Information

Food/Lodging

Hard Labor Creek State Park has 20 rental cottages, 46 regular campsites, and 11 horse campsites; (800) 864-7275; www.gastateparks.org.

51 Twin Bridges Trail

The Twin Bridges Trail winds through low, gently rolling ridges and hollows in a mixed hardwood-pine forest on the Little River arm of Lake Sinclair. The impoundment, a Georgia Power Company reservoir on the Oconee River, was built in 1953. The lake's waters are in sight of the trail for most of the hike.

The trail name originates from the pair of bridges crossing sections of the lake in quick succession on the road at the alternate trailhead. The hike begins at the USDA Forest Service Lake Sinclair Recreation Area campground.

Because of the variety of forest and lakeshore habitat, this trail is an exceptionally productive birding area.

Start: At Camp Loop A
Distance: 3.6 miles out and back
Hiking time: About 2 hours
Difficulty: Easy
Trail surface: Soft loam with tree leaves
Best season: Year-round
Other trail users: Anglers; hunters in season
Canine compatibility: Dogs permitted
Land status: Oconee National Forest
Nearest towns: Milledgeville, Monticello
Fees and permits: Daily parking fee charged
Schedule: The campground at the trailhead is closed Dec–Mar.
Maps: USGS Resseaus Crossroads; Oconee National Forest map
Trail contacts: USDA Forest Service, Oconee Ranger District, 1199 Madison Rd., Eatonton 31024; (706) 485-7110; www.fs.usda.gov/conf

Finding the trailhead: From Monticello go east on SR 212 from its junction with SR 16. Continue 17 miles on SR 212 to Twin Bridges Road. Turn left and follow the signs 1.6 miles to the Lake Sinclair Recreation Area entrance, then go to the Camp Loop A parking area. The trailhead is off the road from the parking area at a marker with trail number 119.

From Milledgeville go north 11.2 miles on SR 212 to Twin Bridges Road; turn right and follow directions above. Trailhead GPS: N33 12.260' / W83 24.044'

The Hike

The white-blazed Twin Bridges Trail is marked number 119. This is a fine morning or afternoon hike for campers or day-use visitors. Small streams, the lakeshore, wildflowers, and wildlife add special interest.

Walk down a gentle slope from Camp Loop A and cross the bridge over a small creek at 40 yards. Along the stream are trout lilies, sometimes called dogtooth violets, which bloom in March. Across the bridge, you go through a small thicket of switch cane and into a mature hardwood forest of yellow poplar, oak, and hickory.

The path next crosses a short boardwalk over a damp area and quickly provides the first view of Lake Sinclair, which remains visible for most of the rest of the hike. Several paths leading off to the left are used by anglers to reach the lake for bank

The view of Lake Sinclair at the primitive camping area at the trail end

fishing. Lake Sinclair is a good fishing lake for largemouth bass and crappie. The tree cover extends right to the edge of the water, providing a nice shady place to fish.

The path soon reaches the first of eight short footbridges or boardwalks that dot the remainder of the trail. Only one of these spans a small creek. The rest are over gullies that are remnants of erosion caused by earlier farming. The old gullies have healed with mosses, ferns, trees, and other soil-retention plants.

Wildflowers are well represented throughout the trail. Among those is the piedmont azalea, with pink flowers on 4- or 5-foot-high bushes blooming in spring. Also look for crane-fly orchids with slender stalks of tiny greenish-yellow flowers blooming in midsummer. Watch for the delicate blooms of blue-eyed grass and tiny yellow blossoms of dwarf cinquefoil in April.

At the fourth bridge a mature yellow poplar is on the left of the trail with a large cavity at the base filled with dirt and decayed wood. Around it and on the facing bank heartleaf, or wild ginger, plants have become established. This small, sweet-smelling plant may last in one place like this for fifteen to twenty years.

Tall loblolly pines, little red cedar trees, and dogwoods are along the rest of the trail. The understory has switch cane, as well as the vines of muscadines and greenbrier.

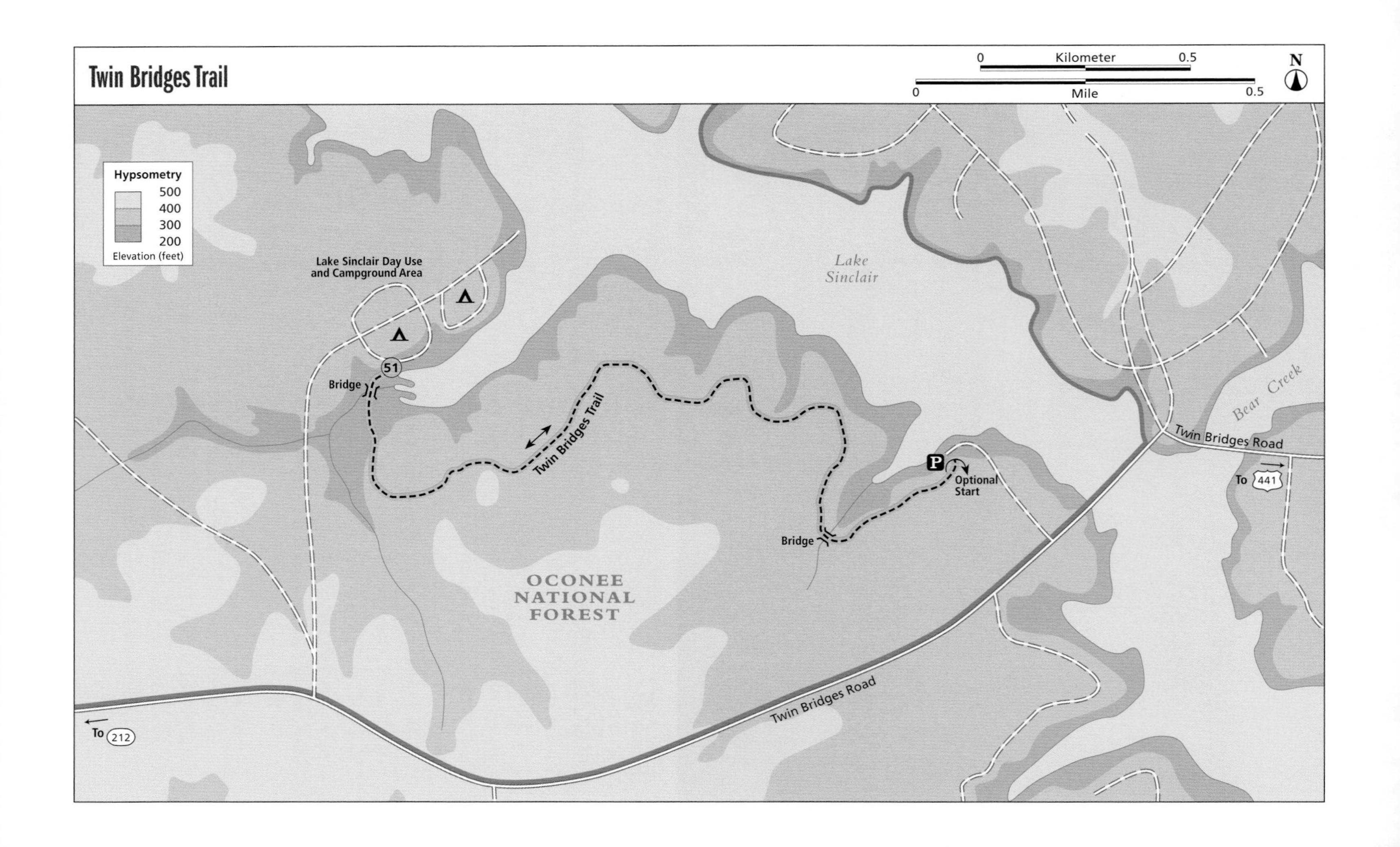
Twin Bridges Trail
0
Kilometer
0.5
0
Mile
0.5
N
Hypsometry
500
400
300
200
Elevation (feet)
Lake Sinclair Day Use
and Campground Area
51
Bridge
Twin Bridges Trail
Lake
Sinclair
Bear Creek
Twin Bridges Road
To 441
P
Optional
Start
Bridge
OCONEE
NATIONAL
FOREST
Twin Bridges Road
To 212

Near the end, the path reaches a dirt road. Turn left on the road and walk to the alternate trailhead at a forest service primitive campground-parking area.

Here you are 0.3 mile from the bridge over the Little River arm of the lake. Across that bridge and another 0.1 mile is the second bridge over Bear Creek.

Miles and Directions

0.0 Start from Camp Loop A on the white-blazed trail. Walk down a gentle slope to a bridge over a small creek.

0.2 The first view of Lake Sinclair appears on the left.

0.3 Reach the first of the footbridges over erosion gullies that are now healed and well vegetated.

0.5 Cross the bridge with the hollow poplar and wild ginger on the left.

1.7 The path enters a dirt road; follow it to the left.

1.8 Reach the primitive camping and parking area. Turn around for the return hike to the recreation area campground.

3.6 Arrive back at Camp Loop A.

52 Watson Mill Bridge State Park Trails

Watson Mill Bridge State Park is named for the 229-foot covered bridge, constructed in 1880, located at its original site across the South Fork of the Broad River, colloquially known as just South Fork River.

The waterpower from the river at this scenic shoal was once used to drive a gristmill for corn and wheat, a cotton gin, a wool factory, and a woodworking shop. In 1905 the hydroelectric powerhouse, millrace canal, and dam were added. The only remains of this era are the canal that was hewn from the granite wall, along with the powerhouse ruins.

This park has a compact series of four short trails on the south side of the river that exhibit the history of early river life and waterpower. The story is amply told with information boards and pamphlets. The trails provide a good cross section of the numerous habitat types as well. The Bottomland, Powerhouse, South Fork River, and Holly Tree Nature Trails can be combined for the 2.2-mile featured hike.

Additionally, to the north of the river there are 4.75 miles of hiking/biking trails and 12 miles of equestrian paths that can be walked.

Start: At the parking area near the southeast end of the covered bridge and dam
Distance: 2.2 miles out and back, with side loops
Hiking time: About 1.5 hours
Difficulty: Easy
Trail surface: Loamy dirt; walkways, bridges, and steps
Best season: Year-round
Other trail users: Hikers only
Canine compatibility: Leashed dogs permitted
Land status: Georgia DNR, State Parks & Historic Sites Division
Nearest towns: Comer, Elberton, and Athens
Fees and permits: Daily parking fee
Schedule: Park hours 7 a.m.–10 p.m., year-round
Maps: USGS Carlton; small map of the park with the hiking and biking trails available at the park office
Trail contacts: Watson Mill Bridge State Park, 650 Watson Mill Rd., Comer 30629; (706) 783-5349; www.gastateparks.org

Finding the trailhead: From Elberton, go west 13.6 miles on SR 72. At the park sign, turn left (south), cross the railroad track, and immediately turn right on Watson Mill Road. It is an additional 0.7 mile to the park entrance, with the covered bridge 0.4 mile farther south.

The trailhead for the South Side Trails is at the parking area on the east side of the road at the south end of the covered bridge. Trailhead GPS: N34 01.549' / W83 04.458'

The Hike

The South Side Trails are an interconnected system of paths exploring the natural and human history of the park. From the parking lot trailhead below the dam, the path begins on the Powerhouse Trail. At the junction with the Holly Tree Nature Trail,

The Watson Mill Covered Bridge and old mill dam, the centerpiece of the state park, is viewed from the Powerhouse Trail.

stay to the left and cross a footbridge over the millrace canal. Good views are afforded of the covered bridge and dam, with water flowing over the grand shoals below them.

Forty yards farther along, leave the Powerhouse Trail and turn left onto the Bottomland Trail. Here the path descends steeply down wooden steps toward the river. The area is characteristic of the Piedmont Plateau physiographic province and its associated flora. Chain ferns, spleenworts, Christmas ferns, and many spring flowers thrive in the moist riverside habitat. Dog-hobble and mountain laurel are among the shrubs growing in the moist shade. At times the river may overflow parts of this trail.

Large riverine trees—beeches, ironwoods, yellow poplars, sycamores, and water oaks—provide shade during the warm months. An exceptionally large loblolly pine is right beside the trail.

Look for tracks of deer, raccoons, squirrels, beavers, and otters in the soft, sandy soil along the path.

At the junction where the Bottomland and Powerhouse Trails again intersect, turn left on the Powerhouse Trail. The path now follows the millrace canal for 50 yards to cross the dam at the powerhouse ruins. As you walk along the canal, notice the exposed granite walls on both shores. During the warm months you may see frogs and toads as they hop into the canal waterway.

At the powerhouse ruins a connector trail runs to the right to the Holly Tree Nature Trail. The hike continues to the left and is now on the South Fork River Trail.

The well-used South Fork River Trail has no blazes, but it does have directional signs at intersections. It continues downstream for a third of a mile to Pioneer Camp 3 at the mouth of Big Clouds Creek.

Along the way the path passes a large observation deck with excellent views of the river. If you have time to sit here for a while, you may see a wood duck, other water birds, beavers, and turtles.

Next the trail crosses a footbridge over a large gully with a nice view of an attractive cove of hardwood trees and then reaches the lower junction with the Holly Tree Nature Trail on the right. Continuing down the path to the left takes you to the mouth of Big Clouds Creek.

Trees along the trail include beech, ash, hickory, yellow poplar, sycamore, and water oak—all providing food and nesting sites for the animals. Along the way is a variety of flowering plants. Heartleaf and elephant's-foot are visible most of the year. Trilliums, Solomon's seals, false Solomon's seals, trout lilies, and hepaticas bloom here in spring.

When the trail emerges into the pioneer campground, turn left along the gravel road and follow it to the last campsite at the creek mouth. There is no directional sign here, but the trail passes through the campsite and turns to the right, upstream along Big Clouds Creek.

The trail continues up the creek past Pioneer Camp 2 and ends at Pioneer Camp 1. The path passes under a piece of history in the form of the old, abandoned Whitsel Hollow Road steel bridge. Only a few steel bridges of this type are left. The bridge is now covered with vines of muscadine, honeysuckle, and trumpet creeper and provides roosting and nesting places for birds.

Big Clouds Creek flows through a typical bottomland hardwood forest, a productive habitat for plants and animals. There are many animal tracks left by deer, squirrels, beavers, and wild turkeys in the soft sandy-clay path. Thick patches of switch cane grow along the trail.

In places the creek changes character and tumbles over granite boulders. In the quiet water above and below the small cataracts are good places to fish for small bass, sunfish, and catfish.

From Pioneer Camp 1, backtrack to the South Fork River and return upstream. At the junction with the Holly Tree Nature Trail turn left onto that pathway. This trail runs sharply uphill on the ridge side, offering a drier, more upland habitat.

Near the powerhouse ruins a connector trail runs to the right to join the Powerhouse Trail. At this intersection, continue straight on Holly Tree Nature Trail. When the Holly Creek Nature Trail dead-ends into the Powerhouse Trail, turn left to reach the trailhead and the end of the hike.

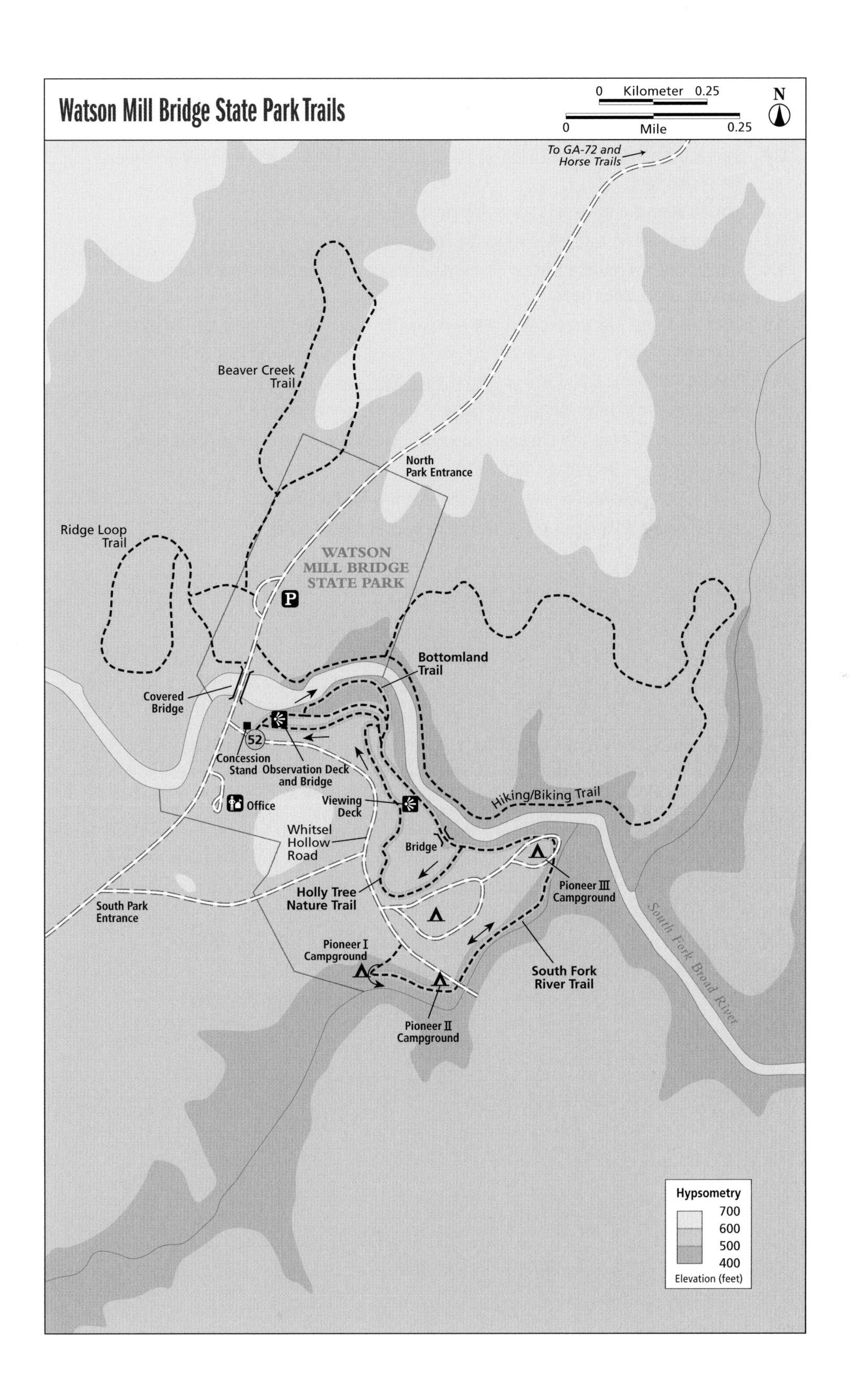

Watson Mill Bridge State Park Trails
0 Kilometer 0.25
0 Mile 0.25
N
To GA-72 and Horse Trails
Beaver Creek Trail
North Park Entrance
Ridge Loop Trail
WATSON MILL BRIDGE STATE PARK
P
Bottomland Trail
Covered Bridge
52
Concession Stand
Observation Deck and Bridge
Office
Viewing Deck
Hiking/Biking Trail
Whitsel Hollow Road
Bridge
Pioneer III Campground
Holly Tree Nature Trail
South Park Entrance
Pioneer I Campground
South Fork River Trail
South Fork Broad River
Pioneer II Campground
Hypsometry
700
600
500
400
Elevation (feet)

Miles and Directions

0.0 Start at the parking area trailhead; at 70 yards pass the junction with the Holly Tree Nature Trail on the right.

0.1 Turn left down the stairs onto the Bottomland Trail.

0.3 At this intersection, turn left to rejoin the Powerhouse Trail.

0.4 Arrive at the powerhouse ruins; continue downstream onto the South Fork River Trail and pass the observation deck.

0.5 Cross the bridge over the erosion gully and pass the second junction with the Holly Tree Nature Trail.

0.7 Pass Pioneer Camp 3 and turn upstream along Big Clouds Creek.

1.0 Pass under the old steel bridge, and come in view of Pioneer Camp 2.

1.0 Reach the end of this trail turnaround point at Pioneer Camp 1 and begin backtracking.

1.7 Turn left onto the Holly Creek Nature Trail.

2.0 Pass the connector trail on the right leading to the powerhouse ruins.

2.2 Turn left onto the Powerhouse Trail and arrive back at the trailhead.

Options

All of the paths on the north side of the river are hiking/biking or equestrian trails.

The **Ridge Loop Trail** is a 0.8-mile trek that takes roughly 30 minutes to walk. The trailhead is at the parking area on the west of the road at the north end of the covered bridge.

The **Beaver Creek Trail** begins at a second parking area, a gravel loop off Watson Mill Road, 0.1 mile north of the covered bridge. This trail covers 1.5 miles, forming a loop that takes 1 hour to walk.

The **Hiking/Biking Trail** is a 2.5-mile loop on the north side of the South Fork River. The return portion of the trail parallels the river upstream. The path begins on the east side of Watson Mill Road at the north end of the covered bridge and takes 1.5 hours to walk.

Access to 12 miles of interconnected **Equestrian Trails** is available from the Equestrian Area at the junction of Watson Mill Road and Old Fork Cemetery Road in the north end of the park. Although open to hiking, no dogs are allowed on these paths.

53 Hamburg State Outdoor Recreation Area Trails

Formerly a state park, the Hamburg State Outdoor Recreation Area is located in east Georgia's Washington County. The 741-acre facility is now overseen by the staff of nearby A. H. Stephens State Park.

The centerpieces of the area are 225-acre Hamburg Lake on the Little Ogeechee River and the gristmill located at its dam. The first mill at the site was built in 1825. That structure was replaced by the present mill in 1921. The gristmill continues to grind cornmeal during special events and contains a museum of primitive agricultural tools typical of rural Georgia.

Hamburg also offers a boat ramp, picnic area, and 30-site self-registration campground.

There are five trails totaling 3.3 miles of walking paths in the area. The 0.1-mile Hamburg Trail runs along the east side of the lake, while the 0.1-mile Blue, 1.0-mile Red, and 1.1-mile White Trails form connected loops on the north side. The 1/2-Mile Trail is on the south side of the lake. The featured hike combines the 0.1-mile Hamburg, 0.1-mile Blue, 1.0-mile Red, and 1.1-mile White Trails into a 2.9-mile lollipop trek.

Start: In the picnic area just east of the gristmill
Distance: 2.9-mile lollipop
Hiking time: About 1.5 hours
Difficulty: Easy
Trail surface: Dirt and sand
Best season: Mar–Oct
Other trail users: Hikers only
Canine compatibility: Leashed dogs permitted
Land status: Georgia DNR, State Parks & Historic Sites Division
Nearest towns: Sandersville, Sparta
Fees and permits: Daily parking fee
Schedule: Area open 7 a.m.–10 p.m. year-round; campground open Mar 15–Nov 30
Maps: USGS Warthen NE; park map available online at www.gastateparks.org/hamburg
Trail contacts: A. H. Stephens State Park; (706) 456-2602; www.gastateparks.org

Finding the trailhead: From exit 54 on I-20, go south on SR 22 for 21.1 miles. In Sparta, turn east on SR 16 and travel 12.1 miles to the intersection with SR 248. Turn right (south) and drive 6.8 miles to the park entrance on the right. The trailhead for the Hamburg Trail is just east of the gristmill in the picnic area. Trailhead GPS: N33 12.436' / W82 46.703'

The Hike

The featured hike starts out on the Hamburg Trail, covers the loops of the Red and White Trails, traverses the Blue Trail, and returns to the trailhead on the Hamburg Trail.

From the trailhead, begin walking east, crossing a boardwalk as the path leaves the picnic area and skirts the east side of Hamburg Lake. This portion of the path offers

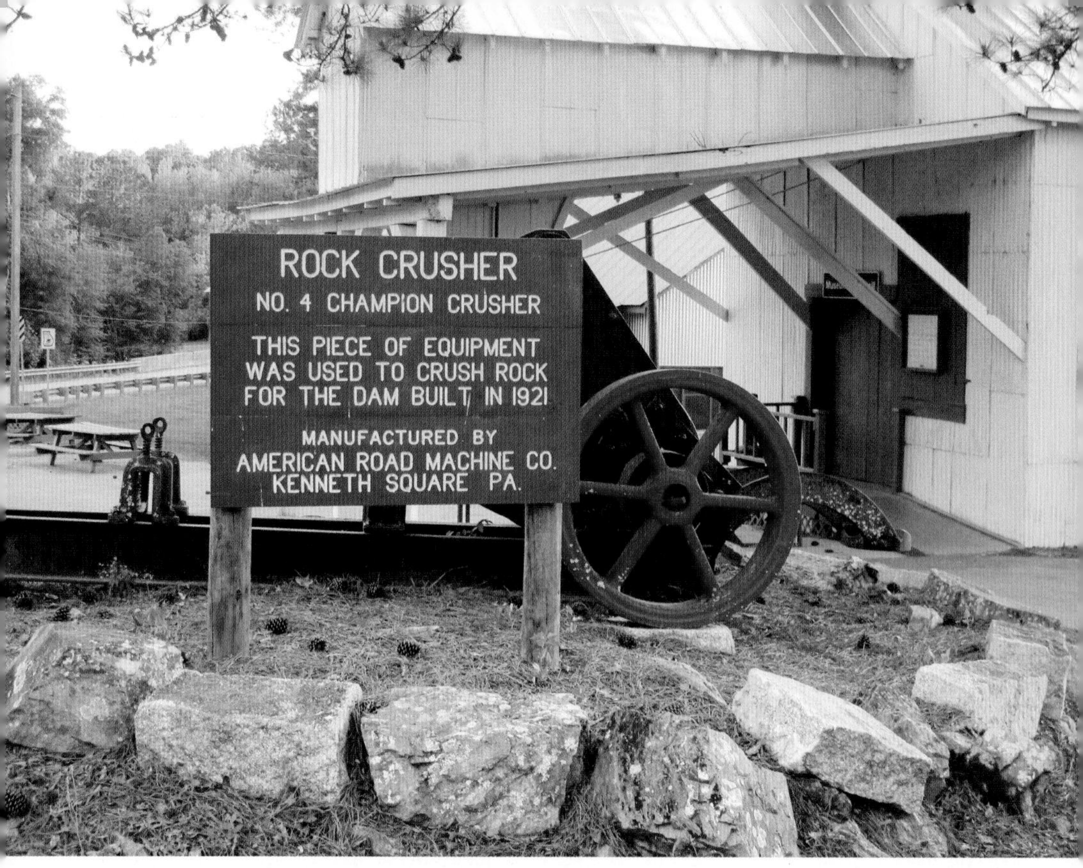

Hamburg's gristmill also serves as an agricultural equipment museum.

good views of the millpond and the gristmill at the dam. In the warmer months, turtles, alligators, and wading birds can be spotted in and along the shore of the lake.

Upon reaching the junction where the Blue Trail runs to the right, stay left on the Hamburg Trail. At the second intersection, the Hamburg Trail dead-ends into the Red Trail. Turn left to walk counterclockwise.

The entire pathway along this hike is through an oak-hickory forest, with the biggest trees being white oaks. Some very large loblolly pines also are interspersed in the woodland, along with sweet gums. The understory of smaller trees contains dogwoods and American holly. Tangles of greenbrier vines are also common.

Shortly you pass an observation deck on the left that offers more views of the lake and gristmill. Beyond, the path later passes through a grass-covered wildlife clearing. The trail then follows a cove on the lake and up a wet-weather creek to the junction with the White Trail.

Turn left onto the White Trail and walk 100 yards to the beginning of the loop portion of that path. Turn to the left to walk it counterclockwise. This trail goes back down to a bench and panoramic view at the water, where the path turns north along the lakeshore. A couple of wildlife clearings are situated along this portion of the hike. These feature open grass and sedge fields.

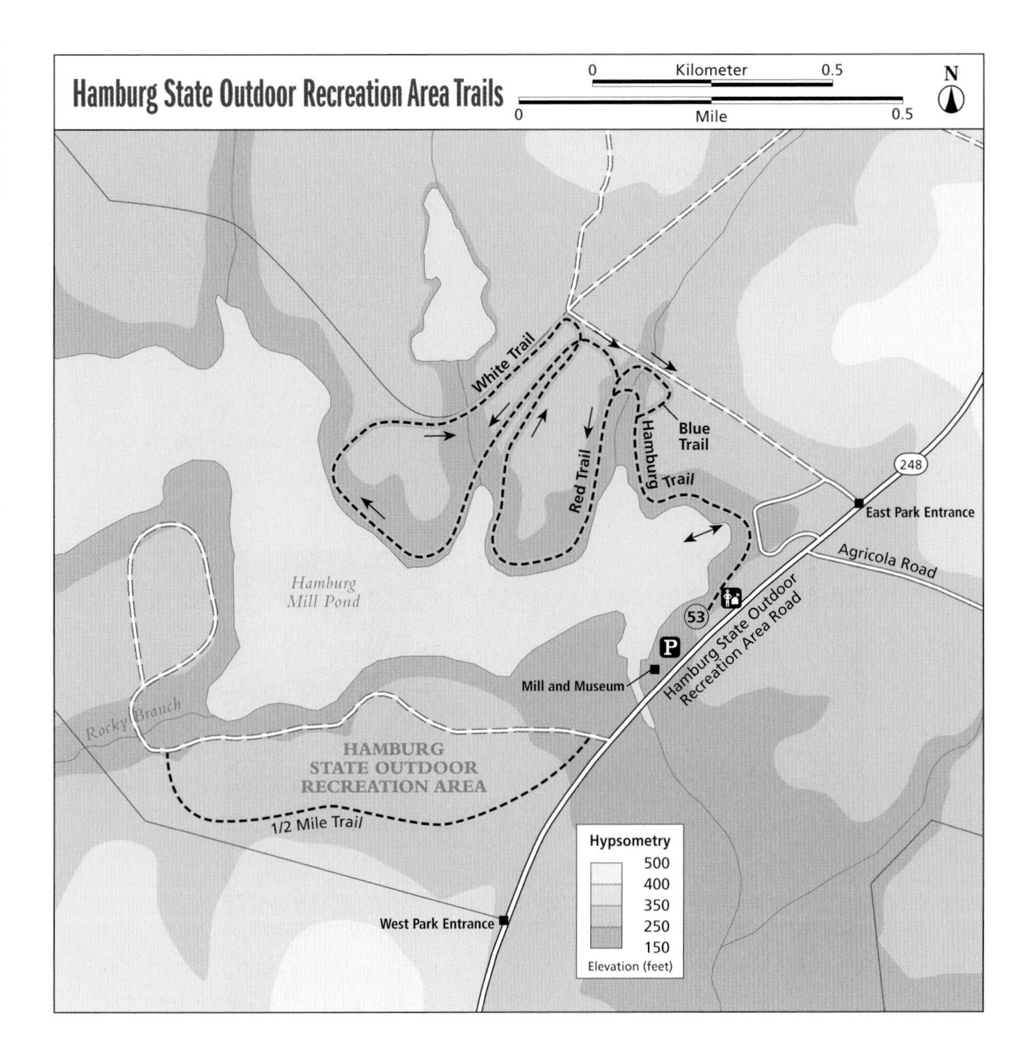

After running along the water for 0.4 mile, the path turns inland to the east. This portion of the hike is again in hardwood forest. At the close of the White Trail loop, turn left to walk back to the junction with the Red Trail and make another left.

Upon reaching the intersection with the Blue Trail, turn left to cross the footbridge. At the end of the Blue Trail, turn left onto the Hamburg Trail and proceed back to the trailhead.

Miles and Directions

0.0 Walk east from the Hamburg Trailhead, out of the picnic area and across the boardwalk.

0.3 Pass the intersection with the Blue Trail; stay to the left.

0.5 Turn left onto the Red Trail.

0.6 Reach the observation deck on the lake.

0.8 Pass through the wildlife clearing.
1.1 Turn left onto the White Trail and 100 yards later turn left at the loop intersection.
1.3 Reach the bench overlook on the lake.
1.7 The trail leaves the lakeshore.
2.1 Close the White Trail loop and return to the Red Trail; turn left.
2.5 Turn left onto the Blue Trail and cross the footbridge.
2.6 Turn left onto the Hamburg Trail.
2.9 Arrive back at the trailhead.

Options

The **1/2-Mile Trail** is on the south side of Hamburg Lake. This path connects the campground to a parking lot near the area entrance.

A view of the gristmill and dam from a vantage point on the Hamburg Trail

54 Richard B. Russell State Park Trails

Richard B. Russell State Park covers 2,508 acres on a peninsula formed by the embayment of Vans and Coldwater Creeks on Lake Richard B. Russell. Lake Russell is a 25,650-acre reservoir on the Savannah River and the border with South Carolina.

Prior to impoundment in 1980, several Native American sites were excavated in the lake bed. The Ruckers Bottom site yielded artifacts, including Clovis points, indicating that Indians used the area as early as 10,000 years ago.

The focal point of the hiking trails in the park is the Blackwell Bridge. Constructed in 1917, it is the last remaining steel bridge in Elbert County. A historical marker now describes the structure.

The park has five hiking trails stretching a total of 5.1 miles. The Blackwell Bridge Trail is the featured hike.

Start: At the east end of the beach parking lot
Distance: 1.3-mile loop
Hiking time: About 1 hour
Difficulty: Easy
Trail surface: Dirt, with short asphalt paved and rubberized surface sections
Best season: Year-round
Other trail users: Hikers only
Canine compatibility: Leashed dogs permitted
Land status: Georgia DNR, State Parks & Historic Sites Division
Nearest town: Elberton
Fees and permits: Daily parking fee
Schedule: Park hours 7 a.m.–10 p.m., year-round
Maps: USGS Lowndesville; trail map available from the park office
Trail contacts: Richard B. Russell State Park, 2650 Russell State Park Rd., Elberton 30635; (706) 213-2045; www.gastateparks.org

Finding the trailhead: From Elberton go north 1.2 miles on SR 77 to SR 368 (Ruckersville Road). Turn right and go 7.7 miles, then turn right on Russell State Park Road to the park entrance. The office and information center is on the right. Continue 4 miles to the beach parking area. The Blackwell Bridge Trailhead is at the east corner of the parking area. Trailhead GPS: N34 09.703' / W82 44.609'

The Hike

The featured Blackwell Bridge Trail takes you away from the main park activity area to a pleasant walk along the lake to the historic bridge. There are no blazes, but the path is easily followed. The trail is basically under a hardwood forest, so even in the heat of summer the hike is mostly shaded.

The principal trees are oaks, maples, sycamores, sweet gums, black gums, yellow poplars, and dogwoods. Shrub vegetation beneath is high-bush huckleberries, blueberries, and hawthorns.

Spring wildflowers begin to show under the leafless trees in late February and continue until May. Bloodroots, trilliums, and dwarf irises grow in the moist coves.

The trail crosses historic Blackwell Bridge over an arm of Lake Richard B. Russell.

Other common plants seen are Christmas ferns and spleenworts, as well as patches of the almost-white pincushion moss and reindeer-moss lichen. The latter plant occurs from the arctic to north Florida.

This second-growth forest has become good habitat for white-tailed deer, gray or fox squirrels, opossums, and raccoons. It is also a fine birding area during spring and fall migrations, with many species of songbirds, hawks, owls, and crows. Near the lake coves you may see egrets, herons, ducks, and geese.

The Blackwell Bridge Trail begins with an asphalt-paved path down to a footbridge and information sign with a map at the start of the loop. The trail then changes to a rubberized surface.

From the footbridge the path follows the lakeshore to the right in a counterclockwise direction around coves and points. The lake is visible for much of the way, especially in the winter when the leaves are off the trees.

The trail emerges from the forest into a grassy area on the lakefront at the park's Group Shelter. The path turns right off the rubberized trail (which continues up to the shelter) to continue along the lakeshore and intersect the old road to Blackwell Bridge. Drop down the hill on the old road to the bridge. Besides being a piece of local history, the bridge offers a great view of the Van Creek arm of the reservoir.

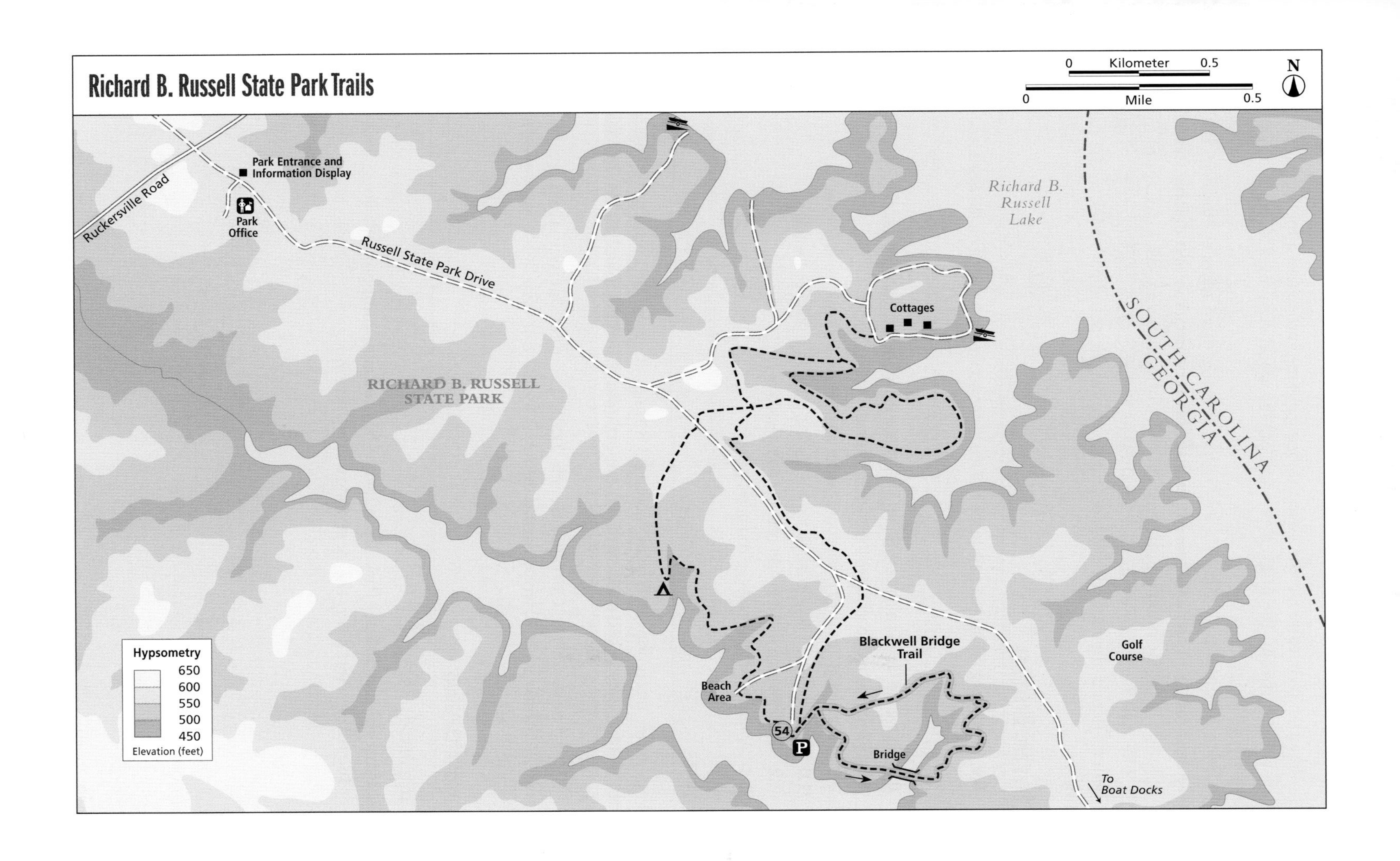
Richard B. Russell State Park Trails
0 Kilometer 0.5
0 Mile 0.5
N
Ruckersville Road
Park Entrance and Information Display
Park Office
Russell State Park Drive
RICHARD B. RUSSELL STATE PARK
Richard B. Russell Lake
Cottages
SOUTH CAROLINA
GEORGIA
Blackwell Bridge Trail
Golf Course
Beach Area
54
P
Bridge
To Boat Docks
Hypsometry
650
600
550
500
450
Elevation (feet)

The trail now turns up the cove the bridge spans and crosses a footbridge over a wet-weather stream. Turning left the trail offers a good view back down the cove to Blackwell Bridge.

From here the path climbs a low ridge, crossing three more footbridges before passing through an area of exposed granite. This very attractive and durable stone has been used in public buildings throughout the world, including the US Capitol.

The trail next crosses another footbridge and the drive leading to the Group Shelter. Then, at the close of the loop, turn right on the paved path back to the parking area.

Miles and Directions

0.0 Start along the asphalt path to the trail loop intersection and turn right on the shredded-rubber surface.

0.2 Pass the first good view of the lake.

0.4 Leave the paved path at the Group Shelter and follow the old road to the steel bridge.

0.6 Reach the vista back down the cove to Blackwell Bridge.

0.9 Pass through the large granite boulders for which Elbert County is world famous.

1.0 Cross the paved drive to the Group Shelter. This is the high point on the trail.

1.2 Close the loop and turn right onto the paved walkway.

1.3 Arrive back at the trailhead and parking area.

Options

Four other interconnected trails totaling 3.8 miles allow you to walk to almost any of the amenities in the park, with the opportunity to see plant and animal life along the way.

Those trails are the **Cottage/Beach Trail,** 1.6 miles one way; **Cottage Loop Trail,** 1.3-mile loop; **Campground Spur,** 0.5 mile one way; and **Campground/Picnic Trail,** 0.5 mile one way.

Local Information

Accommodations

Richard B. Russell State Park has a 28-site RV and tent campground, along with 20 rental cottages; (800) 864-7275; www.gastateparks.org.

55 Mistletoe State Park Trails

The park takes its name from Mistletoe Junction, a local area that derived its name from the large, extensive growth of mistletoe in the oak trees. Young men and women used to meet here during the holiday season and pick the mistletoe.

The woodlands in the park are the result of forest regeneration after farms were abandoned in the mid-1930s, and they consist of old and young growth pine and hardwoods. The area is excellent for birding. Deer, turkeys, squirrels, chipmunks, foxes, raccoons, and opossums may be seen if you walk quietly.

An interconnected group of easy to moderate trails offers campers and hikers almost 15 miles of pathways with very little change in elevation. You pass through a variety of wooded and open areas. You cross two small streams without bridges and go through frequent changes in habitats, adding to the variety and interest of the hikes.

A combination of a portion of the Cliatt Creek Nature Trail Loop and the Rock Dam Trail is the featured hike. A kiosk across the road from the park office has a map of the trail and other useful information about the area.

Start: At the kiosk across the road from the park office
Distance: 6.0-mile lollipop
Hiking time: About 3 hours
Difficulty: Moderate
Trail surface: Clay loam
Best season: Year-round
Other trail users: Mountain bikers
Canine compatibility: Leashed dogs permitted
Land status: Georgia DNR, State Parks & Historic Sites Division
Nearest town: Thomson
Fees and permits: Daily parking fee
Schedule: Park hours 7 a.m.–10 p.m., year-round
Maps: USGS Leah and Woodlawn; park map with trails available at the park office
Trail contacts: Mistletoe State Park, 3725 Mistletoe Rd., Appling 30802; (706) 541-0321; www.gastateparks.org

Finding the trailhead: From exit 175 off I-20, go north 7.8 miles on SR 150 (Cobbham Road) to Winfield. Turn left (north) onto Mistletoe Road and then go 2.9 miles to the park entrance. Turn left and go about 250 yards to the information kiosk and trailhead across the road from the park office. Trailhead GPS: N33 38.578' / W82 23.116'

The Hike

Begin from the trailhead kiosk on the white-blazed Cliatt Creek Nature Trail Loop. Walk southeast toward the park entrance, across the roads, and into a mixed hardwood-pine forest, with a few older white oak trees that most frequently mark the sites of former farmhouses. Those made the best shade trees and were not as subject to lightning strikes as pines and taller, faster growing hardwoods like sweet gum and yellow poplar.

The Rock Dam forms a natural bridge for crossing Bohler Creek.

You go through former farmland with terraces constructed to stop erosion and spread the water better to the crops. Much of this land grew corn, cotton, and tobacco into the late 1930s. The small farms were abandoned because the land was worn out and no longer could support farm families.

The fallow fields rapidly gave way to tree species like loblolly pine, sassafras, and persimmon, as well as a few red cedars. From these more recent clearings, you go into an older hardwood forest of beech, maple, yellow poplar, oaks, and hickories. In this area you also see frequent wax myrtle, Elliott blueberry, greenbrier, muscadine vines, and dogwoods.

At the junction marked with a sign and large boulder, the Cliatt Creek Nature Trail Loop turns off to the left.

Follow the Rock Dam Trail to the right, dropping down to the floodplain of Cliatt Creek to run along and then across the stream. Dogwoods and mayapples bloom all along the trail here in early April. Later the piedmont azaleas show their soft-pink blossoms.

The trail climbs to the top of a ridge through a stand of young pines, and the Return Loop Trail then turns off to the left. This trail gives you the option of cutting the Rock Dam Trail short and returning to the trailhead kiosk. The main trail continues on the blue-blazed path.

All along the trail there are large boulders, part of the erosion-resistant gneiss and granite formations that extend from Augusta diagonally across the state to Columbus. You pass an exceptionally large, dome-shaped rock on the ridge and in the spring see numerous wild petunias abloom in a delicate purple shade. Watch for bright orange butterfly weeds along the path in April and May.

Traversing the low ridge, the trail crosses several small erosion gullies before dropping down into a large gully that leads to Bohler Creek. At the mouth of the gully is a pleasant, open hardwood cove with large loblolly pines, beeches, yellow poplars, and an impressive rock outcrop. This is particularly beautiful in spring when the trout lilies, hepaticas, trilliums, and other spring wildflowers are in bloom. Azaleas, dogwoods, and dwarf pawpaws bloom later in spring.

The path next passes backcountry Campsite No.1 and then crosses Bohler Creek on the rock dam. This natural dam is formed by a single large boulder that extends from bank to bank, creating a pretty little waterfall. There is no bridge at this crossing, and it may be necessary to get your shoes wet to cross over.

Once more you leave the moist, shaded creek bottom and climb a low ridge, following old roadbeds. In this area you see more of the great boulders that have weathered into many shapes and sizes. A large, elongated boulder known as Split Rock sits at the farthest end of the trail loop. It is beneath a large hickory tree and has wild ginger around its base and a colony of resurrection ferns growing on top.

Next the trail descends down past Campsites No. 2 and 3 to the head of an embayment of Clarks Hill Lake. Between those two sites you pass a 50-foot-deep erosion gully on the right.

Turning away from the lake, the path then goes across a drier hillside, paralleling Clarks Hill Lake. Along the way the path skirts around the highest knoll on the way back to Cliatt Creek.

After fording that creek on exposed metamorphic amphibolite bedrock, the trail rejoins the Cliatt Creek Nature Trail Loop. Turn left and follow the signs back to the common trailhead.

Miles and Directions

0.0 Start at the kiosk trailhead and follow the Cliatt Creek Nature Trail Loop to the large rock and trail junction.

0.7 Turn right and head upstream on Cliatt Creek.

0.8 Drop down a steep bank to cross Cliatt Creek.

1.0 Pass the large domed rock on the right.

1.4 Intersect the Return Loop Trail on the left.

2.2 The trail drops into a deep erosion gully and follows it down to Bohler Creek.

2.3 Pass Campsite No.1 and cross Bohler Creek on the Rock Dam.

3.1 Split Rock is on the right of the path.

3.6 Recross Bohler Creek and reach Campsite No. 2.

3.9 The path skirts to the left of a very big and deep erosion ditch.

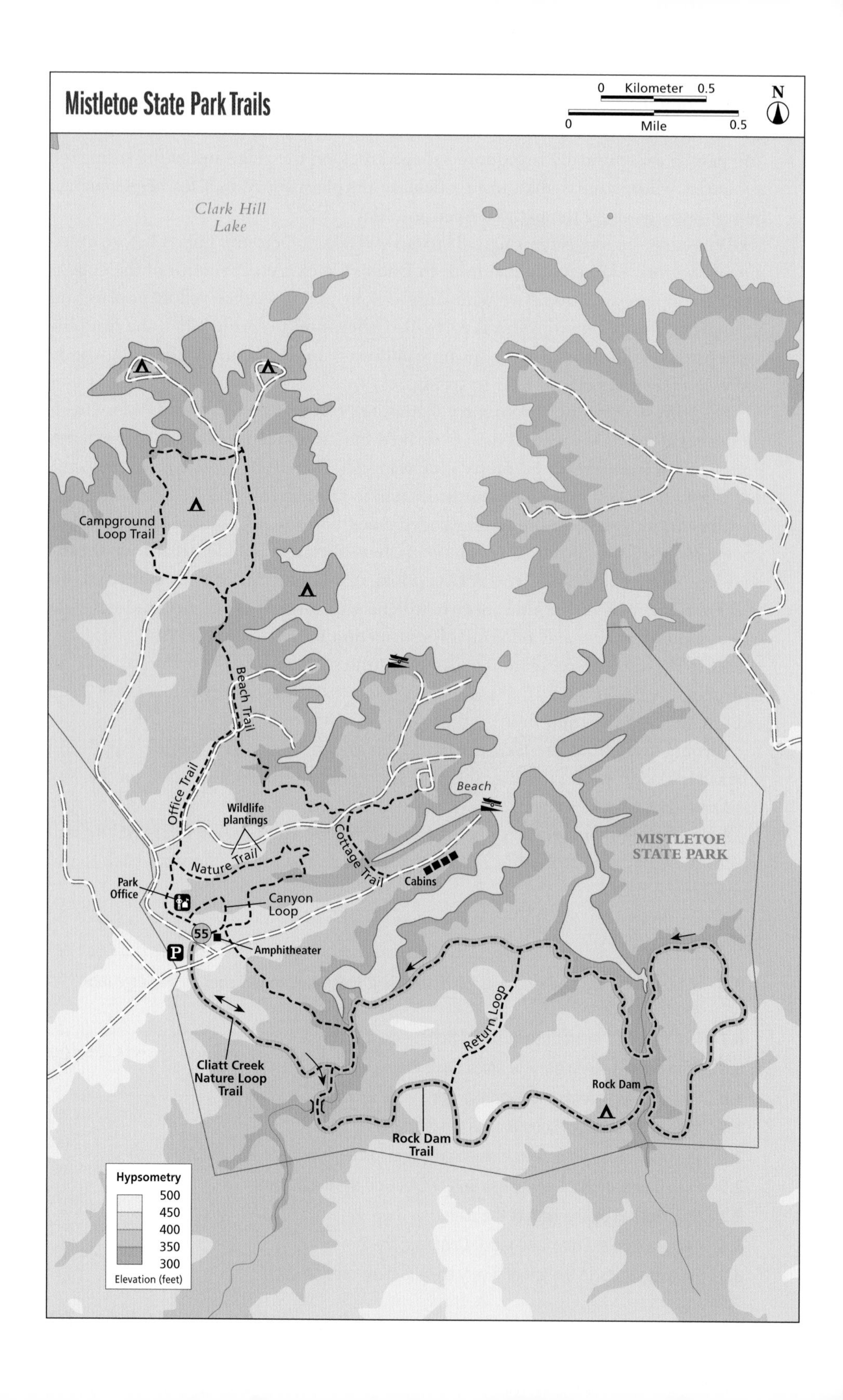
Mistletoe State Park Trails
0 Kilometer 0.5
0 Mile 0.5
N
Clark Hill Lake
Campground Loop Trail
Beach Trail
Office Trail
Wildlife plantings
Nature Trail
Cottage Trail
Beach
Cabins
Park Office
Canyon Loop
55
Amphitheater
P
MISTLETOE STATE PARK
Return Loop
Cliatt Creek Nature Loop Trail
Rock Dam
Rock Dam Trail
Hypsometry
500
450
400
350
300
Elevation (feet)

4.2 Pass to the right of Campsite No. 3.

4.5 The Return Loop Trail intersects from the left.

4.8 Walk along a steep ridge on left with the lake on your right.

5.2 Ford Cliatt Creek and turn left. Continue to the trail junction at the big rock to close the loop, where you then turn right for the trailhead.

6.0 Arrive back at the kiosk trailhead.

Options

The **Cliatt Creek Nature Trail Loop** is a 2.8-mile loop hike marked with white blazes. The path shares a trailhead with the Rock Dam Trail. The trail offers views of Clarks Hill Lake and a walk around a large system of erosion gullies.

The **Return Loop Trail** cuts across the center of the Rock Dam Trail loop, providing a shorter 3.4-mile loop hike.

The **Canyon Loop** starts out sharing the path with the Cliatt Creek Nature Trail. This 0.7-mile lollipop runs from the park office to an overlook at a very large and deep erosion gully.

A portion of the Rock Dam Trail runs down an erosion ditch to Bohler Creek.

Several of the park's other trails are connectors offering hiking options to the various facilities. Those are the **Beach Trail,** 1.9 miles one way; **Campground Loop Trail,** 1.5-mile loop; **Office Trail,** 0.5 mile one way; **Cottage Trail,** 0.3 mile one way.

56 Augusta Canal National Heritage Area Trail

The Augusta Canal Trail is one of the most historic of Georgia's hiking paths, following the waterway that was constructed in the 1840s. The hiking/biking trail runs from the headgates that release water into the canal downstream to the Augusta waterworks pumping station. You walk on what was originally the path used by draft animals to pull cargo boats upstream to the locks.

Expect to see canoeists and kayakers on the canal and the Savannah River. There is a commercial outfitter offering boat rentals at the headgate park.

At the start of the trail, looking across the diversion dam on the river to the South Carolina shore, you can see a fish ladder. Constructed in 1852, the structure allows striped bass, white bass, and American shad to continue their spawning migration upriver.

The trek to the pump station is through an almost pristine natural setting that's ideal for a half-day outing. This hike covers part of a much longer, historically significant multiuse trail along the old canal and on city streets.

Start: At the headgates of the lock and dam
Distance: 7.0 miles out and back
Hiking time: About 3 hours
Difficulty: Easy
Trail surface: Hard, sand and clay
Best season: Year-round
Other trail users: Bikers, joggers
Canine compatibility: Leashed dogs permitted
Land status: Augusta Canal National Heritage Area
Nearest town: Augusta
Fees and permits: None
Schedule: Dawn to dusk, year-round
Maps: USGS Martinez, Augusta West, and Augusta East; map with canal and Augusta Canal history available from Augusta Canal Authority
Trail contacts: Augusta Canal Authority, 1450 Greene St., Suite 400, Augusta 30901; (706) 832-0440; www.augustacanal.com

Finding the trailhead: From I-20 turn north on Washington Road. Immediately turn right on Stevens Creek Road, which makes a sharp left turn to the north at a traffic light at 0.3 mile. Next go 2.8 miles to Evans South Lock Road (also called Evans to Locks Road). Turn right (east) and go 1 mile to Columbia County's Savannah Rapids Park and Pavilion.

The trailhead is at the historic lock and dam and is reached by walking 0.2 mile along the Augusta Canal Walk from Savannah Rapids Park parking area across the canal to the locks. Trailhead GPS: N33 33.094' / W82 02.308'

An alternate trailhead is at the southern end of the path at the parking lot for the Augusta waterworks pump station. Leaving a shuttle vehicle there creates a 3.5-mile one-way hike. Alternate trailhead GPS: N33 30.856' / W82 00.170'

The Hike

History, scenery, birding, and wildlife watching are a few of the fascinating things waiting for you while hiking this rustic and urban hiking trail. Wildlife includes deer,

At the trailhead the headgate regulates water levels in the historic Augusta Canal.

wild turkeys, beavers, muskrats, river otters, raccoons, and squirrels. Gulls, herons, wood storks, egrets, cormorants, and ducks can be seen along and over the river.

The forest between the trail and Savannah River is full of river-bottom hardwood trees. It also holds several of the largest loblolly pines you ever will see. The thin strip of land along the canal bank was originally free of trees to allow passage for the ropes used to pull the barges. Today the canal shore is dominated by sweet gum and sycamore trees draped with Spanish moss. Also along the trail are staghorn sumac, Virginia creepers, and patches of cabbage-like common mullein that feature yellow spikes of flowers in the spring. It is possible occasionally to see a Cherokee rose, Georgia's state flower, along the trail.

As you begin downstream, across the canal you can look into the mouth of Reed Creek as it tumbles into the canal, looking very much like a mountain trout stream.

Next you pass a century-old rock quarry that continues in operation on the opposite side of the canal. Active since the initial canal construction, the quarry is operated today by Martin-Marietta. This is also the county line between Columbia and Richmond Counties. The islands visible in the river were occupied by various Native American peoples in the past.

At this point the canal shore is frequently lined with silk trees, which are often called mimosas. In the spring these are covered in delicate pink blossoms.

Along the way, I-20 crosses over the trail. The underside of the bridge over the canal is a favored nesting area for swallows that build mud nests on the concrete. The birds also feed on insects over the canal.

At the pump station, reverse course to return to the main trailhead. Or you can end the hike here.

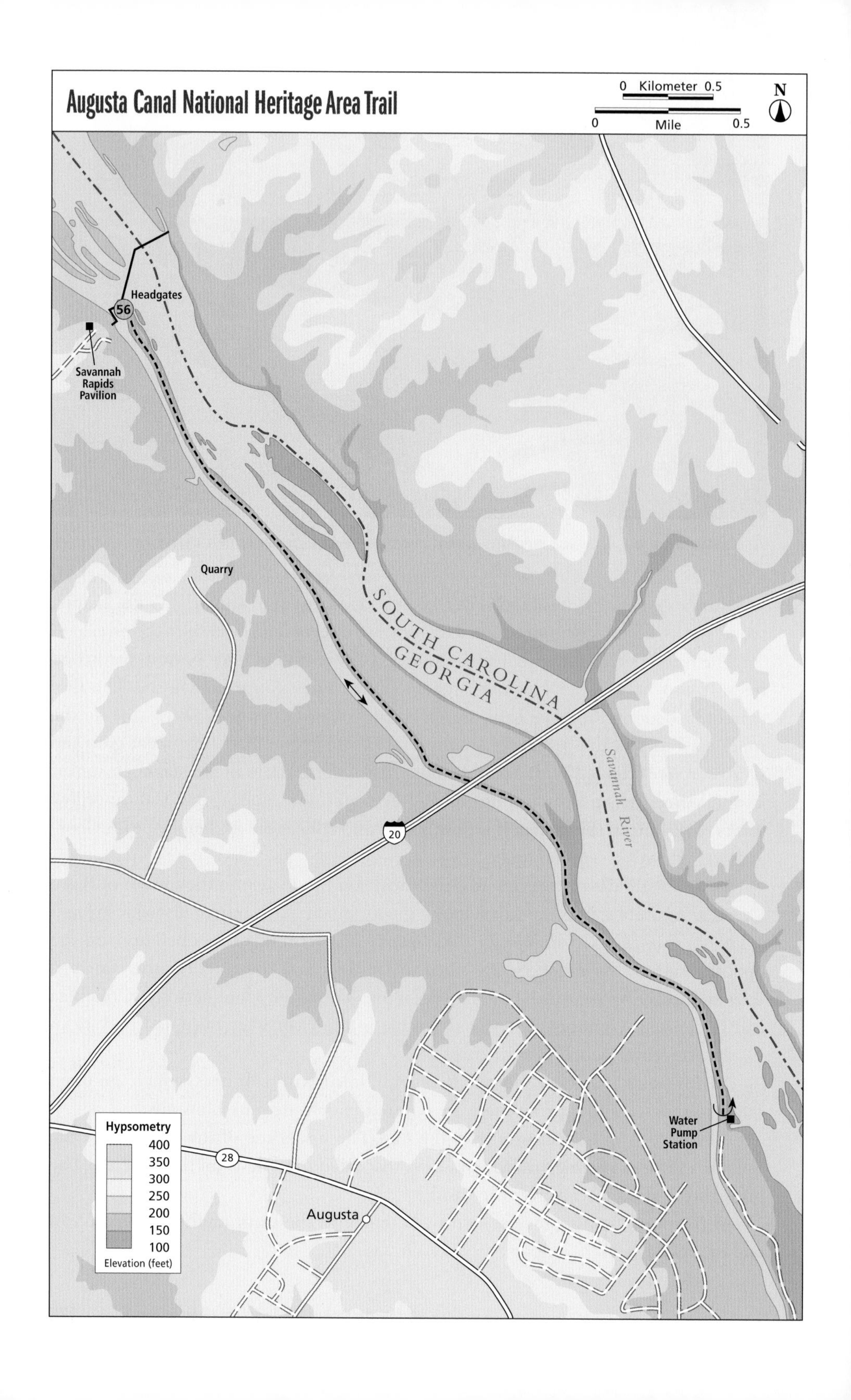
Augusta Canal National Heritage Area Trail
0 Kilometer 0.5
0 Mile 0.5
N
Headgates
56
Savannah Rapids Pavilion
Quarry
SOUTH CAROLINA
GEORGIA
Savannah River
20
Water Pump Station
28
Augusta
Hypsometry
400
350
300
250
200
150
100
Elevation (feet)

To walk the rest of the canal into Augusta proper, go through the fenced parking area and continue on the multiuse trail.

Miles and Directions

0.0 Start at the headgates for the lock and dam.

0.3 A pedestrian bridge connects across the canal to the Augusta River Walk beside the mouth and falls of Reed Creek.

0.6 On the right, pass the quartzite granite quarry.

0.8 The towpath crosses over the first of several floodgates along its length.

1.3 The canal turns away from the river, and a side trail runs to the left to the river shore.

2.1 Pass under the I-20 bridge that spans the canal and Savannah River.

2.6 You are now back closer to the riverbank at an open park area with picnic tables on the left. Warren Lake, fed by Rock Creek, enters the canal on the right, and a second floodgate is just past the park.

3.1 A metal handrail runs along the left of the trail, where you have a grand view of the shoals running from upstream at the I-20 bridge down to islands adjacent to the overlook.

3.5 Reach the Augusta Water Pump Station and the alternate trailhead. This is the turnaround point for walking back to Savannah Rapids Park.

7.0 Arrive back at the headgates.

The diversion dam on the Savannah River at the beginning of the canal and trail

Options

There are several other walking trails that connect to or are part of the Augusta Canal Trail. Those are the **Mill Trail, Downtown Riverwalk Trail, Lake Olmstead Trail,** and the **New Bartram Trail.** The Augusta Canal Authority offers detailed maps of the trail system at their visitor center and online at www.augustacanal.com.

Honorable Mentions

G Ocmulgee Bluff Horse, Hike, and Bike Trail System

Composed of more than 30 miles of interconnected multiuse trails, the best hiking venue is the Ocmulgee River Trail. This trail is 3.0 miles of easy walking through the bottomland hardwoods and pines of the Ocmulgee River. The trail is managed by the USDA Forest Service for both hiking and horseback riding.

Explore the riverbank of the historically important Ocmulgee River. Spring wildflowers, birding, wildlife watching, camping, fishing, and small- and big-game hunting in season are all available. What this trail lacks in grand scenery, it makes up in interesting wildlife and wildflower habitat. Deer, raccoons, foxes, gray squirrels, and other mammals are evident from the many tracks left in the soft sandy and silt loam of the riverbank. Wild turkeys, wood ducks, hooded mergansers, woodcocks, quail, and other game birds may be seen or heard. An amazing variety of songbirds use the area as residents and during the spring and fall migrations. Beavers, minks, muskrats, and even an occasional otter may be seen along the river's edge, with turtles sunning on the exposed logs in the river. The hillsides above the floodplain are excellent areas for spring wildflowers. Trout lilies (also called dogtooth violets) bloom on the floodplain in late February and early March.

Interconnected Kinnard Creek and Wise Creek Trails are accessible from the Ocmulgee River Trail. The Kinnard Creek Trail is designated for horseback riding, although hikers are welcome to use the trail. Wise Creek is for both hikers and equestrians.

For more information: Chattahoochee-Oconee National Forests, Oconee Ranger District, 1199 Madison Rd., Eatonton 31024; (706) 485-7110; www.fs.usda.gov/conf

DeLorme: Georgia Atlas and Gazetteer: Page 34 B3

H Ocmulgee National Monument Trails

Six miles of easy trails interconnect to provide access to the significant areas within the monument. The well-marked Human Cultural Trails make it easy for you to visit all the key features in the lives of the earliest Americans. From these trails you can walk the Wildflower Trail to the McDougal Mound, the Opelofa Trail around the wetland area, the Loop Trail around a wooded knoll of hardwoods and pines, or walk the River Trail that, at this writing, is being reclaimed from two disastrous floods.

Located on the eastern edge of Macon on US 80 East, this national monument is convenient to local residents, especially students who frequently take field trips to the area. Evidence of 12,000 years of human habitation is wonderfully interpreted on the grounds and in the fine visitor center, which houses a major archaeological museum.

Between AD 900 and 1100, the skilled farmers known as Mississippians built the mounds so evident at this site.

The park was established as a memorial to the antiquity of man in this southeast corner of the United States. The trails connect all archaeological and natural history features. Since the mounds are located on the floodplain of the Ocmulgee River, the only significant elevation changes are in various mounds, such as the 45-foot-high Temple Mound. This is a fine place to watch for birds and deer, along with squirrels and other small mammals.

For more information: Ocmulgee National Monument, 1207 Emory Hwy., Macon 31217-4399; (478) 752-8257; www.nps.gov/ocmu

DeLorme: Georgia Atlas and Gazetteer: Page 34 G6

I Bobby Brown Outdoor State Recreation Area Trails

Bobby Brown State Outdoor Recreation Area was formerly a state park and is located on a forested peninsula formed by the Savannah and Broad Rivers at the headwaters of Clarks Hill Lake. The tip of the peninsula is the site of the colonial town of Petersburg, the third-largest town in the state in 1790. The park is named for Robert T. Brown, USN, who lost his life during World War II.

The 2.2-mile trail is ideal for family hiking. It is relatively easy, with only two short, steep sections. Part of the trail follows the path William Bartram trod in 1791 while he was exploring the region for useful plants to be sent back to England for commercial purposes.

Well-made footbridges cross all low and wet areas, and the trail follows contours as it crosses the low ridges. Clark Hill Lake can be seen through the trees for most of the way. An observation platform at the end of the peninsula provides full view of the lake, surrounding you on three sides. From here you may see bald eagles, ospreys, ducks, geese, herons, and other birds associated with Clarks Hill Reservoir. An information board tells about the colonial town of Petersburg and the Petersburg boat used to take people, cotton, and produce to Augusta during the last years of the 1790s and early 1800.

For more information: Call Elijah Clark State Park at (706) 359-3458; www.gastateparks.org.

DeLorme: Georgia Atlas and Gazetteer: Page 31 B9

Metro Atlanta

From the trail at the crest of Kennesaw Mountain, it is possible to see Atlanta's skyline and Stone Mountain on the horizon.

57 Sweetwater Creek State Park Trails

Sweetwater Creek State Park has a wilderness feel, offering many species of wildflowers and wildlife, a beautiful forest, and cascading Sweetwater Creek—all only minutes from downtown Atlanta. Sweetwater Creek is a fast-flowing stream that winds its way through a granite-boulder streambed in a well-protected wooded valley.

During the Civil War, cloth was manufactured at the New Manchester Manufacturing Company for Confederate troops. This proved the factory's undoing. Gen. William T. Sherman ordered the factory and town to be burned on July 9, 1864. The mostly women and children working at the mill were told to pack for a long trip, loaded into wagons, and eventually placed in a prison camp in Louisville, Kentucky. The town of New Manchester never was rebuilt.

The 2,549-acre park features picnicking, as well as boating and fishing on 215-acre George H. Sparks Reservoir. There also are 9 miles of hiking trails within the park.

The Red/History Trail offers a walk through old New Manchester down to Sweetwater Falls. The Blue Trail provides an alternate access to the falls on the overlooking ridges. The Yellow Trail crosses the creek onto the opposite ridges, and the White Trail runs through woodlands and fields from the interpretive center to the waterfall.

The featured trail is a loop combining the Red/History and White Trails.

Start: At the parking area near the interpretive center
Distance: 3.9-mile loop
Hiking time: About 1.5–2 hours
Difficulty: Mostly easy to moderate; a few strenuous sections
Trail surface: Clay loam, with rocky and gravel sections
Best season: Year-round
Other trail users: Hikers, joggers
Canine compatibility: Leashed dogs permitted
Land status: Georgia DNR, State Parks & Historic Sites Division
Nearest town: Lithia Springs
Fees and permits: Daily parking fee
Schedule: Park hours 7 a.m.–sunset, year-round
Maps: USGS Austell, Campbellton, Mableton, and Ben Hill; trail map available from the park office
Trail contacts: Sweetwater Creek State Park, 1750 Mount Vernon Rd., Lithia Springs 30122; (770) 732-5871; www.gastateparks.org

Finding the trailhead: From Atlanta take I-20 West to exit 44 at Thornton Road. Turn left and go 0.4 mile to Blairs Bridge Road. Turn right and go 2.1 miles to Mt. Vernon Road. Turn left and go 1.3 miles to the park entrance on the left. Go 0.7 mile on Factory Shoals Road to the interpretive center and parking area. The parking area is the trailhead for all trails. Trailhead GPS: N33 45.206' / W84 37.685'

The Hike

The park's trails are well blazed and are interpreted in a leaflet, available at the park office. Numbered markers correspond to the interpretive leaflet. More than 120

The ruins of the New Manchester Mill are the focal point on the Red/History Trail.

wildflowers bloom along the trails in the park from early February to mid-June. There is a large wooden trail map at the trailhead.

A tree-covered gravel walkway leaves the parking area, carrying the Red/History Trail under a canopy of a dozen species of trees. The trail descends the ridge down to Sweetwater Creek, passing the junction with the Yellow Trail on the left.

At the creek the path turns downstream to the right. Through here the creek and valley are just as fascinating as the trail's historical features. The trail quickly reaches the head of the old millrace, which forms a narrow canal between the path and creek. A footbridge crosses the race to a parallel path running downstream on the narrow island to the left. Look for native azaleas and mountain laurels.

After you cross a footbridge, the Blue Trail intersects from the right. Turning onto it takes you back to the parking lot.

The New Manchester Mill ruins now appear on the left on the creek shore. A couple of observation decks are available for viewing the structure. The Blue Trail also runs off to the right and downstream along the ridge side at this point.

The Red/History Trail descends left down several flights of wooden steps to the creek shore. This path now follows the creek right at the water. Along the way it climbs over one rock protrusion that has a cable handrail to permit safe passage. The granite cliffs along the bank and the cascades on the stream are spectacular through here. The rock cliffs support many interesting plants, such as rockcap fern, liverworts, and mosses.

After crossing a wooden footbridge, the trail climbs thirty-nine steps built into the hillside, leading up to an observation deck. Another 0.3 mile along the trail is the overlook for Sweetwater Falls. This drop and slide are favorites with kayakers on the stream.

The Red/History Trail ends here, at the junction with the Blue and White Trails. The Blue Trail runs uphill to the right, while the White Trail continues downstream along the creek. Quickly the path descends seventy-three wooden steps to get back down to water level.

Continue along the creek to the mouth of Jacks Branch. The trail runs up the valley along this tumbling brook flowing over gravel and granite. Large chain ferns, cinnamon ferns, Christmas ferns, and other moist-soil plants are abundant along the branch. Be aware there is a bridge over Jacks Branch near its mouth that carries a foot trail farther downstream. This path is not part of the park's regular trail system and is not connected to the other trails at any other point.

Climbing steadily up the side of the ridge, the path crosses a footbridge and then reaches the dam on Jacks Lake, a long, narrow pond frequented by beavers, turtles, wood ducks, and herons.

The trail next skirts the lake on an unpaved road overlooking the water. The trail remains on this old road for most of the rest of the hike.

The unpaved road leads through a forest and into open fields known as the Jacks Hill Area. The field edges with young trees like persimmon, sumac, loblolly pine, and oaks add an interesting diversion from the more mature forest. Several service roads are crossed or branch off the trail. It is necessary to keep the white blazes in sight.

Along the way the hike passes the foundation of an old home place on the right. This region is ablaze in yellow in the early spring when the massive beds of jonquils are blooming.

After going through pine stands and some hardwoods, the trail crosses two paved drives in the picnic and playground area before reaching the parking area and trailhead.

Miles and Directions

0.0 Start downhill toward the creek from the trailhead and parking area.

0.1 Pass the Yellow Trail on left, reach the creek shore, and turn right.

0.3 Reach the head of the millrace and bridge across the race on the left.

0.5 Cross a footbridge and come to the intersection with the Blue Trail and the observation decks for the factory ruins.

0.6 The Blue Trail splits off to the right, and the Red/History Trail goes left down the wooden stairs to the creek bank.

0.7 Pass the rock protrusion with cable handrail.

0.8 Cross the footbridge and climb the steps to the observation deck.

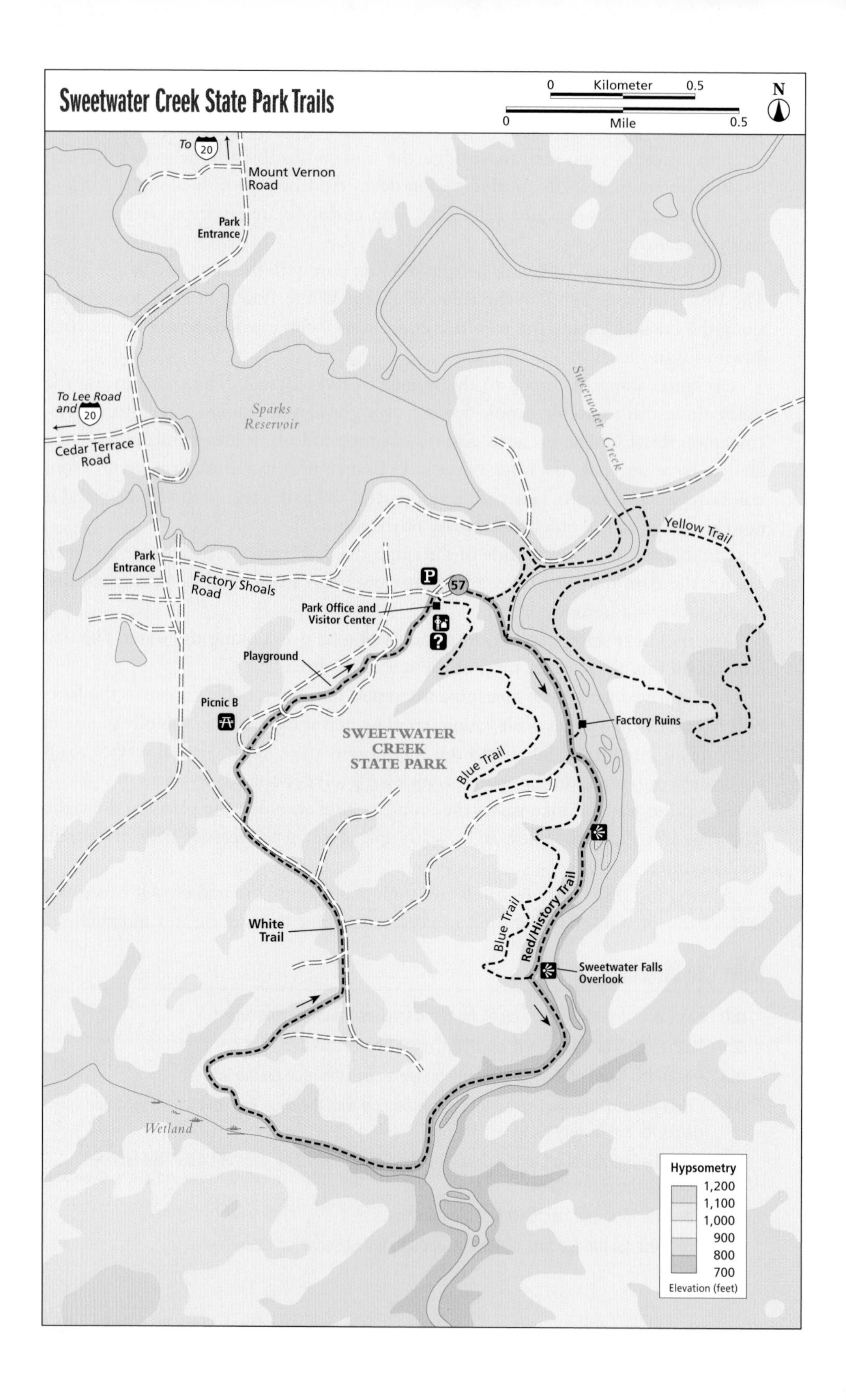

Sweetwater Creek State Park Trails
0 Kilometer 0.5
0 Mile 0.5
N
To 20
Mount Vernon Road
Park Entrance
To Lee Road and 20
Cedar Terrace Road
Sparks Reservoir
Sweetwater Creek
Yellow Trail
Park Entrance
Factory Shoals Road
P
57
Park Office and Visitor Center
Playground
Picnic B
SWEETWATER CREEK STATE PARK
Blue Trail
Factory Ruins
White Trail
Blue Trail
Red/History Trail
Sweetwater Falls Overlook
Wetland
Hypsometry
1,200
1,100
1,000
900
800
700
Elevation (feet)

Sweetwater Falls draws both hikers and kayakers to Sweetwater Creek.

1.0 Reach the end of the Red/History Trail at the Sweetwater Falls Overlook. Continue downstream on the White Trail.

1.1 Climb down the seventy-three steps to the creek bank.

1.7 Make a 90-degree right turn, leaving Sweetwater Creek to go up Jacks Branch.

1.9 Cross a footbridge and reach the dam on Jacks Lake.

2.5 After a long climb, reach the first wildlife clearing in the Jacks Hill Area.

2.7 Pass the old home foundation on the right.

3.4 Cross a paved park drive and enter the picnic and playground area.

3.7 Cross a second paved park drive.

3.9 Arrive back at the parking area to close the loop at the trailhead.

Options

The 2.0-mile **Blue Trail** intersects the Red/History Trail at two points near the mill ruins and again at Sweetwater Falls. It can be combined with the Red/History hike to create a 3.0-mile loop covering the creek bank and the ridges above. This trail begins in the interpretive center parking lot, a few yards south of the main trailhead.

The **Yellow Trail** is not associated with the historical significance of Sweetwater Creek; rather it forms a 3.0-mile lollipop from the common trailhead and offers a more nature-oriented hike. After splitting off the Red/History Trail, the path crosses the Army Bridge over Sweetwater Creek. The trail then circles an upland ridgetop on the eastern side of the creek.

58 Kennesaw Mountain National Battlefield Park Trails

Kennesaw Mountain National Battlefield Park covers 2,923 acres of rolling hills just northwest of Atlanta. From June 19 to July 2, 1864, it was the site of a bloody Civil War battle between the Confederate Army of Tennessee under Gen. Joseph E. Johnston and the Union Army of the Tennessee commanded by Gen. William T. Sherman.

Reminders of those days of conflict are visible throughout the park and dictate land use today. More than 8 miles of trenches, rifle pits, and other earthworks in the Cheatham Hill region are some of the best preserved from the period.

Kennesaw Mountain rises abruptly 1,000 feet above the surrounding Piedmont Plateau to the southeast and the Ridge and Valley area to the northwest. Along with neighboring Little Kennesaw Mountain and Pigeon Hill, the three heights add changes of elevation to the park's hikes.

The visitor center houses a museum, while historic plaques and monuments are found throughout the park.

The trail system features 15.8 miles of paths and is considered one of the nation's best urban hiking destinations. All of the hikes, however, are day treks. No camping is allowed.

There are more than twenty officially named paths, but combinations of these can be broken down into five longer options.

The 9.5-mile West Trail runs from the visitor center to Kolb Farm Trail. The East Trail connects those same two points and is 7.4 miles in length. The Visitor Center to Pigeon Hill, Cheatham Hill to Kolb Farm, and Burnt Hickory to Cheatham Hill Loops all are composed of portions of the East and West Trails.

The featured trail is the Visitor Center to Pigeon Hill Loop, a 5.7-mile trail covering the northern end of the park.

Start: At the visitor center and museum
Distance: 5.7-mile loop
Hiking time: About 2 hours
Difficulty: Easy to moderate, with short strenuous stretches on the mountainsides
Trail surface: Hard-packed dirt, with some paved and gravel stretches
Best season: Year-round
Other trail users: Joggers
Canine compatibility: Leashed dogs permitted
Land status: National Park Service
Nearest towns: Marietta
Fees and permits: None
Schedule: Park hours, dawn to dusk, year-round
Maps: USGS Marietta; hiking trail map available online at www.nps.gov/kemo/planyourvisit/maps.htm
Trail contacts: Kennesaw Mountain National Battlefield Park, 900 Kennesaw Mountain Dr., Kennesaw 30152; (770) 427-4686 Ext. 0; www.nps.gov/kemo/index.htm

Kennesaw Mountain Trail Club; www.kennesawmountaintrailclub.org.

Finding the trailhead: For the Visitor Center to Pigeon Hill Loop, from exit 269 on I-75, go west on Barrett Parkway for approximately 3 miles. Turn left onto Old US 41 and go 1.4 miles to the intersection with Stilesboro Road. Turn right and the visitor center is immediately on the left. Trailhead GPS: N33 58.946' / W84 34.680'

A series of four cannons sits along the path at the top of Kennesaw Mountain.

The Hike

From the trailhead at the visitor center, begin climbing steadily up the face of Kennesaw Mountain on the Kennesaw Mountain Trail. Halfway up, the trail merges into an old road running across the mountainside. Soon the path leaves the old road, turning uphill to the right. At this point it passes through a rock formation that offers an overlook of the town of Marietta.

Switching back up the mountain, the trail passes another outcrop with a bench for resting. Along this north face of the mountain, the forest is dominated by chestnut oak trees. Virginia creepers are present in the rocky areas.

As you reach the parking lot near the mountain crest, a stone overlook provides a great view of the Atlanta skyline to the southeast. A paved walkway now leads up to the peak of the mountain.

Along the way the path passes three of the vintage cannons in their earthworks pointing to the north. On top of the mountain the trail splits into a short paved loop running around the crest.

Sweeping views are available of Atlanta to the southeast and the Allatoona Mountains to the northwest. Some of the rocks bear very old carvings left by early tourists. Such actions are illegal today.

The paved trail ends at the fourth cannon, with the path reverting to packed dirt as it continues down the steep back slope. Where the trail crosses Kennesaw Mountain Drive coming up the mountain, a panorama of Little Kennesaw's crest appears. This also is the end of the Kennesaw Mountain Trail and the beginning of the Little Kennesaw Mountain Trail.

Walking through the swell between the mountains, continue up a gentle slope to a very large flat rock near the top of Little Kennesaw. Here you see prickly pear and lamb's ear growing along the trail. At the peak of Little Kennesaw, the four additional cannons of Fort McBride face the north of the mountain.

The descent down the back side of Little Kennesaw is quite steep, rocky, and uneven. It passes a number of red cedar trees as the trail switches back and forth down the slope, going through one extremely large rock outcrop.

Finally the path levels out on top of Pigeon Hill, reaching the junction with a shortcut trail on the left running to the Camp Brumby Trail. Go straight on the path that now becomes the Pigeon Hill Loop. The trail runs amid Confederate rifle pits, large boulders, and twisted trees on the crest of Pigeon Hill.

As the pathway drops off Pigeon Hill, it crosses an area of exposed rocks with more prickly pear and bear grass. At the next junction, turn sharply left onto the Pigeon Hill Cut-off. The Pigeon Hill Loop continues straight down the slope as part of the Burnt Hickory to Cheatham Hill Loop Trail.

The trail soon passes another intersection with the Burnt Hickory to Cheatham Hill Loop going to the right. Turn to the left onto the Camp Brumby Trail on an old road and quickly pass the other end of the shortcut trail from Pigeon Hill. The hike then passes through a long stretch of oak, hickory, and pine forest. At one point the right side of the trail consists of board fences at the back of a neighborhood.

Also before you leave this old road, grassy clearings appear on the left at the site of the ruins of the Civilian Conservation Corps's Camp Brumby, dating from the 1930s when the park was first developed.

After exiting the old road to the left, the path passes the junction with the Camp Brumby Cut-off Link. The trail to the right runs to Kennesaw Avenue and Marietta. Turn left onto the Cut-off Link. Upon entering a large grassy field, the path skirts the left side of the opening as it follows the foot of the mountain back to the visitor center and trailhead.

Miles and Directions

0.0 Begin climbing the mountain from the visitor center.

0.2 Enter the old roadbed.

0.4 Exit the road at the rock outcrop and Marietta overlook.

0.6 Pass the second rock outcrop.

0.8 Skirt the mountaintop parking area.

1.0 Reach the crest of Kennesaw Mountain.

1.2 Cross the paved drive between the mountains.

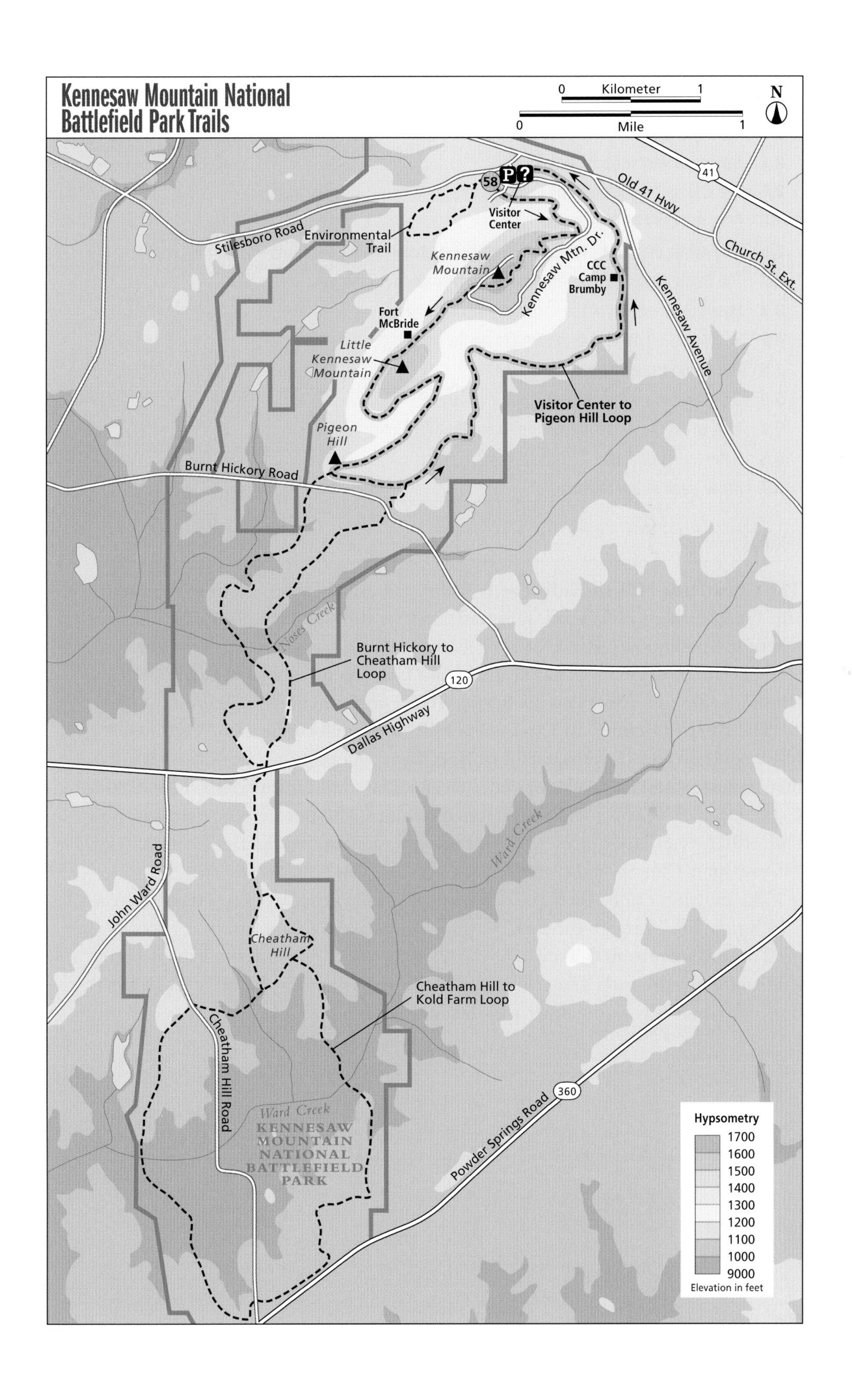

Kennesaw Mountain National Battlefield Park Trails
0 Kilometer 1
0 Mile 1
N
Old 41 Hwy
41
Church St. Ext.
Visitor Center
58
Stilesboro Road
Environmental Trail
Kennesaw Mountain
Kennesaw Mtn. Dr.
CCC Camp Brumby
Kennesaw Avenue
Fort McBride
Little Kennesaw Mountain
Visitor Center to Pigeon Hill Loop
Pigeon Hill
Burnt Hickory Road
Noses Creek
Burnt Hickory to Cheatham Hill Loop
120
Dallas Highway
Ward Creek
John Ward Road
Cheatham Hill
Cheatham Hill to Kold Farm Loop
Cheatham Hill Road
360
Powder Springs Road
Ward Creek
KENNESAW MOUNTAIN NATIONAL BATTLEFIELD PARK
Hypsometry
1700
1600
1500
1400
1300
1200
1100
1000
9000
Elevation in feet

1.6 The large flat rock straddles the trail on Little Kennesaw Mountain.
1.7 Pass Fort McBride at the mountain peak.
2.1 Traverse a very large rock outcrop.
2.5 The shortcut connector trail is on the left.
2.6 Pass the crest of Pigeon Hill.
2.8 Turn left at the trail intersection to continue on the Visitor Center to Pigeon Hill Loop.
3.2 The Burnt Hickory to Cheatham Hill Loop splits off to the right.
3.3 Pass the other end of the shortcut trail on the left.
4.2 Backyard neighborhood fences are on the right.
4.8 The Camp Brumby ruins are on the left.
5.0 Go left off the old roadbed.
5.1 Turn left at the junction with the Camp Brumby Cut-off Link.
5.5 Enter the open field.
5.7 Arrive back at the trailhead.

Options

The **Cheatham Hill to Kolb Farm Loop** trail usually is walked from the parking area on Cheatham Hill Road. This trail traverses the southern portion of the park where the preliminary Battle of Kolb Farm took place on June 22, 1864, between Confederate Gen. John Bell Hood and Union Gen. Joseph Hooker. The historic Kolb farmhouse lies just across Powder Springs Road from the trail's southernmost point.

The **Burnt Hickory to Cheatham Hill Loop** trail connects the Visitor Center to Pigeon Hill and Cheatham Hill to Kolb Farm Loops. It can be walked as a 6.0-mile figure eight, with small loops on each end. The southern end of the hike is along Confederate earthworks with interspersed cannons. The northern portion has more hills, with several creek crossings. It features the sites of the Hardage Sawmill, New Salem Baptist Church, and Confederate Gen. Leonidas Polk's headquarters.

The trail also can be used as a connector with the other two loop trails to create a 15.8-mile hike through the park.

The **Environmental Trail** offers a 1.3-mile walk featuring the natural history and habitats of the park. The trailhead is at the visitor center's picnic area. This path does not connect with the other park hikes.

59 Panola Mountain State Park Trails

The centerpiece of the park is the granite dome of Panola Mountain. The mountain rises to 940 feet of elevation, but that is only 260 feet above the South River, which flows along its northern edge.

Of the several similar domes in the vicinity, Panola is the only one left undisturbed. Unique granite outcrops and endemic plants and animals are associated with this peculiar habitat. The 1,635-acre facility borders a rapidly growing residential area and provides excellent educational outdoor activities for its neighbors. The park's nature center has excellent displays of local geology, plants, and wildlife, while park personnel offer frequent nature walks for children and adults.

Three trails totaling 4.9 miles offer interpretive walks through this unique habitat. The Rock Outcrop, Watershed, and Panola Mountain Trails provide information on the area's geology, fauna, flora, and history. The Fitness and 3-D Target Trails also are in the park.

The park also is tied to the nearby Davidson–Arabia Mountain Nature Preserve and the town of Lithonia by the paved, 12-mile, 10-foot-wide multiuse Arabia Mountain Trail.

The featured hike is a double loop composed of the Watershed and Rock Outcrop Trails.

Start: At the rear of the nature center
Distance: 1.4-mile double loop
Hiking time: About 1 hour
Difficulty: Easy
Trail surface: Dirt and gravel
Best season: Year-round
Other trail users: Hikers only
Canine compatibility: No dogs permitted
Land status: Georgia DNR, State Parks & Historic Sites Division
Nearest towns: Lithonia, Stockbridge
Fees and permits: Daily parking fee
Schedule: Park hours, 7 a.m.–dusk, year-round
Maps: USGS Redan and Stockbridge; page-size map of the park available at the park nature center
Trail contacts: Panola Mountain State Park, 2600 SR 155 Southwest, Stockbridge 30281; (770) 389-7801; www.gastateparks.org

Finding the trailhead: From exit 68 on I-20, take Wesley Chapel Road south for 0.3 mile to Snapfinger Road. Turn left and go 1.8 miles. At this point the road picks up SR 155; continue straight for 5 miles more. The entrance for Panola Mountain State Park is on the left. All trails share the same trailhead at the nature center. Trailhead GPS: N33 37.575' / W84 10.300'

The Hike

Combining the 0.9-mile Watershed and 0.5-mile Rock Outcrop Trails creates a double-loop hike that takes you through the major habitat types in the park. The paths are best walked in a counterclockwise direction beginning with the Watershed Trail.

The authors examine a large boulder that has a split, called a joint, running its length.

On either trail wildlife such as deer, squirrels, rabbits, raccoons, opossums, skunks, and chipmunks may be seen, along with lizards and other reptiles. Butterflies abound during the summer months, feeding on the wide variety of flowering plants.

The red-blazed Watershed Trail leads off to the right behind the nature center and passes through a mixed pine-hardwood forest with undergrowth of sweet gum, sassafras, maple, yellow poplar, and dogwood, along with honeysuckle and muscadine vines. Strawberry bush is common, with its strikingly colorful fruits in fall. Ferns are abundant and include bracken, Christmas, wood, and cinnamon varieties, as well as brown-stemmed spleenwort. Also look for the blue blossoms of elephant's-foot in the spring. The plant's leaves grow flat to the ground.

Climb a set of stone steps at the point a connector trail from the parking lot enters from the right and continue to the left. At the next junction where the loop portion of the Watershed Trail starts, turn right.

Quickly a fence appears on the right of the trail beside a deep erosion gully. This is the first of many such reminders of past farming activities on the land. Next the trail forks, just before crossing a footbridge. The left fork leads about 40 yards to an observation deck affording a good perspective of the deepness of the eroded ravines.

Returning to the fork, turn left across the bridge and continue downhill. After crossing a bridge over another gully, the path reaches a small creek bottom. Here the

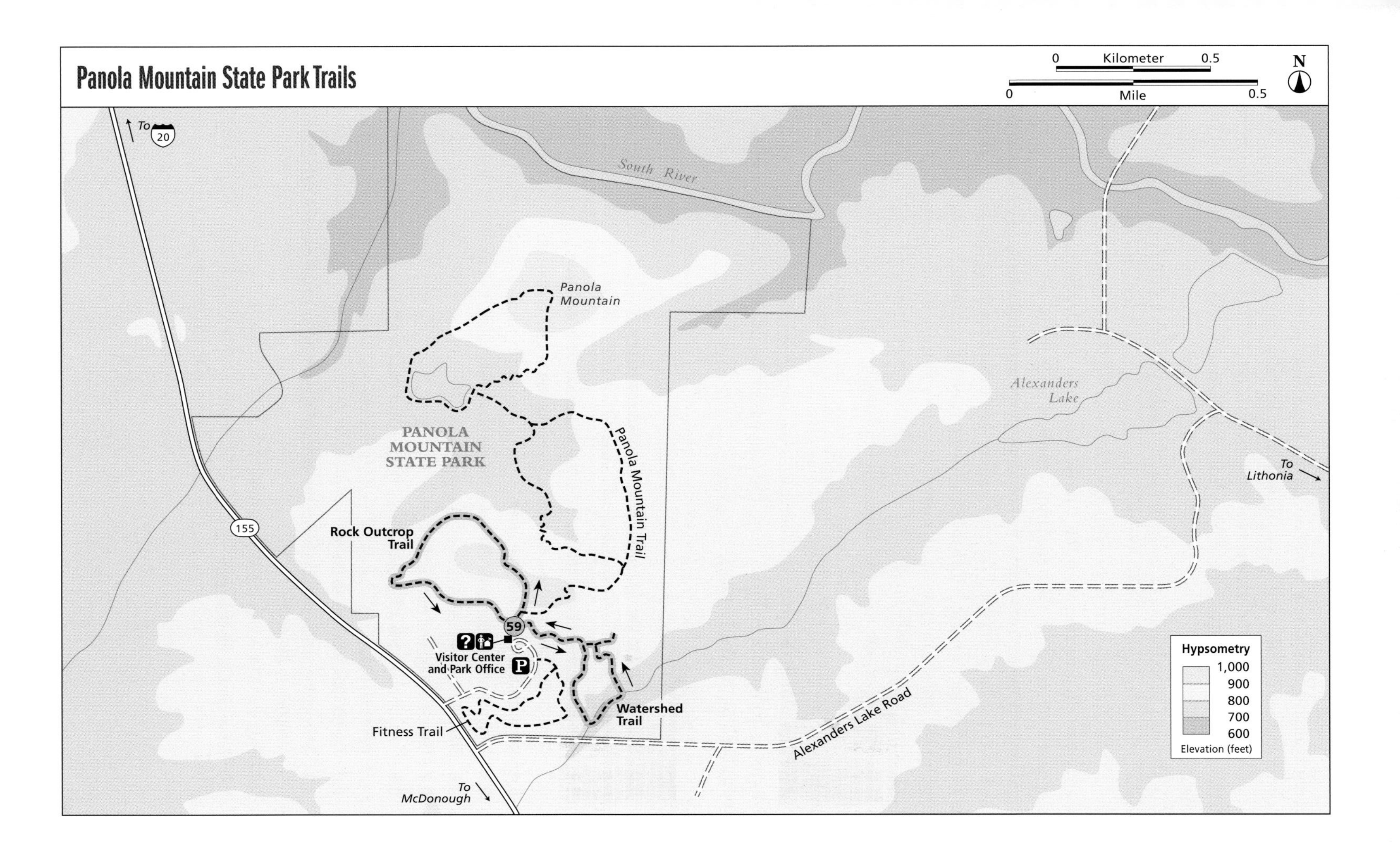
Panola Mountain State Park Trails
0 Kilometer 0.5
0 Mile 0.5
N
To 20
South River
Panola Mountain
PANOLA MOUNTAIN STATE PARK
Panola Mountain Trail
Alexanders Lake
To Lithonia
155
Rock Outcrop Trail
59
Visitor Center and Park Office
P
Watershed Trail
Fitness Trail
Alexanders Lake Road
To McDonough
Hypsometry
1,000
900
800
700
600
Elevation (feet)

forest is almost completely hardwoods with large sweet gums, yellow poplars, beeches, several species of oaks, and an occasional large loblolly pine.

The path crosses the stream twice on footbridges, with another observation deck between them. Large patches of New York ferns grow in the moist alluvial soil along the creek.

The trail then begins to gain elevation, passing another observation deck on the right before closing the loop. At this point, turn right and walk back to the trailhead.

At the trailhead, turn right onto the white-blazed Rock Outcrop Trail and immediately pass the junction with the Panola Mountain Trail leading off to the right. At the next intersection, a shortcut connector trail leads to the left.

The path now passes through boulder-strewn woods leading to an observation deck over the large exposed sheet of granite. Just before reaching the open rock, there is a large boulder on the left that has a fissure running completely through it.

During late summer and fall, masses of yellow flowers, locally known as Confederate daisies and found only on and around these granite domes, add spectacular color to the otherwise gray rock outcrops. Other plants around the rocks are sparkleberry, American beauty berry, and common ragwort. The last also has a yellow flower in spring.

Farther along the path another overlook station offers a grand view of Stone Mountain to the north. From there the trail passes the other end of the shortcut and loops back to the trailhead.

Miles and Directions

0.0 Start downhill to the right on the red-blazed Watershed Trail.

0.1 Pass the junction with the parking lot connector.

0.2 Turn right to begin the Watershed Trail loop and reach the fenced gully.

0.3 Arrive at the footbridge and side trail to the observation deck on the left.

0.4 Cross the first bridge over the creek.

0.5 Pass the observation deck and cross the second creek bridge.

0.6 The upland observation deck is on the right.

0.7 Close the loop and turn right.

0.9 Turn right onto the white-blazed Rock Outcrop Trail and pass the junction with the Panola Mountain Trail.

1.0 The shortcut trail runs to the left.

1.2 Arrive at the observation deck over the exposed granite and then the overlook with Stone Mountain to the north.

1.3 Pass the other end of the shortcut trail.

1.4 Arrive back at the trailhead.

The authors overlook the exposed granite from the observation deck.

Options

The 1.0-mile **Fitness Trail** is a loop with a number of exercise devices placed along it course.

The 3.5-mile, double-loop lollipop **Panola Mountain Trail** is designed to provide a closer look at the undisturbed 100-acre granite dome atop the mountain. To protect the natural condition of the very fragile plant communities, the trail is available only as a scheduled guided hike. The staff leaders interpret the special features throughout the 3-hour hike. Call (800) 864-7275 to arrange a guided hike.

60 Davidson-Arabia Mountain Nature Preserve Trails

Davidson–Arabia Mountain Nature Preserve encompasses 2,550 acres and another of the prominent rock outcrops called monadnocks—isolated hills standing above the surrounding area. These rock outcrops host a unique environment with a wide variety of microhabitats that support a number of endemic plant and animal species.

Arabia Mountain is said to be one hundred million years older than its two local granite-dome cousins—Panola and Stone Mountains. Arabia is noted for the swirling tidal gray rock pattern characteristic of Lithonia gneiss, formed when the mountain's original gneiss was partially melted to form a rock that incorporates both igneous and metamorphic features in a granite-gneiss.

The history of human settlement in this region is intimately connected to its geological resources, starting more than 7,000 years ago with the quarrying and trading of soapstone. Included in the park is the former rock quarry donated by the Davidson family, who operated it until 1972.

Arabia Mountain is home to two federally protected species (black-spored quillwort and pool sprite) as well as several other rare plants unique to the granite-outcrop environment, such as Georgia oaks and the brilliant red diamorpha, which is also known as Small's stonecrop.

Other plants you can expect to find here are sunnybells, sparkleberry, and fringe tree. Mosses and lichens are well adapted to the harsh rock outcrop as well. A plant endemic to these mountains that is quite noticeable is the yellow daisy-like flower called the Confederate daisy that blooms in masses in late summer.

There are eight hiking trails in the preserve, as well as a portion of the long multi-use Arabia Mountain Trail. These trails have been designed to expose you to as many of the different habitats as possible and the history of the area.

The featured hike combines the 1.2-mile Forest and 1.0-mile Mile Rock Trails to create a loop beginning and ending at the Davidson–Arabia Mountain Nature Center.

Start: At the information sign beside the nature center
Distance: 2.4-mile loop
Hiking time: About 1 hour
Difficulty: Easy
Trail surface: Dirt and sandy loam; natural, uneven granite and exposed quarry stone surface
Best season: Mar–June; Oct–Dec
Other trail users: Hikers only
Canine compatibility: Leashed dogs permitted
Land status: DeKalb County, Natural Resources Management Office
Nearest towns: Lithonia, Conyers
Fees and permits: None
Schedule: Preserve hours 7 a.m.–dusk, year-round
Maps: USGS Conyers and Redan; map of Davidson-Arabia Mountain Nature Preserve available at nature center; Arabia Mountain Trail map available from the PATH Foundation at http://pathfoundation.org/trails/arabia-mountain/

Trail contacts: Davidson-Arabia Mountain Nature Preserve, 3787 Klondike Rd., Lithonia 30038; (770) 492-5220; www.co.dekalb.ga.us/naturalresources/wonders.html

Finding the trailhead: From Atlanta take I-20 East to exit 74 (Evans Mill Road and Lithonia). Turn east and go 0.1 mile on Evans Mill Road. Turn right to the south on Woodrow Drive. At 0.8 mile turn right onto Klondike Road and go 1.2 miles to the Davidson-Arabia Mountain Nature Preserve sign. Turn right into the parking area for the nature center and trailhead. Trailhead GPS: N33 40.329' / W84 07.005'

The Hike

The yellow-blazed Forest Trail begins at the Davidson–Arabia Mountain Nature Center information sign, crosses a short boardwalk, and goes through a pleasant pine-hardwood forest to Arabia Lake. You go to the right of and parallel to the wide, paved multiuse Arabia Mountain Trail, crossing it at 0.2 mile to continue on toward the lake.

The most impressive forest feature here is the thickness of the undergrowth and the large loblolly pines. You continue northwest on a soft pine needle and leaf, loam trail, passing through an area of large, old, gnarled pines showing the scars of past fires that were common seventy years ago. Openings in the undergrowth give you views of small areas of exposed granite, lined with trees and supporting patches of moss and lichens, along with bunches of flowering plants.

The trail next goes down a few feet to parallel a little intermittent creek. The path eventually crosses the small streambed, where water may puddle up in the trail during wet weather. Just beyond the crossing, the trail forks; take the left fork to continue on the east side of Arabia Lake. The right fork offers access to the west shore of the lake.

Continuing on the trail, the lake is now on the right. You may see resident wood ducks, great blue herons, or any of the local or migrant waterbirds. The path crosses a couple of exposed rock faces along the way, one of which stretches right to the edge of the water. This is a small, clear lake impounded more than a hundred years ago to support quarry operations. There are some old metal structures standing in the water that date from World War II. Georgia Tech used these, under contract with the US Navy, to test underwater explosives.

Continue south along the lakeshore to the junction with the Mile Rock Trail at the dam.

Turn right at this intersection to continue on the Forest Trail. The path drops down past the stone spillway of the lake to follow Stephenson Creek downstream. The trail runs through a pleasant, moist habitat with many flowering plants, ferns, and lichens. After crossing a couple of footbridges, the trail ends at the junction with a long boardwalk portion of the Arabia Mountain Trail.

Reverse course, walk back to the intersection with the Mile Rock Trail, and turn right. This trail begins by passing through a gazebo beside the first rock cairn. The path is across open granite and is not blazed; rather it has roughly thirty stone cairns that serve as trail markers, without which it would be quite difficult to follow the designated path.

The Mile Rock Trail crosses the Lithonia gneiss in the old rock quarry, where the path is marked with cairns.

The pathway leads across smooth quarried sections, as well as uneven areas over scattered large stones of cut granite. Patches of the red diamorpha are abundant, along with small round pockets that hold water.

At the point the trail turns sharply north, the remains of the old quarry office and weigh station are on the right, with the Arabia Mountain Trail running on the other side of the structure. To stay on the Mile Rock Trail, continue to follow the cairns. Shortly, on the left you have a larger, deeper pool with permanent water. This is the Frog Pond. An information plaque explains the significance of this small water hole.

Upon passing the remains of another historic quarry building, the trail quickly exits the granite to enter a pine and hardwood forested area. The trail is a well-defined path that takes you along an old railroad bed associated with the quarry. Stay to the left where a spur trail turns off to the right. When the trail dead-ends into the paved Arabia Mountain Trail, turn right and walk to the nature center.

Miles and Directions

0.0 Start at the Davidson-Arabia Mountain Nature Center, crossing the short boardwalk.

0.2 Cross the paved Arabia Mountain Trail.

0.7 Cross the small stream that floods the path, and pass the trail junction for the spur leading to the west side of Arabia Lake.

0.8 Arrive at Arabia Lake, cross the exposed rock face, and pass the metal structure standing in the water.

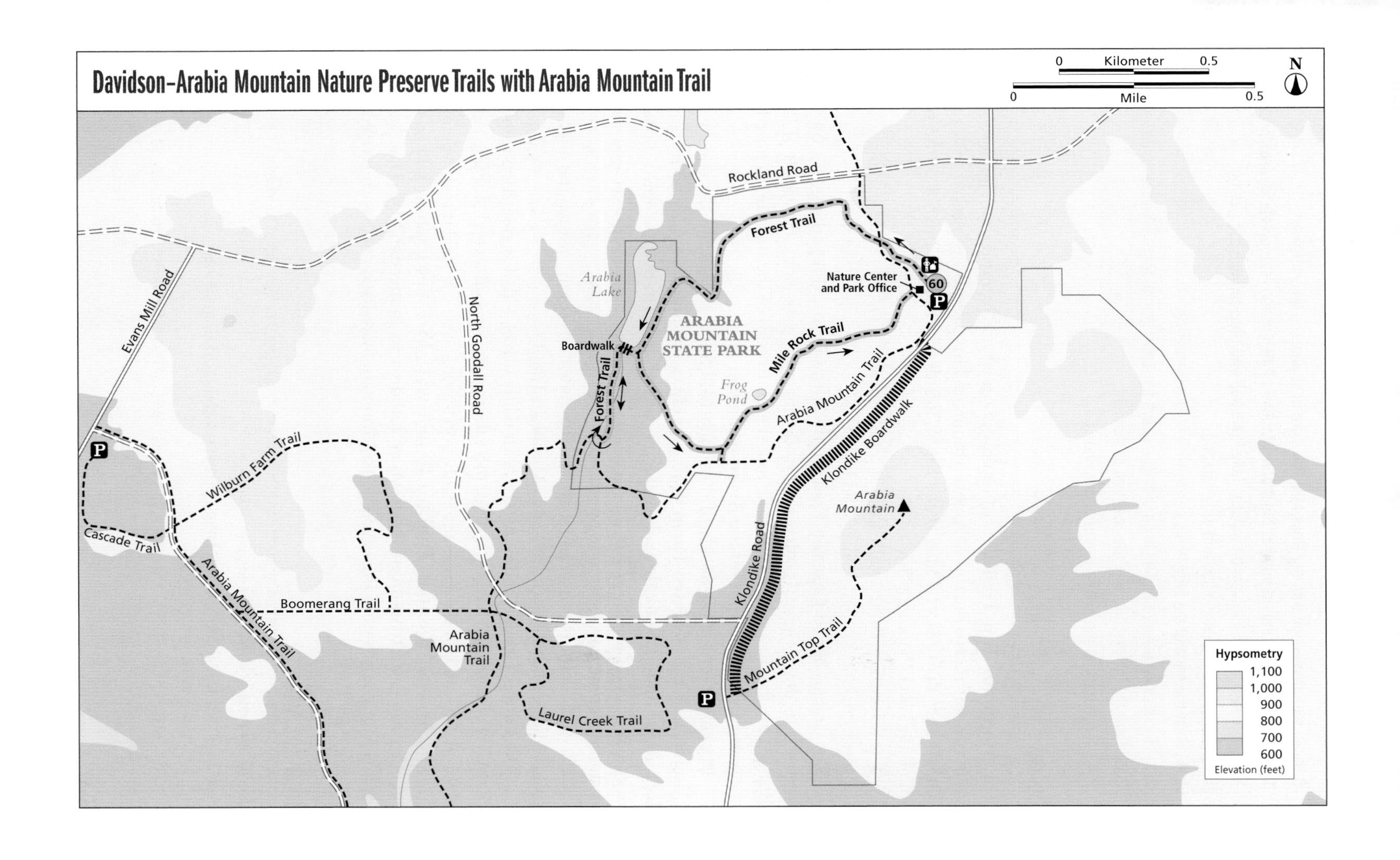
Davidson–Arabia Mountain Nature Preserve Trails with Arabia Mountain Trail
0
Kilometer
0.5
0
Mile
0.5
N
Rockland Road
Forest Trail
Nature Center
and Park Office
60
P
Arabia
Lake
ARABIA
MOUNTAIN
STATE PARK
Mile Rock Trail
Boardwalk
Forest Trail
Frog
Pond
Arabia Mountain Trail
Klondike Boardwalk
Arabia
Mountain
Klondike Road
Mountain Top Trail
Evans Mill Road
North Goodall Road
Wilburn Farm Trail
Cascade Trail
Arabia Mountain Trail
Boomerang Trail
Arabia
Mountain
Trail
Laurel Creek Trail
Hypsometry
1,100
1,000
900
800
700
600
Elevation (feet)

0.9 At the intersection with the Rock Mile Trail, turn right past the lake spillway.

1.2 Reach the turnaround point at the Arabia Mountain Trail junction and reverse course.

1.4 Turn right at the intersection with the Mile Rock Trail and pass through the gazebo.

1.7 Pass the old quarry office and weigh station.

1.8 Skirt the edge of the Frog Pond.

2.1 The historic quarry building is on the right. Leave the open granite for the forested area.

2.2 Pass the intersection with the spur trail to the right.

2.4 Arrive back at the nature center and trailhead.

Options

The **Mountain Top Trail** is a 1.0-mile out-and-back pathway leading from the south parking area to the top of Arabia Mountain. This path also is marked with rock cairns rather than blazes. Once at the top, a 360-degree view is offered of the surrounding lower Piedmont forests.

The **Klondike Boardwalk** spans 0.5 mile from the visitor center parking lot to the south parking lot, paralleling Klondike Road for the entire distance.

The orange-blazed **Cascade Trail** begins at the Evans Mill parking area on the west side of the preserve. It offers a 0.8-mile one-way walk along the shoals of Pole Bridge Creek, across from the historic mill site. Both ends of the trail are anchored to the paved Evans Mill Spur off the Arabia Mountain Trail.

Beginning on the north side of the Evans Mill Spur, across from the end of the Cascade Trail, the **Wilburn Farm Trail** provides a 1.6-mile one-way (with a short loop in the middle) walk through of the remains of the farm that occupied the land beginning in the late 1800s. The other end of this orange-blazed path is at a junction with the Boomerang Trail.

The red-blazed **Boomerang Trail** is a 0.5-mile connector between the multiuse Evans Mill Spur and the main Arabia Mountain Trail.

The **Laurel Creek Trail** is marked with white blazes. This 1.8-mile loop runs off the Arabia Mountain Trail to explore the valley of its namesake creek and the ridge above it.

The **Arabia Mountain Trail** is a 10-foot-wide, 18.4-mile multiuse biking and hiking path. It stretches from the town of Lithonia to Stonecrest Mall, Davidson–Arabia Mountain Nature Preserve, Panola Mountain State Park, and South Rockdale Community Park.

Local Information

Local Events/Attractions

Arabia Mountain National Heritage Area; www.arabiaalliance.org

CHATTAHOOCHEE RIVER NATIONAL RECREATION AREA

The Chattahoochee River begins as a spring in Chattahoochee Gap at the Appalachian Trail, high in the North Georgia mountains near the end of Jacks Knob Trail. It collects water from hundreds of tributaries along its meandering course before it reaches Atlanta as the largest and most important water source for that metropolitan area.

The Chattahoochee River National Recreation Area was established in 1978 to preserve the river corridor and provide recreation under management of the National Park Service. Sixteen tracts of land have been developed for recreation on the 48 miles of river flowing through the north and west regions of metro Atlanta. Four of the tracts with hiking trails are discussed here. Most of the other units have similar hiking trails.

A detailed map of the Chattahoochee River from Buford Dam down to Atlanta is available from the National Park Service. It shows access roads to all the units of land administered by the Park Service. The map can be found at www.nps.gov/chat.

The flow of the Chattahoochee River is controlled for hydroelectric-power generation at Buford Dam. Depending on water releases, the river may be very full or quite low with many rocks exposed in the shoals. The water discharged from Buford Dam is cold—50 to 60 degrees—year-round. The Georgia Department of Natural Resources, Wildlife Resources Division manages the river for a very popular rainbow and brown trout fishery. Visit www.georgiawildlife.com/fishing/ for more information on the fishing.

For more information:

River Through Atlanta Guide Service, 710 Riverside Rd., Roswell 30075; (770) 650-8630; www.riverthroughatlanta.com.

Upper Chattahoochee Riverkeeper, 3 Puritan Mill, 916 Joseph E. Lowery Blvd. NW, Atlanta 30318; (404) 352-9828; www.chattahoochee.org. An independent environmental organization whose mission is to advocate and secure protection of the Chattahoochee River, its tributaries, and its watershed.

The Chattahoochee Cold Water Tailrace Fishery Foundation, Inc., 710 Riverside Rd., Roswell 30075; (770) 650-8630; www.chattahoocheefoodwebs.org. Dedicated to protecting the cold-water trout fishery in the Chattahoochee River and supporting the work of the Georgia Wildlife Resources Division and the National Park Service effort to manage these waters.

61 West Palisades Trail

The West Palisades Unit comprises 302 acres along 1.5 miles of Cochran, Thornton, and Devils Race Course Shoals on the Chattahoochee River. Both the West and East Palisades Units derive their names from the high cliffs along this part of the stream. The trail follows the riverbank and then moves into the rocky palisades uplands. A varied habitat of dense woods, tumbling streams, and rocky cliffs make this area especially interesting.

In sight of Atlanta's skyscraper skyline, you have an almost backwoods-type hiking experience. Cliff-edge views of the Chattahoochee River and stream-edge trails make this a very popular morning or afternoon hike for local residents. Others drive miles just for the experience, which includes wildflowers, birding, fishing for trout, and nature photography.

Start: At the upstream end of the parking area at the trailhead marker for the Rottenwood Creek Multi-use Trail
Distance: 4.7-mile double-loop lollipop
Hiking time: About 2–2.5 hours
Difficulty: Easy to moderate; one short, steep section
Trail surface: Sandy loam; one portion of old broken pavement
Best season: Year-round
Other trail users: Mountain bikes, anglers
Canine compatibility: Leashed dogs permitted
Land status: Chattahoochee River National Recreation Area (CRNRA)
Nearest town: Smyrna
Fees and permits: Daily parking fee
Schedule: Park opens dawn to dusk, year-round
Maps: USGS Fayetteville; page-size map available from the CRNRA office at Island Ford or online at www.nps.gov/chat
Trail contacts: National Park Service, Chattahoochee River National Recreation Area, 1978 Island Ford Pkwy., Atlanta 30350; (678) 538-1200; www.nps.gov/chat

Finding the trailhead: From exit 19 on I-285, travel south on US 41 (Cobb Parkway) to the Chattahoochee River bridge. Turn right just before the bridge into the Paces Mill Unit of the CRNRA. The trailhead is at the upstream end of the parking area. Trailhead GPS: N33 52.277' / W84 27.215'

The Hike

The trail begins on the west side of the river across from the toe of Long Island. The first portion of the trail shares the path with the paved Rottenwood Creek Multi-use Trail and is wheelchair accessible. Once off the paved portion, the West Palisades Trail is blue blazed, with most of the marks on stakes beside the path.

After you pass under the I-75 bridge, a good vista upstream of the Chattahoochee River is presented, looking toward the bend at the Whitewater Creek Unit of the CRNRA. A footbridge crosses Rottenwood Creek, and the path continues straight, leaving the paved trail that turns left to follow Rottenwood upstream. Continue upriver, walking under a typical riverbank forest of sycamore, sweet gum, water oak, river birch, ironwood, and box elders. The ridge to the left of the trail supports many wildflowers, including azalea, mountain laurel, dogwoods, trout lilies, trilliums, Solomon's seal, phlox, and violets. Privet shrubs have invaded the riverbank in places, forming dense thickets. Large yellow poplars, loblolly pines, and an occasional deciduous magnolia are in the coves leading away from the river. In October the hickories, maples, sassafras, dogwoods, sumacs, and red oaks put on a beautiful show of color.

The deep bend pool at Diving Rock in Sandy Bottom

Short spur trails used by fishermen lead to the riverbank. Look for great blue herons feeding in the river and for mammal tracks in the moist sandy-clay areas. Belted kingfishers, wood ducks, and Canada geese can be seen regularly along this portion of the trail. Signs of beaver activity are common.

At an intersection marked with a directional stake, the trail turns off to the left. Most of the trail junctions have a map mounted on a post showing where you are. The trail now begins a 0.4-mile climb to the ridge above the river valley. At the next intersection you have completed half of the first loop; turn right and continue the climb.

Mountain laurel, rhododendron, and several species of ferns dot the passage as you climb to the ridgeline with its chestnut oaks, white oaks, and hickories. It is easy to imagine yourself in the more remote mountains instead of metropolitan Atlanta. The sound of traffic gives way to the murmurs of the river and forest.

At the point the trail turns sharply to the right, an old paved driveway goes to the left, leaving the park service property. Keep to the right until the trail crosses the headwaters of tiny Trout Lily Creek.

The path then reaches a gravel service road used by park service vehicles only. It follows the bed of the old James Hayes Road, leading steeply downhill toward the river and the area known as Sandy Bottom. A couple of the steepest portions have old, broken concrete pavement. At the bottom of the hill is the intersection at the beginning of the second loop. Turn right to walk it in a counterclockwise direction.

After crossing a footbridge and a boardwalk, the trail turns sharply back upstream along Thornton Shoals. Next is a deep bend of the river with a small boat ramp. On the opposite shore is Diving Rock, where rafters stop in the warmer months to take the 20-foot plunge into the water from an overhanging boulder.

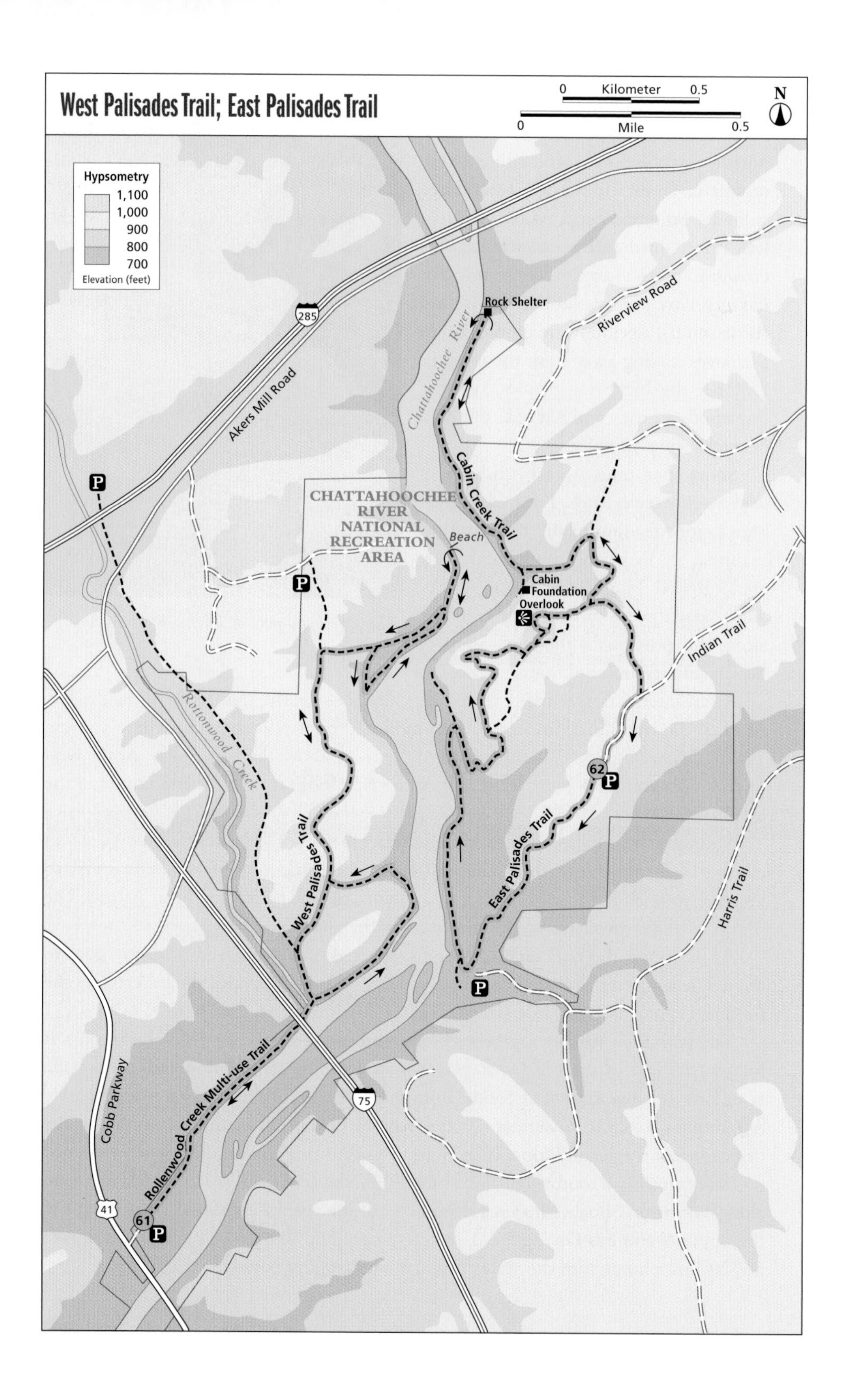
West Palisades Trail; East Palisades Trail
0 Kilometer 0.5
0 Mile 0.5
N
Hypsometry
1,100
1,000
900
800
700
Elevation (feet)
285
Akers Mill Road
Chattahoochee River
Rock Shelter
Riverview Road
Cabin Creek Trail
CHATTAHOOCHEE RIVER NATIONAL RECREATION AREA
Beach
Cabin Foundation
Overlook
Indian Trail
Rottenwood Creek
West Palisades Trail
East Palisades Trail
62
Harris Trail
75
Cobb Parkway
Rottenwood Creek Multi-use Trail
41
61
P

The path next passes the junction at the upper end of the second loop, continuing up an old roadbed to a sandy beach at the foot of Devils Race Course Shoals. From the beach, retrace your path back to the loop intersection and turn right past a building containing restrooms. These are provided for rafters and canoeists on the river.

The next junction closes the second loop; turn right and climb back up the service road to where the trail exits to the left. Continue to retrace your earlier path back to the intersection at the first loop. Turn right and follow the very rutted trail downhill to its junction with the Rottenwood Multi-Use Trail. Turn left and follow the paved path back to the trailhead.

Miles and Directions

0.0 Start from the parking lot along the Rottenwood Creek Multi-use Trail.

0.6 Pass under the I-75 bridge, over the footbridge across Rottenwood Creek, and continue straight, leaving the paved path.

1.0 Turn left at the intersection, climbing away from the river.

1.2 Turn to the right at this intersection, ending half of the first loop.

1.7 Pass the old paved drive leading to the left out of the park. Stay to the right.

1.8 Cross Trout Lily Creek.

1.9 Turn right onto the service road, walking downhill to the river.

2.1 Reach the intersection for the second loop and turn right.

2.2 Cross the footbridge.

2.3 Cross a boardwalk and turn sharply upstream along Thornton Shoals.

2.4 Pass the boat ramp and view of Diving Rock.

2.5 Reach the other end of the second loop; continue straight on the old roadbed.

2.7 Turn around at the beach at Devils Race Course.

2.8 Turn right at the intersection and pass the restrooms.

2.9 Close the second loop and turn right up the service road.

3.1 Turn left off the service road.

3.8 At the intersection on the first loop, turn right.

4.1 Turn left on the paved Rottenwood Creek Multi-use Trail.

4.7 Arrive back at the trailhead and parking area.

The I-75 bridge over the Chattahoochee from the footbridge over Rottenwood Creek

62 East Palisades Trail

The East Palisades Unit comprises 393 acres of hardwood forest with rock outcrops, ravines, and a narrow river floodplain. The East Palisades Trail has a number of connecting trails in the interior of its loop. The main trail and most of these connectors all have blue blazes.

Roughly 5 miles of forest footpaths wind along the steep bluffs overlooking the east side of the river. Only short sections of the East Palisades Trail are steep and strenuous for hiking. The elevation change from the river to the highest point in the unit is about 290 feet.

An observation deck provides a panoramic view of the river shoals from the top of the bluff. River boatmen in the eighteenth and nineteenth centuries called these rapids Devils Race Course Shoals. They named the granite palisades the Devils Stairsteps.

The featured hike is a combination of the 2.8-mile East Palisades Trail loop and 1.0-mile one-way Cabin Creek Trail.

See map page 304.
Start: At Indian Trail parking area
Distance: 4.6-mile out and back, with a loop at the beginning
Hiking time: About 3–4 hours
Difficulty: Mostly moderate, with short strenuous stretches
Trail surface: Dirt and sandy loam
Best season: Year-round
Other trail users: Joggers
Canine compatibility: Leashed dogs permitted
Land status: Chattahoochee River National Recreation Area (CRNRA)
Nearest town: Roswell
Fees and permits: Daily parking fee
Schedule: Park opens dawn to dusk, year-round
Maps: USGS Sandy Springs; page-size map available from the National Park Service office and from www.nps.gov/chat
Trail contacts: National Park Service, Chattahoochee River National Recreation Area, 1978 Island Ford Pkwy., Atlanta 30350; (770) 399-8070; www.nps.gov/chat

Finding the trailhead: Exit I-285 at Northside Drive (exit 22). Follow this residential road south to Indian Trail. Turn right and go 0.5 mile to the dead end in the parking area at the trailhead. Trailhead GPS: N33 53.043' / W84 26.213'

The Hike

Beginning at the Indian Trail parking area, the path follows an old roadbed for a few yards before dropping down in a series of switchbacks to Whitewater Creek and the river. A bridge on the left crosses Long Island Creek to an alternate trailhead at the Whitewater Creek parking area (Trailhead GPS: N33 52.706' / W84 26.510').

At the river, the path is only a few feet from the bank. This is a good place to look for tracks of muskrats, beavers, raccoons, minks, and other mammals using the river's edge. The exposed rocks visible when the river is running low, or the whitewater

A panorama of Devils Race Course Shoals is offered from the observation deck.

when the river is up, are Long Island Shoals and Thornton Shoals. Large patches of shrubs, switch cane, and honeysuckle grow in the wet areas along the bank. Through here you cross two short boardwalks and one footbridge.

After crossing a second footbridge over Charlies Trapping Creek, you reach the first of a number of trails intersecting from the right. At each of these, take the path to the left.

The path soon begins the climb up along the palisades. This is the steepest portion of the trail.

Once on the top of the high bluff you pass a wintertime overlook, and then the trail turns left down to the observation deck. From the deck you get a grand view of the river and appreciate the height of the bluffs.

The main channel of the river below going through Devils Race Course is not natural. It was blasted out with dynamite to allow for the passage of flatboats in the 1800s.

Exiting the overlook, you turn left. Shortly you pass the junction with the Cabin Creek Trail and turn left. Descending a ridge from the junction, the path goes through a beautiful mature hardwood forest of large yellow poplars, white oaks, chestnut oaks, and an occasional deciduous magnolia with exceptionally large leaves. Orange flame azaleas, honeysuckle, and mountain laurel bloom along the trail in the spring.

The path crosses a bridge over Cabin Creek and then 100 yards farther enters an old roadbed to follow the stream down to the river. Along the way you pass the junction of a trail on the right that connects to Riverview Road. However, there is no parking at the road on the other end of this trail.

At the mouth of the creek, the stone foundation of a cabin is on the left. The trail now turns upriver across a stone bridge. As it continues, the path next crosses a bridge over Mountain Heath Creek and then runs between a rock cliff on the right and a stand of bamboo on the left. Some of these plants are 5 to 6 inches in diameter.

The trail ends on top of a stone outcrop and rock shelter at the recreation area property boundary. Retrace your path back to the junction with the East Palisades Trail. At the intersection, turn left to reach Indian Trail. A right turn onto that road leads back to the trailhead.

Miles and Directions

0.0 Start from the parking area at the end of Indian Trail.

0.4 After you come down from about 180 feet in elevation to a boardwalk, Long Island Creek is on the left.

0.6 Pass the footbridge leading over Long Island Creek to the alternate trailhead. Begin walking up the Chattahoochee River's east bank.

0.7 Cross the first of several boardwalks over wet areas and continue upstream.

1.0 Cross the bridge over Charlies Trapping Creek.

1.2 The loop trail turns sharply back to the right as you begin an ascent to the overlook. A fisherman's trail runs off to the left at the bend of the pathway, so take care to follow the blazes uphill.

1.3 Reach a trail junction. The trail to the left runs about 150 yards down to the river to a rocky point overlooking Thornton Shoals. This is a one-way trail. Return to the main path and start climbing through several switchbacks.

1.8 Arrive at the top of the bluff with a winter vista of the river. From spring through fall the foliage blocks the view.

2.0 Follow the trail sharply to the left down to the observation deck.

2.1 Reach the deck. Take the trail to the left as you exit the deck to continue.

2.2 Reach the Cabin Creek Trail junction and turn left.

2.3 Cross the first bridge over Cabin Creek.

2.5 Pass the junction with Riverview Road connector trail.

2.6 Cross the second bridge over the creek; reach the river, stone foundation, and stone bridge at the mouth of Cabin Creek. Turn right and walk upstream along the river.

2.7 Cross the bridge over Mountain Heath Creek.

3.1 Reach the rock outcrop and shelter at the turnaround point.

4.0 Arrive back at the junction with the East Palisades Trail. Turn left.

4.3 Turn right onto Indian Trail.

4.6 Reach the trailhead at the parking lot.

63 Johnson Ferry North Trail

The Johnson Ferry Unit of the Chattahoochee River National Recreation Area (CRNRA) comprises 108 acres entirely on the floodplain of the Chattahoochee River. This unit also provides a picnic area, along with boat ramp and launch area for canoes and rafts on the river.

The trail is on the west side of the river upstream from Johnson Ferry Road. This is an exceptionally good birding area with aquatic, open, brushy and forested habitats. Ducks, herons, beavers, muskrats, raccoons, opossums, otters, turtles, frogs, and toads are some of the wildlife associated with the wet area and river. The forested area attracts many songbirds. Several benches are positioned along the riverside portion of the trail for wildlife viewing.

A single-loop, blue-blazed trail takes you around the unique and extensive wetland area with several creek crossings. For half the distance you are in almost constant view of the river. After the turn along the banks of Mulberry Creek, the return is via a very straight walk through brushy cover and larger trees.

Start: The path begins at a trailhead sign, gate, and large rock at the north end of the parking area.
Distance: 1.7-mile loop
Hiking time: About 1 hour
Difficulty: Easy
Trail surface: Sandy loam; short gravel section
Best season: Year-round
Other trail users: Hikers only
Canine compatibility: Leashed dogs permitted
Land status: Chattahoochee River National Recreation Area
Nearest town: Sandy Springs
Fees and permits: Daily parking fee
Schedule: Unit open dawn to dusk, year-round
Maps: USGS Sandy Springs; page-size map available from the park service office at Island Ford or from www.nps.gov/chat
Trail contacts: National Park Service, Chattahoochee River National Recreation Area, 1978 Island Ford Pkwy., Atlanta 30350; (678) 538-1200; www.nps.gov/chat

Finding the trailhead: From I-285 take exit 25 (Roswell Road) and go north on Roswell Road 1.7 miles to Johnson Ferry Road. Turn left and go 2.2 miles and cross the Chattahoochee River Bridge. Immediately across the bridge, turn right at the sign for the Johnson Ferry North parking area. Follow the gravel road through the gate to the boat ramp and parking area. Trailhead GPS: N33 56.806' / W84 24.220'

The Hike

This trail is an easy but interesting path that goes around a natural wetland area. From the trailhead at the parking area, walk past the information sign, gate, and large rock onto an old gravel roadbed. This is to the right of the return loop of the trail, which is also on an old gravel road.

The first part of the trail is on an old gravel roadbed.

During spring and summer, you may see killdeers in the gravel and grassy areas.

Roughly 200 yards into the hike, the path merges with the return loop as they both cross a culvert over Nannyberry Creek. From there the trail turns right and approaches the riverbank.

Spur trails made by fishermen lead off the main path at irregular intervals. During periods when the water in the river is very clear or low, it is possible to see a dark V-shaped area crossing the channel. This is the remains of a fish trap used by early settlers. It is believed that white settlers learned to build and use fish traps from the Indians.

Privet shrubs and switch cane grow in dense thickets along the trail close to the river. The privet is an escaped horticultural plant. The cane is native and in the past extended in great patches along many of the rivers of the Southeast. The large canebrakes of the past were used extensively by both wildlife and humans.

After crossing a cleared gas line right-of-way and continuing past a bench, the trail reaches a sign marking River Mile 311 in the edge of the water. These miles are measured from the Woodruff Dam on Lake Seminole in southwest Georgia, where the Chattahoochee and Flint Rivers join to form the Apalachicola River.

Beyond the river marker the trail turns left to cross a culvert over Arrowhead Creek. It then returns to the river shore. Two more benches along the bank are passed before the trail crosses over Owl Creek on yet another culvert. There's also another bench just north of this crossing.

Just before reaching Mulberry Creek, the main trail turns to the left. A well-beaten fisherman's path continues ahead toward the mouth of the creek, so be careful to follow the blue blazes. As you walk along Mulberry Creek, the area is alive with yellow jonquils in the late winter months. A pipe crosses the creek to the right, with another well-worn path continuing at the other end of the pipe. That trail leaves the park property, following the river upstream.

Continuing toward the ridge, the path comes to a four-way junction. A trail continues straight ahead up the creek valley, and another fords the creek to the right.

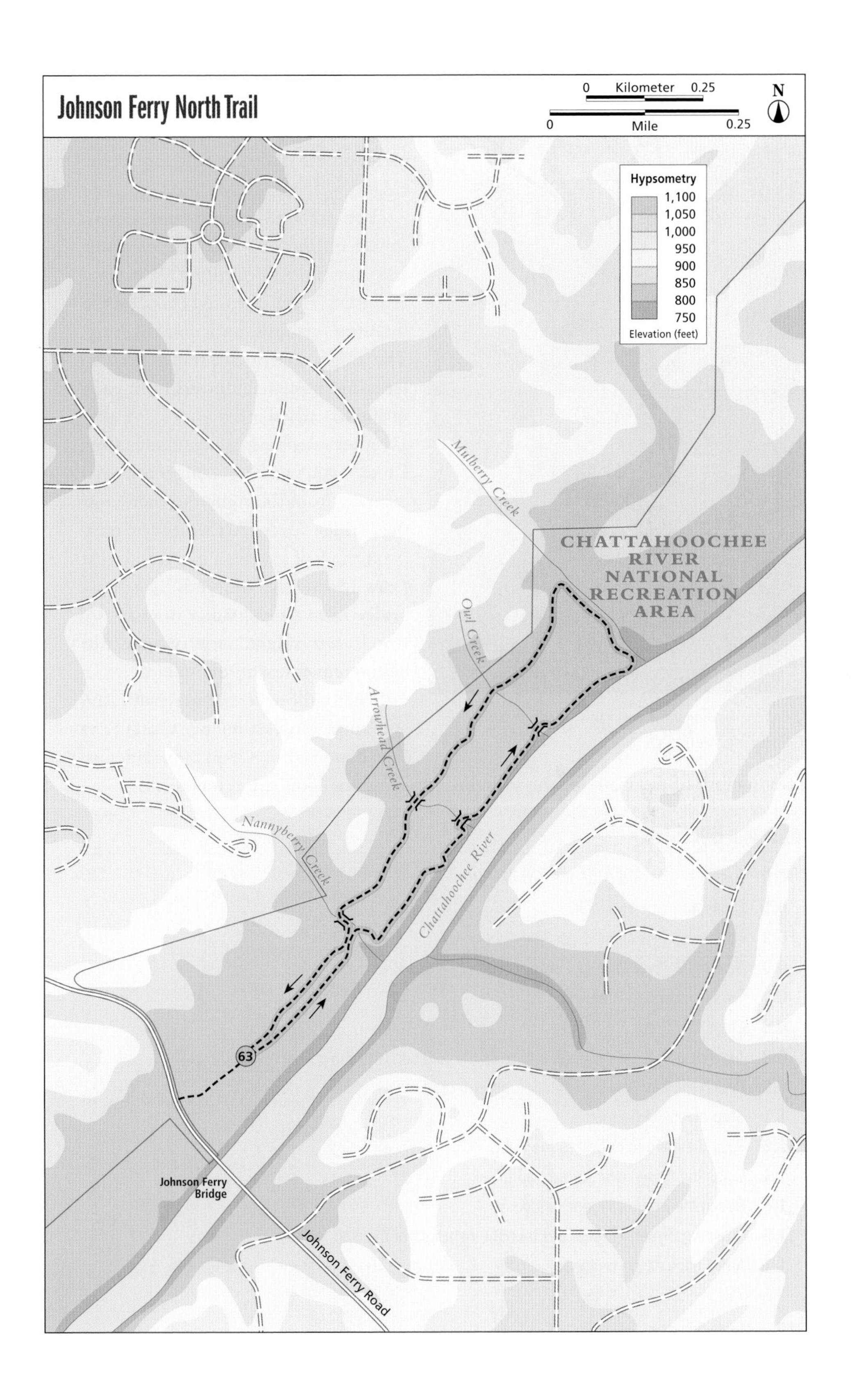

Johnson Ferry North Trail
0 Kilometer 0.25
0 Mile 0.25
N
Hypsometry
1,100
1,050
1,000
950
900
850
800
750
Elevation (feet)
Mulberry Creek
CHATTAHOOCHEE RIVER NATIONAL RECREATION AREA
Owl Creek
Arrowhead Creek
Nannyberry Creek
Chattahoochee River
63
Johnson Ferry Bridge
Johnson Ferry Road

The first half of the loop offers many views of the Chattahoochee River.

Both of those leave the park property. Turn sharply left to follow the blue blazes on the trail along the foot of the ridge.

You are now hiking back downstream on the opposite side of a wet, and sometimes flooded, area. Watch for cardinals, yellow-breasted chats, brown thrashers, catbirds, and mockingbirds. The ridge side of the trail is rich in ferns and hosts wildflowers from early spring to early winter.

After stepping across tiny Owl Creek, you pass a connector trail entering from the right and then cross the bridge over Arrowhead Creek. Next the trail reaches a boardwalk that turns to the left and ends at a footbridge over a small water flow. In the woods to the right are what appear to be the remains of an old stable.

The trail next merges with the outbound loop to recross the culvert over Nannyberry Creek. Once across, take the fork to the right for the walk back to close the loop at the trailhead.

Miles and Directions

0.0 Pass the sign and gate at the trailhead.

0.1 Cross Nannyberry Creek.

0.2 Pass through a cleared gas line right-of-way.

0.3 Reach the River Mile 311 sign.

0.4 Cross Arrowhead Creek.

0.6 Cross Owl Creek.

0.8 Turn left up Mulberry Creek and pass the junction with the trail across the pipe.

0.9 Reach the four-way trail junction and turn left.

1.1 Step across Owl Creek.

1.2 Pass the connector trail to the right.

1.3 Cross the bridge over Arrowhead Creek.

1.4 Reach the boardwalk and bridge.

1.5 Cross Nannyberry Creek and take the right fork of the trail.

1.7 Arrive back at the trailhead.

64 Island Ford Trail

The 297-acre Island Ford Unit of the Chattahoochee River National Recreation Area (CRNRA) has been retained in as natural a condition as possible for almost a century, first by the original private owners and later by the National Park Service. The mature hardwood forest at this site is a fine example of what the Piedmont area of Georgia might have looked like before it was cleared and developed.

This is a great natural area, especially for a highly residential portion of metropolitan Atlanta, to find a variety of spring and summer wildflowers, trees, and wildlife. The area also contains a number of rock shelters along the river, as well as shoals within the stream.

Visitors use the site as start or finish points for paddling trips on the Chattahoochee, for picnicking along the shore, or wading in pursuit of rainbow and brown trout.

The unit contains a system of interconnected trails, none of which bear names. All the trails have signs with maps at junctions and are easy to follow. The featured hike is a combination of several of these paths, creating a double-loop trek beginning and ending at the parking lot at the CRNRA office. The trail combination enables you to see a wide variety of habitats in a relatively small area.

Start: At the information sign in front of the CRNRA office
Distance: 2.2-mile double loop
Hiking time: About 1–1.5 hours
Difficulty: Easy to moderate
Trail surface: Mostly clay or sandy loam
Best season: Mar–Dec
Other trail users: Anglers
Canine compatibility: Leashed dogs permitted
Land status: Chattahoochee River National Recreation Area
Nearest town: Roswell
Fees and permits: Daily parking fee
Maps: USGS Sandy Springs; page-size map available from the park service office or from www.nps.gov./chat
Trail contacts: National Park Service, Chattahoochee River National Recreation Area, 1978 Island Ford Pkwy., Atlanta 30350; (678) 538-1200; www.nps.gov./chat

Finding the trailhead: From I-285 take exit 27 and follow SR 400 north 5 miles to exit 6 (North Ridge Road). Turn right and go back across SR 400. Turn right at the traffic light to Roberts Road. Go 1.2 miles to the National Park Service entrance sign; turn right on Island Ford Parkway. The trailhead is 1.1 miles ahead, where the parkway dead-ends at the CRNRA office. Trailhead GPS: N33 59.234' / W84 19.502'

The Hike

The Island Ford Trail provides a pleasant hike in a mature hardwood forest and along the shoals of the Chattahoochee River. The path takes you through all the habitat types with flat, easy walks and moderate climbs in the hilly upland. It is almost all shaded during the warm months and an open forest canopy in winter.

The trail parallels the Island Ford shoals on the river.

Start from the information sign in front of the CRNRA office, following the paved pathway around the left side of the building. Once past the office the trail reaches the junction where the second smaller loop on the trail closes from the right. Turn left here and descend the steps toward the river.

As you climb down the hill, a picnic pavilion with a massive stone barbecue pit appears on the left. This structure predates the park service acquisition of the property. Continue down to a trail junction at the foot of the hill. The trail to the left follows a small stream up toward a small lake. This moist cove is full of spleenworts and Christmas ferns. The forest canopy is composed of dogwoods, redbuds, yellow poplar, white oak, American beech, maples, sweet gums, and loblolly pines.

From the junction turn right and follow the creek to the riverbank and another junction. The smaller loop of the trail goes to the right here; turn left across a footbridge and walk downstream along the river. Quickly you pass another trail joining on the left. This one also leads uphill to the lake.

For the next 0.2 mile the trail hugs the riverbank offering views of the shoals and the island that splits the river into two channels. During most seasons Canada geese, kingfishers, and mallard ducks are present in or over the water. Water-tolerant river birch, ironwood, sycamore, and red maple trees grow right to the riverbank. Mosses, liverworts, and ferns help stabilize the bank.

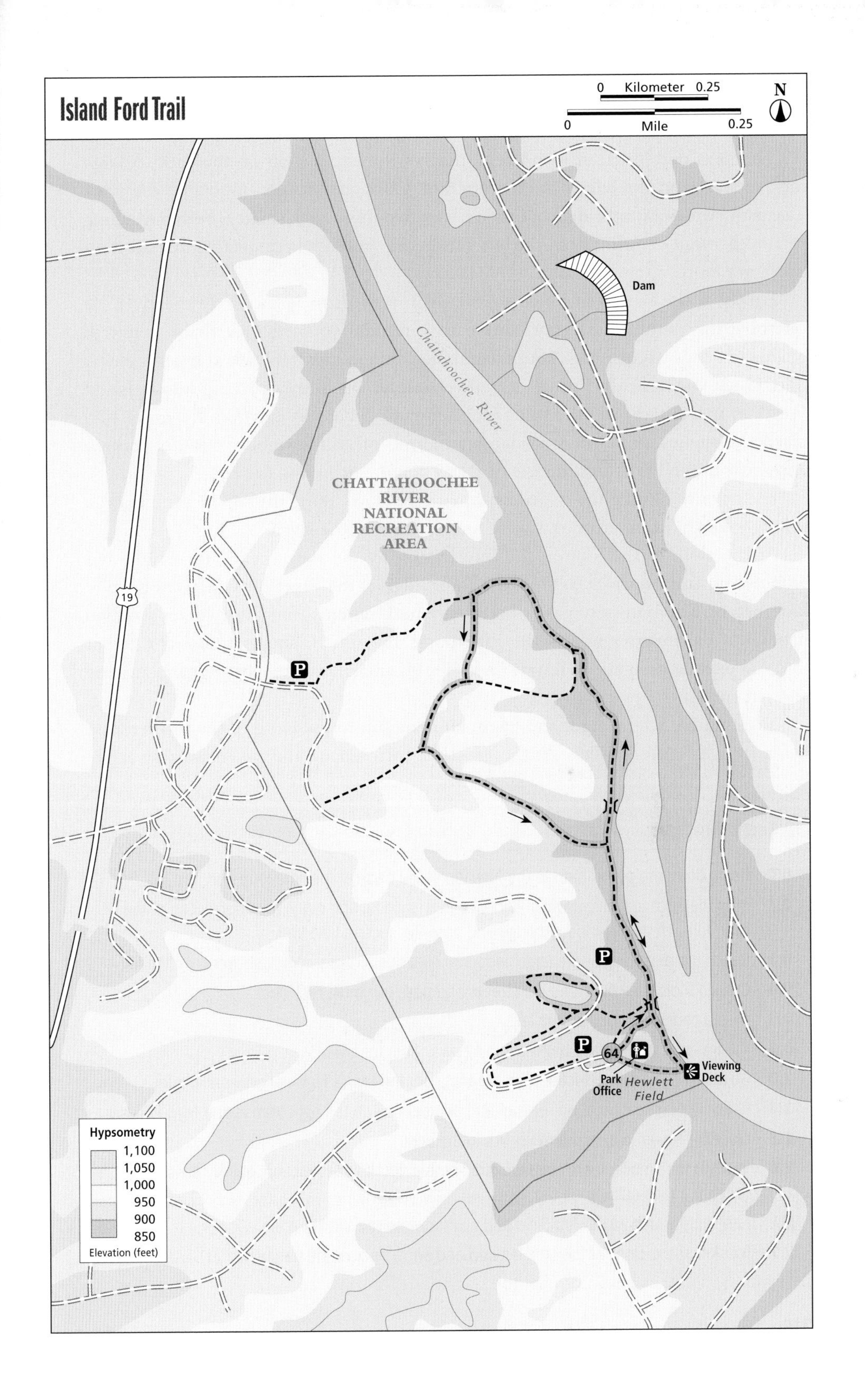

Island Ford Trail
0 Kilometer 0.25
0 Mile 0.25
N
Dam
Chattahoochee River
CHATTAHOOCHEE RIVER NATIONAL RECREATION AREA
19
P
64
Park Office
Hewlett Field
Viewing Deck
Hypsometry
1,100
1,050
1,000
950
900
850
Elevation (feet)

This is also a popular stretch with wading anglers. In the warmer months expect to see swimmers and rafters on the water as well.

The next trail junction is the beginning of the larger loop on the path. A large rock shelter is on the left of the intersection. Continue straight, following the river. The path crosses a footbridge and then passes two more rock shelters before reaching yet another trail entering from the left. This is one of several connectors that shortcut the larger loop.

Finally, at the next trail junction, the main path turns left to leave the river. Be careful at this point, for a fisherman's path continues down the riverbank. The trail gradually bends to turn back south, climbing through a switchback as it gains elevation. Once you're headed south, a trail coming down from a parking lot on Island Ford Parkway enters from the right. Continue straight at this junction. When the trail reaches its highest point on the ridge, a trail forks off to the right to another parking area. Bear to the left at this intersection and begin descending the ridge.

Just prior to closing the large loop, the trail follows along the top of a mini gorge through which Summerbrook Creek tumbles toward the river.

At the close of the loop at the intersection by the rock shelter, turn right and retrace your steps upriver to cross the footbridge at the junction where the smaller loop begins. The trail now passes between a rock outcrop and the river. A wooden handrail is on the river side of the path along this stretch. The trail next comes out into the open at the grassy Hewett Field. This is an activity area that features a canoe and raft launch.

Turn sharply to the right and begin climbing up to the close of the smaller loop behind the CRNRA office. At the junction, turn left on the paved walk to arrive back at the trailhead.

Miles and Directions

0.0 Begin down the paved path to the junction at the close of the little loop and turn left.

0.1 Pass the historic picnic pavilion and lake trail junction, and reach the intersection at the river; turn left across the footbridge and pass the second lake trail.

0.3 Reach the beginning of the larger loop and continue straight; a rock shelter is on the left.

0.4 Cross a footbridge over a feeder stream and pass two more rock shelters.

0.7 Pass a connecting trail on the left.

0.8 The trail now turns left to begin climbing away from the river.

1.0 Go straight at the intersection with the trail from the Island Ford Parkway parking lot.

1.3 Reach the highest point on the trail and another trail on the right from Island Ford Parkway.

1.8 Close the larger loop and turn upriver to the right.

2.0 To begin the smaller loop, continue straight through the trail junction, quickly passing beneath a rock outcrop on the right.

2.1 Turn sharply right at Hewlett Field and climb toward the CRNRA office.

2.2 Turn left at the close of the smaller loop and arrive back at the trailhead.

Honorable Mention

J Chattahoochee River National Recreation Area: Cochran Shoals Unit Trails

The Cochran Shoals Unit comprises 968 acres, the largest and most popular park along the Chattahoochee River National Recreation Area (CRNRA). There are fields, woodlands, wetlands, and river habitats. This is a good birding and wildlife-watching trail.

Ten miles of interconnected trails offer a variety of natural and historic attractions. Most of the trail system is on jogging, fitness, and bike trails. The wheelchair-accessible fitness trail is a 2.5-mile loop that follows close to the river. Two other trails, about 1.5 miles each, lead away from the heavily used areas into forested hiking paths. The degree of difficulty varies from easy to moderate. The ruins of the old Marietta Paper Mill add historic interest to the area.

The Cochran Shoals area is located close to major office and residential areas of Atlanta, and hundreds of hikers, bikers, joggers, and others use it daily. All trails can be reached on foot from three parking areas on the west side of the river. The unit is accessible year-round.

This area is just north of the I-285 bridge across the Chattahoochee River. A page-size map is available from the park service office.

For more information: National Park Service, Chattahoochee River National Recreation Area, 1978 Island Ford Pkwy., Atlanta 30350; (678) 538-1200; www.nps.gov/chat

DeLorme: Georgia Atlas and Gazetteer: Page 20 H2

Southwest Georgia

The clay and sand soils of Southwest Georgia are highly erodible, creating some impressive mosaics of color.

65 Providence Canyon State Outdoor Recreation Area Trails

About 40 miles south of Columbus, Providence Canyon is one of the former state parks that were changed to state outdoor recreation areas.

The rolling topography and the geological formation, coupled with clearing the land in the early 1800s for lumber and farming, caused severe erosion gullies. The soils found on the area are very soft and easily eroded. By 1850 the gullies were 3 to 5 feet deep. Once the water cut through the erosion-resistant surface layers, the softer sandy soils of the Providence Formation wore away rapidly. This has resulted in a canyon 150 feet deep with exposed sides that are exceptionally colorful. The formation is frequently called "Georgia's Little Grand Canyon."

Most of the park's 1,003 acres have been reforested and are no longer eroding. The hills now are covered with a wide variety of plants, from large loblolly and longleaf pines to mature deciduous trees and showy rhododendrons and azaleas.

Two loop trails totaling 9.7 miles offer a remarkable hiking experience. The Canyon Loop Trail gives you a close-up visit to the exposed 100-foot-plus canyon walls. The featured Backcountry Trail shares part of the path with Canyon Loop in circling the entire canyon. This longer trail also has two pioneer and six backpack campsites along it. Hikers on this trail must sign the registry at the trailhead before starting to hike.

Start: At the office/interpretive center
Distance: 6.7-mile loop
Hiking time: About 3-3.5 hours
Difficulty: Easy to moderate; a few very short, steep grades
Trail surface: Clay loam, sand, and sandy clay
Best season: Mar-June; Oct-Dec
Other trail users: Hikers only
Canine compatibility: Leashed dogs permitted
Land status: Georgia DNR, State Parks & Historic Sites Division
Nearest town: Lumpkin
Fees and permits: Camping fee
Schedule: Recreation area hours, Sept-Apr, 7 a.m.-6 p.m.; May-Aug, 7 a.m.-9 p.m.; office/interpretive center open weekends only, Mar-May and Sept-Nov, 8 a.m.-5 p.m.
Maps: USGS Lumpkin; page-size maps available at the interpretive center or online at www.gastateparks.org
Trail contacts: Providence Canyon State Park, 8930 Canyon Rd., Lumpkin 31815; (229) 838-6870; www.gastateparks.org

Finding the trailhead: From US 27 just west of Lumpkin, turn west on SR 39. The park entrance is on the left at 6.2 miles. The joint trailhead is on the canyon rim behind the office/interpretive center. Trailhead GPS: N32 04.138' / W84 54.801'

The Hike

The Backcountry Trail goes into the canyon on the joint path with the Canyon Loop Trail, beginning at the sign-in registry station behind the office/interpretive center. The hike begins by descending through two switchbacks and crossing a bridge over a small brook before reaching the canyon floor.

The Providence Canyon walls are colorfully arrayed in red, white, and yellow clay deposits.

The trees on the dry slope are white, southern red, and blackjack oaks; shortleaf and loblolly pines; and hickories. Dogwoods, blueberries, hawthorns, and numerous wildflowers grow beneath the taller trees.

At the canyon floor, the red-blazed Backcountry Trail splits off to the right and away from the steeper walls. The white-blazed Canyon Loop crosses the headwater of Turner Creek and continues straight.

As the Backcountry Trail parallels Turner Creek it can be difficult to tell the stream from the path in wet weather. The alluvial bed of sandy clay that eroded from the canyon walls can turn into a quagmire of mud.

As you walk down the canyon, the walls become less pronounced and open away to the sides and are covered by forest. The canopy on this part of the trail contains a large number of sycamore trees. At the point the connector trail to the pioneer campsites intersects from the right, a single low-growing palm tree is on the right of the path.

Upon reaching the mouth of the canyon, turn left to cross Turner Creek on a footbridge that was constructed as an Eagle Scout project. This is at the lowest point of the hike.

The path turns sharply to the east and begins climbing to the rim of the canyon. About halfway up the incline a bench is on the left, offering a respite from the ascent and a wintertime view back down to Turner Creek. Reaching the crest of the ridge, the path passes the trail shelter of Campsite 6.

The trail now is in a forested area that surrounds the canyon with large trees and denser shrub thickets. The ground is more level as the path passes the spur to the right for Campsite 5 and then reaches Campsite 4. Look for the scratching and diggings of armadillos in the sandy soil along this portion of the trail.

From here the trail again begins to climb, passing Campsite 3 and then Campsite 2, which is the highest-elevation camping spot on the hike. The path next passes through an intersection to make a sharp right turn at this point. The spur that goes straight ahead is a shortcut that lessens the hike by about 0.7 mile.

The trail now makes a loop to the east and passes Campsite 1. The forest becomes more open, with terraces and rock piles suggesting earlier agricultural activity. Next the path intersects an old roadbed with a gate on the right side of the trail. Make a sharp turn to the left following the roadbed as it begins the descent into a pleasant cove of more mature trees and spring flowers. The other end of the shortcut appears on the left.

At the point the trail leaves the roadbed to the left, the path begins paralleling the right side of a deep erosion gully dropping steeply down into one of the canyon arms. A small stream is in the bottom, lined with stands of switch cane. The trail crosses the flow and begins a steep climb back up to the canyon rim. On a level shelf about a third of the way up, another bench is provided for taking a breather.

When the trail reaches the canyon rim, it soon passes the first overlook, providing a view of the white, yellow, and red clay walls for which the canyon is noted. Each of the colors along the canyon wall represents a different age and composition. Iron ore, manganese, kaolin, mica, and sandy clays are just a few of the substances contributing to the many colors you see.

There are a total of sixteen overlooks and observation decks along the rest of the hike.

Just past the junction with the Canyon Loop Trail that climbs up from the bottom of the gorge, a reminder of earlier times along the canyon rim is encountered. At the site of an old home place, 200 yards of the path is littered with the remains of several abandoned vehicles. These predate state ownership, but biologists decided to leave the debris in place because it serves as dens and nesting places for a wide range of small mammals, birds, and reptiles.

Continuing along the canyon rim, the trail frequently has red cedars growing along the way. Soon the path comes into a clearing with a historic marker, a parking lot, and one of the observation decks. Just beyond, the trail then passes through the area's picnic grounds and group shelter.

From this point the path continues to skirt the canyon rim with frequent overlooks until arriving back at the trailhead.

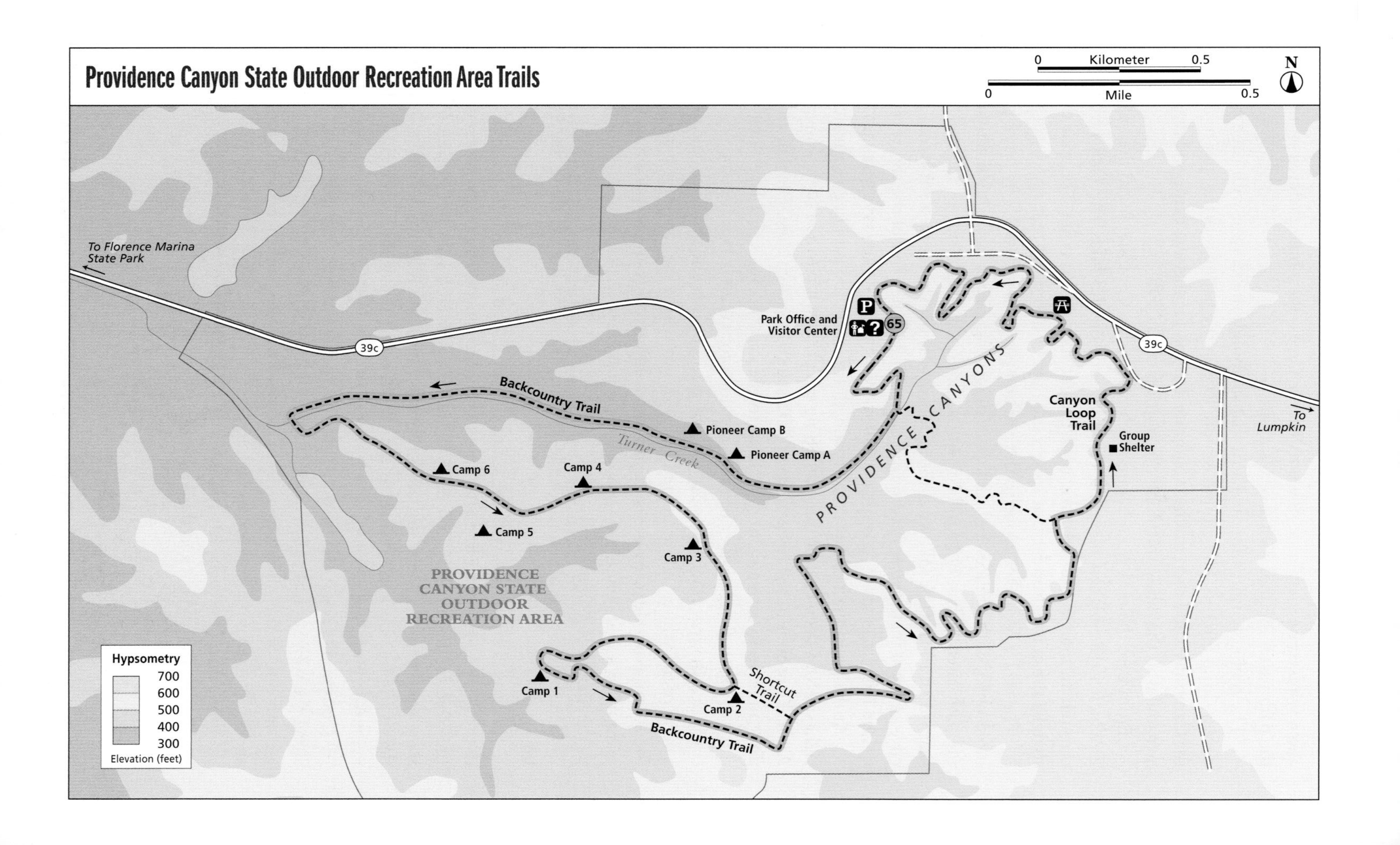
Providence Canyon State Outdoor Recreation Area Trails
0
Kilometer
0.5
0
Mile
0.5
N
To Florence Marina State Park
39c
Park Office and Visitor Center
65
Backcountry Trail
Pioneer Camp B
Pioneer Camp A
Turner Creek
Camp 6
Camp 4
Camp 5
Camp 3
PROVIDENCE CANYONS
Canyon Loop Trail
Group Shelter
To Lumpkin
PROVIDENCE CANYON STATE OUTDOOR RECREATION AREA
Camp 1
Camp 2
Shortcut Trail
Backcountry Trail
Hypsometry
700
600
500
400
300
Elevation (feet)

Miles and Directions

0.0 Start at the steps of the office/interpretive center. The Backcountry and Canyon Loop Trails descend to the canyon floor on a shared path.

0.2 Cross a bridge over a small brook.

0.3 Reach the canyon floor and turn right on the red-blazed Backcountry Trail.

1.2 Pass the spur trail to the pioneer camps on the right.

1.8 Cross the Eagle Scout footbridge over Turner Creek and begin to climb through a forest area.

2.1 Campsite 6 is on the left.

2.3 Pass the spur trail for Campsite 5 on the right.

2.4 Campsite 4 is on the left.

2.6 Pass Campsite 3 on the right and begin to climb.

3.0 At the intersection with the shortcut trail, turn right; Campsite 2 is on the left.

3.4 Campsite 1 is on the right.

3.9 Intersect an old roadbed that is gated to the right; turn left on the road and pass the other end of the shortcut trail.

4.1 Leave the roadbed; make a sharp left turn and descend into a forest cove.

4.4 Cross the stream; turn right and begin to climb back uphill.

4.8 Reach the canyon rim.

4.9 Pass the first overlook.

5.3 Rejoin the white-blazed Canyon Loop Trail and pass the junk vehicles at the old home place.

5.7 Reach the historic marker, parking lot, and overlook.

5.8 Pass the group shelter and picnic area.

6.7 Arrive back at the trailhead to close the loop.

Options

The **Canyon Loop Trail** offers a 3.0-mile, 1- to 2-hour hike beginning at the shared trailhead behind the office/interpretive center. After splitting off from the Backcountry Trail, this white-blazed path explores the upper canyon with its colorful walls. It then climbs back up to the east rim of the canyon to rejoin the Backcountry Trail.

A total of nine short side paths veer up into the various arms of the canyon. Rhododendron and the rare plumleaf azalea grow in the canyon arms, along with thick stands of alders.

66 Kolomoki Mounds State Historic Park Trails

This unusual park is an important archaeological site as well as a scenic recreation area. The mounds here were built between AD 250 and 950 by the Swift Creek and Weeden Island Indians. Among the mounds is Georgia's oldest great temple mound. The park museum is designed so that you are actually inside an excavated portion of a mound.

Along with the early American history and artifacts, the park offers four hikes totaling 7.1 miles. Two of the trails take you along the edge of Lakes Kolomoki and Yahola, beside a wetland habitat with marsh grasses and shrubs. The other two loop trails offer views of the mounds, with explanatory displays, as well as a walk through an upland white oak forest. The featured hike is on Spruce Pine Trail.

Start: At the dam on Lake Yahola
Distance: 3.1-mile loop
Hiking time: About 2–2.5 hours
Difficulty: Easy to moderate
Trail surface: Hard sandy clay
Best season: Oct–June
Other trail users: Hikers only
Canine compatibility: Leashed dogs permitted
Land status: Georgia DNR, State Parks & Historic Sites Division
Nearest town: Blakely
Fees and permits: Daily parking fee
Schedule: Park hours 7 a.m.–10 p.m., year-round
Maps: USGS Blakely North; page-size map available at the lodge office and online
Trail contacts: Kolomoki Mounds State Historic Park, 205 Indian Mounds Rd., Blakely 39823; (229) 724-2151; www.gastateparks.org.

Finding the trailhead: The park entrance is 6 miles north of Blakely on US 27. Continue on the entrance drive until you reach the intersection with Second Kolomoki Road and turn right. The trailhead for the Spruce Pine Trail is at the parking lot on the left, beside the boat ramp on Lake Yahola. Trailhead GPS: N31 27.859' / W84 55.211'

The Hike

The Spruce Pine Trail offers the park's most varied terrain and habitat. This path is part of Georgia's Southern Rivers Birding Trail. Walking this trail provides views of both Lakes Kolomoki and Yahola, with blue herons and other wading birds present along the shores. A variety of songbirds also inhabits the woodlands. In the drier areas look for armadillo diggings and gopher tortoise burrows.

The forest is dominated by large spruce pines, mixed with loblolly pines, magnolias, water oaks, and dogwoods. Wild azaleas are abundant in the understory.

After crossing the Lake Yahola dam, the trail splits. Follow the orange-blazed path to the right in a counterclockwise direction, and make the first crossing of Second Kolomoki Road.

Soon you reach Lake Kolomoki, passing an observation deck and then a pier jutting out into the lake. For the next 0.5 mile the path crosses through several little hollows with boardwalks in the bottoms.

An observation deck overlooks Lake Kolomoki on the Spruce Pine Trail.

The trail then climbs out of the bottoms to a 200-yard-long upland clearing that is pockmarked with gopher tortoise burrows. From there the trail crosses a wooden footbridge before reaching another crossing of Second Kolomoki Road. Beyond the road are several hundred yards of open ground beneath tall loblolly pines.

Upon reaching the shore of Lake Yahola, some pretty vistas of the lake are on the right. The trail is up on some rather steep bluffs above the water, and the surrounding forest has abundant southern magnolias.

At the point the trail closes the loop, turn right back across the dam to the trailhead.

Miles and Directions

0.0 Start at the trailhead at the boat-ramp parking lot on Lake Yahola and cross the dam.

0.1 Turn right where the loop trail splits.

0.2 Cross Second Kolomoki Road.

0.4 First view of Lake Kolomoki appears on the right.

0.6 Pass the observation pier on Lake Kolomoki.

1.2 Enter the upland clearing.

1.4 Cross a wooden footbridge.

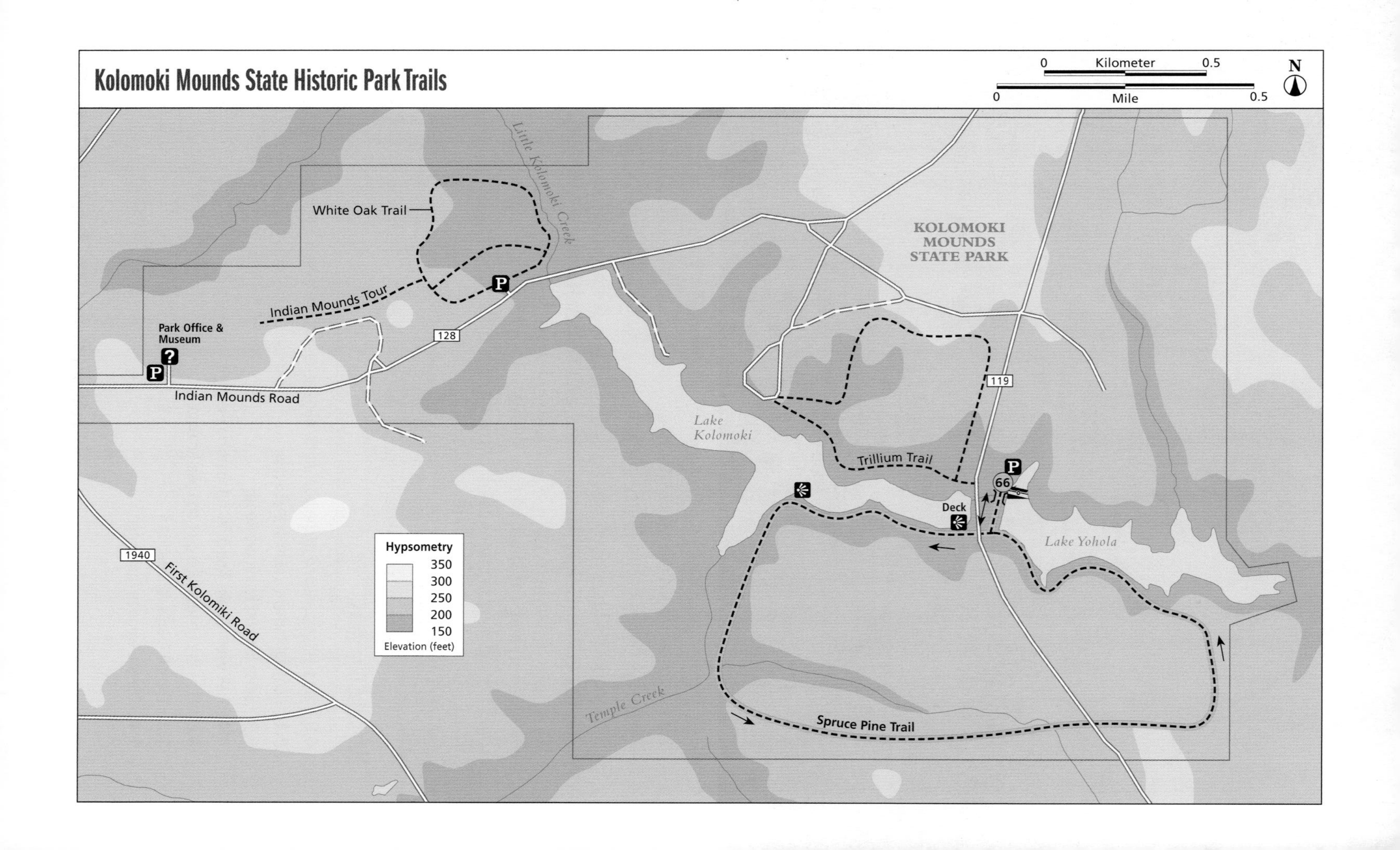
Kolomoki Mounds State Historic Park Trails
0
Kilometer
0.5
0
Mile
0.5
N
White Oak Trail
Little Kolomoki Creek
KOLOMOKI
MOUNDS
STATE PARK
Indian Mounds Tour
Park Office &
Museum
128
119
Indian Mounds Road
Lake
Kolomoki
Trillium Trail
66
Deck
Lake Yohola
1940
First Kolomiki Road
Hypsometry
350
300
250
200
150
Elevation (feet)
Temple Creek
Spruce Pine Trail

Pass right by the Temple Mound on the White Oak Trail.

1.9 Cross Second Kolomoki Road again.
2.4 Reach the shore of Lake Yahola.
3.0 Close the loop and turn right.
3.1 Arrive back at the trailhead.

Options

The 1.3-mile **Trillium Trail** begins at the Georgia-Pacific Amphitheater, is blazed in yellow, and features twenty interpretive stations along the path. Walked in a counterclockwise direction, it begins along the north shore of Lake Kolomoki, meandering along a couple of spring-fed branches that drain into the lake and crossing several bridges over the flows.

The **Mound Tour** forms a 1.4-mile loop beginning at the park museum. Traveled in a clockwise direction, you walk over open grass fields, passing a total of eight Indian mounds and their interpretive signs. You also have the option of climbing the steep eighty-one steps leading to the top of the 56-foot high Temple Mound.

The **White Oak Trail** is a 1.3-mile loop beginning at the group picnic shelters beneath tall spruce pines decked with Spanish moss. The green-blazed path then runs through a forest of white oaks, loblolly pines, and small magnolias near Little Kolomoki Creek and then past the Indian mounds.

67 Seminole State Park Trails

Located in the very southwestern corner of Georgia and south of Bainbridge, Seminole State Park sits on the shores of Lake Seminole. A portion of the 37,500-acre reservoir that opened in 1957 forms one border of this 604-acre park.

The park contains the featured Gopher Tortoise Loop Trail (1.9 miles), along with two shorter connector paths for a total of 2.2 miles. Though not a long distance, the featured trail is well worth hiking, as it contains a rich and varied environment of flora and fauna.

Start: At an intersection on the park's entrance drive, just before reaching the lakeside cabins; the parking lot is on the left side of the drive.
Distance: 1.9-mile lollipop
Hiking time: About 1 hour
Difficulty: Easy
Trail surface: Sandy loam
Best season: Sept–June
Other trail users: Mountain bikers, joggers
Canine compatibility: Leashed dogs permitted
Land status: Georgia DNR, State Parks & Historic Sites Division
Nearest town: Bainbridge
Fees and permits: Daily parking fee
Schedule: Park hours 7 a.m.–10 p.m., year-round
Maps: USGS Fairchild and Reynoldsville; trail map available at the park office
Trail contacts: Seminole State Park, 7870 State Park Dr., Donalsonville 39845; (229) 861-3137; www.gastatparks.org

Finding the trailhead: Take SR 253 southwest from Bainbridge for 21.5 miles to the park entrance on the left. After you pass Picnic Shelter No. 4 on the right, the trailhead is at the parking lot on the left of the park road. Trailhead GPS: N30 48.300' / W84 52.163'

The Hike

The Gopher Tortoise Loop Trail runs through a picture-perfect example of longleaf pine and wiregrass habitat that does have a number of tortoise burrows along the way. Besides these land-dwelling reptile's excavations, the trail is lined with nest boxes that are heavily used by eastern bluebirds in the spring months. Indigo snakes and eastern diamondback rattlesnakes are also indigenous to this habitat, often taking up residence in the tortoise burrows. Overhead, red-tailed hawks are often sighted.

Along the way the trail passes near the raised platform of the Treehouse Camping area and later skirts the pioneer campground.

Signs posted along the trail identify some of the more prominent plant species.

At the outer end of the loop the trail crosses a long bridge over Seminole Pond. This small lily-pad-filled lake offers sightings of beavers, alligators, herons, egrets, and red-winged blackbirds. There is an observation deck built on the side of the bridge near its middle.

The Gopher Tortoise Loop Trail runs through a terrain of longleaf pines and wiregrass.

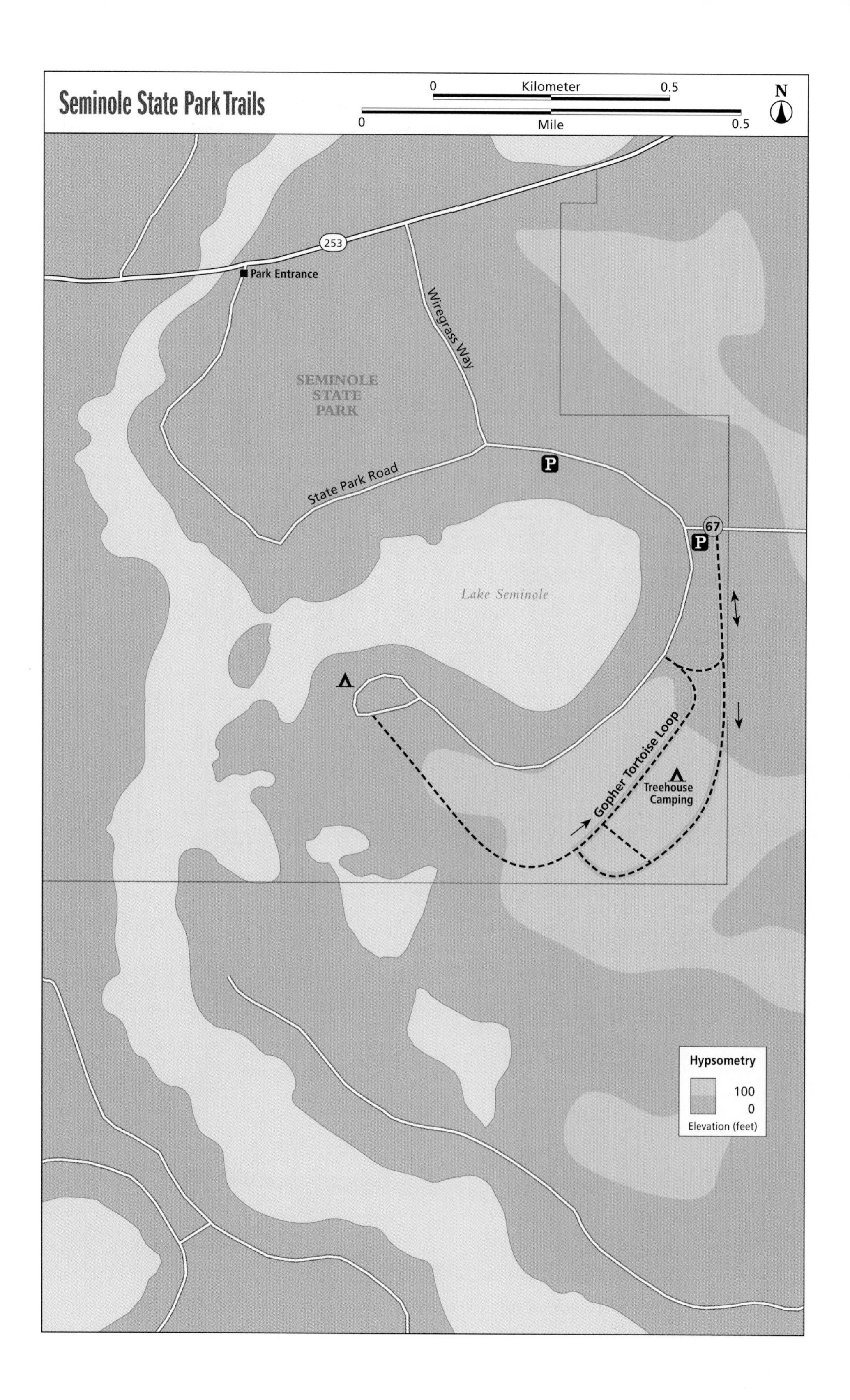

Seminole State Park Trails
0
Kilometer
0.5
0
Mile
0.5
N
253
Park Entrance
Wiregrass Way
SEMINOLE
STATE
PARK
State Park Road
P
67
P
Lake Seminole
Gopher Tortoise Loop
Treehouse
Camping
Hypsometry
100
0
Elevation (feet)

Just prior to the bridge, a side trail enters on the right. This connector forms the Seminole Pond Loop that circles one end of the lake. On the back side of the lake, you pass the junction with the trail leading to the campground.

The path now is headed back toward the trailhead. As it finishes skirting the west side of Seminole Pond, the other end of the pond loop trail intersects from the right.

Continue on the main trail to the junction that closes the loop. Turn left and walk back to the trailhead.

Miles and Directions

0.0 The trailhead is at the parking lot off the park's entrance drive.

0.1 The loop begins at this junction. Continue clockwise to the left.

0.7 Pass close by the Treehouse camping platform on the right of the path.

0.9 Reach the junction with the Seminole Pond Loop, which branches off to the right. Immediately ahead is the 120-yard-long wooden footbridge across Seminole Pond.

1.1 The connector trail to the campground enters from the left. After another 130 yards ahead, the other end of the Seminole Pond Loop enters from the right side.

1.8 Complete the loop at the trail junction and turn left to the parking lot.

1.9 Arrive back at the trailhead.

Options

The **Seminole Pond Loop** trail runs for 0.3 mile, most of which is on the same path as the Gopher Tortoise Loop Trail. The trail crosses the footbridge and circumnavigates a large cove on the pond. This part of the pond is dominated by lily pads and is a good area for spotting alligators.

The 0.2-mile **Campground Connector** runs from the outer end of the Gopher Tortoise Loop Trail to the park's campground.

68 Sprewell Bluff Wildlife Management Area Trails

The day-use area of the Sprewell Bluff Wildlife Management Area (WMA) was formerly a state park, but for budgetary reasons it was transferred in 2012 to the Georgia Wildlife Resource Division for management as part of the WMA. An agreement was then signed, under which the Department of Natural Resources (DNR) retains ownership but Upson County operates and maintains the old state park property. The 1,372-acre tract is located on the Flint River at the eastern end of the Pine Mountain Formation, which is the southernmost granite ridge in the state.

The Flint River borders the tract, twisting and turning its way through a valley between the sharp forested ridges and bluffs, forming an area of scenic beauty. Animals on the tract include white-tailed deer, squirrels, raccoons, skunks, and wild turkeys.

The main access at the day-use area has a long, sandy, pebble-and-rock beach on the inside of a wide bend in the river. It is equipped with restrooms, picnic tables, and a playground.

Sprewell Bluff has two trails totaling 4.6 miles. The Longleaf Pine Loop Trail follows the river downstream from the day-use area and returns on the adjacent ridge. The featured Natural Dam Trail runs upriver from the access and also ventures up on the ridge for its return.

Start: At the west end of the day-use area by the river
Distance: 3.0 miles out and back, with a loop in the middle
Hiking time: About 1.5 hours
Difficulty: Easy to moderate
Trail surface: Dirt and clay
Best season: Mar–June; Oct–Dec
Other trail users: Anglers
Canine compatibility: Leashed dogs permitted
Land status: Georgia DNR, Wildlife Resources Division
Nearest town: Thomaston
Fees and permits: Daily parking fee
Schedule: Trails open year-round
Maps: USGS Roland and Sunset Village
Trail contacts: Thomaston-Upson Recreation, 101 Civic Center Dr., Thomaston 30286; (706) 647-9691

Finding the trailhead: From Thomaston go west on SR 74 (West Main Street) for 5.6 miles to Old Alabama Road. Turn left (west) and go 3.9 miles to Sprewell Bluff Road, which is a continuation of Old Alabama Road. At 2.3 miles you pass the parking area on the right for the alternate trailhead. The road ends 0.3 mile farther at the day-use area and main trailhead. The Natural Dam Trail begins at the south end of the parking lot. Trailhead GPS: N32 51.171' / W84 28.883'

The Hike

Start at the day-use area for the Natural Dam Trail. Walk through the gap in the wood-beam fence marking the end of the parking area. There are no blazes, but once the path reaches the woods it is well trodden and easy to see.

The overlook platform offers a good view of the upstream shoals on the Flint River.

As you pass through an open park area, the sparse tree cover is composed of sweet gums, maples, oaks, and pines. Very shortly the path begins to climb up a rocky 130-foot-high bluff. Here the trees are chestnut oaks, black oaks, hickories, sourwoods, dogwoods, and shortleaf pines. Under the trees throughout the trail are red buckeyes, dwarf pawpaws, azaleas, and sparkleberry bushes. Mountain laurel blooms in April and May on the rock bluff.

On a rock outcrop jutting toward the river, a well-constructed overlook platform affords excellent views of the river shoals and surrounding ridges. Leaving the overlook, the path continues up the bluff and past the intersection with a trail coming down the hillside from the right. This is the return route of the loop portion of the path.

Finally reaching the crest of the bluff, the trail then drops steeply down to the river again. Here the trees are water-tolerant hickories, sycamores, and water oaks. Mayapples, trilliums, bloodroots, and anemones are abundant in season.

The trail continues up the river around overflow ponds with temporary standing water. During flood stage, the river may be out of its banks and temporarily cover the trail. In the late winter and spring wet season, these areas are important to the tree-nesting wood ducks and hooded mergansers.

Farther along, a side trail enters from the right. This is a shortcut connector within the loop. Continue straight, and then the trail bends sharply to the left toward the river. The path leads out to a large sand-and-rock beach on the river shore.

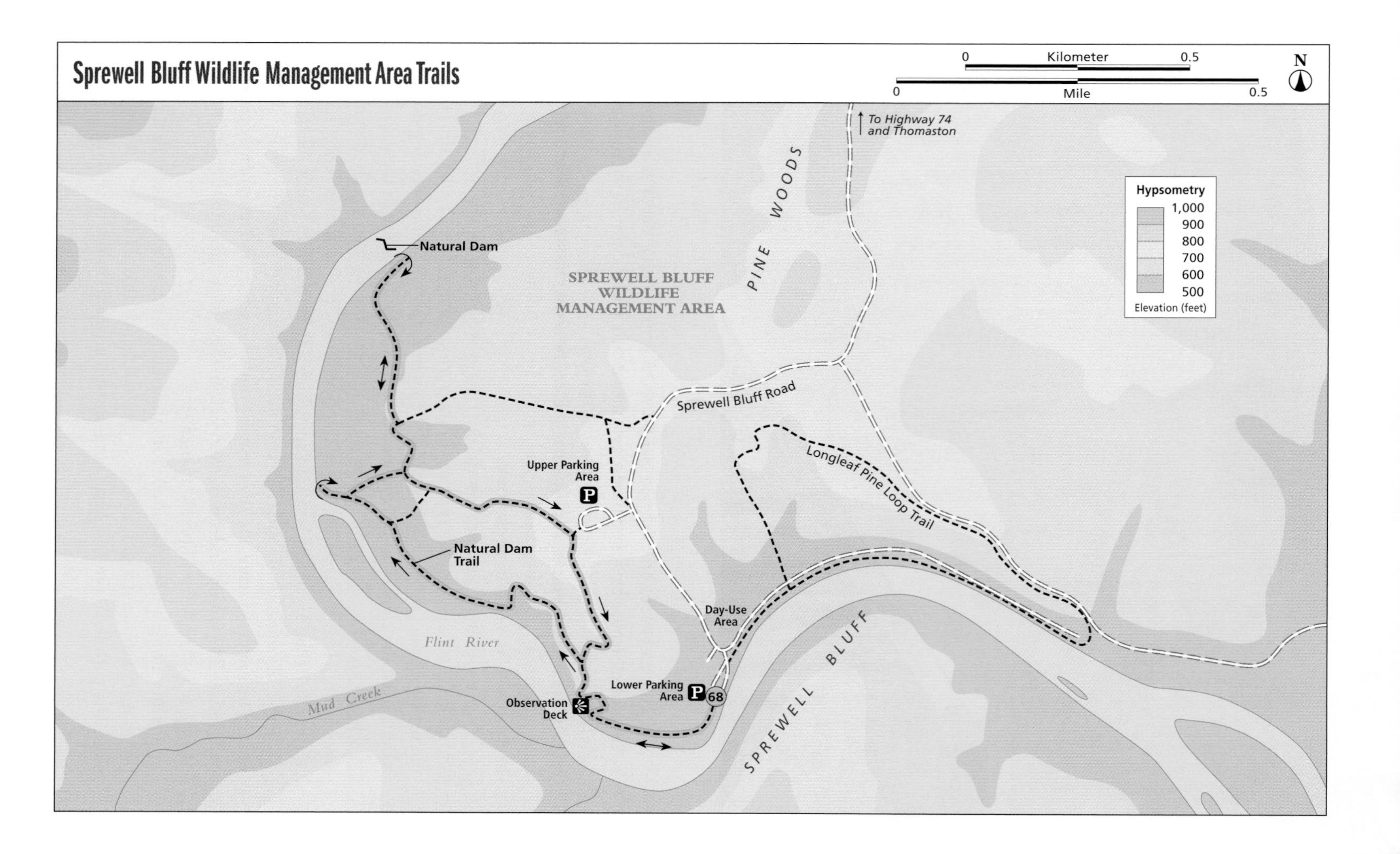

Sprewell Bluff Wildlife Management Area Trails
0
Kilometer
0.5
0
Mile
0.5
N
To Highway 74
and Thomaston
Hypsometry
1,000
900
800
700
600
500
Elevation (feet)
PINE WOODS
SPREWELL BLUFF
WILDLIFE
MANAGEMENT AREA
Natural Dam
Sprewell Bluff Road
Longleaf Pine Loop Trail
Upper Parking
Area
P
Natural Dam
Trail
Flint River
Mud Creek
Day-Use
Area
Lower Parking
Area
68
Observation
Deck
SPREWELL BLUFF

Turning back from the beach, the trail next reaches the junction at the other end of the loop. Follow the arrow on the trail sign to the left to continue upriver to the Natural Dam. At 70 yards farther along, an old road appears on the right. That overgrown roadbed leads up onto the ridgetop and the alternate parking area.

The trail continues along the river, passing a picnic table just before crossing a boardwalk. The path then reaches the turnaround point at the Natural Dam. A large band of rocks spans the entire river width here, creating a 2- to 3-foot drop as the water pours over the stone barrier.

Reversing course, retrace your steps back to the loop junction and turn left. The trail now begins climbing steeply up the hillside away from the river and quickly passes the other end of the shortcut connector trail within the loop. After gaining 130 feet of elevation, the path passes the alternate parking lot on the left at the top of the ridge. The trail then turns back downhill to close the loop. Turn left to walk past the overlook platform and back to the trailhead.

Miles and Directions

0.0 Start at the wood-beam fence at the west end of day-use area.

0.2 Reach the overlook platform on the rock bluff.

0.3 The closing portion of the loop trail intersects from the right.

0.4 The trail drops off the bluff and back to river level.

0.7 The shortcut connector trail is on the right.

0.8 The path reaches the sand-and-rock beach on the river shore.

0.9 Pass the intersection with the upstream end of the loop portion of the trail. Turn to the left.

1.0 The old roadbed to the alternate parking area is on the right.

1.3 Reach the picnic table and cross the boardwalk.

1.6 This is the turnaround point at the Natural Dam. Reverse course and walk downstream.

2.2 Reach the junction for the loop portion of the trail, turn left away from the river, and pass the other end of the shortcut connector trail.

2.5 The alternate parking area is on the left at the highest point of the hike.

2.7 Close the loop and turn left.

3.0 Arrive back at the trailhead.

Options

The **Longleaf Pine Loop Trail** begins near the boat ramp at the east end of the day-use area. The 1.6-mile lollipop takes 1 hour to walk. The opening portion of the trail follows the river downstream, crossing bridges over several feeder branches before reaching a picnic area and old canoe landing. It then climbs up onto the ridge above the river for the return. Along the way the path passes a natural rock chair, old homesite, and longleaf pine restoration area.

69 Reed Bingham State Park Trails

Reed Bingham State Park is in South Georgia, about midway between the ocean and the Alabama line. The centerpiece of the 1,613-acres facility is the 375-acre impoundment on the Little River, which provides visitors with boating, swimming, and fishing opportunities. Other amenities are a campground, picnic areas, playgrounds, miniature golf, and a kayak trail on the lake and river.

The park is a favored wintering area for black and turkey vultures. As many as 2,000 to 3,000 of these large birds sometimes can be seen soaring above the area. Other wildlife common to the park are rare gopher tortoises, alligators, deer, armadillos, raccoons, beavers, squirrels, bobcats, foxes, and rabbits. The lake provides good fishing for largemouth bass, crappie, bluegill, and redbreast sunfish.

Seven unpaved combination walking and biking trails provide 5.5 miles of hiking. Six of those are interconnected. The 0.4-mile Turkey Oak Trail and 0.9-mile Upland Loop are designed to show specific land and habitat types. The 1.0-mile Little River and 0.7-mile Birdwalk Trails include long boardwalks that bring you especially close to open aquatic areas. The 1.0-mile Yearling Trail and 0.5-mile Red Roberts Loop are the newest marked paths, offering walks along the Little River corridor in the northern portion of the park.

Combined, these trails exhibit just about all the typical habitats of this portion of Georgia. There are bay swamps, flat woods, river swamp, upland pinewoods, turkey oak–pinewoods on sand ridges, mixed southern hardwoods, and old fields.

The featured hike is a combination trail covering a portion the Upland Loop and all of the other connected paths.

Start: At the parking area at the trailhead of the Upland Loop at the northern end of the park's entrance drive
Distance: 5.3-mile lollipop
Hiking time: About 2–2.5 hours
Difficulty: Easy
Trail surface: Hard sand and boardwalks
Best season: Oct–June
Other trail users: Hikers, bikers
Canine compatibility: Leashed dogs permitted
Land status: Georgia DNR, State Parks & Historic Sites Division
Nearest town: Adel
Fees and permits: Daily parking fee
Schedule: Park hours 7 a.m.–10 p.m., year-round
Maps: USGS Adel; page-size map showing the trails available in the park office or at www.gastateparks.org
Trail contacts: Reed Bingham State Park, 542 Reed Bingham Rd., Adel 31620; (229) 896-3551; www.gastateparks.org

Finding the trailhead: From Adel take exit 39 off I-75; go 5.3 miles west on SR 37 to Evergreen Church Road. Turn right and go 0.3 mile to Reed Bingham Road. Turn left and go 0.4 mile to the park boundary; continue 0.1 mile and turn right on the park entrance drive. Go another 1.3 miles to the end of the drive at the parking area for the trailhead of the Upland Loop. Trailhead GPS: N31 10.423' / W83 32.129'

The lake in Reed Bingham State Park viewed from the park office

The Hike

All of the trails, except the Yearling Trail and Red Roberts Loop, have interpretive markers along them. Pamphlets keyed to and explaining these marked sites are available at the park office.

Begin walking north from the Upland Loop trailhead on the green-blazed path. You quickly pass a junction with the yellow-blazed Turkey Oak Trail entering from the right. Keep left at this intersection.

The next junction is with the Little River Trail, which splits off to the left. Turn onto the Little River Trail and begin following the red blazes. The path continues north, heading toward the lake. A side trail to the left soon appears, leading out to an observation deck on the water.

After visiting the deck, return to the main trail and turn left to continue walking along the lakeshore. Watch for elephant's-foot with its leaves lying flush on the ground. Also, in the late summer the purple berries of American beauty berry plants are evident along the path.

Toward the upper end of the lake, another side trail to the left leads to a second observation deck. This one is on the floodplain of the Little River, offering a good location for spotting aquatic bird species.

Continuing along the path brings you to a short boardwalk and the junction where the purple-blazed Birdwalk Trail begins. This path bends around to the right, almost immediately intersecting the Yearling Trail. There is a rest station and small pond at this junction. Turn left here to follow yellow blazes on Yearling Trail as it heads upriver.

This trail next crosses a 280-yard-long boardwalk, taking you into the fascinating wetland habitat of the river swamp. Beyond the boardwalk the path passes a covered rest station that offers a good place for birding in a pine-hardwood forest. The trail then climbs onto the low ridges of the river bluffs. The southern mixed hardwood forest features large southern magnolias and many spring wildflowers that add aroma and color to the hike. Just before the junction with the Red Roberts Loop, an overlook from one of the bluffs offers a great view of the Little River on the left of the trail.

At the intersection with the Red Roberts Loop, turn left to walk the orange-blazed path clockwise. After crossing a footbridge, you pass an alternate trailhead and parking lot that is accessed from Roundtree Bridge Road (Trailhead GPS: N31 11.507' / W83 31.261').

Continue around the loop, passing over a short boardwalk on the south side before closing the loop. Turn left and retrace your path along the Yearling Trail to its junction with the Birdwalk Trail.

Turn left and follow the purple blazes on the Birdwalk Trail. The path goes through a pitcher plant savanna harboring insectivorous plants that grow in moist, sandy, and acid soil. Hooded and trumpet pitcher plants trap insects in their long leaves. The tiny sundews trap insects with sticky beads of plant juices on their leaves. The bladderwort, another insectivorous plant, grows in areas with shallow, standing water.

Many species of frogs here are usually heard before you see them. In the wetland areas, chain, cinnamon, and royal ferns grow in abundance.

Along the way you cross two boardwalks, each of which is close to 200 yards long and one of which has a rest station at its midpoint. Then, after passing another rest station, the path reaches the intersection with the Upland Loop. Turning left here provides a 0.3-mile shortcut back to the trailhead.

For the main hike, turn right, following the green blazes through upland pinewoods. Fires that blackened trunks of the pine trees but did not kill them are a very important part of the Coastal Plain ecology, maintaining natural grasses, herbaceous plants, and shrubs in this area.

Watch for evidence of digging and scratching marks left by armadillos searching for insects, their primary food source. You may see gopher tortoise holes, identified by the low mound of sand and clay excavated from the holes.

Just after passing another of the rest stations, arrive at the junction with the yellow-blazed Turkey Oak Trail. The path straight ahead leads to the junction of the Upland Loop and Little River Trails. To continue the main hike, turn left on the Turkey Oak Trail.

This path takes you through pine flat woods and along a turkey oak–pinewoods sand ridge. This is the driest of the park's habitats; most of the trees, except for the pines, are quite small due to the lack of nutrients in the well-drained sandy soils.

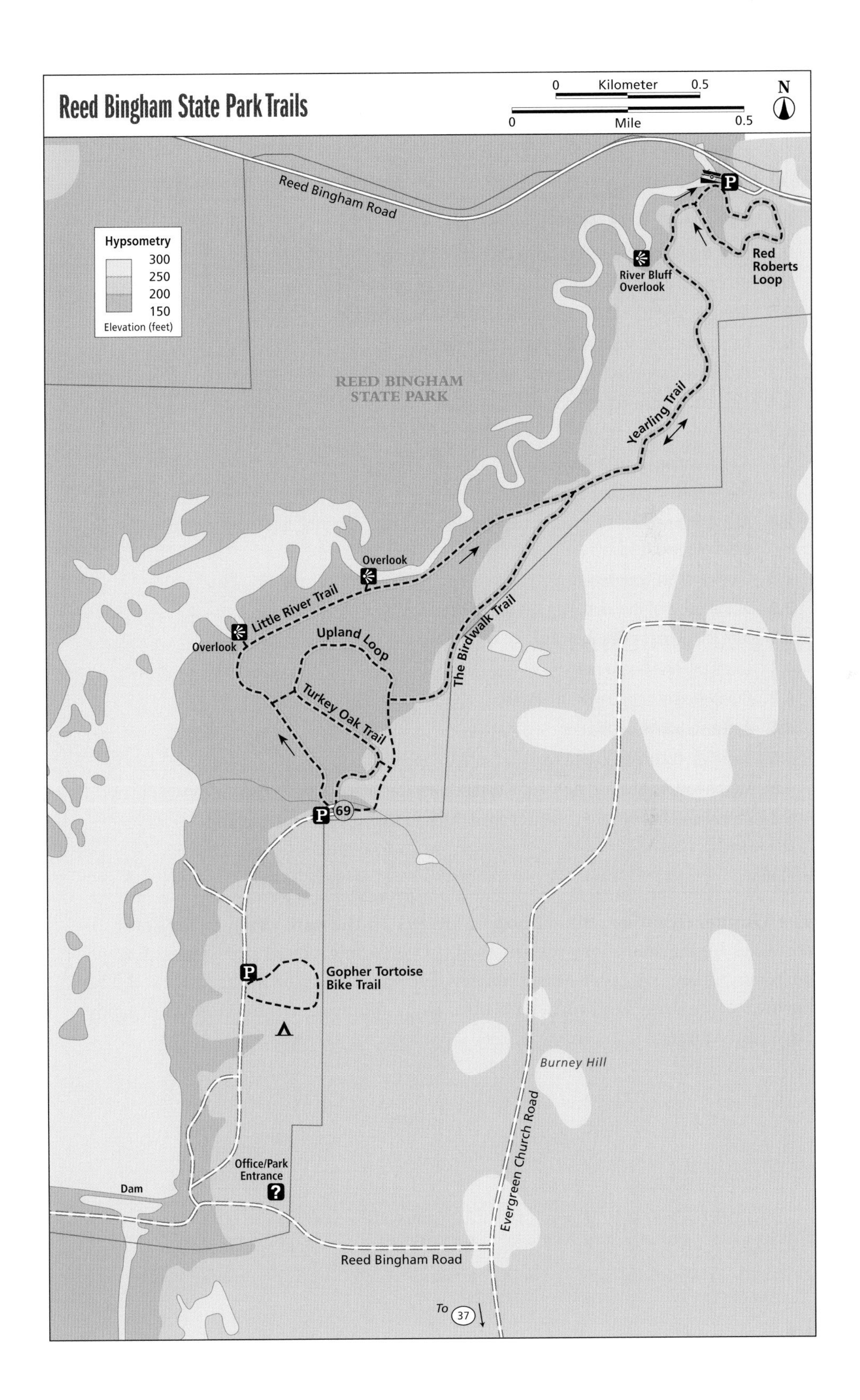
Reed Bingham State Park Trails
0 Kilometer 0.5
0 Mile 0.5
N
Reed Bingham Road
Hypsometry
300
250
200
150
Elevation (feet)
REED BINGHAM STATE PARK
River Bluff Overlook
Red Roberts Loop
Yearling Trail
Overlook
Little River Trail
Overlook
Upland Loop
The Birdwalk Trail
Turkey Oak Trail
69
Gopher Tortoise Bike Trail
Burney Hill
Evergreen Church Road
Office/Park Entrance
Dam
Reed Bingham Road
To 37

Upon reaching the next junction with the Upland Loop, turn left to complete the hike at the trailhead.

Miles and Directions

0.0 Walk north from the Upland Loop trailhead.

0.1 Pass the junction with the Turkey Oak Trail on the right.

0.3 Reach the intersection with the Little River Trail and turn left.

0.5 Take the side trail to the left to the lake observation deck.

0.8 Reach the river observation deck connector trail.

1.3 Cross the boardwalk to the junction with the Birdwalk Trail.

1.4 Turn left at the junction with the Yearling Trail.

1.5 Cross the long boardwalk.

1.7 A rest station is on the right.

2.3 The river bluff overlook is on the left.

2.4 At the intersection, turn left on the Red Roberts Loop, cross the footbridge, and pass the alternate trailhead.

2.8 Cross a short boardwalk.

2.9 At the close of the loop, turn left on the Yearling Trail.

3.9 Turn left onto the Birdwalk Trail.

4.1 Cross the first boardwalk.

4.2 Cross the second longer boardwalk.

4.4 A rest station is on the left.

4.5 Turn right onto the Upland Loop.

4.9 Pass a rest station and turn left onto the Turkey Oak Trail.

5.3 At the junction with the Upland Loop, turn left to arrive back at the trailhead.

Options

The **Gopher Tortoise Bike Loop** is located on the park drive, to the south of the other hiking trails. This well-marked, 1.0-mile interpreted path passes through wiregrass, turkey oaks, post oaks, and a few live oaks that grow in the sandy soil. The burrows of the large land turtles are obvious by the nearly white mounds of sandy clay at the entrance.

Honorable Mention

K George T. Bagby State Park Trails

The park is on the shore of Lake Walter F. George, a 48,000-acre US Army Corps of Engineers reservoir on the Chattahoochee River. The park features a 60-room lodge, conference center, restaurant, 18-hole golf course, boat dock at the lodge, and a marina.

There are two hiking trails totaling 2.8 miles. Both trailheads are at the park lodge.

The 1.7-mile Chattahoochee Trail is a lollipop though a second-growth pine-oak forest. The path has blue blazes. Tucked into the forest along the way is a gazebo with a wheelchair ramp and a series of numbered interpretive stations. One of those features a replica moonshine still.

The white-blazed 0.9-mile Lake Loop at first hugs the reservoir's edge while spanning wetlands and a lily-pad pond on boardwalks. It then turns uphill through an oak-hickory forest before returning to the trailhead.

Both trails have firm enough beds to permit wheelchair access to most of their lengths.

For more information: George T. Bagby State Park and Lodge, Rte. 1, Box 201, Fort Gaines 31571; (912) 768-2571; www.gastateparks.org

DeLorme: Georgia Atlas and Gazetteer: Page 48 G1

Southeast Georgia

Flat hikes on sandy soil characterize Southeast Georgia, with the trails extending even to the beaches of barrier islands.

70 Little Ocmulgee State Park Trails

This 1,360-acre Southeast Georgia park is best known for its 18-hole Wallace Adams Golf Course, Pete Phillips Lodge, and lake on the Little Ocmulgee River. It also features picnic areas, playgrounds, and rental cabins.

However, Little Ocmulgee also offers some great natural areas. The park is an excellent example of a Coastal Plain sandy ridge habitat. At one time this area was at the edge of the ocean. As the ocean receded, the beach dunes were left behind as today's sandy ridges.

This habitat supports such wildlife as gopher tortoises, indigo snakes, white-tailed deer, gray and fox squirrels, and both water- and land birds. The 265-acre lake offers good warm-water fishing. Flora ranges from a canopy of picturesque trees festooned with Spanish moss, right down to insectivorous pitcher plants at the swamp's edge.

The park has four trails, providing 4.4 miles of hiking. The featured Oak Ridge Trail passes through towering longleaf pines and stunted scrub oaks as it climbs onto and back down the park's sand ridge.

Start: At the Group Shelter 2 parking area
Distance: 2.1-mile lollipop
Hiking time: About 1.5 hours
Difficulty: Easy
Trail surface: Sandy loam
Best season: Sept–June
Other trail users: Hikers only
Canine compatibility: Leashed dogs permitted.
Land status: Georgia DNR, State Parks & Historic Sites Division
Nearest town: McRae
Fees and permits: Daily parking fee
Schedule: Park hours 7 a.m.–10 p.m., year-round
Maps: USGS McRae; detailed trail map available at the Pete Phillips Lodge and park office
Trail contacts: Little Ocmulgee State Park, 80 Live Oak Trail, Helena 31037; (912) 868-7474; www.gastateparks.org

Finding the trailhead: From McRae travel 2 miles north on US 319/441. The park entrance is on the left. The main trailhead is at the Group Shelter 2 parking area. Trailhead GPS: N32 05.687' / W82 53.747'

The Hike

The Oak Ridge Trail begins by descending into a small bay swamp and through a beautiful stand of longleaf pines draped with Spanish moss. Along the sides of the trail, a large shrub called yaupon holly grows in tight thickets. This holly has red berries in the fall and provides a winter supply of food for birds and other wildlife.

The Oak Ridge Trail is blazed in red, but at the beginning it also has the yellow blazes of the Short Loop Trail. This early part of the path has a number of interpretive stations keyed to the guide pamphlet for the Short Loop. After the two trails separate, a set of stations is then keyed to another pamphlet for the Oak Ridge Trail. Pamphlets for both trails are available online from the park's website or from the park office.

Sandy ridge habitat is found on the northern end of the Oak Ridge Trail loop.

After crossing a bridge on the trail you reach the point where the loop splits. Turn right to walk the path in a counterclockwise direction, continuing to see both red and yellow blazes.

The trail soon comes out of the forest and into open sandy terrain, just before the Short Loop turns off to the left. The main trail now bears only red blazes.

The path now begins to climb onto the top of a sand ridge, where it follows the bed of an old road.

Gopher tortoises dig burrows in this sandy terrain. The holes are very easily spotted because of the small mounds of white sand at the entrance. The gopher tortoise once existed throughout the lower Coastal Plain. Today it survives almost exclusively on the undeveloped, protected lands of state and federal parks.

The scrubby oaks here are dwarfed because of the nutrient-deficient sand. Although these trees are only 10 to 20 feet high, they may be very old and just don't get any larger. Lightning fires occurring over thousands of years in the Coastal Plain produced the wiregrass–longleaf pine habitat and the plants and animals it supports. Along the path you see many turkey oaks and some prickly pear cacti.

This trail area is under a continual "fire ecology" management program to maintain the native plant species that have evolved from frequent natural fires. Deer, armadillos, raccoons, rabbits, squirrels, and a number of birds frequent the area.

The trail makes a sharp left turn, now gradually heading downhill toward the park's impoundment on the Little Ocmulgee River.

A side trail soon appears that runs 20 yards to the right to an observation deck in the tupelo gum swamp at the head of the lake. The water here is full of swamp and water tupelo gums, along with some bald cypress.

In the spring you may hear wild turkeys clucking and gobbling in the distance. Also watch for colorful migrant songbirds, such as the bright yellow and black prothonotary warbler.

Return to the main trail and continue to the right. Soon you cross a wooden boardwalk and reach the other end of the Short Loop Trail. The trail again has both red and yellow blazes.

Continue beside the lake, watching for insectivorous pitcher plants growing at the shallow edge. Several breaks in the lakeshore foliage offer good views of the water.

The lake is excellent habitat for wood ducks, gallinules, herons, egrets, and anhingas. Vultures roost in the trees along the lakeshore and may flock in great numbers in the winter. They spend the winter here, as do migratory ducks and moorhens.

A short side trail runs off to the right to more closely follow the lakeshore but quickly rejoins the main path 100 yards farther along.

When the loop closes, turn right to reach the trailhead.

Miles and Directions

0.0 Leaving the trailhead, walk through a magnificent stand of tall longleaf pines festooned with Spanish moss.

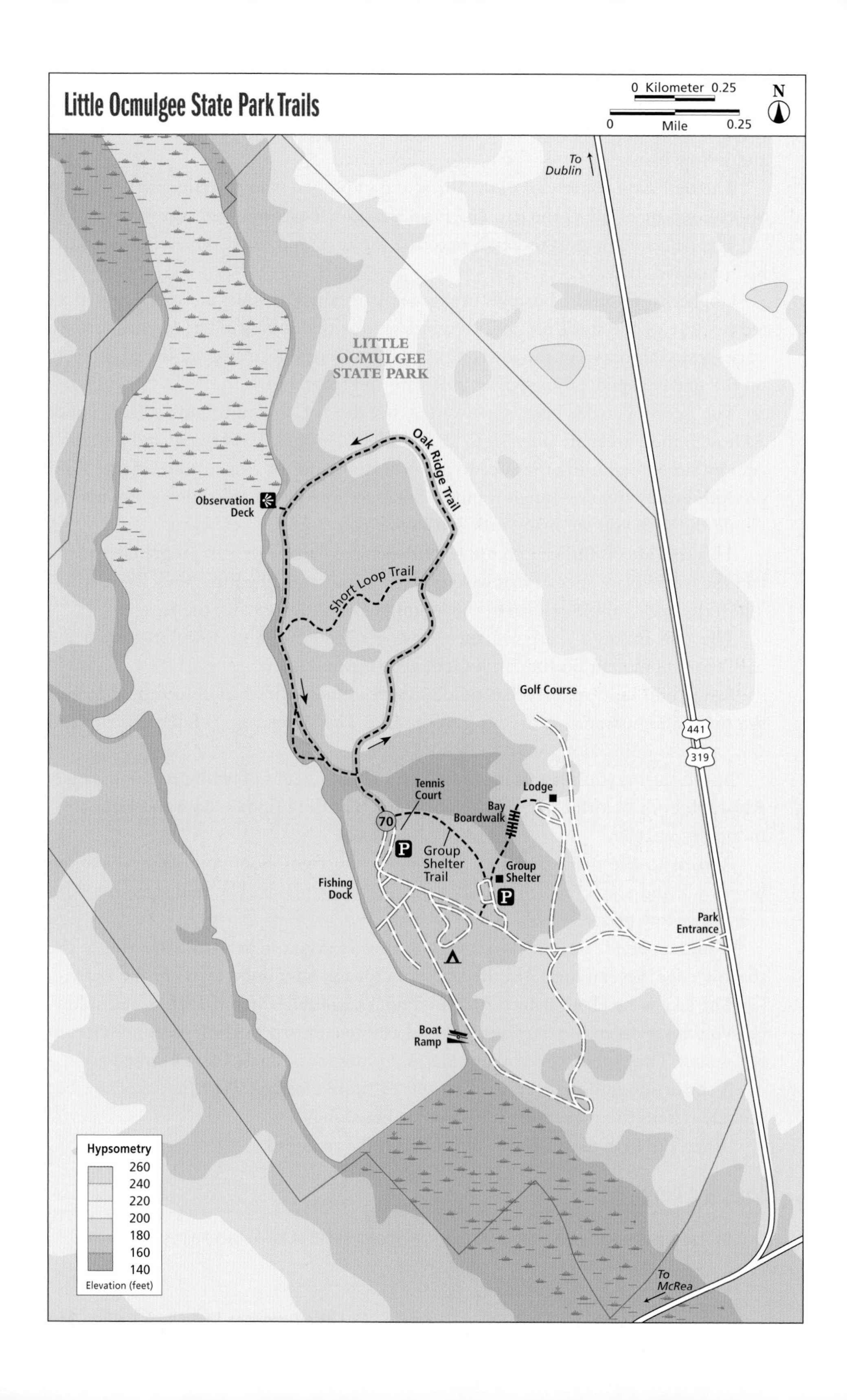
Little Ocmulgee State Park Trails
0 Kilometer 0.25
0 Mile 0.25
N
To Dublin
LITTLE OCMULGEE STATE PARK
Oak Ridge Trail
Observation Deck
Short Loop Trail
Golf Course
441
319
Tennis Court
Lodge
Bay Boardwalk
70
Group Shelter Trail
Group Shelter
Fishing Dock
Park Entrance
Boat Ramp
Hypsometry
260
240
220
200
180
160
140
Elevation (feet)
To McRea

0.1 The trail forks here. Follow the arrows to the right.

0.5 The trail exits the forest into sand hill terrain.

0.6 Pass the junction for the Short Loop Trail connector.

1.0 Reach the peak of the sand hill.

1.3 Pass the trail junction on the right for the observation deck in the Tupelo gum swamp.

1.5 Reach the other end of the Short Loop Trail entering from the left.

1.8 Pass the junction with the side trail to the right that follows along the lake and then rejoins 100 yards ahead.

2.0 Close the loop and turn right.

2.1 Arrive back at the trailhead.

Options

The yellow-blazed **Short Loop Trail** shares the same trailhead, as well as much of its path, with the Oak Ridge Trail. Once it bears off to the left, it travels on its own for 0.5 mile before rejoining the Oak Ridge Trail. This creates a 1.7-mile lollipop shape.

The **Group Shelter Trail** is a 0.3-mile path through the forest connecting the Oak Ridge and Short Loop trailhead to the Bay Boardwalk and access to the Pete Phillips Lodge. This trail has no blazes but is easy to follow.

The **Bay Boardwalk** is a 0.3-mile wooden walkway with eighteen interpretive stations. It runs from the park lodge to Group Shelter 1. As the name implies, the path leads through forest terrain featuring three species of bay plants: loblolly, swamp, and sweet bay.

Local Information

Food/Lodging

The Pete Phillips Lodge, located within the park, has 60 rooms and a restaurant; (229) 868-7474; www.georgiastateparks.org/lodges.

71 General Coffee State Park Trails

General Coffee State Park was named for nineteenth-century local planter and politician Gen. John E. Coffee and is a fascinating area of sand ridges and river swamp. The park also contains a working pioneer homestead exhibit, fishponds, picnic areas, playgrounds, campgrounds, and rental cabins.

Several bridges and boardwalks provide access deep into the Seventeen Mile River swamp that passes through the park. The flora and fauna of the river swamp and sand ridge make walking the four trails totaling 6.4 miles most interesting experiences.

The featured hike combines the 1.5-mile West River Swamp and 1.3-mile Gopher Loop Trails.

Start: At the large wooden sign with a map of the trail near Picnic Shelter 4
Distance: 4.3-mile lollipop
Hiking time: About 2 hours
Difficulty: Easy
Trail surface: Sandy loam
Best season: Sept–June
Other trail users: Hikers only
Canine compatibility: Leashed dogs permitted.
Land status: Georgia DNR, State Parks & Historic Sites Division
Nearest town: Douglas
Fees and permits: Daily parking fee
Schedule: Park hours 7 a.m.–10 p.m., year-round
Maps: USGS Douglas North; maps of the park and trails available from the park office and trading post
Trail contacts: General Coffee State Park, 46 John Coffee Rd., Nicholls 31554; (912) 384-7082; www.gastateparks.org

Finding the trailhead: At the intersection of US 441 and SR 32 in Douglas, go east 4.5 miles on SR 32 to the park entrance on the left. Go 0.4 mile on the park access road. The trailhead is near Picnic Shelter 4, to the right of the road. Trailhead GPS: N31 30.890' / W82 45.618'

The Hike

From the trailhead follow the blue blazes of the West River Swamp Trail as they lead across two boardwalks and penetrate the thick vegetation along the edge of the swamp.

The river swamp habitat is best seen from the bridge at the start of the East River Swamp Trail that takes off to the right soon after starting along the main path. This structure provides a vista of a relatively undisturbed swamp. Such wet lowlands are a crucial part of the Coastal Plain river system. This is the Seventeen Mile River, which joins the Satilla River on the way to the Atlantic Ocean.

Trees in this moist-soil area are large buttressed tupelo and cypress, red maple, yellow poplar, live and water oaks, as well as slash and longleaf pines. Trees in the swamp are much taller than those on the sandy ridge. This difference is so great that from a distance the "ridge" does not stand out above the swamp.

The burrow of a gopher tortoise on the Gopher Loop Trail

Sphagnum moss along with chain and royal ferns grow in the very wet areas. Titi and wax myrtle make up most of the shrub vegetation, along with an occasional dense thicket of privet hedge that has escaped cultivation.

Continue on the main trail, crossing two more boardwalks. As the habitat changes from the river swamp on the right to the sandy ridge to the left, palmetto and wax myrtle bushes are more evident, along with larger water and live oaks. This is where the rare greenfly orchid lives as an epiphyte on the limbs and trunks of the larger oaks.

Leaving the river swamp, the path moves into the sandy ridge plant and animal community where gopher tortoises and armadillos burrow into the soft, sandy soil. Burrows created by the tortoise to escape heat and cold are used by the endangered indigo snake, frogs, diamondback rattlesnakes, insects, and spiders. The tortoise is a native that has been here for many thousands of years, while the armadillo has lived here less than one hundred years, having extended its range eastward from the Mississippi River.

Once the trail joins the Gopher Loop Trail, the blazes change to green. Follow those blazes to the right in a counterclockwise direction. Some blazes are painted on trees, but others are green metal posts. Other paths and jeep trails cross this trail, leading to various campgrounds in the park and to the small lakes on Seventeen Mile River. The main trail, however, is well marked and easy to follow.

On the ridge, the trees are more stunted and the soil so well drained that it is dry most of the time. Turkey oaks, scrubby post oaks, and longleaf pine are the common

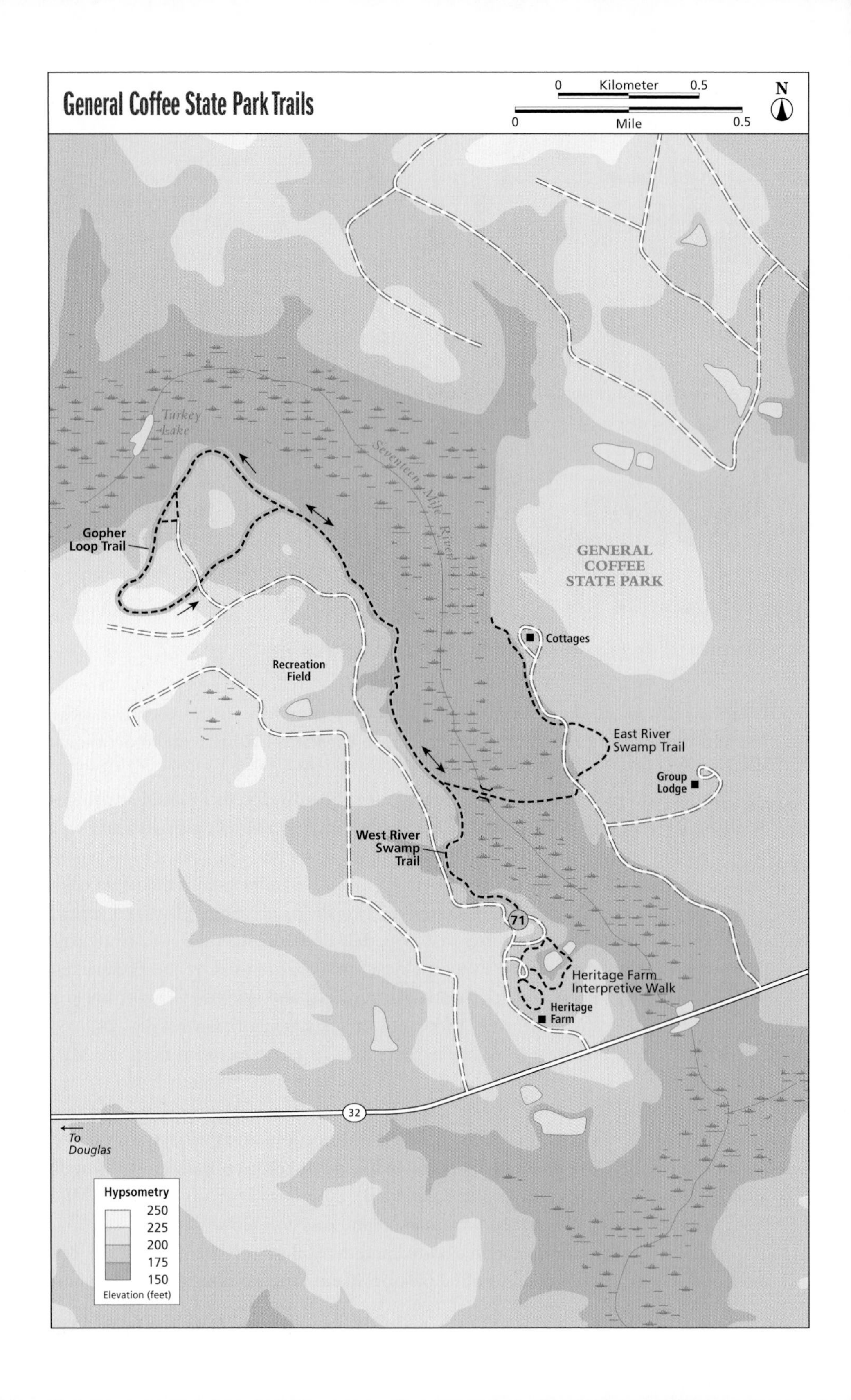
General Coffee State Park Trails
0
Kilometer
0.5
0
Mile
0.5
N
Turkey Lake
Seventeen Mile River
Gopher Loop Trail
GENERAL COFFEE STATE PARK
Cottages
Recreation Field
East River Swamp Trail
Group Lodge
West River Swamp Trail
71
Heritage Farm Interpretive Walk
Heritage Farm
32
To Douglas
Hypsometry
250
225
200
175
150
Elevation (feet)

trees along the loop. One of the more common shrubs is the sparkleberry, with its silver-underside leaves that seem to sparkle when moved by the wind.

At the end of the loop turn right and backtrack on the West River Swamp Trail to the trailhead.

Miles and Directions

0.0 Start near Picnic Shelter 4 at the wooden sign showing the trail.

0.4 The trail on the right is the beginning of the East River Swamp Trail.

1.0 The path moves away from the swamp, climbing onto the drier ridge area. Watch for the greenfly orchids growing on the oak limbs and trunks.

1.5 Take the right fork at the beginning of the Gopher Loop Trail.

1.7 Pass the junction with an old road that bisects the loop.

2.2 Reach the crest of the sandy ridge and the pioneer camping area.

2.3 Cross the spur road into the tortoise area.

2.8 Close the loop and turn right to return to the trailhead on the West River Swamp Trail.

4.3 Arrive back at the trailhead.

Options

The red-blazed **East River Swamp Trail** is a must-do hike. The two boardwalk sections across the Seventeen Mile River alone make it worth the 1.6-mile out-and-back trek. Several colonies of greenfly orchids also are on the trees along this path. The trail turn-around point is at a gigantic southern magnolia tree behind the park cottages.

The **Heritage Farm Interpretive Walk** is an option for a historical tour. This 0.5-mile path around a small fishing pond passes a pioneer homestead consisting of 11 buildings with live domestic animals and depicting farm life in this part of Georgia during the nineteenth century.

This giant southern magnolia marks the end of East River Swamp Trail.

72 Okefenokee National Wildlife Refuge Trails

The Okefenokee National Wildlife Refuge provides a doorway to more than 400,000 acres of one of the oldest and best preserved freshwater wetland areas in the United States. Interpretive displays in the visitor center describe human and natural history, botanical diversity, and the unparalleled wildlife in the refuge.

Winter is the best time for migratory waterfowl, including sandhill cranes, the beginning of osprey nesting, and the presence of many wading birds. Spring is prime season for wildflowers, wading-bird rookeries, and great numbers of migrating warblers. Spring is also when the swamp's abundant alligators begin sunning. In summer listen for the fascinating sounds of more than a dozen species of frogs, including green tree, pig, carpenter, and cricket frogs.

The late fall and winter are often the best times to visit the Okefenokee in order to avoid mosquitoes, biting flies, and other insect pests.

The only way to really see the swamp is by boat or canoe. However, a series of trails offers the opportunity to see the fringe areas and get a feel for life near the "Land of the Trembling Earth."

All told, the refuge contains nine trails totaling 9.8 miles of hiking. The featured hike is a combination of a portion of the 0.7-mile Canal Diggers Trail and the entire 4.3-mile Longleaf Pine Trail.

Start: At the visitor center
Distance: 4.5 miles one way
Hiking time: About 2 hours
Difficulty: Easy
Trail surface: Sandy soil
Best season: Oct–Mar
Other trail users: Hikers only
Canine compatibility: Leashed dogs permitted
Land status: US Fish and Wildlife Service
Nearest town: Folkston
Fees and permits: Daily parking fee
Schedule: Year-round except for Christmas Day; the main gate is open Nov through Feb, one-half hour before sunrise until 5:30 p.m.; Mar through Oct, one-half hour before sunrise until 7:30 p.m.; visitor center open 9:00 a.m.–5:00 p.m.
Maps: USGS Chesser Island and Chase Prairie; trail maps available at the visitor center or online at www.fws.gov/okefenokee
Trail contacts: Okefenokee National Wildlife Refuge, 2700 Suwannee Canal Rd., Folkston 31537; (912) 496-7836; www.fws.gov/okefenokee

Finding the trailhead: From exit 3 on I-95, go 21.5 miles west on SR 40 to Folkston. Take US 1/23 (Okefenokee Drive) west for 7.4 miles. Turn left onto Suwannee Canal Road (also called Okefenokee Parkway on some maps). At 3.7 miles pass the fee station and continue 1.5 miles to the visitor center. Trailhead GPS: N30 44.293' / W82 08.383'

The Hike

The featured trail can be started at either end. The eastern trailhead of the Longleaf Pine Trail is shared with the Phernetton Trail from a parking area on Okefenokee

The Longleaf Pine Trail is the longest in the refuge, running through pine stands with wiregrass and saw palmettos.

Parkway near its junction with Okefenokee Drive. The trailhead for the Canal Diggers Trail is at the visitor center. The preferred starting point is at the visitor center.

Begin walking east on the Canal Diggers Trail. This 0.7-mile path follows the upland portion of the Suwannee Canal and then turns south to cross the water and loops back to the visitor center. A pamphlet available at the visitor center describes the history of the canal, which was an aborted attempt many years ago to drain the swamp.

Continue along this northern side of the loop through the picnic area. The path then leads through a low area across the remnant canal and the paved Swamp Island Drive. A short distance farther is the trail junction with the Longleaf Pine Trail. The path to the right leads 35 yards to the western trailhead of the Longleaf Pine Trail. Continue straight through the intersection, with the Canal Digger Trail and Longleaf Pine Trail now sharing the pathway.

A bit farther the trail crosses a bridge back over the canal and reaches a trail intersection. At this point the Canal Diggers Trail turns south, crosses the canal, and bends back toward the visitor center. Continue to the left on the Longleaf Pine Trail as it leaves the canal.

The trail now begins traversing a very long stretch of longleaf pine habitat, with understory composed of wiregrass and patches of saw palmetto. There is very little variation in the foliage along the rest of this trail.

Crossing Okefenokee Parkway, the path makes a big bend to the north of the road before popping out on the sand surface of Swamp Perimeter Road. After running south on this road for 40 yards, the trail turns off to the left and continues in a southeast direction to eventually cross over Okefenokee Parkway again.

Making a sharp bend to the east, the path parallels the parkway to a parking lot and alternate access point. The trail then begins a long, very gradual descent that loses 80 feet of elevation along the rest of the hike. After 100 yards, the path passes through a deep sand gully, with the refuge office in sight across Okefenokee Parkway to the left.

When the trail runs into a sand road, turn right on the road and cross over the canal on a culvert. Once across, make a left turn back onto the trail. The trail now parallels a portion of the canal with quite steep banks. Soon a gap in the foliage along the canal opens to reveal a 30-foot drop down to the waterway. Just beyond this point the dredged part of the canal ends; the small Starland Creek continues to the east.

The trail next makes a sharp turn to the left, crossing a bridge over Starland Creek. When the path meets Okefenokee Parkway, turn to the right and walk along the shoulder for roughly 300 yards before turning right and back into the woods.

From here the pathway twice repeats the cycle of returning to the road shoulder before turning back south. The third time it comes to the road, the trail crosses to the north side and reaches a junction with the Phernetton Trail. At the intersection take the left fork as the two trails run on the same path in a bend away from the road and then back to the turnaround point at the roadside parking lot.

If you haven't arranged a shuttle, reverse course and return to the visitor center for a 9.0-mile hike.

Miles and Directions

0.0 Start at the Canal Diggers trailhead at the visitor center.

0.1 Walk through the picnic area.

0.2 Cross Swamp Island Drive and pass the connector path to the Longleaf Pine trailhead to the right.

0.4 Cross the bridge over the Suwannee Canal.

0.5 Reach the intersection where the Canal Diggers Trail splits off to the right. Turn to the left.

0.7 Cross the Okefenokee Parkway.

1.2 Turn right on sand Swamp Perimeter Road, walk 40 yards, and exit onto the trail on the left.

1.5 Cross back to the south side of Okefenokee Parkway.

1.6 Turn sharply left to parallel the paved parkway.

1.8 Reach the parking area and roadside trail access, then walk through the deep gully with the park office across the road to the left.

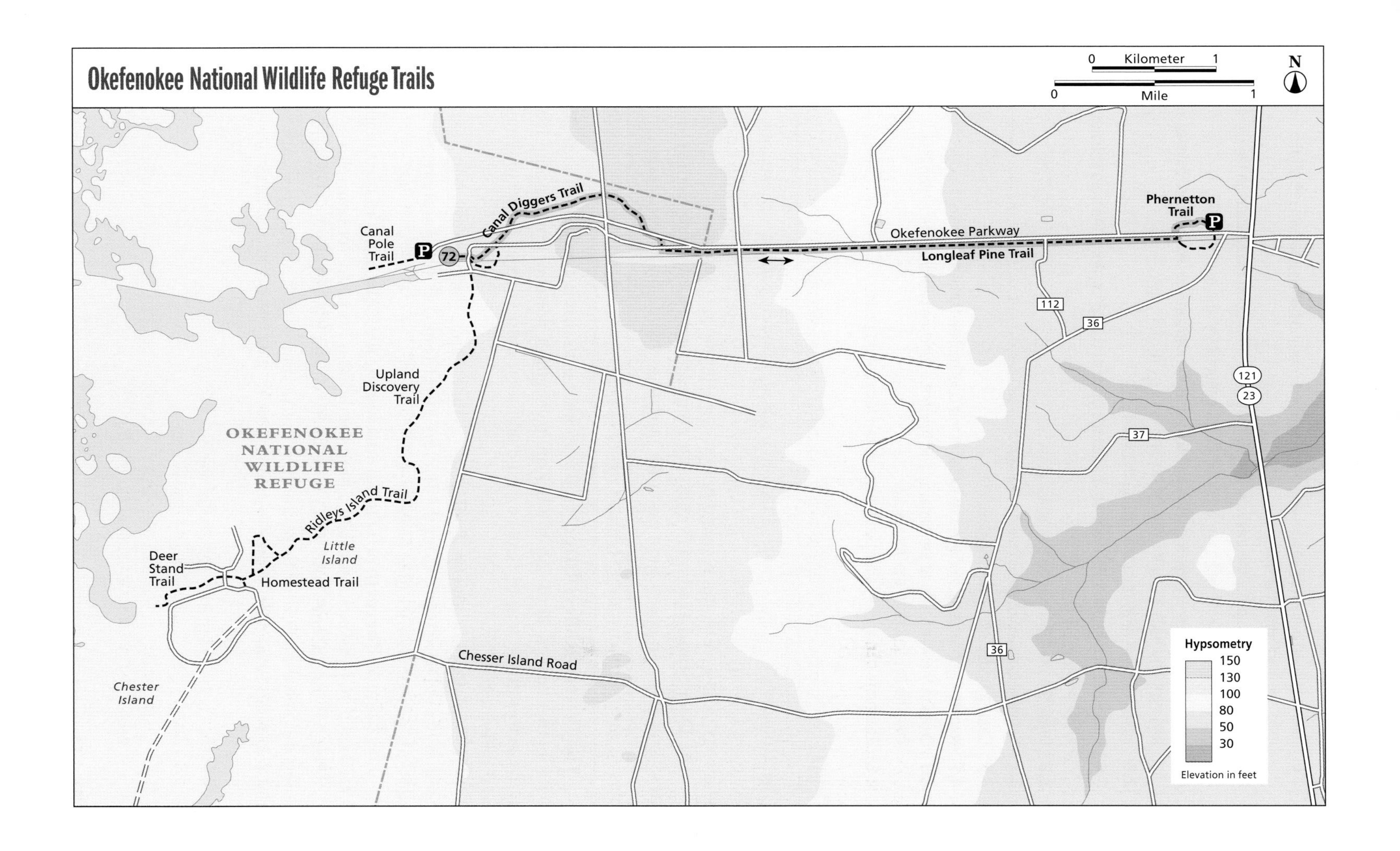
Okefenokee National Wildlife Refuge Trails
0 Kilometer 1
0 Mile 1
N
Canal Pole Trail
P
72
Canal Diggers Trail
Okefenokee Parkway
Longleaf Pine Trail
Phernetton Trail
P
112
36
121
23
37
36
Upland Discovery Trail
OKEFENOKEE NATIONAL WILDLIFE REFUGE
Ridleys Island Trail
Little Island
Deer Stand Trail
Homestead Trail
Chester Island
Chesser Island Road
Hypsometry
150
130
100
80
50
30
Elevation in feet

2.0 Turn right onto the gated sand road, cross a culvert over the canal, and turn left off the road and back onto the trail.

2.3 Gaze off the left side of the trail into the 30-foot-deep drop down to the water in the canal.

2.4 The Suwannee Canal ends; tiny Starland Creek continues to the east.

2.6 Cross a bridge over a drainage ditch and turn sharply north; at the Okefenokee Parkway, turn right and walk along the road shoulder.

2.8 Follow the trail away from the road to the south.

3.4 Turn north across another bridge on a drainage ditch and begin walking the road shoulder to the east.

3.6 Leave the road, walking to the right.

3.7 Begin walking along an old sand roadbed.

3.9 Cross a bridge over a dry drainage ditch.

4.1 You are again walking along the shoulder of the Okefenokee Parkway.

4.3 Cross to the north side of the parkway and reach the junction with the Phernetton Trail. Take the left fork from the intersection.

4.5 Reach the parking lot, alternate trailhead, and turnaround point.

Options

The **Boardwalk** is a 0.7-mile walk on a raised wooden path to an overlook on Seagrove Lake in the swamp. The boardwalk, however, burned in the Honey Prairie wildfire of April 2011 and is closed until reconstruction is complete.

The **Deer Stand Trail** is 0.5 mile long, connecting the Boardwalk to the Homestead Trail. It has an observation tower for watching wildlife on its north side.

The **Homestead Trail** spans 0.7 mile as it runs through and around the preserved family farm of the Chesser family on their namesake island.

The 1.6-mile **Ridleys Island Trail** is another path that is closed due to the 2011 wildfire that burned all the boardwalks on its length. It stretches from Swamp Island Drive across the swamp to Ridleys Island and then onto Chesser Island to connect to the Homestead Trail.

The **Upland Discovery Trail** is a 0.2-mile nature loop on the east side of Swamp Island Drive, across from the Ridleys Island Trailhead. It features nest trees of the endangered red-cockaded woodpecker.

The 1.3-mile **Phernetton Trail** forms a loop at the eastern end of the Longleaf Pine Trail. The path circles through a pine stand that is home to fox squirrels.

The 0.3-mile **Cane Pole Trail** is a paved, wheelchair-accessible path running along the Suwannee Canal to platform at the swamp edge. This path begins beside the boat ramp behind the visitor center.

73 George L. Smith State Park Trails

George L. Smith State Park is best known for Parrish Mill, a refurbished combination gristmill, sawmill, covered bridge, and dam built in 1880. Visitors can walk the self-guided tour through the old mill, and it is still used on special occasions to grind corn.

Watson Pond is a 412-acre impoundment on Fifteen Mile Creek. Its waters provide power to the mill and offer visitors boating and fishing opportunities, along with three canoe paths. Other amenities are rental cabins, campgrounds, picnic areas, and playgrounds.

There are five marked hiking trails totaling 7.9 miles in the park. These paths are located on the lower Coastal Plain in an area of old dunes that supports a dwarf oak forest, characterized by longleaf pines, turkey oaks, and wiregrass. The gopher tortoise and the several species of animals associated with the tortoises' burrows are sometimes encountered on hikes.

The featured Deer Run Trail is a flat hike alongside Fifteen Mile Creek, through the wiregrass and longleaf pine plant community, and back along the millpond shore.

Start: At the office parking area
Distance: 3.3-mile loop
Hiking time: About 1.5 hours
Difficulty: Easy
Trail surface: Sandy clay
Best season: Year-round
Other trail users: Hikers only
Canine compatibility: Leashed dogs permitted
Land status: Georgia DNR, State Parks & Historic Sites Division
Nearest town: Twin City
Fees and permits: Daily parking fee
Schedule: Park hours, 7 a.m.–10 p.m., year-round
Maps: USGS Twin City; map of the park with trails available at the park office
Trail contacts: George L. Smith State Park, 371 George L. Smith State Park Rd., Twin City 30471; (912) 763-2759; www.gastateparks.org

Finding the trailhead: From exit 104 on I-16, take SR 23 north 1.5 miles to downtown Metter. Continue north on SR 23 for 11.4 miles and turn left onto George L. Smith State Park Road. At 1.7 miles this road leads into the park. The Deer Run Trailhead is in front of the park office. Trailhead GPS: N32 32.686' / W82 07.509'

The Hike

To start the Deer Run Trail, walk through the mill house and covered bridge and check out the displays depicting early farm life of the region. The trail then continues crossing the earthen dam.

At this point you come to a junction. The path straight ahead is the 0.7 Mile Trail that bisects the Deer Run loop. It follows the abandoned, sandy route of Mill Pond Road, which was formerly a county road. The path to the left is the Deer Run return loop. Turn right past the sign with the map of the trail to begin the Deer Run loop in a counterclockwise direction. The path is marked with blue blazes.

After passing the old pond dam, the Deer Run Trail runs through a forest thick with Spanish moss.

On the right, the moist soil supports dense vegetation of titis, water oaks, maples, magnolias, and black and water tupelo trees. On the left are the well-drained, sandy soils of the ancient dunes, with turkey oaks, longleaf pines, sparkleberry bushes, reindeer lichens, and bracken ferns.

A side path to the right runs down to a small springhead. The spring is a tributary of Fifteen Mile Creek. Royal, cinnamon, and sensitive ferns surround the short footbridge over the spring at the turnaround point.

Returning to the main path, turn right and watch for the tracks of white-tailed deer, rabbits, gray and fox squirrels, raccoons, opossums, armadillos, bobcats, otters, and foxes in the sand. During the warm months you may see a number of different butterflies, including the giant swallowtail.

When the trail reaches a bench, the path makes a sharp turn to the left. Just beyond, a sand road crosses the trail. Continue straight across on the path.

The trail now leaves the dense vegetation and goes through the more open, sandy, drier habitat with dwarf turkey oaks and longleaf pines, wiregrass, and an occasional Spanish bayonet. In the spring, watch for blooming red mint, which is also called scarlet wild basil, a favorite of hummingbirds. This also is the typical home of the gopher

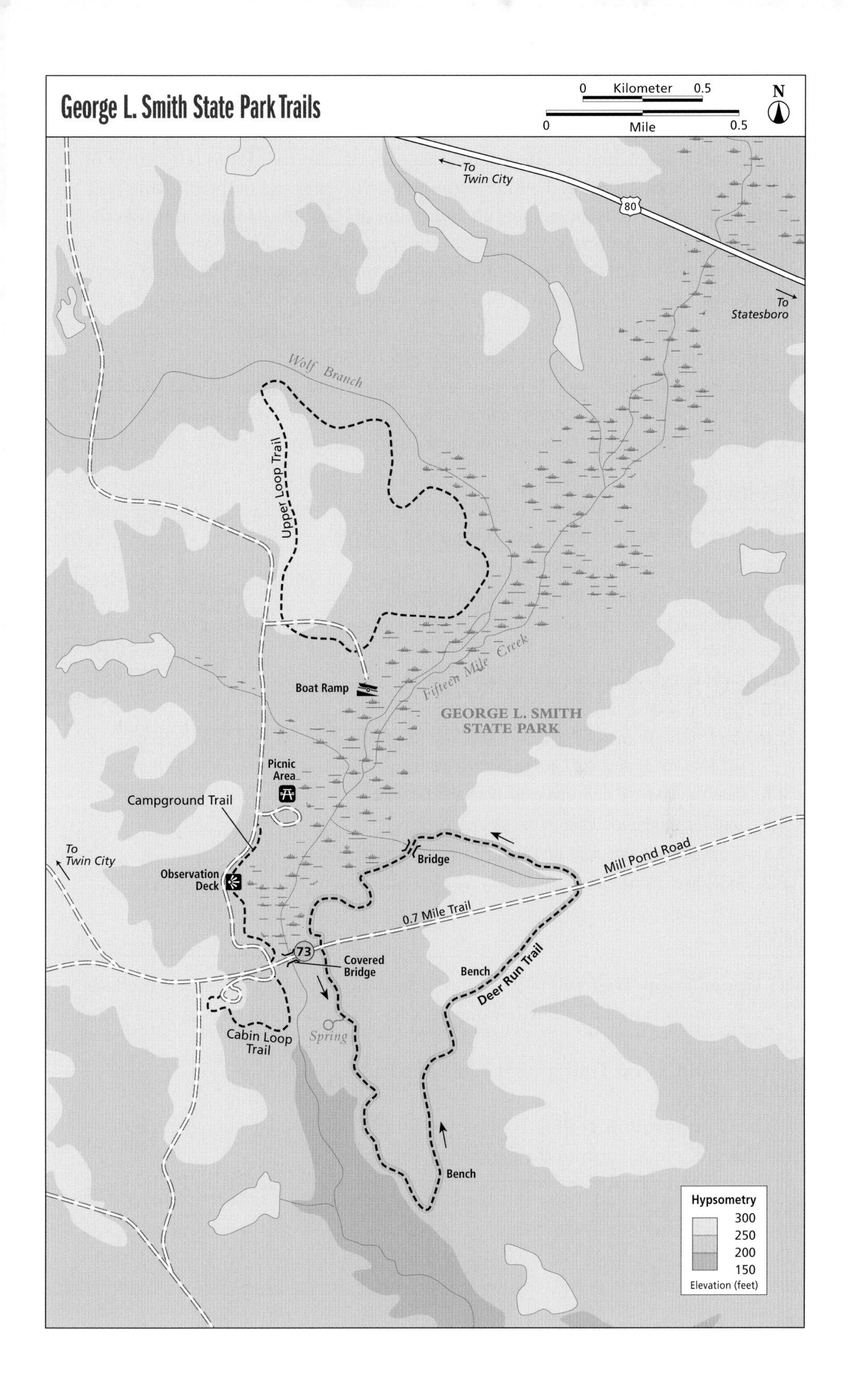
George L. Smith State Park Trails
0 Kilometer 0.5
0 Mile 0.5
N
To Twin City
80
To Statesboro
Wolf Branch
Upper Loop Trail
Boat Ramp
Fifteen Mile Creek
GEORGE L. SMITH
STATE PARK
Picnic Area
Campground Trail
To Twin City
Observation Deck
Bridge
Mill Pond Road
0.7 Mile Trail
73
Covered Bridge
Bench
Deer Run Trail
Spring
Cabin Loop Trail
Bench
Hypsometry
300
250
200
150
Elevation (feet)

tortoise. Their burrows are used by endangered indigo snakes or eastern diamondback rattlesnakes.

At another bench, the trail begins following an old sand road through a stand of longleaf pines until it reaches the intersection with the other end of the 0.7 Mile Trail. Turning left takes you back to the mill and trailhead. Continue straight through the intersection for the main trail.

The pathway now bends around to the west, coming to the dam of an old pond. As you pass below it, you cross a footbridge beneath trees heavily festooned with Spanish moss. The dense vegetation gives a jungle-like appearance. To the right is a swamp area with wood duck nest boxes standing on poles.

From here the trail snakes its way to the south and parallel to the lakeshore through a patch of switch cane. At the intersection at the close of the loop, turn right and walk back through the covered bridge to the trailhead.

Miles and Directions

0.0 Start at the fence in front of the park office.

0.2 Turn right at the trail intersection.

0.4 Reach the side trail to the right for the springhead.

1.0 Pass a bench and turn sharply to the left. The trail begins to climb into the old dune habitat.

1.1 Cross an old, sandy road; stay straight on the trail.

1.5 Come to another bench where the trail begins following an old sand road.

2.0 Cross the wide unpaved surface of Mill Pond Road to continue the loop. Turn left on the 0.7 Mile Trail to shortcut back to the trailhead.

2.5 Pass the old pond dam and cross a small footbridge.

2.6 Look for wood duck boxes in the swamp to the right.

3.1 Close the loop, turn right, and walk through the covered bridge.

3.3 Arrive back at the trailhead.

Options

The **Upper Loop Trail** covers 2.7 miles, beginning at the boat ramp on the lake. The path connects to the primitive camping sites in the park and takes about 1 hour to walk.

The **Cabin Loop Trail** spans 0.7 mile, circling the cottage area to the south of the park office.

The **Campground Trail** is a one-way, 0.5-mile path leading along the lakeshore from the park office north to the park's camping area.

The **0.7 Mile Trail** is the connector path that bisects the Deer Run Trail to offer shorter options for walks.

74 Magnolia Springs State Park Trails

Magnolia Springs State Park offers visitors both outdoor activities and a bit of history. Magnolia Springs gives the park its name and gushes an estimated nine million gallons of water per day into Spring Mill Branch. Additionally, 28-acre Magnolia Lake offers fishing and boating opportunities.

The spring, branch, and lake are home to a wide variety of fish, plant life, alligators, and turtles, along with shore- and wading birds. This area supports nesting colonies of the endangered red-cockaded woodpeckers, as well as gopher tortoises, deer, beavers, squirrels, and armadillos.

Any trip to Magnolia Springs State Park should include a visit to the aquarium at the Bo Ginn Fish Hatchery and Aquatic Education Center, located across a footbridge over Spring Mill Branch from the park.

The park also contains the site of a Civil War prison, as well as campgrounds and rental cabins.

The Beaver, Fort Lawton Historic, Hiking/Biking, and Woodpecker Woods Nature Trails are located in Magnolia Springs, providing a total of 4.5 miles of hiking paths. The Beaver Trail is the featured hike in the park.

Start: At the boat ramp on Magnolia Lake
Distance: 1.3-mile lollipop
Hiking time: About 1 hour
Difficulty: Easy
Trail surface: Sandy loam
Best season: Sept–June
Other trail users: Mountain bikers
Canine compatibility: Leashed dogs permitted
Land status: Georgia DNR, State Parks & Historic Sites Division
Nearest town: Millen
Fees and permits: Daily parking fee
Schedule: Park hours 7 a.m.–10 p.m., year-round.
Maps: USGS Millen; trail maps available from the park office
Trail contacts: Magnolia Springs State Park, 1053 Magnolia Springs Dr., Millen 30442; (912) 982-1660; www.gastateparks.org.
Special considerations: Both Magnolia Springs and Magnolia Lake have healthy populations of alligators. Around the spring they often lounge virtually on the trails and should be given a wide berth when passing.

Finding the trailhead: From Millen, start at the intersection of SR 17 and US 25 North. Go 5 miles north on US 25 North, and turn right into the park entrance on Magnolia Springs Drive. Continue along the drive to the boat ramp at Magnolia Lake to access the Beaver Trail. Trailhead GPS: N32 53.031' / W81 57.205'

The Hike

The Beaver Trail starts at the boat ramp and fishing pier on Magnolia Lake. Begin walking along the east side of the lake past the racks where rental boats are stored. The path then crosses a boardwalk over a small wooded swamp of tupelo, cypress, maple,

Alligators are plentiful in Magnolia Springs State Park and should be given a wild berth.

water oaks, sweet gum, hickory, and dogwood trees. Many are festooned with Spanish moss. The understory has titi, buttonbush, and muscadine vines. In the spring look for red trumpet honeysuckle blossoms.

At 150 yards the return loop of the trail enters from the right. Turn left and walk the path in a clockwise direction.

As the trail hugs the edge of the lake, watch for great blue herons, little blue herons, egrets, and anhingas. Keep an eye open for wood ducks anytime of the year and many other duck species during winter.

Continuing along the lakeshore, the path remains in the woods, where dead trees serve as dens for wildlife and attract birds like the large, showy pileated woodpeckers. The large longleaf pines provide habitat needed by the endangered red-cockaded woodpecker too.

Near the upper end of the lake a short spur off the main trail turns to the left to an observation platform standing well above the water level. This provides an excellent view of the lake habitat that is home to beavers, turtles, frogs, and alligators. Waterbirds are usually abundant, and kingfishers are often seen. The overlook is especially interesting during winter when the migratory waterbirds are in residence.

As you resume the hike, the soil changes to the dry sandy ridge condition that is a remnant of the ancient sand dunes of a former ocean beach. Prickly pear cacti, small twisted turkey oaks, and a few tall longleaf pines with their enormous cones

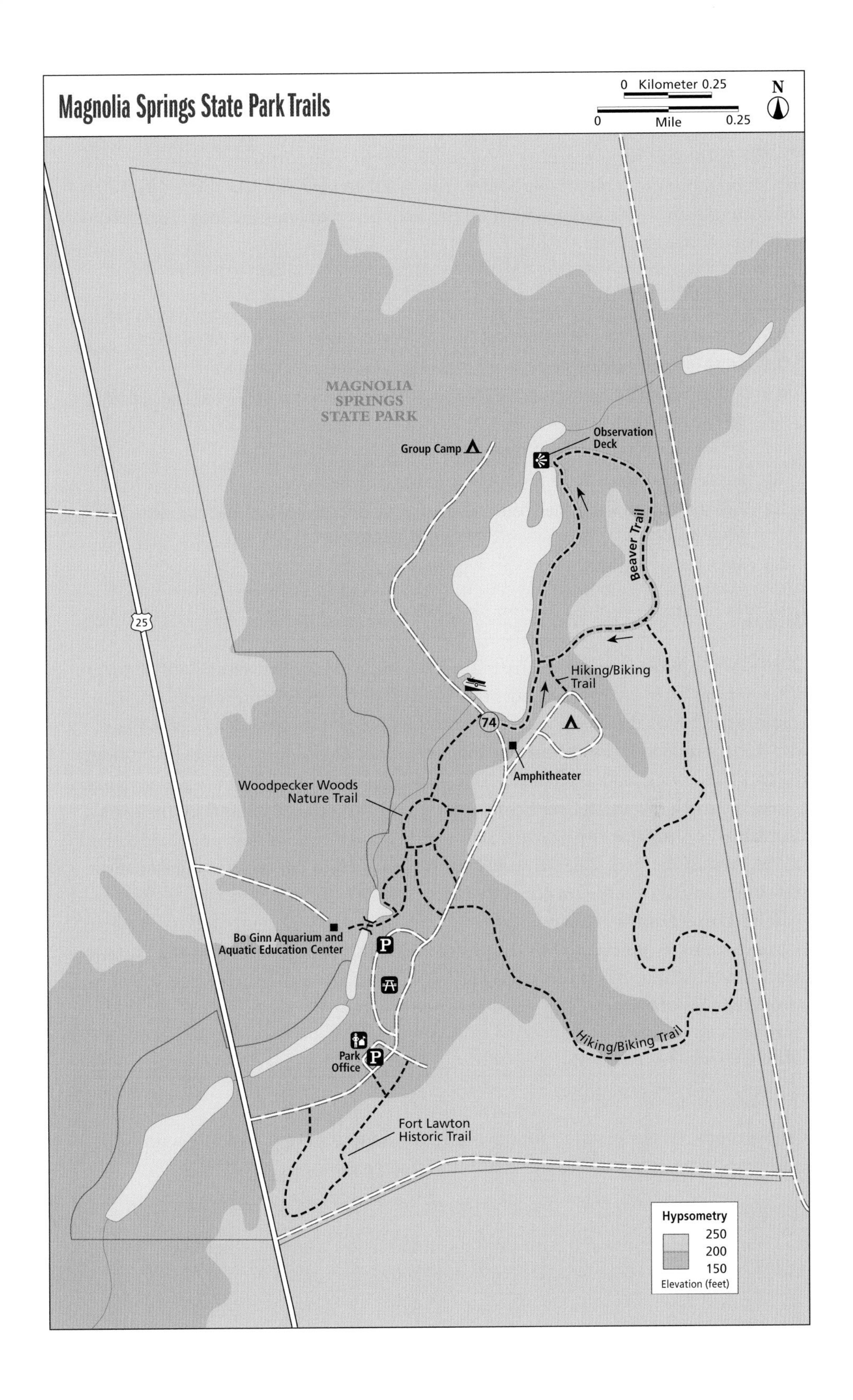
Magnolia Springs State Park Trails
0 Kilometer 0.25
0 Mile 0.25
N
MAGNOLIA
SPRINGS
STATE PARK
Group Camp
Observation
Deck
Beaver Trail
Hiking/Biking
Trail
74
25
Amphitheater
Woodpecker Woods
Nature Trail
Bo Ginn Aquarium and
Aquatic Education Center
Park
Office
Hiking/Biking Trail
Fort Lawton
Historic Trail
Hypsometry
250
200
150
Elevation (feet)

appear here. Also watch for holes leading into gopher tortoise burrows along this sandy stretch.

The path next turns sharply to the south. At the point it passes a junction with the Hiking/Biking Trail, the path veers east, back toward the lake. After passing a connecting path to the campground on the left, the trail closes the loop. Turn left to walk back to the trailhead.

Miles and Directions

0.0 Start at the parking area for the boat ramp on Magnolia Lake and cross the boardwalk.

0.1 At the junction marking the beginning of the loop, take the trail to the left.

0.5 A short trail on the left leads to the observation deck. Return to the main trail and turn left up a gentle incline.

0.7 Arrive at the crest of the ancient sand dunes.

1.0 Reach the junction with the Hiking/Biking Trail on the left.

1.2 Pass the junction with a short path on the left to the campground and reach the point where the trail loop closes. Turn left to return to the trailhead.

1.3 Arrive back at the start.

Options

The 0.7-mile **Woodpecker Nature Trail** begins at the crystal-clear pool of Magnolia Springs. An interpretive boardwalk gives you a great observation point for viewing the life of the spring area. The trail then loops through a drier upland area.

The 0.9-mile loop **Fort Lawton Historic Trail** begins just across the road from the park office. During the Civil War, this site was used as a Confederate prison camp. Camp Lawton was located here because of the ample supply of water from the spring. Remnants of the 40,000-prisoner camp and the fortifications that protected it can still be seen in the park. The camp history is explained in pamphlets available at the park office and also in the on-site museum.

The **Lime Trail** is a 1.0-mile path through an upland palmetto and oak habitat. Running from its junction with the Beaver Trail, this path connects to the parking area at the playground and rest station across the road from the park office. It can be combined with the Beaver Trail for a 2.9-mile hike.

Local Information

Accommodations

For overnight visits, the state park offers 26 RV and tent campsites, along with 5 cottages. For details and reservations visit www.gastateparks.org.

Attractions

Bo Ginn Fish Hatchery and Aquatic Education Center, 1061 Hatchery Rd., Millen 30442; (478) 982-4168; www.fws.gov/camplawtonsite/boginn.html

75 Crooked River State Park Trails

Crooked River State Park is one of only a few places along Georgia's coastal marshes and live oak forests where you can hike. The trails in this small 500-acre park are short, but they provide a good cross section of the varied habitat of the Atlantic Coast area.

The park sits on a bluff overlooking its namesake river in the extreme southeast corner of the state near the town of St. Marys. It is also close to the Kings Bay Naval Submarine Base and Cumberland Island National Seashore.

The state park has campgrounds, playgrounds, picnic areas, rental cabins, a miniature golf course, and a nature center. It is the jump-off point for a kayak trail on the Crooked River as well.

The park's five trails offer more than 3.0 miles of easy hiking. They provide exposure to the mystical maritime forest of live oaks and Spanish moss, a walk through more open palmetto-pine landscape, a trek along a freshwater wetland area, or a short stroll out to the river bluff. Pamphlets available at the park office describe the Bay Boardwalk, Palmetto, and Sempervirens Trails.

The featured Sempervirens Trail loops along the marsh, then into a maritime-forested area, as well as skirting some open pine and palmetto habitat.

Start: Just east of Cabin 11 at the end of the park drive
Distance: 1.2-mile lollipop
Hiking time: About 1 hour
Difficulty: Easy
Trail surface: Sand and sandy loam
Best season: Oct–June
Other trail users: Hikers only
Canine compatibility: Leashed dogs permitted
Land status: Georgia DNR, State Parks & Historic Sites Division
Nearest town: St. Marys
Fees and permits: Daily parking fee
Schedule: 7 a.m.–10 p.m., year-round
Maps: USGS Harrietts Bluff; Crooked River State Park map available at the park office
Trail contacts: Crooked River State Park, 6222 Charlie Smith Sr. Hwy., St. Marys 31558; (912) 882-5256; www.gastateparks.org
Special considerations: During the warm months, prepare for various biting flies, mosquitoes, no-see-ums, and ticks when hiking these trails. Be sure to bring a good repellent. There are fewer annoying insects in the cooler months, and ticks are much less of a problem if you stay on the trail.

Finding the trailhead: From exit 3 on I-95, take SR 40 east for 2 miles. Turn left on Kings Bay Road and go 2.8 miles to SR 40 Spur. Turn left and drive 3.4 miles to the park entrance on the right. Follow the park drive 0.8 mile to its end at the Sempervirens Trailhead and parking area. Trailhead GPS: N30 50.764' / W81 32.795'

The Hike

Sempervirens is Latin for "forever green," which does characterize this nature walk through varied habitats. The trail features five Georgia Champion Trees. This program recognizes the largest known trees of each species found in the state. The ones located

The trail along the river has a tropical feel to it, and some unusual but natural sights.

along the path are staggerbush lyonia, Florida soapberry, myrtle oak, Chapman oak, and Carolina holly.

Start the hike at the parking area and an interpretive sign designed as an Eagle Scout project. Go down a rather straight and sandy old road with palmettos on one side and young live oaks, wax myrtles, and bracken ferns on the other. The white sand, pine needles, and oak leaves make the roadway easy to walk on.

After a short distance the path reaches the junction with a connector path to the Palmetto Trail entering from the right. Continue straight past the intersection on the sand road.

Next you come to a four-way intersection on the trail. The pathway coming in from the right is the return loop of the Sempervirens, while the main trail continues straight ahead. Turn to the left and follow the spur trail out to the marsh edge and a birding platform. The structure's upper deck provides a panoramic view of the marsh and Crooked River. Look for such birds as clapper rails, gallinules, herons, and egrets. Gulls and terns are usually flying over the marsh and river as well.

Walk back to the junction with the main trail and turn left. At the next intersection the path straight ahead is a shortcut through the interior of the Sempervirens Trail. Turn to the left to leave the sand road and enter a mature live oak hammock with some large southern magnolia trees. Spanish moss, large grapevines, a smattering of palmettos, smaller hollies, and wax myrtles give the area a tropical atmosphere. A

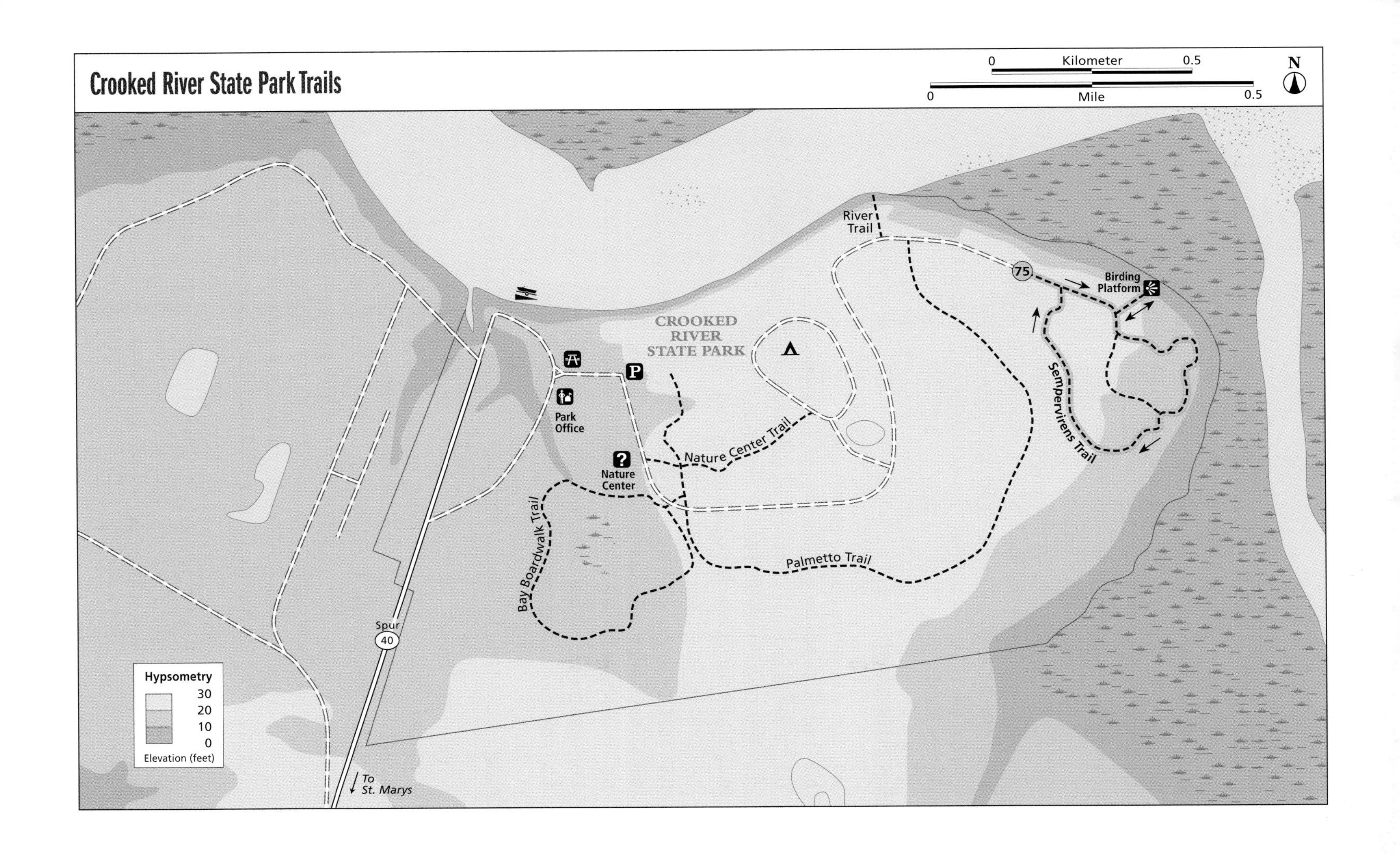
Crooked River State Park Trails
0
Kilometer
0.5
0
Mile
0.5
N
CROOKED
RIVER
STATE PARK
River
Trail
75
Birding
Platform
Sempervirens Trail
Nature Center Trail
Palmetto Trail
Bay Boardwalk Trail
Park
Office
Nature
Center
Spur
40
To
St. Marys
Hypsometry
30
20
10
0
Elevation (feet)

total of eleven short boardwalks crossing wet areas are encountered on this portion of the hike.

As the path bends out toward the river, a short side trail on the left leads to a sandy overlook at the marsh edge. If the tide is low, an army of fiddler crabs scurrying about can create the sense that the ground is moving in front of you.

Retrace your steps back to the main trail and turn left. The path bends back inland, crossing more of the boardwalks until reaching another trail junction. Here the interior shortcut rejoins the main trail from the right. Turn left at the intersection.

As the trail makes a sharp turn at its southern end, the path begins running to the north. To the left, pinewoods with a palmetto understory begin to parallel the rest of the hike. Along this section you are likely to encounter gopher tortoise burrows and see the scratch marks and smaller holes made by armadillos.

At the junction where the loop closes, turn left and walk back along the sand road to the trailhead.

Miles and Directions

0.0 Start at the parking area and information sign.

0.1 Pass the junction with the connecting path on the right that leads to the Palmetto Trail.

0.2 At this intersection turn left to walk the side trail to the birding platform. Retrace your steps to the main trail and turn left.

0.3 Turn left at this intersection to leave the sand road.

0.4 Cross the first of eleven short boardwalks.

0.5 Reach the junction with the side trail on the left to the marsh overlook.

0.6 Cross the last boardwalk and turn left at the trail junction.

0.7 The trail turns north along the pine and palmetto woodlands.

1.0 Close the loop and turn left on the sand road.

1.2 Arrive back at the trailhead.

Options

The **Palmetto Trail** is a 1.5-mile one-way path running from the picnic area near the miniature golf course to a parking area across the park drive from Cabin 5. The trail runs exclusively through a pine and palmetto woodland.

The **Bay Boardwalk Trail** covers 1.4 miles, traversing an evergreen and hardwood wetland in the western portion of the park. Beginning at the nature center, the green-blazed path leads across a couple of long boardwalks and then past an observation tower before running through a drier upland area and back to the trailhead.

The white-blazed **Nature Center Trail** connects the nature center to the park's campground.

The **River Trail** is a very short path with red blazes. It runs from the parking area at the eastern trailhead of the Palmetto Trail, north across the park drive to a vantage point on the bluff overlooking the Crooked River.

76 Cumberland Island National Seashore Trails

Cumberland Island National Seashore is located on the largest and southernmost of Georgia's barrier islands. With its maritime forests, dunes, beaches, marshes, and human history, it provides an unparalleled and entertaining escape from the mainland.

Although inhabited by humans for thousands of years, Cumberland Island is still in a near-wilderness state. The island is 16 miles long and 3 miles wide at its widest point. Unpaved Grand Avenue is the single thoroughfare on the island, running from the Dungeness Ruins on the south end to Cumberland Wharf at the north end.

The island was named by James Oglethorpe in honor of the Duke of Cumberland, and after the American Revolution, war hero Gen. Nathanael Greene settled on it. He and his wife built a four-story tabby home called Dungeness.

In the 1880s Thomas Carnegie, the younger brother of steel baron Andrew Carnegie, bought much of the island and built a new Dungeness mansion. The ruins of that estate are still present on the southern end of Cumberland.

There are some grandfathered private tracts on the island, and the northern end is a federally mandated wilderness area. Visitors are limited to foot travel or bicycling on Grand Avenue, North Cut Road, and the road to Plum Orchard. Plum Orchard is another of the Carnegie family homes on the island and is open for tours.

Sea Camp Beach is the only developed campground, with restrooms, cold showers, and drinking water. Four primitive campgrounds are located in backcountry sites.

A system of roughly twenty named trails provides hikers with many miles of paths.

The featured hike is the Dungeness Loop on the south end, consisting of the Dungeness, Beach, Cemetery, Marsh, Sea Camp, and River Trails, combined with a beach walk. This route takes you through most of the island's habitat types to the two ferry docks, the Sea Camp Campground, and the Dungeness ruins.

Start: At the Dungeness Dock
Distance: 4.5-mile loop
Hiking time: About 1.5–2 hours
Difficulty: Easy
Trail surface: Sand or sandy loam
Best seasons: Year-round
Other trail users: Hikers only
Canine compatibility: No dogs permitted
Land status: National Park Service
Nearest town: St. Marys
Fees and permits: Entrance, ferry, and camping fees; ferry and camping reservations required; camping permits required
Schedule: The ferry from St. Marys makes two trips per day Mar–Nov. Only one trip is provided Dec–Feb, and no service is available on Tues and Wed.
Maps: USGS Cumberland Island North, Cumberland Island South, Fernandina Beach; island maps with hiking trails available at the visitor center in St. Marys
Trail contacts: Cumberland Island National Seashore, 101 Wheeler St., St. Marys 31558; (912) 882-4336; www.nps.gov/cuis
Special considerations: No supplies are available on the island, so you need to bring everything needed for day hiking or camping with you. Drinking water and restrooms are available at the Dungeness Dock, Sea Camp Ranger Station, and Sea Camp Beach campground.

If you miss the last ferry in the afternoon, you will have to charter a boat for the trip back to the mainland.

Sunscreen and insect repellent are necessities in the warmer months.

Finding the trailhead: From exit 3 on I-95, go east for 10 miles on SR 40. When the road ends at the waterfront on the St. Marys River, the ferry dock is immediately to the right. The ferry ride to Cumberland Island takes 45 minutes. Disembark at the Dungeness Dock, which serves as the trailhead for the featured hike. Trailhead GPS: N30 45.237' / W81 28.417'

The Hike

Before beginning the hike, visit the Ice House Museum at the trailhead. The old ice house contains displays recounting the story of Dungeness mansion and the lifestyle of the Carnegies. Also pick up a pamphlet at the dock that is keyed to numbered posts along the Dungeness Trail, explaining the points of interest.

Start out on the Dungeness Trail walking along the packed sand of Coleman Road directly in front of the ferry dock. The road is canopied by old, large live oaks. To the sides of the road the understory is thick with palmetto fans.

At the intersection with Grand Avenue, turn right and walk to the south. Continue on the road until it passes through the gate for the Dungeness mansion. While inspecting the ruins, keep an eye out for wild horses grazing on the surrounding lawns. These feral horses have inhabited the island for decades.

At the front of the mansion, turn right and walk to the small tabby house and percola. The house is thought be the oldest on the island, predating Dungeness. It was used first as a gardener's house and later as an office by the Carnegies.

Reverse your course and walk back in front of Dungeness, continuing past it on the sand road headed toward the beach. At the junction with the Beach Trail, turn to the right. At the next intersection, turn right onto the Cemetery Trail.

A short distance down this path you reach the Greene-Miller Cemetery, where Nathanael Greene's wife, Catherine, and some of her descendants are buried. Also, at one time Revolutionary War Gen. Henry "Lighthorse Harry" Lee was interred here. While sailing along the coast in 1818, the general took sick and came ashore at Dungeness. He later died and was buried in the cemetery. In 1913 his body was moved to Virginia, where he was reburied next to his equally famous son, Robert E. Lee.

Continue on the trail past the graveyard as it skirts the marsh. When it intersects with the Marsh Trail, stay to the right, now walking on a boardwalk over the marsh. At the midpoint of this long boardwalk an observation deck overlooks the water and spartina grass. At the end of the boardwalk, turn sharply left and continue toward the beach.

Shortly you arrive at a junction with the Beach Road. Turn right and quickly ascend onto another long boardwalk over the sand dunes. At the end of this boardwalk

The ruins of the Dungeness mansion are a highlight of hiking the southern end of Cumberland Island.

continue along the Beach Road until it emerges onto the beach on the Atlantic Ocean. Turning north, the next 1.3 miles of the hike are on the beach. Shelling is good on this beach, with welks, tiger eyes, sand dollars, and other shells abundant. Usually dolphins can be seen rolling just beyond the surf, while brown pelicans, gulls, and terns cruise above the water.

At the Sea Camp Trail junction, turn inland and walk over the dunes on another boardwalk. You are now back under the canopy of live oaks as you walk through the campground and past the bathhouse. After leaving Sea Camp, the trail continues west past the junction on the right with the Parallel Trail and then crosses Grand Avenue. The name *Parallel* is derived from that path's course to the north, paralleling Grand Avenue.

The Sea Camp Trail comes to its end at the Sea Camp Ranger Station and dock on the Cumberland River. Next turn to the left and begin heading south on the River Trail. This path passes through more maritime forest habitat as it follows the river back to the trailhead at Dungeness Dock.

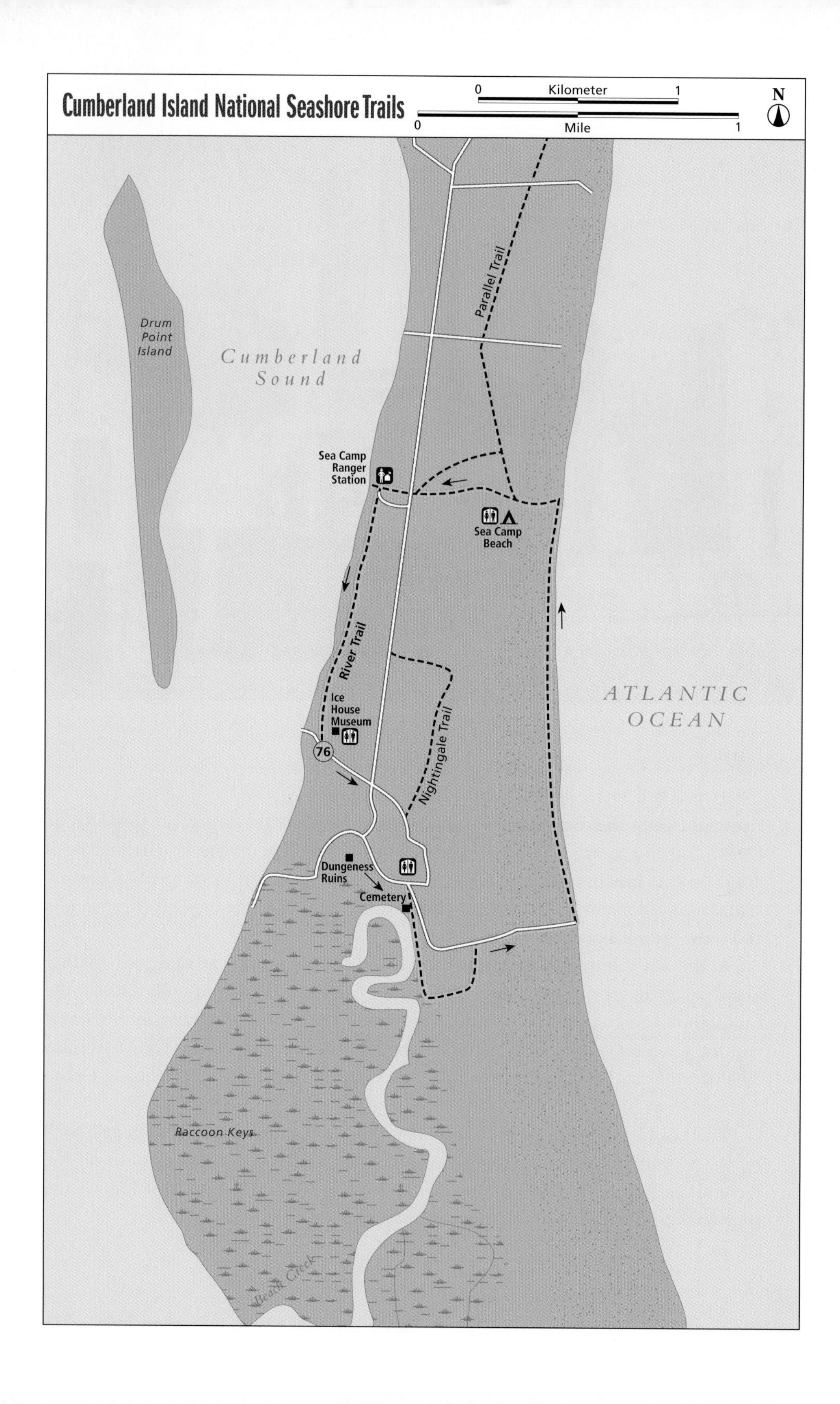

Cumberland Island National Seashore Trails
0
Kilometer
1
0
Mile
1
N
Drum
Point
Island
Cumberland
Sound
Parallel Trail
Sea Camp
Ranger
Station
Sea Camp
Beach
River Trail
Ice
House
Museum
76
Nightingale Trail
ATLANTIC
OCEAN
Dungeness
Ruins
Cemetery
Raccoon Keys
Beach Creek

Encounters with the wild horses of Cumberland Island are common occurrences when trekking on the isle.

Miles and Directions

0.0 Walk east from Dungeness Dock on Coleman Road.

0.3 Turn right onto Grand Avenue.

0.5 Reach the Dungeness ruins and grounds; turn left onto the Beach Road.

0.8 Stay to the right on the Beach Road.

0.9 Turn right onto the Cemetery Trail.

1.0 Pass the Greene-Miller Cemetery.

1.1 Reach the end of the Cemetery Trail and turn right onto the boardwalk of the Marsh Trail.

1.2 Exit the boardwalk and turn sharply to the left.

1.3 Turn right onto the Beach Road.

1.4 Start across the boardwalk over the dunes.

1.5 Reach the end of the dune boardwalk.

1.6 The Beach Road ends on the beach; turn left and walk north.

3.0 At the Sea Camp Trail turn to the west over the dunes on a boardwalk.

3.3 Pass the Sea Camp bathhouse.

3.5 Reach the junction with the Parallel Trail and Grand Avenue.

3.7 At the Sea Camp Ranger Station and dock, turn left to walk south on the River Trail.

4.5 Arrive back at the trailhead.

77 Harris Neck National Wildlife Refuge Trails

Harris Neck National Wildlife Refuge (NWR) is part of the seven tracts of the Savannah Coastal Refuge Complex, most of which is located on barrier islands requiring boat rides to reach. Harris Neck's 2,824 acres are the exception because there is road access. The NWR has half a dozen information panels along the trails and a visitor contact station at the refuge office.

The property contains a historic African-American cemetery dating back to just after the Civil War, when freed slaves farmed the land. There are also ruins of the Lorillard Mansion at Thomas Landing. They were a wealthy family from the Northeast who owned a portion of the refuge land in the early twentieth century.

In the late 1930s the Federal Aviation Administration constructed an emergency-landing runway here for commercial air traffic from Miami to New York. At the outbreak of World War II, it was converted to a military air base for antisubmarine patrols along the mid-Atlantic coastline. The area then became a national wildlife refuge in 1962.

Although almost obliterated by vegetation, the triangle of runways is still discernible today and provides some of the best wildlife watching and birding in the area.

Fifteen miles of interconnected roads and trails provide a paved Wildlife Drive and eight named walking trails. However, the disjointed layout of the area makes the hiking trails more like a maze than an interconnected system.

The featured trail is a North Loop, composed of the Historic Trail, the Goose Pond Trail, and a portion of the Bunting Loop, as well as a short stretch of the Wildlife Drive. This hike is designed to provide a good cross section of the habitats and historic areas of the refuge.

Start: At the parking area at Thomas Landing in the northeast corner of the refuge
Distance: 3.4-mile loop
Hiking time: About 1–1.5 hours
Difficulty: Easy
Trail surface: Dirt, paved, and unpaved roads; sandy loam
Best season: Oct–June
Other trail users: Bikers; motor vehicles on the Wildlife Drive; hunters in season
Canine compatibility: No dogs permitted
Land status: US Fish and Wildlife Service
Nearest town: Eulonia
Fees and permits: None
Schedule: Roads and trails open sunrise to sunset daily, year-round
Maps: USGS Shellmans Bluff, Seabrook, St. Catherines Sound, and Sapelo Sound; page-size map of the refuge available at the refuge office
Trail contacts: Savannah Coastal Refuges Complex, 684 Beech Hill Ln., Hardeeville, SC 29927; (843) 784-2468; www.fws.gov/southeast/
Special considerations: Take care to protect yourself from biting insects and ticks. Mosquitoes, deerflies, and gnats can be bad from late spring through early fall. The freshwater ponds on the refuge also hold alligators.

Finding the trailhead: From I-95 take exit 67 (South Newport) and go south on US 17 for 1.1 miles to Harris Neck Road (SR 131). Turn left onto Harris Neck Road and go 6.5 miles to the entrance of the NWR on the left. Follow the one-way Wildlife Drive to its intersection with two-way Thomas Landing Loop Road. Turn left; the North Loop trailhead is at the end of the Thomas Landing Loop. Trailhead GPS: N31 38.483' / W81 15.431'

The Hike

The North Loop hike begins on the Historic Trail at the information panel about the Lorillard mansion at Thomas Landing. The grand mansion and other buildings were razed because of their unsalvageable condition by the time Harris Neck was obtained by the US Fish and Wildlife Service. The only thing that remains of its original glory is an elaborate fountain and a small concrete pool, both of which are immediately encountered on the trail. Several ornamental plants from the mansion's gardens have continued to reproduce amid the native plants.

The trail then meanders to the northwest through thick undergrowth, generally paralleling the South Newport River on the right. Making a sharp turn to the left, the path then travels to the southwest through a forest of old live oaks covered with Spanish moss, until breaking out of woods onto a pad paved with concrete. To the right is a large concrete bunker with thick walls and dating from World War II.

Turn left on the concrete pad to continue the hike. At the next junction on the trail, you have reached the old eastern runway of the air base. Turn right here. The pathway now carries both the Goose Pond and Airfield Perimeter Loops. At the intersection at the northern end of the runway, turn back sharply to the southwest onto the Goose Pond Loop, walking along the old interior taxiway of the air base. The Airfield Perimeter Loop splits off to continue to the west.

The trail now has Goose Pond on the right and soon passes Greenhead Pond on the left. These freshwater ponds are home to alligators and otters, and they hold migrating ducks during the fall months. The old fields and shrubby habitat through here are good birding areas for spotting upland species. Expect to also see signs of deer, armadillos, rabbits, and feral pigs.

At the next junction turn left, continuing along another old paved taxiway. This part of the Goose Pond Loop shares the path with the Wildlife Drive. A vista of Greenhead Pond to the left and Teal Pond to the right soon comes into view. Endangered wood storks and other wading birds are often present on either or both ponds.

When the trail reaches the Airfield Perimeter Loop running north and south, the Goose Pond Loop and Wildlife Drive turn left to join it. Make that left turn to follow the joint trail to the next intersection. Here you turn right on the Wildlife Drive as it leaves the loop trails. When the drive makes a turn to the south, continue straight ahead onto the Bunting Loop. Walk along an old driveway that passes through an area that formerly contained the air base barracks and other buildings. It is now a forest of loblolly pines and live and willow oaks. As the trail's name implies, painted buntings are often seen along the path.

The fountain on the Historic Trail at Harris Neck is at the site of the Lorillard mansion.

The Bunting Loop forms a horseshoe shape before running back into the Wildlife Drive to the south. There also is a connector portion that runs through the interior of the loop from the north to the south. You soon pass the northern end of that connector trail on the right. Continue straight, walking around the loop. Upon reaching the southern end of the connector trail, turn right, then when it dead-ends back into the main trail, turn left.

You now are retracing your earlier path along the Bunting Loop to the Wildlife Drive. Next follow the drive back to its junction with the Goose Pond and Airfield Perimeter Loops. Turn right to follow those paths to the junction with the Historic Trail. Another right turn takes you back along the Historic Trail to the trailhead.

Miles and Directions

0.0 Begin walking on the Historic Trail behind the information panel at Thomas Landing.

0.1 Pass the old fountain and concrete pool of the Lorillard mansion.

0.4 Turn sharply to the southwest away from the South Newport River.

0.6 Reach the concrete pad of the old airfield and turn left.

0.7 Turn right onto the Goose Pond and Airfield Perimeter Loops.

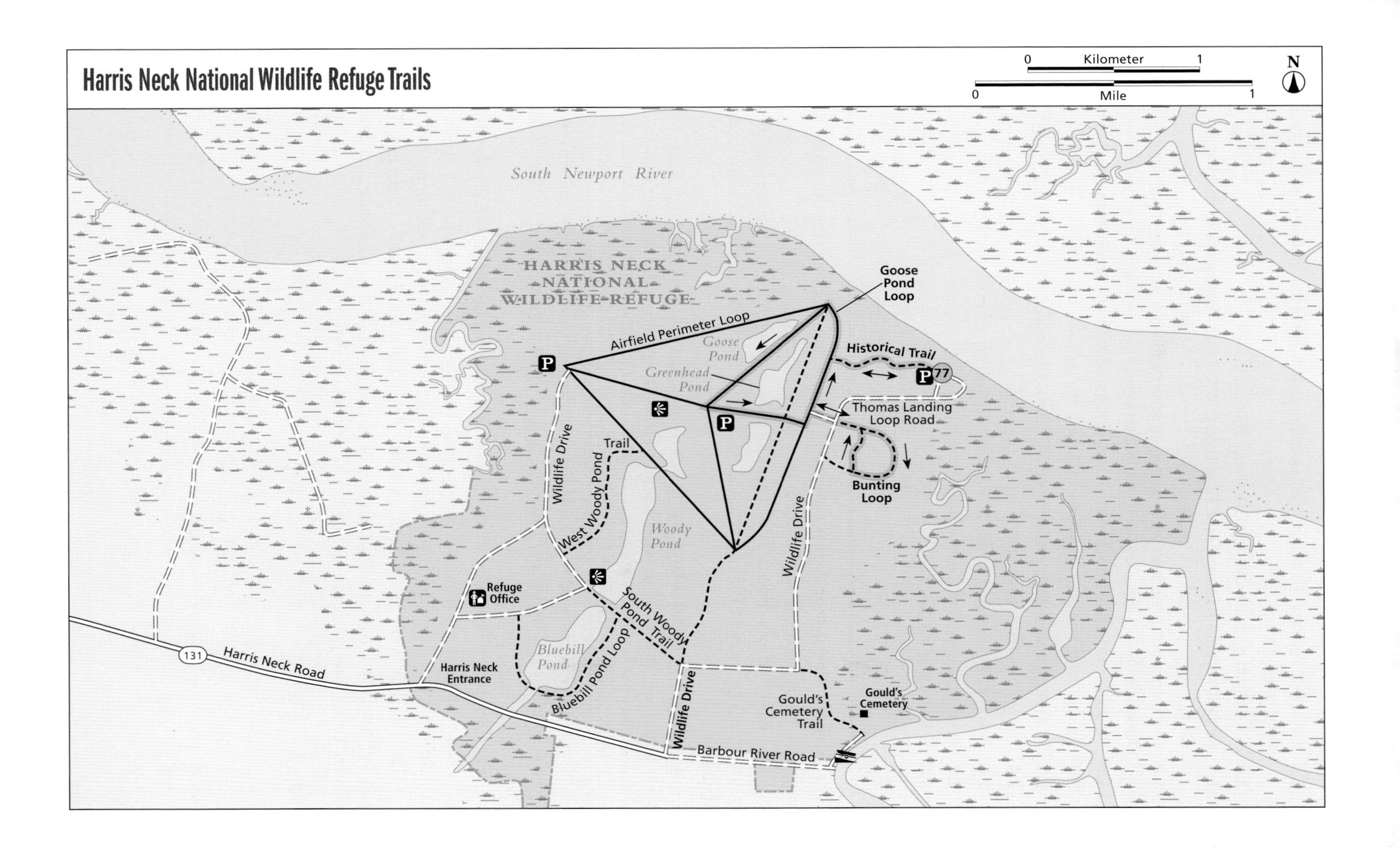
Harris Neck National Wildlife Refuge Trails
0
Kilometer
1
0
Mile
1
N
South Newport River
HARRIS NECK NATIONAL WILDLIFE REFUGE
Goose Pond Loop
Airfield Perimeter Loop
Goose Pond
Greenhead Pond
Historical Trail/
77
Thomas Landing Loop Road
Bunting Loop
Wildlife Drive
Trail
West Woody Pond
Woody Pond
Refuge Office
South Woody Pond Trail
Bluebill Pond
Bluebill Pond Loop
131
Harris Neck Road
Harris Neck Entrance
Gould's Cemetery Trail
Gould's Cemetery
Barbour River Road

0.9 The Airfield Perimeter Loop continues west; turn sharply left to the southwest on the Goose Pond Loop.

1.0 Goose Pond is on the right and Greenhead Pond on the left.

1.4 Turn left, continuing on the Goose Pond Loop that now runs concurrent with the Wildlife Drive.

1.8 Turn sharply to the left, then make the turn to the right to leave the Goose Pond and Airfield Perimeter Loops. You are on the Wildlife Drive.

1.9 The Wildlife Drive turns sharply to the right; continue straight onto the Bunting Loop.

2.0 Pass the north end of the connector trail across the loop.

2.3 Turn right to walk north on the connector trail across the loop.

2.4 Turn left onto the main Bunting Loop.

2.6 Reach the junction with the Goose Pond and Airfield Perimeter Loops and turn right.

2.8 At the junction with the Historic Trail turn right.

3.4 Arrive back at the trailhead.

Options

The **Airfield Perimeter Loop** covers 3.0 miles running along the three old runways that form a triangle in the north portion of the refuge.

The **West Woody Pond Trail** runs 0.6 mile one way along its namesake pond, connecting the Airfield Perimeter Loop to the Wildlife Drive near the visitor contact station.

The **Bluebill Pond Loop** forms a 1.1-mile circle around that body of water, with both ends anchored on the Wildlife Drive near the visitor contact station. On the northern part of the trail, Woody Pond is on the north side of the trail. It offers opportunities for sighting wood storks and alligators.

The **South Woody Pond Trail** does not appear on the refuge trail maps but spans 0.3 mile as it connects the Bluebill Pond Loop to the eastern side of the Wildlife Drive.

The **Gould's Cemetery Trail** appears as a road on the refuge trail map, but it is closed to vehicle traffic and is now a trail. It runs for 0.2 mile one way from the Wildlife Drive to the historic African-American cemetery that is still in use.

The Bluebill Pond Loop, South Woody Pond Trail, and Gould's Cemetery Trail can be combined with short stretches of the Wildlife Drive to create a 3.3-mile **South Trails Loop** beginning at the visitor contact station.

78 Fort McAllister State Historic Park Trails

Fort McAllister was a large earthen fortification during the Civil War, designed to block the Union Navy from access to the Ogeechee River and Savannah. The fort did its job well, withstanding frequent bombardments from the sea. In fact, the fort was not taken by the Union until Gen. William T. Sherman arrived on the coast at the end of his March to the Sea in late 1864 and stormed it from the land side. Today the fort is open for tours.

Fort McAllister State Historic Park covers 1,725 acres between the Ogeechee River on the north and Redbird Creek to the south. Besides the fort, the park features a museum, fishing pier, boat ramps on the Ogeechee and Redbird Creek, rental cottages, and primitive, pioneer, and RV campgrounds.

The park's two trails offer just shy of 4 miles of hiking. The Redbird Creek Trail, running through a maritime forest and along the creek's associated marsh, is the featured hike.

Start: Just south of the fee station at the road to the group shelter
Distance: 2.9-mile lollipop
Hiking time: About 1 hour
Difficulty: Easy
Trail surface: Sand and sandy loam; gravel roadbed
Best season: Oct–June
Other trail users: Hikers only
Canine compatibility: Leashed dogs permitted
Land status: Georgia DNR, State Parks & Historic Sites Division
Nearest town: Richmond Hill
Fees and permits: Daily parking fee
Schedule: Park hours 7 a.m. to 10 p.m., year-round
Maps: USGS Oak Level; full-page park and Redbird Creek Trail maps available at the museum and office
Trail contacts: Fort McAllister State Historic Park, 3874 Fort McAllister Rd., Richmond Hill 31324; (912) 727-7275; www.gastateparks.org
Special considerations: Insect repellent strongly recommended for spring through fall hiking

Finding the trailhead: From exit 90 on I-95, go east for 6.3 miles on SR 144. Turn left onto SR 144 Spur, which dead-ends into the park. The Redbird Creek Trail starts just south of the fee station at the road to the group shelter. Trailhead GPS: N31 53.306' / W81 12.050'

The Hike

The Redbird Creek Trail begins at a stake at the start of the gravel road running to the park's group shelter. At a gate on the road, the trail exits to the right, entering the forest to make a sweeping turn to the west, before arriving at the saltwater marsh. Along the way the path has a canopy of mostly oaks and some loblolly pines. Smaller yaupon holly, cabbage palms, and cedar trees also are present. The understory is heavy with palmettos.

Fort McAllister was a Confederate fort guarding the entrance to the Ogeechee River and Savannah during the Civil War.

The trail crosses a footbridge over a marsh creek and arrives at the beginning of the loop section. The path turns sharply south toward Redbird Creek as you walk to the right on the trail.

At the next intersection, turn right onto a connector trail to an observation tower at the edge of the marsh. This platform offers a view to the south across the spartina grass to Redbird Creek. The vantage point is good for spotting several species of egrets and herons on the marsh.

An orange-blazed side trail splits off to the north from the tower. This path runs 50 yards to Primitive Campsite No. 1.

Retrace your steps back to the main trail and turn right. As you walk along the edge of the marsh, watch for the indigenous saltwort growing by the trail. The small vine-like plant thrives in the salty environment.

As the trail makes a sharp turn back to the north, an excellent view of the marsh to the east is presented. The path then skirts the marsh to the junction with another orange-blazed trail on the right. This trail leads to Primitive Campsite No. 2.

The trail next crosses two footbridges over tidal areas before closing the loop. Turn right across the bridge at this point and walk back to the trailhead.

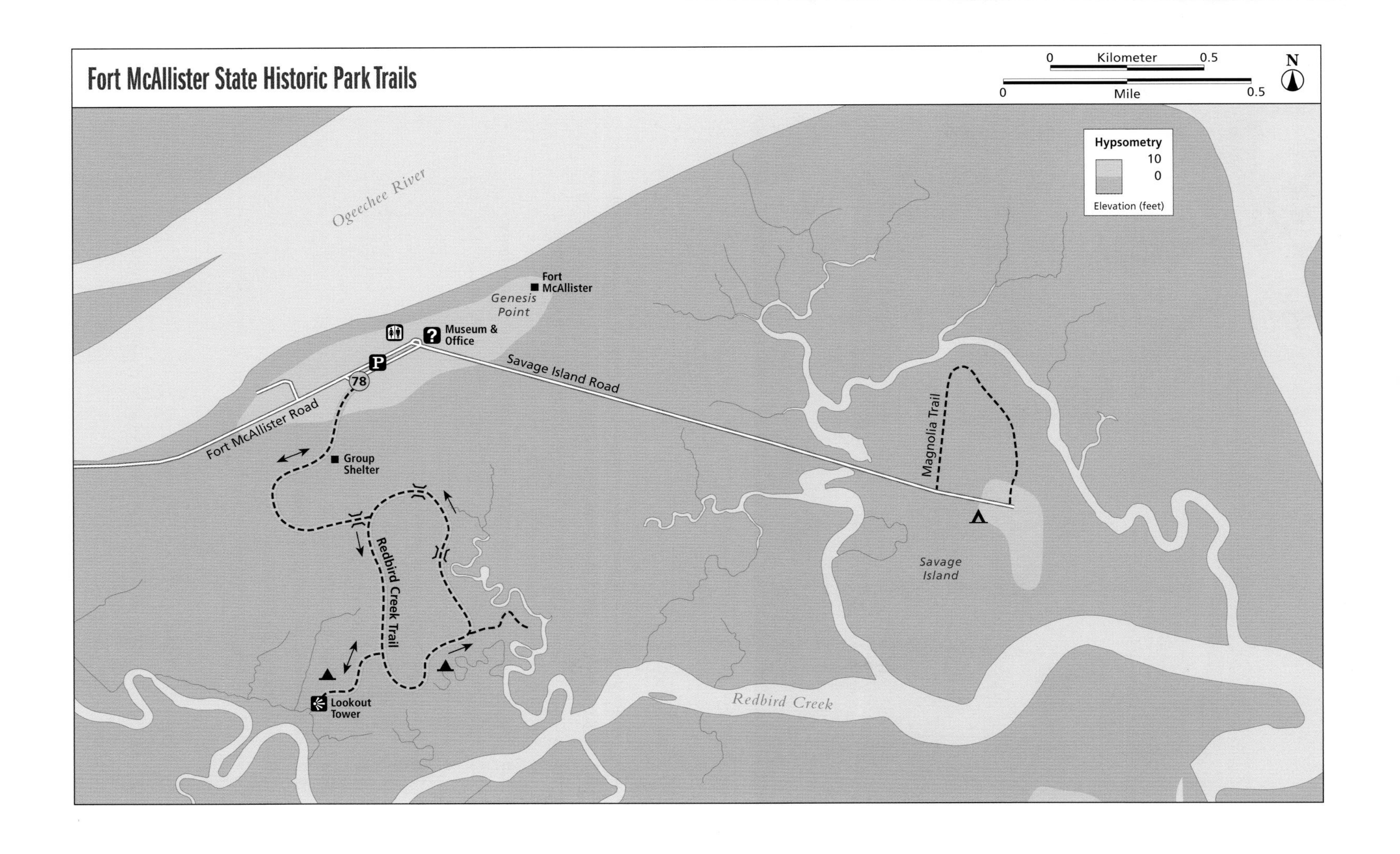

Fort McAllister State Historic Park Trails
0
Kilometer
0.5
0
Mile
0.5
N
Hypsometry
10
0
Elevation (feet)
Ogeechee River
Fort McAllister
Genesis Point
Museum & Office
P
78
Savage Island Road
Fort McAllister Road
Group Shelter
Redbird Creek Trail
Lookout Tower
Magnolia Trail
Savage Island
Redbird Creek

The observation deck on the trail overlooks the marsh along Redbird Creek.

Miles and Directions

- **0.0** Begin walking south from the trail marker at the entrance to the group shelter road.
- **0.1** The trail turns right and leaves the road at a gate.
- **0.7** Cross a footbridge and reach the beginning of the loop. Turn right to walk counterclockwise.
- **1.0** Turn right at the junction with a side trail running to the observation tower.
- **1.2** Reach the observation tower; a side trail leads north to Primitive Campsite No. 1.
- **1.4** Arrive back at the main trail and turn right.
- **1.5** An excellent marsh view is on the right.
- **1.7** Pass the intersection with a side trail to Primitive Campsite No. 2 on the right.
- **1.9** Cross a footbridge over a tidal creek.
- **2.1** Cross another footbridge.
- **2.2** Close the loop and turn right across the bridge.
- **2.9** Arrive back at the trailhead.

Options

The **Magnolia Trail** is a 0.9-mile nature trail to the east of the park campground. Both ends of the path are located on the east end of the campground loop road.

79 Skidaway Island State Park Trails

Skidaway is a barrier island south of historic Savannah, separated from the mainland by Skidaway Narrows. The 588-acre state park contains several types of coastal habitat due to freshwater estuaries and saltwater marshes in the area.

Spanish moss–draped live oaks and stately longleaf pines overhead, and cabbage palms and palmettos below, give the trails on the island a subtropical atmosphere. A flower peculiar to the salt marsh is the sea oxeye, a yellow daisy-like flower that blooms from late spring to summer.

Skidaway Island is home to such wildlife as deer, raccoons, alligators, and gray and fox squirrels and provides excellent wildlife-viewing and birding areas.

Additionally the park provides glimpses of how humans have used the area, along with recreation facilities for continued enjoyment of the island. Picnic areas, campgrounds, playgrounds, and an interpretive center are in the park.

The Skidaway path system consists of five trails stretching for just a bit more than 6 miles. The feature hike is on the longest of those, the Big Ferry Trail.

Start: At a large trail sign near pioneer campground entrance road
Distance: 2.8-mile lollipop
Hiking time: About 1–1.5 hours
Difficulty: Easy
Trail surface: Sandy clay and sandy loam; some gravel roads, wooden bridges, and boardwalks
Best season: Year-round
Other trail users: Hikers; bicyclist
Canine compatibility: Leashed dogs permitted
Land status: Georgia DNR, State Parks & Historic Sites Division
Nearest town: Savannah
Fees and permits: Daily parking fee
Schedule: 7 a.m.–10 p.m., year-round
Maps: USGS Isle of Hope; trail maps and interpretive leaflets available at the park office
Trail contacts: Skidaway Island State Park, 52 Diamond Causeway, Savannah 31411-1102; (912) 598-2300; www.gastateparks.org
Special consideration: Insect repellent is strongly advised during spring through fall.

Finding the trailhead: From Savannah, take I-16 east about 6 miles to exit 164A, which becomes DeRenne Avenue. Turn right on Truman Parkway. Take the Whitefield Avenue exit and turn right. Turn left at State Park Road. Skidaway State Park entrance is straight ahead. The Big Ferry Trail begins at the entrance to the pioneer campground road. Trailhead GPS: N31 57.222' / W81 03.003'

The Hike

The interconnected loops of the featured Big Ferry Trail take you past a Prohibition-era moonshine still, shell middens left by early Native Americans, and Civil War earthworks. There are six numbered posts along the trail, keyed to the park map indicating these and other points of interest. Additionally, a plant-walk pamphlet can be picked up at the interpretive center, which identifies twenty-five plants along the way. Each of these is marked with small green numbered posts.

The remains of an illegal liquor still are located along the Big Ferry Trail.

The Big Ferry Trail starts at the park road for the pioneer campground. The old dirt road leads to the abandoned site of the Big Ferry landing. Before bridges were built, all access to Georgia's barrier islands was by ferry or private boat.

Spanish moss, cabbage palm, wax myrtle, and bay trees are abundant along the trail.

The well-marked path passes the junction with the Connector Trail coming in from the left, then reaches the intersection with the return portion of the first loop path. Stay to the right to walk the outbound side of the loop.

The trail crosses a wooden footbridge over a freshwater slough before reaching the close of the first loop. Beyond, on the left of the trail, is a shell midden dating from the Gaule Indian occupation of the area.

Upon reaching the very short second loop, again stay right. A wood rail fence is on the right, behind which the old moonshine still is on display. The loop then quickly ends and the hike continues to the right.

Upon reaching the junction for the third loop, walk the trail to the left in a clockwise direction. Toward the outer edge of the loop the trail reaches a series of Confederate earthworks. This fortification housed the soldiers manning a mortar battery protecting Savannah's "back door" from a waterborne invasion.

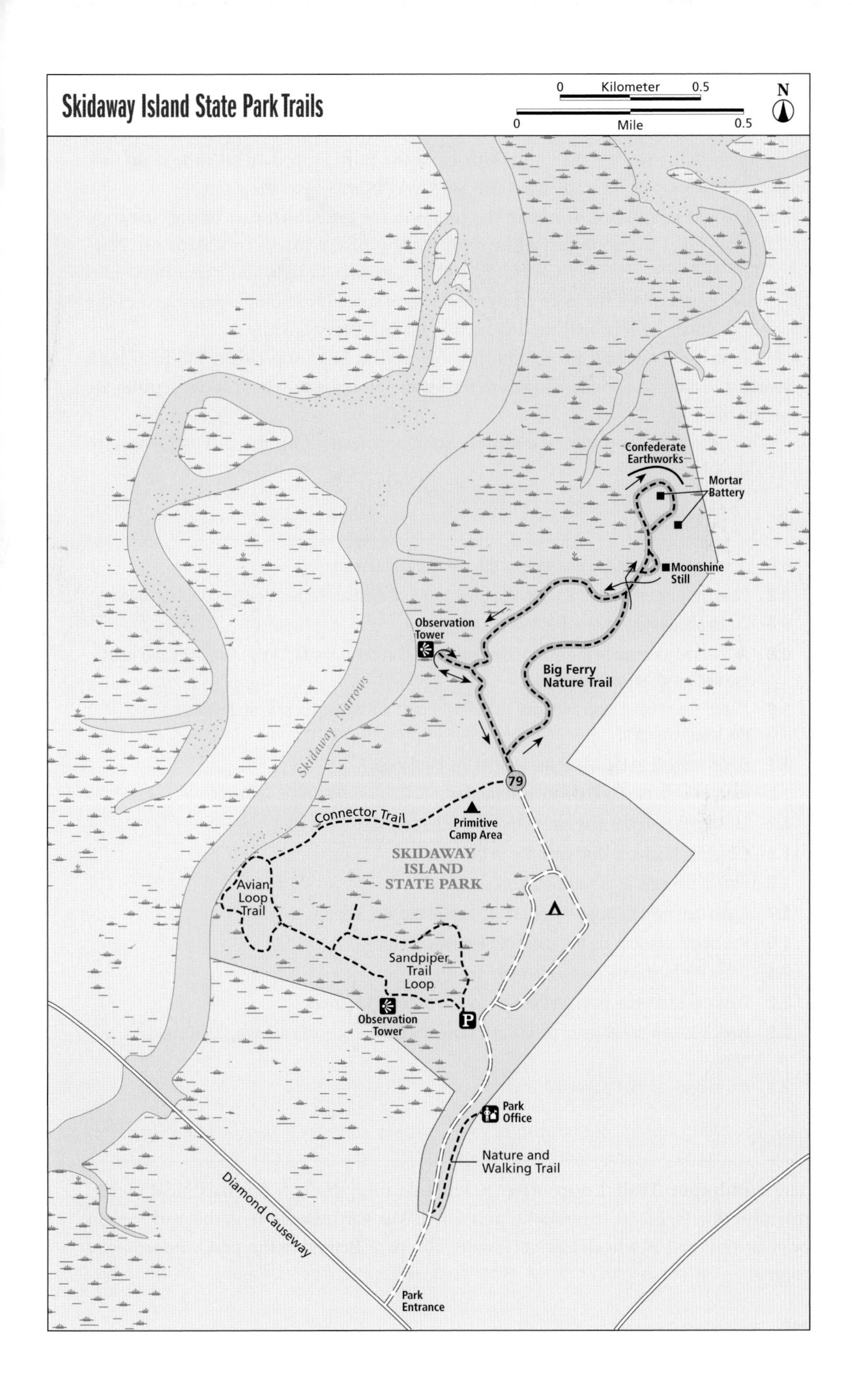
Skidaway Island State Park Trails
0
Kilometer
0.5
0
Mile
0.5
N
Confederate Earthworks
Mortar Battery
Moonshine Still
Observation Tower
Big Ferry Nature Trail
Skidaway Narrows
79
Connector Trail
Primitive Camp Area
SKIDAWAY ISLAND STATE PARK
Avian Loop Trail
Sandpiper Trail Loop
Observation Tower
P
Park Office
Nature and Walking Trail
Diamond Causeway
Park Entrance

Leaving the fortifications to continue around the loop, a side trail intersects from the left. Follow this trail to the location of the Confederate mortar battery. Returning to the main trail, turn left. Walking south, close the third loop, then take the right fork at the second loop as the trail skirts the Skidaway Narrows to the right.

Stay to the right upon reaching the junction for the return part of the first loop and pass an open overlook providing a great view of the marsh and Skidaway Narrows. The trail next crosses a footbridge over a saltwater slough, and a trail then splits off to the right. Follow this path to an observation tower providing a panorama of the creek and marsh. This is near the site of the old Big Ferry landing.

Back at the main trail turn right. Just before the first loop closes, the path leads between the alligator ponds. These are freshwater sloughs in which those reptiles are sometimes seen.

When the first loop closes, continue straight ahead along the dirt road back to the trailhead.

Miles and Directions

0.0 Start at the sign at the entrance of the pioneer camp road.

0.2 Pass the junction with the Connector Trail and turn right at the beginning of the first loop.

0.4 Cross a footbridge over a freshwater slough.

0.8 At the trail junction at the end of the outbound portion of the first loop, turn right and pass the shell midden on the left.

1.0 Reach the second loop and walk to the right past the old liquor still; at the outer end of the loop turn right.

1.1 Begin walking to the left at the start of the third loop.

1.2 Pass through the Confederate earthworks.

1.3 Turn left to walk the side trail to the mortar battery site.

1.5 Close the third loop and continue to the right.

1.6 Stay to the right at the second loop junction.

1.7 Again turn right to begin the return portion of the first loop.

1.9 Reach the overlook on the shore of Skidaway Narrows.

2.1 Cross the footbridge over a saltwater slough.

2.2 Pass the connector path on the right for the observation tower.

2.5 Walk between the alligator ponds and close the first loop; continue straight on the dirt road.

2.8 Arrive back at the trailhead.

Options

The **Sandpiper Trail Loop** offers a 1.2-mile hike through salt flats, tidal creeks, maritime forest, island hammocks, and Civil War earthworks. It is the park's most popular trail and is wheelchair accessible. The path begins at the park's interpretive center.

The Sandpiper Trail Loop runs around and across a system of tidal creeks.

The **Avian Loop Trail** covers 0.7 mile and connects to the Sandpiper Trail Loop. The path crosses a sand causeway spanning the park's largest tidal creek. It then skirts the Intracoastal Waterway.

The **Connector Trail** is 0.6-mile long, running from the Avian Loop to the Big Ferry Trail. Along the way it passes a freshwater pond and runs through a forest of invasive Chinese tallow, which is known as the "popcorn tree."

The **Nature & Walking Trail** is a short stroll that parallels the entrance road near the park office.

Honorable Mentions

L Big Hammock Natural Area Trails

The sandy ridges of Georgia's Coastal Plain are a pleasant relief from the otherwise flat topography. Big Hammock is one of the largest and least disturbed of these unique areas. A number of plant and animal species are endemic to these sandy soils.

Two loop trails, 1.3 miles and 1.0 mile, lead you through the most impressive parts of this distinctive habitat. The main yellow-blazed nature trail has a number of interpretive stations. The blue-blazed shorter loop runs off the nature trail and farther into the floodplain of the nearby Altamaha River.

Entering the woods from the road, the trail leads to the right through the moist base of the sand ridge, where bracken ferns, titis, and other moisture-tolerant plants occur. A boardwalk spur trail leads into and through a cypress head before making the short climb up the ridge.

Turkey oaks and clumps of wiregrass are indicative of the sandy soils of the ancient dunes. There is little herbaceous growth here, although prickly pear cactus, Georgia plume, and sand spikemoss are present. The gopher tortoise is a primary inhabitant of the sand hills, along with the armadillos, a more recent arrival.

You cross the crest of the sand dune and the path leads down the slope into another valley between successive dunes or ridges. In the valley, the forest type changes abruptly to tall longleaf pines, ironwood, maples, white oaks, and live oaks with resurrection ferns on their limbs.

For more information: Wildlife Resources Division, Game Management Section, Fitzgerald 31750; (229) 426-5267; www.gohuntgeorgia.com

DeLorme: Georgia Atlas and Gazetteer: Page 54 D1

M Hofwyl-Broadfield Plantation Historic Site Trails

This site is a must if you are visiting the Georgia coast. The plantation was preserved by the efforts of Ophelia Dent, the last heir of the site, who left it to the state of Georgia for use as a historic site.

The land first was developed for rice culture in the early 1800s, and rice continued to be grown here until 1913. Because of the canals and flooded fields, rice plantations attract both resident and migratory waterbirds. In fact, the bobolink was once known as the ricebird because of the great numbers that stopped to eat the grain before harvest. Many migrating passerine birds stop on their flights up and down the Atlantic Coast. The bird populations make this one of the stops on the Colonial Coast Birding Trail.

There are 4.0 miles of walking trails at the site. Those are the 0.6-mile Rice Field Nature Trail, 0.4-mile Plantation House Trail, and a 2.7-mile hiking trail with a 0.3-mile Lake Loop connector.

An admission fee is charged.

For more information: Hofwyl-Broadfield Plantation State Historic Site, 5556 US 17 North, Brunswick 31525; (912) 264-7333; www.gastateparks.org

DeLorme: Georgia Atlas and Gazetteer: Page 63 C7

N Sapelo Island Trails

Sapelo Island is a 16,500-acre barrier island with grand maritime forests of live oaks festooned with Spanish moss. Longleaf and slash pines are found on the higher, drier ground.

Sapelo is a limited-access island, as designated by Georgia DNR. The only access for hiking or staying overnight is via a ferry operated by the Department of Natural Resources, Wildlife Resources Division. It leaves the mainland from the dock at the Sapelo Island Visitor Center for Marsh Landing on the island. Reservations must be made in advance.

Many of the residents of the African-American community of Hog Hammock on Sapelo are descendants of slaves of Thomas Spalding, who owned the island prior to the Civil War. Several families in Hog Hammock provide overnight accommodations and other services, such as guided tours.

The Reynolds Mansion on the island is managed by the State Parks & Historic Sites Division and can be reserved for group events and conferences.

The Nanny Goat Nature Trail begins 0.1 mile from the mansion and offers a 2.5-mile out-and-back walk in the tidal zone salt marsh, ancient and active dunes, and along the beach. Key points along the trail are interpreted with descriptive markers and with a leaflet available from the Sapelo Visitor Center on the mainland.

The visitor center can also provide a list of island residents who provide tours and accommodations, as well as details on the Reynolds Mansion.

For more information: Sapelo Island Visitor Center, Rt. 1, Box 1500, Darien 31305; (912) 437-3224; www.gastateparks.org

Delorme: Georgia Atlas and Gazetteer: Page 63 A9-10, B9-10

Hike Index

About the Authors

A native of Chattanooga, Tennessee, Donald W. Pfitzer retired from the US Fish and Wildlife Service as an assistant regional director of the Southeast Region after thirty-three years as a fish and wildlife biologist and public affairs officer. He has a master's degree in entomology and botany and has produced thirteen wildlife movies for television for the Tennessee Game and Fish Commission. In 1955 he originated and hosted the first outdoor television program in the Southeast, *Woods and Waters,* and has written many technical and popular articles on fish, wildlife, and nature in general.

Jimmy Jacobs (left), Don Pfitzer (right)

Don is a member and past president of the Southeastern Outdoor Press Association and the Georgia Outdoor Writers Association. He also is a member of the Outdoor Writers Association of America, charter member of the Georgia Conservancy, and a member of the Georgia Hunting and Fishing Hall of Fame. He continues to be active in environmental education, writing, and photography.

Jimmy Jacobs is a lifelong Georgian, born in Atlanta and now living in Marietta. He was the editor of *Georgia Sportsman* magazine for more than two decades and is an outdoor columnist for the *Atlanta Journal-Constitution* newspaper.

A member of the Georgia Outdoor Writers Association and Southeastern Outdoor Press Association, he has authored five guidebooks to fishing the southeastern states and one volume of Southern humor and nostalgia.

About the Photographer

Polly Dean is a native of south Florida, attended the University of Georgia, and never left the state. She makes her home in Marietta. She is an award-winning freelance photographer and writer, as well as a member of the Georgia Outdoor Writers Association and Southeastern Outdoor Press Association.

Polly Dean